Living and Working
in
London

A Survival Handbook

Edited by
Di Tolland

SURVIVAL BOOKS • LONDON • ENGLAND

First published 2000
Second Edition 2004
Third Edition 2007

Cover illustration, cartoons & maps © Jim Watson
Cover Photograph © Zsolt Nyulazsi (www.shutterstock.com)

Survival Books Limited
26 York Street, London W1U 6PZ, United Kingdom
☎ +44 (0)20-7788 7644, 🖨 +44 (0)870-762 3212
✉ info@survivalbooks.net
🖳 www.survivalbooks.net
To order books, please refer to page 429

British Library Cataloguing in Publication Data.
A CIP record for this book is available from the British Library.
ISBN 10: 1-905303-09-2
ISBN 13: 978-1-905303-09-0

Printed and bound in India by Ajanta Offset

ACKNOWLEDGEMENTS

M y sincere thanks to those who contributed to the successful publication of this book, including Clare O'Brien, David Hampshire, Elizabeth Opalka, Dougal Robertson, Kerry Laredo, Sian Astrop, Valerie Baxter, Tamsin Gregory, Jason Grimsley, Susan Hardcastle, Sandra Horniman, Charlie Masson Smith, Mill Millward, Nick Williams and everyone else who contributed in any way and whom I've omitted to mention. The excellent colour photographs were kindly supplied by VisitLondon (⌨ www.visitlondon.com). Finally, a special thank-you to Jim Watson for the superb cover, maps, cartoons and illustrations.

OTHER TITLES BY SURVIVAL BOOKS

Living & Working Series

America; Australia; Britain; Canada; European Union; Far East; Germany; Gulf States & Saudi Arabia; Ireland; Italy; New Zealand; Spain; Switzerland

Buying a Home Series

Australia & New Zealand; Bulgaria; Cyprus; Florida; France; Greece; Italy; Portugal; South Africa; Spain

Lifeline Guides

Brittany; Costa Blanca; Costa del Sol; Dordogne/Lot; Normandy; Poitou-Charentes; Provence

Other Titles

The Alien's Guide to Britain;
The Alien's Guide to France;
The Best Places to Live in France;
The Best Places to Live in Spain;
Buying or Renting a Home in London;
Buying or Renting a Home in New York;
Buying, Selling & Letting Property;
Foreigners in France;
Foreigners in Spain;
Making a Living in France;
Making a Living in Spain;
Renovating & Maintaining Your French Home;
Retiring in France;
Retiring in Spain;
Rural Living in France;
Shooting Caterpillar's in Spain;
Wild Thyme in Ibiza

Order forms are on page *429*

WHAT READERS & REVIEWERS

When you buy a model plane for your child, a video recorder, or some new computer gizmo, you get with it a leaflet or booklet pleading 'Read Me First', or bearing large friendly letters or bold type saying 'IMPORTANT – follow the instructions carefully'. This book should be similarly supplied to all those entering France with anything more durable than a 5-day return ticket. It is worth reading even if you are just visiting briefly, or if you have lived here for years and feel totally knowledgeable and secure. But if you need to find out how France works then it is indispensable. Native French people probably have a less thorough understanding of how their country functions. – Where it is most essential, the book is most up to the minute.

LIVING FRANCE

Rarely has a 'survival guide' contained such useful advice. This book dispels doubts for first-time travellers, yet is also useful for seasoned globetrotters – In a word, if you're planning to move to the USA or go there for a long-term stay, then buy this book both for general reading and as a ready-reference.

AMERICAN CITIZENS ABROAD

It is everything you always wanted to ask but didn't for fear of the contemptuous put down – The best English-language guide – Its pages are stuffed with practical information on everyday subjects and are designed to complement the traditional guidebook.

SWISS NEWS

A complete revelation to me – I found it both enlightening and interesting, not to mention amusing.

CAROLE CLARK

Let's say it at once. David Hampshire's Living and Working in France is the best handbook ever produced for visitors and foreign residents in this country; indeed, my discussion with locals showed that it has much to teach even those born and bred in l'Hexagone. – It is Hampshire's meticulous detail which lifts his work way beyond the range of other books with similar titles. Often you think of a supplementary question and search for the answer in vain. With Hampshire this is rarely the case. – He writes with great clarity (and gives French equivalents of all key terms), a touch of humour and a ready eye for the odd (and often illuminating) fact. – This book is absolutely indispensable.

THE RIVIERA REPORTER

A mine of information – I may have avoided some embarrassments and frights if I had read it prior to my first Swiss encounters – Deserves an honoured place on any newcomer's bookshelf.

ENGLISH TEACHERS ASSOCIATION, SWITZERLAND

HAVE SAID ABOUT SURVIVAL BOOKS

What a great work, wealth of useful information, well-balanced wording and accuracy in details. My compliments!

THOMAS MULLER

This handbook has all the practical information one needs to set up home in the UK – The sheer volume of information is almost daunting – Highly recommended for anyone moving to the UK.

AMERICAN CITIZENS ABROAD

A very good book which has answered so many questions and even some I hadn't thought of – I would certainly recommend it.

BRIAN FAIRMAN

We would like to congratulate you on this work: it is really super! We hand it out to our expatriates and they read it with great interest and pleasure.

ICI (SWITZERLAND) AG

Covers just about all the things you want to know on the subject – In answer to the desert island question about the one how-to book on France, this book would be it – Almost 500 pages of solid accurate reading – This book is about enjoyment as much as survival.

THE RECORDER

It's so funny – I love it and definitely need a copy of my own – Thanks very much for having written such a humorous and helpful book.

HEIDI GUILIANI

A must for all foreigners coming to Switzerland.

ANTOINETTE O'DONOGHUE

A comprehensive guide to all things French, written in a highly readable and amusing style, for anyone planning to live, work or retire in France.

THE TIMES

A concise, thorough account of the DOs and DON'Ts for a foreigner in Switzerland – Crammed with useful information and lightened with humorous quips which make the facts more readable.

AMERICAN CITIZENS ABROAD

Covers every conceivable question that may be asked concerning everyday life – I know of no other book that could take the place of this one.

FRANCE IN PRINT

CONTENTS

1. CHOOSING THE AREA   19

Barking & Dagenham   22
Barnet   25
Bexley   27
Brent   29
Bromley   30
Camden   33
City Of London   35
Croydon   36
Ealing   38
Enfield   40
Greenwich   41
Hackney   44
Hammersmith & Fulham   45
Haringey   47
Harrow   49
Havering   51
Hillingdon   53
Hounslow   55
Islington   57
Kensington & Chelsea   58
Kingston-Upon-Thames   59
Lambeth   63
Lewisham   65
Merton   66
Newham   68
Redbridge   70
Richmond-Upon-Thames   72
Southwark   74
Sutton   76
Tower Hamlets   77
Waltham Forest   79
Wandsworth   81
Westminster   83

2. ARRIVAL & SETTLING IN 87

Permits & Visas 89
Immigration 93
Customs 93
Retirement 96
Police Registration 96
Council Tax Registration 97
Embassy Registration 98
Finding Help 98
Checklists 99

3. GETTING THERE & GETTING ABOUT 103

Air 106
Sea 109
Rail 111
Underground 118
Buses 121
River Ferries 123
Taxis 125
Driving in London 126
Cycling 133

4. SOMEWHERE TO LIVE 137

Housing Market 139
British Homes 142
Buying Property 144
Rented Accommodation 155
Garages & Parking 164
Utilities 165
Heating & Air-Conditioning 167
Home Security 168
Moving House 170

5. EARNING A LIVING   175

Qualifications   177
Job Hunting   178
Self-Employment & Doing Business   184
Regeneration   191

6. MONEY MATTERS & INSURANCE   195

Banks & Building Societies   197
Mortgages   202
Cost Of Living   208
Council Tax   210
Insurance   213

7. GETTING AN EDUCATION   221

General Information   222
Pre-School   223
Primary & Secondary Schools   224
State Schools   225
Private Schools   228
Religious Schools   231
Specialist Schools   232
International & Foreign Schools   234
Universities & Colleges   235
Vocational Courses   242
English-Language Schools   243
Evening Classes & Distance Learning   243

8. STAYING HEALTHY   247

Emergencies   248
National Health Service   250

Private Health Insurance 252
Private Health Treatment 254
Complementary Medicine 255
Doctors 255
Chemists & Medicines 259
Hospitals & Clinics 261
Cosmetic Surgery 265
Childbirth 265
Dentists 266
Opticians 268
Family Planning Services 270
Sexually Transmitted Diseases 271
Information & Help 272
Births & Deaths 273

9. TIME OFF 277

Art Galleries & Museums 278
Cinemas & Theatres 282
Music 284
Nightlife 287
Parks 290
Pubs & Bars 291
Restaurants & Cafes 293
River Trips & Excursions 297
London For Children 301

10. SPORT & FITNESS 305

Bungee Jumping 307
Cricket 307
Cycling 307
Football 308
Golf 310
Greyhound Racing 311
Gymnasia & Health Clubs 311

Horse Riding 313
Ice Skating 313
Leisure Centres 314
Motorsports 315
Racket Sports 315
Rugby 318
Skiing 319
Swimming Pools 320
Watersports 321
Miscellaneous Sports 321

11. SPEND, SPEND, SPEND 325

West End 328
West London 336
East London 338
North London 339
South London 340
Internet Shopping 341

12. MISCELLANEOUS MATTERS 345

Climate 346
Crime 347
Government 350
Monarchy 353
Pets 354
Police 358
Postal Services 359
Telephone 361
Television & Radio 371
Time Difference 377

APPENDICES 379

Appendix A: Useful Addresses 380
Appendix B: Further Reading 389
Appendix C: Useful Websites 394
Appendix D: Weights & Measures 408
Appendix E: Maps 412

INDEX 418

ORDER FORMS 428

IMPORTANT NOTE

London is huge city with many faces, a variety of ethnic groups, religions and customs, and the UK has continuously changing rules, regulations, interest rates and prices. Note that a change of government in the UK can have far-reaching effects on many important aspects of life. **I cannot recommend too strongly that you check with an official and reliable source (not always the same) before making any major decisions, or taking an irreversible course of action. However, don't believe everything you're told or read (even, dare I say it, herein).**

Useful addresses, websites and references to other sources of information have been included in all chapters and in **Appendices A, B** and **C** to help you obtain further information and verify details with official sources. Important points have been emphasised **in bold print**, some of which it would be expensive, or even dangerous, to disregard. **Ignore them at your peril or cost.** Unless specifically stated, the reference to any company, organisation or product in this book doesn't constitute an endorsement or recommendation.

Editor's Notes

- Times are shown using am for before noon and pm for after noon.

- Unless otherwise stated, prices shown usually include VAT at 17.5 per cent and should be taken as estimates only, although they were mostly correct at the time of publication.

- His/he/him also means her/she/her (please forgive me ladies).This is done to make life easier for both the reader and (in particular) the author, and isn't intended to be sexist.

- F requent references are made throughout this book to the Euro pean Union (EU), which (from 1st February 2007) comprises Austria, Belgium, Bulgaria, Cyprus, the Czech Republic, Denmark, Estonia, Finland, France, Germany, Greece, Hungary, Ireland, Italy, Latvia, Lithua nia, Luxembourg, Malta, the Netherlands, Poland, Portugal, Romania, the Slovak Republic, Slovenia, Spain, Sweden and the UK, and to the European Economic Area (EEA), which includes the EU countries plus Iceland, Liechtenstein and Norway.

- All spelling is (or should be) British English and not American English. American English equivalents are given in brackets where these differ significantly from British English words.

- Warnings and important points are shown in **bold** type.

- The following symbols are used in this book: ☎ (telephone), 📠 (fax), 💻 (Internet) and ✉ (email).

- Lists of useful addresses, further reading and useful websites are contained in **Appendices A, B** and **C** respectively.

- For those unfamiliar with the imperial system of weights and measures, metric conversion tables are included in **Appendix D**.

- Maps of the 33 London boroughs and transport links are included in **Appendix E.**

INTRODUCTION

People are drawn to London for many reasons, among which are its rich traditions, unrivalled entertainment, stimulating arts scene, and the abundance of business, career and educational opportunities. It provides more cultural activities than any other city in the world and boasts some of the best known sights – history awaits you around every corner. It's also one of the world's greenest capital cities with some 1,800 parks and open spaces. Nowhere provides a more varied and vibrant nightlife for the young (and young at heart) than London. A confident, cocky (Cockney) city that's constantly re-inventing itself, London is a bustling, vibrant place to live, work or study.

Whether you're already living or working in London or just thinking about it – this is **THE BOOK** for you. Forget about all those glossy guide books, excellent though they are for tourists – this amazing book was written especially with you in mind and is worth its weight in pickled cockles. *Living and Working in London* is designed to meet the needs of anyone wishing to know the essentials of London life, whether you're an immigrant, temporary worker, transferee, business person, student, retiree or long-stay visitor. However long your intended stay in London, you'll find the information contained in this book invaluable.

Reliable and up-to-date information specifically intended for newcomers living and working in London isn't easy to find. Our aim in publishing this book was to help fill this void and provide the practical information necessary for a relatively trouble-free life. You may have visited London as a tourist, but living and working there is a different matter altogether. Adjusting to a different environment and culture and making a home in any foreign country can be a traumatic and stressful experience, and for most people the UK is no exception.

With a copy of *Living and Working in London* to hand you'll have a wealth of information at your fingertips. Information derived from a variety of sources, both official and unofficial, not least the hard won personal experiences of the authors, their families, friends, colleagues and acquaintances. Adapting to life in a new country is a continuous process and this book will reduce your beginner's phase, minimise the frustrations and help you make informed decisions and calculated judgements instead of uneducated guesses and costly mistakes. **Most important of all, it will help save you time, trouble, and money and repay your investment many times over.**

Whatever else it may be, life in London is invariably spiritually, mentally and intellectually stimulating and rarely dull, and, although foreigners may occasionally complain about the Government, the British weather or traffic wardens, most feel privileged to live and work there and wouldn't dream of leaving. I trust this book will help you avoid the pitfalls of life in London and smooth your way to a happy and rewarding future in your new home.

Good Luck!

Di Tolland (Editor)
March 2007

1

CHOOSING THE AREA

1

London is one of the world's great cities, Europe's largest city and one of the most populous on earth – Greater London covers over 610mi^2 (circa 1,580km^2) and has a population of ca. 7.5 million (or more, depending on how you define London). It's the seat of government and home of the British Royal Family, the UK's commercial, cultural and sporting centre, Europe's leading financial market, the 'capital' of the English-speaking world and a world leader in architecture, art, fashion, food, music, publishing, film and television.

London is also Europe's most racially and culturally diverse city and the most cosmopolitan city in the world; one in five Londoners (over a million people) were born outside the UK and between them speak some 200 different languages. Greater London is home to almost half the ethnic minority population of the UK. Its people hail from all corners of the globe, particularly Europe and the Commonwealth countries of Africa, Asia and the West Indies. Not surprisingly, London is a treasure trove of foreign culture and multi-culturalism and almost anyone can feel at home there – it has some 35 communities of over 10,000 people born outside the UK. To add to this cultural potpourri, London's resident population is swelled by a staggering 25 million tourists a year, not to mention the hundreds of thousands of commuters who flock there daily to work.

London is the UK's main employment centre with a huge variety of job opportunities and relatively low unemployment. However, in common with most capital cities, the cost of living is high and prices (particularly property) are among the highest in Europe, although higher salaries compensate to some extent. Like all large cities, London displays stark contrasts of wealth and poverty, although few places offer such endless opportunities to make (or lose) your fortune.

London's failings include pollution, an ageing and over-burdened public transport system, dreadful traffic congestion, substandard housing and homelessness, over-crowding, high crime (in some areas) and racial tension. However, it's the people – the good, the bad and the ugly – who make London what it is and give the city its unique character. Although the British can be infuriating at times, they will invariably charm and delight you with their sense of humour and idiosyncrasies.

The sheer size of London can be daunting. It isn't only vast and labyrinthine, but also chaotic. Central London was originally an assortment of villages and some 250 years ago there were vast spaces between them; today they've merged into an almost seamless metropolis. The surrounding parts of London grew mainly in the Victorian period, when the 'suburbs' were at least partly planned. Here there's more open space and the population density is generally below 2,750 people per square mile (7,000 per square kilometre), compared with up to twice as many in the city centre.

Any attempt to divide London into manageable and comprehensible chunks can only be partially successful. The task is complicated by the overlap between the different artificial divisions that have been created over the years – geographical, cultural, historical, administrative and postal. The customary division of the city is marked by the River Thames, which flows from west to east through its centre. There's a widespread notion that the areas north of the river are more pleasant than those to the south, just as it's generally believed that the West End is superior to the East End, but such generalisations often fail to stand up when you start looking at areas in more detail.

Although Greater London is now 45 years old, many people still consider only the central areas to be proper London, the outer areas belonging to the surrounding ('home') counties. For example, Kingston was originally part of Surrey and Bromley was in Kent, but both towns have since given their names to a London borough. Created in 1965, the boroughs are the administrative areas of Greater London, which is one of the 45 administrative regions (or counties) of England. There are 32 boroughs plus the City of London, which is effectively a borough but has certain peculiarities such as its own police force. (The so-called City of Westminster, on the other hand, is a borough like any other.) The boroughs vary considerably in size but each has a population of between 150,000 and 350,000, with the exception of the City of London, which has just 8,000 residents.

Unofficially, the boroughs are divided between 'inner London' (Camden, City of London, Greenwich, Hackney, Hammersmith & Fulham, Haringey, Islington, Kensington & Chelsea, Lambeth, Lewisham, Newham, Southwark, Tower Hamlets and Wandsworth) and 'outer London' (the remaining 19 boroughs). Inner London boroughs tend to be characterised by a huge gulf between rich and poor, and a wide racial and cultural mix. Outer London boroughs are more suburban with swathes of green belt (areas in which building is restricted) and a predominantly white (and 'white-collar') population.

The creation of the Greater London Authority in 2000 grouped the boroughs into 14 constituencies, listed below, and there are other more or less arbitrary divisions: 16 health authority areas, five police regions, four ambulance service zones and three fire brigade sectors.

Constituency	Boroughs
Barnet and Camden	Barnet, Camden
Bexley and Bromley	Bexley, Bromley
Brent and Harrow	Brent, Harrow
City and East London	Barking and Dagenham, City of London, Newham, Tower Hamlets
Croydon and Sutton	Croydon, Sutton
Ealing and Hillingdon	Ealing, Hillingdon

Enfield and Haringey	Enfield, Haringey
Greenwich and Lewisham	Greenwich, Lewisham
Havering and Redbridge	Havering, Redbridge
Lambeth and Southwark	Lambeth, Southwark
Merton and Wandsworth	Merton, Wandsworth
North East	Hackney, Islington, Waltham Forest
South West	Hounslow, Kingston-upon-Thames, Richmond-upon-Thames
West Central	Hammersmith and Fulham, Kensington and Chelsea, Westminster

Officially, each borough is divided into 'wards' (an administrative district of a parliamentary constituency), although even people who live there often don't know their names. Most people refer instead to districts which in some cases don't appear on maps, but which are either named after places long since swallowed by the outward sprawl of the capital or derive from contemporary 'estate agent speak' (e.g. 'Blythe Village' and 'Brackenbury Village' in the borough of Hammersmith & Fulham and the new 'Limehouse Village' in Docklands). In many cases, these districts straddle borough or county boundaries.

But the most perplexing of London's various partitions is its division into postal areas, each with a different 'postcode' that seldom bears any relationship to counties, constituencies, boroughs, wards or districts! Codes in 'central' London (an area stretching in some cases to the borders of Greater London!) have codes beginning W (for west), NW (north-west), N (north), E (east), SE (south-east) and SW (south-west). (Bizarrely, there are no S or NE codes.) Those in 'outer' London have codes relating to the nearest town where there's a main sorting office, which is in some cases a 'borough' town (BR for Bromley, CR for Croydon, EN for Enfield, HA for Harrow, KT for Kingston and SM for Sutton – OK, so there's no M in Sutton) and in other cases isn't (DA for Dagenham in Bexley, IG for Ilford in Redbridge, RM for Romford in Havering, TW for Twickenham in Richmond and UB for Uxbridge in Hillingdon). Needless to say, postcode boundaries don't always match borough boundaries, so that there are for example HA, TW and WD (Watford) codes as well as UB codes in Hillingdon and DA, CR, SE and TN (Tunbridge) as well as BR codes in Bromley.

As if all this weren't confusing enough, the numbers following the initial letter or letters of postcodes can also be misleading. These normally start at 1 (perversely, Croydon's and Harrown's start at 0 and omit 1!) but their distribution is to all intents and purposes arbitrary.

Originally, the system was based on the initial letter of each sub-district in the alphabet: a district beginning with the letter 'A' was given the number 1 and so on. Many people erroneously believe that the numbers indicate the distance from the centre of London, whereby logically the lowest numbers would be nearest the centre and the highest furthest out. This isn't the case.

To make matters even worse, between 1968 and 1971, some 'central' London codes gained an extra letter, e.g. part of W1 become W1H and these letters have recently changed – no doubt making life easier for the Post Office but, like the repeated telephone number changes (see page 364), costing London residents and business millions of pounds without improving their lives one iota.

Those looking to buy or rent property in London should note that postcodes confer status and there's a 'postcode snobbery' which can significantly inflate or deflate the price of property. You can therefore sometimes save a great deal of money simply by buying a home on the left rather than the right side of a street.

Maps of inner and outer London showing the borough and postcode boundaries are on pages 400 and 400 respectively.

Each London borough has its own website containing a wealth of information, all of which can be accessed via ⌨ http://bubl.ac.uk/uk/england/ london. htm. The addresses of individual sites are www.[borough name].gov.uk, e.g. ⌨ www.brent.gov.uk, except those of Barking & Dagenham (⌨ www. lbbd. gov.uk), City of London (⌨ www.corpoflondon.gov.uk), Hammersmith & Fulham (⌨ www.lbhf.gov.uk), Kensington & Chelsea (⌨ www.rbkc.gov.uk) and Waltham Forest (⌨ www.lbsf.gov.uk). The Greater London Authority's site (⌨ www.london.gov.uk) provides information about the 14 constituencies, and the UpMyStreet Solutions site (⌨ www.upmy street.com), run in conjunction with Thomson Directories, is a mine of information about each postcode area – including the annual number of missed rubbish collections!

Vital statistics for the 33 boroughs that comprise Greater London are listed on the following pages.

BARKING & DAGENHAM

The east London borough of Barking and Dagenham is generally a rather de-prived area. It was once marshland and most of it consists of terraced council houses (public housing owned by the local authority), some of which are now privately owned. The recently completed Barking Barrage has enabled develop-ment to take place along the River Roding in the south-west and there are plans to reclaim more marshland along the north bank of the River Thames over the next two decades for some 4,000 new homes.

Property

The borough's largest housing estate (a development that often refers to council or public housing), Becontree, was built in the '20s and '30s for East End work-ers. It consists of some 27,000 homes, mostly two and three-bedroom red brick houses. Since then other council estates have been constructed to the north, but there's a relatively small amount of private housing, which is nevertheless among the cheapest in London. Barking town offers small Victorian terraced houses and as well as larger Edwardian and '20s to '30s properties. The slightly more upmarket Chadwell Heath has some semi-detached houses (semis), but over 64 per cent of properties in Barking & Dagenham are terraces (the highest proportion in London) and a further 26 per cent flats, most purpose-built. The southern part of Barking & Dagenham will be affected by the Thames Gateway housing scheme (see page 139).

Costs

Average house prices and rents are among the lowest in London (see pages 141 and 160), while council taxes are just below the London average (see page 210).

Communications

Public transport is good in most areas, particularly for commuting into central London. The tube's District Line runs through Barking, Becontree and Dagen-ham, and there are three overground lines: one running into London's Liverpool Street station, one to Fenchurch Street, and another from Barking to Gospel Oak near Hampstead Heath (Camden). Buses are a better bet for travelling north/south and there are good services between the towns of Barking and Dagenham. The main A13 road to Essex cuts across the southern part of the borough, while the A406, known as the 'North Circular Road', forms Barking and Dagenham's western boundary.

Facilities

There's plenty of open space in Barking and Dagenham but it tends to be flat and rather dull. The largest of the borough's 16 parks, Eastbrookend Country Park in the east, boasts a lake and its own Millennium Centre, and the govern-ment is creating attractive walks along the River Roding as well as landscaping the A13. The borough is well supplied with cinemas and leisure centres, al-though there's only one museum, one theatre and one main library (in Barking). If you're looking for somewhere with plenty of good restaurants, Barking and Dagenham isn't for you!

Schools

Barking & Dagenham's state secondary schools are among the fastest-improving in London and its Education Authority has been described by OFSTED as 'a model of clarity'. There are no private schools in the borough.

Shopping

Barking is the best place for shopping, with the new Vicarage Fields centre and a pedestrian precinct. Chadwell Heath has reasonable shops, but Dagenham is best avoided.

Other Information

Council Offices: Civic Centre, Dagenham RM10 7BN (☎ 020-8592 4500, ✉ 3000direct@lbbd.gov.uk).
    Postcodes: IG11, RM6 (part), RM7 (part), RM8, RM9 (part) and RM10.
    Population: 165,000, with a high proportion of people under 20. Barking and Dagenham has a predominantly 'white' population, just 12 per cent belonging to ethnic minorities.
    Unemployment: The percentage of the working-age population that are unemployed is 12 – above the average for London.
    Crime Rate: Barking and Dagenham's crime rates are around average for London (see page 347).

BARNET

The outer London borough of Barnet is one of the largest. Much of its housing sprang up around the Northern tube line, which was built in the early part of the last century. At the end of the line in the far north of the borough, Barnet retains its market town character. In the centre, Totteridge and Mill Hill offer some attractive parts between the main roads. To the west, Edgware and Burnt Oak aren't particularly full of character, but Hendon in the south has distant echoes of its rural past. More up-market are Finchley and Friern Barnet to the east, with Hampstead Garden Suburb in the south-east corner home to the rich and famous. In the extreme south-west of the borough are Golders Green, Cricklewood and Brent Cross, the last two (with West Hendon) being the site of London's largest current housing development, not due to be completed until 2020. Other areas under development are Grahame Park and Stonegrove in the north-west of the borough and Dollis Valley in the north-east.

Property

Property is fairly evenly divided between flats (38 per cent), semi-detached (31 per cent), terraces (20 per cent) and detached houses (11 per cent) and rang-es from the affordable (in Edgware, Brent Cross and parts of Finchley) to the

1

outrageously expensive (in Hampstead Garden Suburb, where London's 'Millionaires' Row', Bishops Avenue, is to be found) and includes every style from modern apartment blocks and ex-council houses to Edwardian and Georgian mansions.

Costs

House prices and rents are just above the London average (see pages 141 and 160), as are council taxes (see page 210).

Communications

The Northern Line remains the main public transport artery, but trains can be infrequent, slow and crowded. Barnet isn't well served by mainline trains, although one of London's two trans-Thames routes (appropriately named Thameslink) links Mill Hill, Hendon and Cricklewood to places as far south as Wimbledon and Sutton via Blackfriars station in the City. Buses run all the way into central London but there are few east/west routes.

The UK's first motorway, the M1, begins in Barnet and other main roads such as the A1 and A41 cut through the borough from north to south. The A5 runs along the boundary between Barnet and Brent, and the North Circular Road (A406) joins the M1 at the busy Brent Cross intersection. Most areas have resident parking zones.

Facilities

There's lots of open space in Barnet, particularly towards the border with Hertfordshire, where there are several golf courses. There are also plenty of museums (including the RAF Museum at Hendon and the Jewish Museum in Finchley), cinemas, leisure centres and libraries, and a major arts and leisure centre due to open in 2004 in North Finchley will provide the borough with a second theatre to add to the Bull Theatre in Barnet town.

Schools

Barnet has a high proportion of state secondary schools providing above average education. There are plenty of private schools in the borough.

Shopping

Barnet is second only to Westminster in terms of the number of retailers within its boundaries. Shops range from the small specialist Jewish shops (and restaurants) in Golders Green and London's only Eastern shopping centre in West Hendon, to the huge 'mall' at Brent Cross. Edgware, Finchley, Hendon and

Barnet town all offer reasonable shopping.

Other Information

Council Offices: The Burroughs, London NW4 4BG (☎ 020-8359 2000, ✉ first.contact@barnet.gov.uk).

Postcodes: N2, N3, N10 (part), N11 (part), N12, N20, NW2 (part), NW4, NW7, NW9 (part), NW11, EN4 (part), EN5 (part), EN6 (part) and HA8 (part).

Population: 327,000 – London's second-most populous borough. Barnet is mainly a prosperous area with a high proportion of middle class families. Almost 25 per cent of its population belong to ethnic minorities, including London's largest Gujerati community, while Golders Green is home to the capital's biggest Jewish community.

Unemployment: The percentage of the working-age population that are unemployed is 5.8 – above the London average of 7 per cent.

Crime Rate: Barnet has the sixth highest overall crime rate, although violent crime is significantly below average (see page 347).

BEXLEY

Bexley (meaning 'clearing in the box wood') is mainly suburban and often rather dull, although there are smarter areas towards its southern end and the boundary with Bromley.

Property

A large proportion of property in Bexley is semi-detached (44 per cent – the highest percentage in London), with 30 per cent terraced, 21 per cent flats (almost all purpose-built) and only 6 per cent detached. Most properties date from the '20s and '30s and vary from the smart (around Sidcup and Blackfen in the south-west) to the shabby (around Erith in the north-east, which, however, are in line for a 'government improvement scheme'). In the centre of the borough, the town of Bexley itself is attractive, with something of a village feel, while neighbouring Bexleyheath and Welling consist mainly of typical '20s and '30s terraces and semis. In the flat marshland to the north-west, Thamesmead offers some attractive modern properties, and elsewhere there are bargains to be found among the tower blocks. The northern part of Bexley will be affected by the Thames Gateway housing scheme (see page 139).

Costs

House prices are generally low (see pages 141 and 160) and council taxes just above average (see page 210).

Communications

The underground doesn't reach Bexley, which is, however, particularly well served by overground trains: Belvedere, Bexley, Bexleyheath, Erith, Falconwood, Sidcup and Welling are linked to various central London terminals (Blackfriars, Cannon Street, Charing Cross, London Bridge, Victoria and Waterloo) and to all parts of Kent in the other direction. Bexley also has reasonable bus services.

The main A2 and A20 roads linking London with the Channel ports slice through the borough and offer escape routes into rural Kent, although they're inevitably heavy with traffic. Parking is increasingly controlled (and charged for) through resident permit zones.

Facilities

There are a number of hills in Bexley, as well as woods, parks and other open spaces, with golf courses in the centre of the borough and walks along the Rivers Cray and Thames. Restaurants are scarce and shopping is little more than adequate. Sports facilities are good and there are no fewer than four theatres and several museums, but only two cinemas.

Schools

Bexley's state secondary schools, which unusually include grammar schools, are mostly high-performing and over-subscribed; to have a chance of admission, a child must usually live within two miles of a school. There are no private secondary schools in the borough.

Shopping

The best shops are in Bexleyheath and the worst in Erith (although it has a popular twice weekly street market); there are hardly any shops at all in Thamesmead.

Other Information

Council Offices: Bexley Civic Offices, Broadway, Bexleyheath DA6 7LB (☎ 020-8303 7777, ✉ customer.services@bexley.gov.uk).

Postcodes: SE2, SE28 (part), DA1 (part), DA5 (part), DA6, DA7, DA8, DA14, DA15, DA16, DA17 and DA18.

Population: 220,000. Bexley is largely well-to-do with a predominantly white population (93 per cent), with a small Asian community centred in Belvedere).

Unemployment: The percentage of the working-age population that are unemployed is 5.0 – well below the London average of 7 per cent.

Crime Rate: Bexley has low crime rates for London and is the sixth lowest for all London Boroughs (see page 347).

BRENT

Brent, which takes its name from the river that runs through it, is a borough of various characters and is neither a typically 'inner' nor a typically 'outer' London borough. The North Circular, London's inner orbital road, splits the borough in half, each half having distinct economic and social characteristics. To the south, areas such as Harlesden, South Kilburn and Stonebridge suffer inner city levels of social deprivation, while parts of the more affluent, leafy suburban north (Brondesbury and Willesden Green, Dollis Hill, Kingsbury and out towards Harrow) boast tree-lined streets and a conservation area modelled on a picture postcard English village (there's even a castle and a thatched cottage!).

Wembley, of course, is home to one of the world's most famous sporting stadiums (currently being rebuilt) as well as the Arena and Conference Centre, which together attract tens of thousands of visitors a week. The planned regeneration of the stadium area could make Wembley one of the newly desirable areas of London. Further east, Neasden has a partly deserved reputation for dullness (and the largest Hindu temple outside India), while Queens Park and Kilburn in Brent's south-east corner are among the capital's upwardly mobile areas.

Property

Brent has a high proportion of flats (48 per cent), more than a third conversions, compared with 24 per cent each of terraces and semis, with a mere 4 per cent of detached houses. The flats around Queens Park are particularly attractive, being mostly in spacious, converted houses and situated close to central London.

Costs

House prices (see pages 141 and 160) are generally below average, but vary widely (houses sell for up to £1 million in upmarket areas) and council taxes are just above average (see page 210).

Communications

Public transport in Brent is generally good. The Bakerloo and Jubilee tube lines serve most areas, but Wembley is practically the only place with overground railway stations – linking with Marylebone and Euston stations. One of London's trans-Thames rail services usefully links Wembley to Clapham Junction, Croydon and places south.

The A406 North Circular Road, which cuts the borough in half, has recently been widened but still tends to jam at peak times. The A5 runs along the boundary with Barnet. Residents' parking permits have been widely introduced in recent years, and there are particularly high fees for second and third cars.

Facilities

Apart from the Wembley Arena, which offers world-class entertainment, there are good theatres and cinemas and reasonable sports facilities (including two boules rinks) in Brent. Its 1,000 acres of open spaces include Queens Park in the south, Gladstone Park with its exotic plants in the east, Roundwood Park (venue of the largest Irish festival outside Ireland), Fryent Country Park in the north and the Brent Reservoir (known as the Welsh Harp on account of its shape) on the border with Barnet. Wembley is notable for its choice of Indian restaurants as well as for a major Asian street market in Ealing Road.

Schools

Brent has 17 secondary schools, of which two are private. Most of the state schools are grant-maintained and most have good educational standards, despite the culturally diverse population (over 120 languages are reckoned to be spoken in the borough). There are three schools for religious groups: Hindus, Jews and Muslims. There are also two colleges of technology, an arts college and a language college. The top performing secondary (according to the government's 2003 performance reports) schools are Claremont High and Preston Manor High.

Shopping

Shopping in Brent tends to be functional, although there's a variety of ethnic shops in Kilburn, Willesden and Wembley. Nearby Brent Cross shopping centre (actually in Barnet) is one of London's largest.

Other Information

Council Offices: Forty Lane, Wembley HA9 9HX (☎ 020-8937 1234, ✉ customer.services@brent.gov.uk).

Postcodes: NW2 (part), NW6 (part), NW9 (part), NW10, HA3 (part), HA9 and HA0.

Population: 270,500. Brent has the most multi-cultural population in London and the second-most in England and Wales, boasting an ethnic majority population (i.e. over half its residents are non-'white'), consisting mainly of people of Asian origin (almost 28 per cent of the total population, mostly in the north and west) and Afro-Caribbeans (20 per cent); over 70 languages are spoken in Brent's schools. The borough also has the highest proportion of Irish-born inhabitants in London (9 per cent), mostly around Kilburn in the south-east. Poverty is a significant problem in the south of the borough; the number of low income households is increasing the gap between rich and poor is widening. Some 70 per cent of people in Harlseden are officially 'poor'.

Unemployment: The percentage of the working-age population that are unemployed is 8.4 – just above the London average of 7 per cent.

Crime Rate: Bent has the 11th highest crime rate of all the London Boroughs (see page 347).

BROMLEY

The largest of London's boroughs, Bromley is generally regarded as being part of Kent – particularly by its inhabitants. But in contrast to almost rural villages like Keston and Farnborough in the south, there's plenty of suburbia elsewhere. Bromley's north-west corner, which borders Lambeth, Southwark and Lewisham, has a rather depressed, inner city feel, although the government is committed to regenerating the areas around Penge, Anerley and Crystal Palace (once one of London's major attractions and the site of several aborted development projects). As you travel east, to Beckenham and Bromley town and then to Hayes and West Wickham, standards (and prices) start to rise, the most up-market parts of the borough being Chislehurst and Petts Wood in the north-east.

Property

Bromley has the highest percentage of detached houses in London (18 per cent), reflecting its high proportion of well-heeled residents. Most of these houses were built during the first third of the 20th century.
The remainder of properties are fairly evenly divided between semi-detached (29 per cent), terraces (25 per cent) and flats (29 per cent).

Costs

Average property prices and rents in Bromley are below the London average (see pages 141 and 160). Council taxes are also relatively low (see page 210).

Communications

Bromley isn't served by the underground, although overground rail stations are well spread and services are good. Anerley, Beckenham, Bromley, Chislehurst, Crystal Palace, Hayes, Orpington, Penge, Petts Wood and West Wickham are variously linked to Blackfriars, Cannon Street, Charing Cross, London Bridge, Victoria and Waterloo stations, and the East London line is expected to be extended as far as Crystal Palace. Buses are also widespread, but most won't take you anywhere near the city centre. The roads are particularly busy around Crystal Palace, where parking can also be a problem, otherwise the borough is mostly permit-free.

Facilities

There's plenty of open space in Bromley, as well as a variety of theatres, concert halls, libraries and museums, but just two cinemas. There are several sports centres – apart from the famous Athletics Stadium at Crystal Palace – and half a dozen golf courses. Chislehurst has a decent selection of restaurants.

Schools

Bromley has only one Local Education Authority-run secondary school, the rest being foundation, private or voluntary-aided schools.

Shopping

Excellent shopping facilities are to be found in Bromley town and good shops in Orpington; other towns are less well served.

Other Information

Council Offices: Bromley Civic Centre, Stockwell Close, Bromley BR1 3UH (☎ 020-8464 3333, ✉ csc@bromley.gov.uk)

Postcodes: SE20, BR1 (part), BR2, BR3, BR4, BR5, BR6, BR7, BR8 (part), CR6 (part), TN14 (part) and TN16 (part).

Population: 300,000 with the second-highest proportion of over 50s among the 33 boroughs. Bromley has a generally affluent, predominantly white population.

Unemployment: The percentage of the working-age population thatare unemployed is 5.5, below the London average of 7 per cent.

Crime Rate: In contrast to its northern neighbours, Bromley boasts a low crime rate (see page 347).

CAMDEN

Camden contains some of London's smartest areas – around Regent's Park to the south-west and Hampstead to the north-east – as well as some of its seediest around King's Cross station to the south-east, one of the capital's unofficial red light districts (which is, however, part of a multi-million pound regeneration project expected to start in 2007 and take at least ten years). A smaller development – of shops, offices and homes, to be called 'Regent's Quarter' – is being undertaken in the area surrounding the Pentonville Road. In the centre of the borough, Camden Town itself, with its colourful markets, has recently become one of the most 'in' places in London. Bloomsbury and Fitzrovia to the south are almost as trendy, while further west Primrose Hill and Belsize Park have attractive areas.

Property

The vast majority of properties in Camden are flats (86 per cent), of which over a third are conversions (i.e. converted from large houses), a further 10 per cent being terraced houses and just 4 per cent detached and semi-detached houses. Property varies from drab council blocks (in Somers Town) to elegant Georgian terraces (Camden Town) and Italianate villas (Belsize Park and Primrose Hill). The King's Cross development project (see above) will create 'affordable' housing on the 60-acre site behind King's Cross and St Pancras stations.

Costs

Property prices and rents vary enormously in Camden: reasonably priced houses can be found in some areas but in others it's possible to pay over £1 million for a three-bedroom flat or house (see pages 141 and 160); council tax rates are also high (see page 210).

Communications

In most parts of Camden you're spoilt for choice when it comes to public transport – which is just as well, because the council is waging war on the use of cars, and parking is a problem throughout the borough. The Northern tube line serves Belsize Park, Hampstead, Tufnell Park and Kentish Town, which is also on an overground line running through Blackfriars and across the river to Wimbledon and Sutton, as well as on a route linking Richmond with east London. A cross-river tram scheme linking Camden Town with Waterloo, Brixton and Peckham is being considered. King's Cross, St Pancras and Euston stations are all in the borough of Camden. King's Cross was given a face-lift in 2004 and St Pancras

1

is to have an international terminal for Eurostar trains, thanks to the Channel Tunnel Rail Link, by summer 2007, when it will be possible to reach Paris by train in just two-and-a-quarter hours.

Facilities

There's no shortage of leisure facilities in Camden, which includes part of London's 'theatreland', as well as the British Museum and the British Library in its new home at St Pancras. Hampstead Heath lies within the borough as does part of Regent's Park, and there are plenty of other green spaces including Primrose Hill, Parliament Hill and Kenwood. Camden has a vast choice of excellent restaurants.

Schools

Camden's state schools are 'excellent', according to the government's latest performance review, which awards the borough a three-star rating, and include no fewer than eight 'beacon' schools (boasting extremely high standards). This means that a large number of pupils 'commute' from neighbouring boroughs. The £21 million redevelopment of Haverstock secondary school is expected to be completed in 2005. There's also a good choice of private schools in and near Hampstead, and Camden houses much of the University of London.

Shopping

For shoppers, there's everything from crafty Covent Garden and ethnic Camden Market (actually five separate markets with a total of over 1,000 stalls) to the computer-heaven of Tottenham Court Road.

Other Information

Council Offices: Judd Street, London WC1H 9JE (☎ 020-7278 4444, ✉ info@camden.gov.uk).

Postcodes: N6 (part), NW1 (part), NW3, NW5, NW6 (part) and WC1.

Population: 211,000, with a high proportion of people between 20 and 35. Camden is the 17th most deprived area in England, yet many of the super-rich live there.

Unemployment: The percentage of the working-age population that are unemployed is 6.4 – just above the London average of 7 per cent. The King's Cross development project (see above) is expected to create 20,000 jobs in the borough by 2020.

Crime Rate: Camden has some of London's highest crime rates, including its highest rate of theft from cars and its second-highest house burglary rate (see page 347). Car theft and violence figures, however, are distorted by the large influx of visitors to the borough, particularly to London's West End.

CITY OF LONDON

The most ancient part of London, dating back to Roman times, 'the City' measures just one mile by one mile and is often referred to as 'The Square Mile' for that reason. This is the financial heart of London and, until quite recently, it consisted of almost nothing but banks and office buildings. Even today, outside working hours, it's a quiet place, with many shops, pubs and restaurants closed in the evenings.

Property

Virtually all the property (99 per cent) in the City of London is purpose-built flats. The largest development is the Barbican, dating from the '70s – a concrete maze broken up by occasional green spaces and ponds – but there are also luxury flats around St Paul's cathedral and Fleet Street, now deserted by the newspapers in favour of Docklands.

Costs

Not surprisingly, the City's few properties are among the most expensive in London to buy or rent (see pages 141 and 160), although council tax rates are the second-lowest in the capital (see page 210).

Communications

Being in the centre of London, the City is naturally well served by public transport and has no fewer than eleven tube stops and four overground terminals: Blackfriars (serving north London, the Midlands and the north of England as well as south London, Sussex, Hampshire and Dorset), Cannon Street (serving south-east London and Kent), Fenchurch Street (serving the East End and Essex) and Liverpool Street (serving Essex and East Anglia). It isn't, however, a place where cars are welcome; in fact access to the City is subject to a charge of £8 per day (see **Congestion Charge** on page 126), there's no resident parking and car parks can cost £12 or more per day.

Facilities

The Barbican has its own Arts Centre (incorporating a theatre, concert hall, museum, art galleries and cinemas) as well as being home to the Guildhall School of Music and Drama. The Museum of London is nearby. There's just one public leisure centre in the City, but umpteen private 'health clubs' for those who can afford them. Green spaces are few and small. Like its shops, the City's restaurants cater mainly for the local office population and choice is limited in the evenings.

Schools

There's only one state school in the City, a primary school, although there are three private schools.

Shopping

Shops cater mostly for the working population, with the exception of the famous Petticoat Lane market (actually in Middlesex Street on the border with Tower Hamlets).

Other Information

Council Offices: The Guildhall London, The Corporation of London, PO Box 270, London EC2 2EJ (☎ 020-7606 3030, ✉ enquiries@corpoflondon.gov. uk).

Postcodes: EC2 (part), EC3 and EC4.

The City of London is unlike the other 32 boroughs in that it's governed by a corporation, which has existed since the Middle Ages, and has its own police force – the City of London Police.

Population: Although some 350,000 people work in the City, its resident population is a mere 8,600 – most of them wealthy. The proportion of people under 20 is by far the lowest of any London borough, and the proportion of people between 20 and 35 among the highest.

Unemployment: The percentage of the working-age population that is unemployed is low at 2.1 – one of the lowest in London, where the average is 7 per cent.

Crime Rate: The City of London isn't covered by the Metropolitan Police, so there are no crime figures to compare with other boroughs. 'Petty' crime is generally low with property theft being the most likely crime, although the risk of terrorist attacks is probably the highest in London.

CROYDON

The outer London borough of Croydon has more than its fair share of drab parts – not least much of Croydon town itself in the centre of the borough – as well as some smarter suburban areas to the south.

Property

Croydon has an even mix of flats (31 per cent), terraces (34 per cent) and semi-detached or detached houses (35 per cent). Large Victorian properties predominate around Upper Norwood and South Norwood in the north, many converted into flats. Thornton Heath and Norbury to the north-west have mostly flats. Shirley Hills, south-east of Croydon town, is one of the borough's smartest areas and there are attractive semi-detached and detached houses around Purley, Selsdon and Coulsdon to the south. The best parts of Croydon town are on the east and south sides.

Costs

Average house prices and rents are around the London average (see pages 141 and 160), and council tax rates just above average (see page 210).

Communications

There are no tube stations but excellent rail services through Croydon town north to central London and south to Gatwick airport. A new 'railway' system called Tramlink (see page 115) runs across Croydon laterally from New Addington (on the border with Bromley) in the east to Mitcham and Wimbledon in Merton to the west. Most bus routes stop short of the city centre. The A23, which becomes the M23 south of Croydon, runs south into Surrey and Sussex.

Facilities

There are lots of parks in the borough, including Lloyd Park near Croydon town, South Norwood Country Park, Happy Valley Park near Coulsdon and the North Downs in the south. There's a fine house and garden at Norwood Grove near Upper Norwood with splendid views. The borough has a reasonable selection of cinemas, libraries, museums and leisure centres, and Croydon town boasts the new Clocktower arts centre as well as the Fairfield Halls – one of the major concert halls outside central London. A new swimming pool and leisure centre is under construction in Thornton Heath. There are probably more golf courses in Croydon than in any other London borough. There are some interesting restaurants in Crystal Palace and Upper Norwood; surprisingly, Croydon town isn't a particularly good place for eating out.

Schools

Croydon has a variety of secondary schools, including state, private, voluntary-aided and foundation schools and the country's only school of performing arts. Standards vary widely.

Shopping

A great deal of money is being spent on Croydon town's shopping centres, which are among the best outside central London; a new centre, called 'Centrale', is due to open in the town centre in April 2004. Otherwise shopping in the borough is rather uninspiring, although there's a new complex in North End.

Other Information

Council Offices: Taberner House, Park Lane, Croydon CR9 3JS (☎ 020-8686 4433, ✉ enquiries@croydon.gov.uk).

Postcodes: SE19, SE25, SW16 (part), CR0, CR2, CR3 (part), CR5, CR7 and CR8.

Population: 340,500 – London's most populous borough. Almost 20 per cent of Croydon's population belong to ethnic minorities, mostly Asian and Afro-Caribbean.

Unemployment: The percentage of the working-age population that are unemployed is 6.3 – just below the London average of 7 per cent.

Crime Rate: Croydon has slightly higher crime rates than its outer London neighbours, but they're below the London average (see page 347). Croydon's town centre is a particular trouble spot with priority to tackle street crime a big importance.

EALING

Ealing boasts interesting buildings, good shops, plenty of open space and good public transport. The borough as a whole is being promoted as a tourist and business destination. Ealing town in the centre is much sought-after, but Bedford Park in the south-east corner is the most expensive area. Acton in the east is less smart but seems to be on the up.

Property

Some 42 per cent of properties in Ealing are flats, 35 per cent terraces, 19 per cent semi-detached houses and just 3 per cent detached houses. Property in Ealing town is largely Victorian, as it is in Acton, where some attractive converted flats are to be found. West Acton has mock Tudor houses and flats, and North Ealing is mainly Edwardian. Near the A40 (Great West Road), Southall in the west and Greenford and Northolt in the north consist of mostly boring '30s semis. West Ealing and Hanwell are among the cheapest areas.

Costs

House prices and rents are comparable with neighbouring Hounslow, although those at the lower end of the market are cheaper (see pages 141 and 160), but council taxes are lower – just above the London average (see page 210).

Communications

One of Ealing's main attractions is its excellent train and tube links. The Central Line runs east/west across the middle of the borough and the Piccadilly Line north/south. Acton and Ealing are on an overground route into London Paddington and Acton is also linked by rail to Richmond and the City Airport in Docklands. The A40 runs across the north of the borough, linking it to central London and Birmingham, but, like all London's arterial roads, it's often badly clogged. The A406 North Circular Road, which cuts through Ealing from north to south, is notoriously busy at Hanger Lane (which is a bottleneck).

Facilities

There are plenty of theatres, cinemas and leisure centres in the borough, but poor library provision. There's also lots of open space, particularly in the north, where there are fine views from Horsenden Hill, and a surprising number of golf courses. Attractive walks can be found along the River Brent and the Grand Union Canal in the south-west of the borough. Shops are good in Ealing and dull in Acton. Southall has many excellent Indian restaurants and there's also a wide range of restaurants in Acton and Ealing.

Schools

A variety of secondary schools, both state and private, include the Greek School of London and the Japanese School. St Augustine's is one of the country's highest-performing private schools.

Shopping

There's a large choice of shops in Ealing, where you can find all the usual high street names and a number of shopping malls. Most of the rest of the borough has uninspiring shopping, with the exception of Southall, which has a wealth of Indian shops selling everything from spices to saris and excellent indoor and outdoor markets.

Other Information

Council Offices: Perceval House, 14/16 Uxbridge Road, Ealing W5 2HL (☎ 020-8825 5000, ✉ customers@ealing.gov.uk).
   Postcodes: W3, W5, W7, W13, UB1, UB2, UB5 and UB6.

Population: 305,000. Ealing's population is mostly middle class. Almost a third of the residents belong to ethnic minorities and the borough has London's biggest Indian population (centred in Southall, where there's also a significant Afro-Caribbean community).

Unemployment: The percentage of the working-age population that are unemployed is 5.3 – just below the London average of 7 per cent.

Crime Rate: Ealing's crime rates are around average for London (see page 347).

ENFIELD

London's most northerly borough, Enfield is a mixture of salubrious suburbs in the west and grim council estates in the east, although the industrial areas around Edmonton and Ponders End are being regenerated. The smart parts are Palmers Green, Oakwood, the rather twee village of Winchmore Hill and Hadley Wood – the most expensive part of Enfield where the odd celebrity may be spotted. In the centre is Enfield town itself, which is more of a county town than a London suburb.

Property

There's everything from grand detached houses in the north-west to grim tower blocks in the east. But even Edmonton and Ponders End have their Victorian terraces and '30s semis. In fact terraces make up 42 per cent of properties in Enfield, flats (which are mostly purpose-built) 32 per cent, semi-detached houses 20 per cent and detached houses the remaining 5 per cent.

Costs

House prices and rents are around the London average, similar to those of neighbouring Brent (see pages 141 and 160), but council taxes are higher than in Brent – just above the London average (see page 210).

Communications

Only the west of the borough is served by the tube; the Piccadilly Line stops at Southgate and Oakwood. Otherwise there are overground rail services from Moorgate and Liverpool Street stations to most parts of the borough.

Few buses make the slow journey to central London. The main A10 bisects Enfield north/south and the A406 North Circular Road cuts east/west across its southern end.

Facilities

Enfield has a reasonable selection of theatres, cinemas and leisure centres as well as several parks: Trent Park Country Park in the west, Whitewebbs Park and Forty Hall Country Park in the north, and Lee Valley Park (as well as the River Lee and a chain of reservoirs) in the east. Towards the Hertfordshire border is the vast open space of Enfield Chase. Enfield has a rather unexciting choice of restaurants.

Schools

There are some good private and selective state secondary schools in the borough.

Shopping

Enfield town has good shopping and there are a number of antiques shops in Winchmore Hill. In contrast, Southgate is dull and Edmonton Green has some of the worst shopping facilities in London.

Other Information

Council Offices: Civic Centre, Silver Street, Enfield EN1 3XY (☎020 8379 1000, ✉ webmaster@efirstop.demon.co.uk).

Postcodes: N9, N13, N14 (part), N21, EN1, EN2 (part), EN3, EN4 (part) and EN7 (part).

Population: 280,500. Enfield's population is mostly white (only 14 per cent belong to ethnic minorities), but there's a significant Indian and Afro-Caribbean population in Enfield town.

Unemployment: The percentage of the working-age population that are unemployed is 4.2 – lower than the London average of 7 per cent.

Crime Rate: The borough's crime rates are just below the London averages (see page 347).

GREENWICH

Greenwich is a curious mixture of the historic and the futuristic, the grand and the derelict. Despite Greenwich town being one of London's principal tourist attractions with its Observatory, National Maritime Museum and Royal Naval College and park (collectively declared a World Heritage Site in 1997 – see 🖳 www.greenwichwhs.org.uk), the borough as a whole is among the most deprived areas in England. The government is addressing the problem through a number of regeneration projects, including those at the Royal Arsenal in Woolwich, Kidbrooke, Thamesmead and Greenwich Peninsula. The last is the site of the ill-fated Millennium Dome sitting at the centre piece on the site of the former Millennium Dome, The 'O2 Arena' now boasts a fully-raised roof and outline. The purpose-built street, which wraps around the complex and will contain a 2,000 capacity Live Music Club, 11 screen cinema, exhibition and theatre spaces as well as bars and restaurants, is now clearly defined. An Olympic Venue, in 2012, The O2 will host the Gymnastics and Basketball finals whilst in 2009, it will play host to the Artistic Gymnastics World Championships. The Peninsula development will also provide 10,000 new homes, almost 40 per cent of them 'affordable', and create an estimated 24,000 new jobs.

Property

Property ranges from grand Victorian and Georgian houses in Blackheath and West Greenwich, small Victorian terraces in East Greenwich, Shooters Hill and Plumstead to the east, and '60s tower blocks in Thamesmead in the north-east. Some of the cheapest properties in London are to be found among the council estates of Abbey Wood in the south. Some 42 per cent of properties in Greenwich are flats (the great majority purpose-built), 39 per cent terraced houses, 16 per cent semi-detached and just 3 per cent detached houses. Most detached houses are found in Kidbrooke (centre) and Charlton (north), the latter enjoying good views across the River Thames to Docklands.

There's a considerable amount of development taking place in Greenwich: up to 1,500 new homes are to be built in the Millennium Village on Greenwich's so-called peninsula (its north-west corner, which protrudes into a bend in the River Thames) near the Dome, and there are plans for 2,500 more along Gallions Reach to add to the recently built starter homes at Thamesmead North. The northern part of Greenwich will be affected by the Thames Gateway housing scheme (see page 141). Several interesting buildings in and around Woolwich are being renovated and converted into housing.

Costs

Property prices and rents in Greenwich are around the London average (see pages 141 and 160). Council taxes are just above average (see page 210). The cheapest rented accommodation is to be found in the east of the borough, in Plumstead, Thamesmead and Woolwich.

Communications

The Docklands Light Railway (DLR) has been extended to Greenwich, with two stops in the borough, Cutty Sark and Greenwich town, and a further extension, from City Airport to Woolwich, has recently been approved and is underway. The Jubilee Line now serves North Greenwich, which is a 15-minute journey from the City. Overground train services are better in some areas than others; Thamesmead, for example, is more than two miles from a station. Bus services are little better, although there are routes across the river to the city centre and river taxi services have recently been revived (see page 121). The A2, the main road from northern Kent, runs through the borough to central London and is bi-sected by the A204 South Circular Road, which connects with the North Circular north of the river via the free Woolwich ferry (see page 122). A new bridge from Thamesmead to Beckton has been approved, although it will take many years to build. Parking is virtually impossible around Greenwich town, particularly at weekends.

Facilities

As well as the attractions of Greenwich town (see above), the borough has many parks, woods and open spaces: Oxleas Woods in the east, Greenwich Park and Blackheath in the west, and Avery Hill near Eltham in the south-west. There are numerous leisure centres but few theatres and cinemas, although a 14-screen cinema has recently opened on the Greenwich Peninsula. The Blackheath Concert Halls do their best to rival those in Croydon and central London and the new Laban Dance Centre in Deptford offers both classes and performances. The Royal Arsenal site in Woolwich incorporates the national museum of the Royal Artillery as well as the borough museum. Most of the best restaurants are to be found in Eltham and Greenwich town.

Schools

With the exception of two 'beacon' schools, Greenwich's secondary schools generally perform poorly and truancy levels are high, although standards are improving. Its primary schools, on the other hand, are among the best in the country. There are some good private schools in the borough as well as six centres offering vocational and academic training for children over 16.

Shopping

There are some interesting shops in Eltham and Greenwich town, the latter also having covered and open-air markets. The Greenwich Peninsula development (see above) incorporates a shopping centre, there's a new retail park in Charl-ton, and the shopping facilities in Woolwich town centre are being revamped.

Other Information

Council Offices: 29–37 Wellington Street, Woolwich, London SE18 6PQ (☎

020-8854 8888, ✉ Frankie.Eldridge@greenwich.gov.uk).
   Postcodes: SE3, SE7, SE9, SE10, SE18 and SE28 (part).
   Population: 225,800. Some 15 per cent belong to ethnic minorities.
   Unemployment: The percentage of the working-age population that are unemployed is 8.3 – just above the London average of 7 per cent.
   Crime Rate: Greenwich's crime rates are around average for London (see page 347).

HACKNEY

Hackney stretches from the City to Haringey and shares with neighbouring Islington such inner city problems as high unemployment and crime rates and poor schools. In response to these, the government is injecting money into Dalston, Haggerston, Hackney Wick and Hackney town itself.

Property

The borough has a good deal of council property including ugly tower blocks, some of which are due to be demolished. Some of the best property is to be found by the Regent's Canal in the south, around Victoria Park (which is actually in Tower Hamlets) to the east and in De Beauvoir Town to the west. There are some large Victorian houses around Stamford Hill to the north and Clapton to the east. Warehouses and factories are being converted into flats in Shoreditch and Hoxton in the south. Flats account for the vast majority of properties in Hackney (77 per cent) and a further 20 per cent are terraced houses. Just 2 per cent of properties are semi-detached and fewer than 0.5 per cent are detached houses, most of these in and around Stoke Newington.

Costs

Hackney has some of the cheapest property in London (see pages 141 and 160), but council taxes are high (see page 210).

Communication

Incredibly, there's only one tube station in Hackney – Old Street on the Northern Line on the Islington boundary, but the borough does have reasonable rail links into Liverpool Street, except in the south-west corner. There's also an overground route running east/west through Dalston, Hackney and Homerton. Fortunately, bus services are good, although most roads are clogged with traffic.

Facilities

Inhabitants of Hackney have access to lovely Victoria Park in Tower Hamlets and to the Regent's Canal. In Clissold Park, near Stoke Newington, there are even deer, but Hackney Marsh consists mostly of football pitches.

Varied entertainment facilities include live circus, art cinemas and the famous Hackney Empire theatre. There are also lots of art galleries and many resident artists open their studios to the public. Hackney has four leisure centres as well as other sports facilities, and the Stoke Newington West Reservoir is to be converted into a water sports centre. Stoke Newington is the place to eat out in Hackney, although there are also plenty of restaurants in Shoreditch and a number of Turkish restaurants elsewhere.

Schools

Hackney has 16 secondary schools, including six private schools, several of which are run by the local Jewish community.

Shopping

Shopping facilities are adequate, the most interesting shops being near Victoria Park (arts and crafts), Stamford Hill (Jewish) and Stoke Newington (ethnic).

Other Information

Council Offices: Town Hall, Mare Street, London E8 1EA (☎ 020-8356 3000, ✉ info@hackney.gov.uk).

Postcodes: E5, E8, E9, EC2 (part), N1 and N16.

Population: 207,000, with a high proportion of people under 20. Hackney is the country's fourth most deprived area, although it's trying to revive itself and attract artists and small businesses as well as middle-class homebuyers. Almost half of the population live in council houses, but some parts – particularly adjacent to Islington – have recently become quite trendy, particularly Stoke Newington. There's a substantial Turkish population in Hackney as well as a large orthodox Jewish community around Stamford Hill and Clapton.

Unemployment: The percentage of the working-age population that are unemployed is 11.3 – one of the highest in London, where the average is 7 per cent.

Crime Rate: Hackney has some of the highest crime rates in London, with one of the capital's highest rate of house burglary and second-highest of stolen cars (see page 347).

HAMMERSMITH & FULHAM

Hammersmith & Fulham started to become fashionable in the '80s and is now solidly respectable. The smarter areas – Hammersmith, Fulham, Parsons Green, Hurlingham, Sands End and the exclusive Chelsea Harbour – are in the south near the river and in the east along the border with Kensington & Chelsea. The further north you go, through Shepherds Bush towards White City and Wormwood Scrubs, the scruffier the borough becomes. In fact, these three areas are the centre of a multi-million pound government regeneration scheme.

Property

Hammersmith & Fulham has a similar property mix to Hackney with just 3 per cent detached and semi-detached houses, 24 per cent terraces and 72 per cent flats, almost half of which are conversions (compared with just a fifth in Hackney). West Kensington and Barons Court in the centre of the borough have mostly flats, as do Sands End in the south-east, although here the buildings are modern. Nearby Chelsea Harbour is an '80s development of exclusive flats, shops, restaurants and a five-star hotel surrounding a small marina with access to the River Thames. In the south-west around Fulham and Parsons Green are mostly Victorian terraces – those along the river at Hurlingham having distinctive terracotta facings. All this is in stark contrast to the unsightly council estate at White City in the north.

Costs

There's a huge range of property prices and rents across the borough: a four or five-bedroom house, for example can be had for as 'little' as £185,000 or as much as £1 million (see pages 141 and 160). Council tax rates are just above the London average (see page 210).

Communications

The District, Piccadilly, Central and Hammersmith & City/Metropolitan tube lines all run through the borough, but there are virtually no overground train links (two lines run along the boundary with Kensington & Chelsea, stopping at West Brompton). Bus services are generally good, but there's invariably heavy traffic on and around the A4, which cuts across the centre of the borough. Hammersmith & Fulham contains no fewer than three major football grounds (Chelsea, Fulham and Queen's Park Rangers) as well as the Olympia Exhibition and Conference Centre, which can cause severe congestion of the transport system.

Facilities

The borough boasts several well-known theatres (Apollo Hammersmith, Lyric and Riverside Studios), but only one mainstream cinema. There isn't much in the way of museums either, although the 'museum borough', Hounslow, is next-door. There are few open spaces and the largest area, Wormwood Scrubs (adjacent to the eponymous prison), is uninteresting. By way of compensation there are attractive walks along the River Thames and three leisure centres. Fulham, Parsons Green, Hammersmith and Shepherds Bush all have a good selection of restaurants, pubs and wine bars.

Schools

Hammersmith & Fulham's 14 secondary schools include three private schools, a theatre school and a school (Twynholm) offering a curriculum leading to the National Christian Education Certificate. Standards vary considerably, although the Local Education Authority has been highly praised for its effort to improve them.

Shopping

The smartest shops are along the New Kings Road in Fulham and at Chelsea Harbour. Hammersmith and Shepherds Bush have extensive but not very user-friendly shopping centres. There are six-day markets in the North End Road east of Hammersmith and in Goldhawk Road in Shepherds Bush.

Other Information

Council Offices: Town Hall, King Street, London W6 9JU (☎ 020-8748 3020, ✉ information@lbhf.gov.uk).

Postcodes: NW10 (part), SW6, W6, W12 and W14 (part).

Population: 177,000 with a low proportion of people under 20 but a high proportion of people between 20 and 35. Despite the 'Yuppie-land' reputation of parts of the borough (particularly Fulham), Hammersmith & Fulham is the 18th most deprived area in England.

Unemployment: The percentage of the working-age population that are unemployed is 9.2 – just above the London average of 7 per cent.

Crime Rate: Crime rates are around the London averages for violence and stolen cars but above average for house burglary and theft from cars (see page 347).

HARINGEY

Haringey is less popular than its southern neighbours, Islington and Camden, and is generally considered as part of inner London. Some of London's wealthiest citizens can be found in Highgate in the south-west and some of its poorest in Tottenham in the north-east. The government is pouring millions into new housing, shops and leisure facilities in the latter area.

Property

Haringey has 52 per cent flats (almost half of which are conversions), 41 per cent terraced houses, 5 per cent semi-detached and just one per cent detached. There are some lovely Georgian residences among the mix of properties in Highgate, which is marginally less expensive than Hampstead in neighbouring Camden, and splendid Edwardian properties in Muswell Hill, Alexandra Palace and Crouch End in the west. In the north, Wood Green, Noel Park and their more up-market neighbour Hornsey offer Victorian terraces, while up-and-coming Finsbury Park in the south-east has plenty of large conversion flats. Housing in Tottenham in the north-east mostly consists of drab council estates, but Victorian and Edwardian terraces can also be found. The cheapest properties are around White Hart Lane, where Tottenham Hotspur football club has its ground.

Costs

House prices in Haringey are near the average for London (see pages 141 and 160), but council taxes are high (see page 210).

Communications

The Victoria and Piccadilly tube lines run through the borough, but some parts (e.g. Muswell Hill) are a good walk from a station. Two overground rail routes run north/south through the borough – one centrally, the other down the eastern side – and a third runs east/west across the southern part of the borough. There are good bus services to central London. The A1 cuts across the southwest corner of the borough and the A10 forces its way up through the east end. There's only one controlled parking area, in Wood Green.

Facilities

Haringey is reasonably well provided with theatres, cinemas, museums and sports facilities and boasts the recently rebuilt Alexandra Palace exhibition centre in Alexandra Park, which provides fabulous views over London. Haringey's many other open spaces include Finsbury Park in the south, Highgate Woods in the south-west and the River Lea on the border with Waltham Forest. There's a reasonable choice of restaurants, particularly Turkish and Greek around Finsbury Park, Hornsey and Wood Green.

Schools

Haringey's secondary schools, two of which are private, have varying standards.

Shopping

There's a large mall at Wood Green and reasonable shopping in Highgate, Hornsey and Finsbury Park, but the best shops are in Muswell Hill and Crouch End. A new retail centre is planned for Tottenham, where there are several interesting Afro-Caribbean shops.

Other Information

Council Offices: Civic Centre, High Road, Wood Green, London N22 8LE (☎ 020-8489 0000, ✉ customer.services@haringey.gov.uk).
Postcodes: E5, E8, E9, N4, N6 (part), N8, N10 and N16.
Population: 225,00, with a high proportion of people between 20 and 35. Almost a third of the borough's inhabitants belong to ethnic minorities, with significant Afro-Caribbean, Asian, Greek and Turkish communities.
Unemployment: The percentage of the working-age population that are unemployed is 10.4 – among the highest in London, where the average is 7 per cent.
Crime Rate: Haringey's crime rates are generally just above the London average, although it has the capital's highest rate of house burglary (see page 347). Finsbury Park station has long been a trouble spot although improved CCTV is helping.

HARROW

Most people in Harrow actually believe they live in Middlesex, even although Middlesex ceased to exist in 1965 and isn't marked on any current map. Harrow is famous for its public school – which is actually in Harrow-on-the-Hill, the smartest part of the borough. Elsewhere there's dull '20s and '30s suburbia, which stretches from South Harrow in the south through Harrow town and Wealdstone to Harrow Weald in the north. Further out still, around Stanmore in the north-east and Pinner in the north-west, are more open areas.

Property

Harrow boasts one of the highest levels of owner-occupied property in the UK. Harrow-on-the-Hill in the south-east of the borough has mostly Victorian and Edwardian properties, many converted into flats. There are some attractive modern flats to be found among the '30s semis in and around Harrow town just to the north, and bargain buys to be had in South Harrow (south-west) and Wealdstone (centre). In the north-west, Pinner and Hatch End offer semi-detached and detached '30s Tudor-style houses as well as more modern townhouses. Stanmore to the north-east boasts some of the borough's grandest properties as well as more modest semis and detached houses. Overall, Harrow has a high proportion of semi-detached houses (39 per cent) with a further 11 per cent detached. The remainder are equally divided between flats (27 per cent) and terraced houses (23 per cent).

Costs

Harrow has average house prices and rents for London (see pages 141 and 160), but council tax rates are the second-highest in London (see page 210).

Communications

The Bakerloo, Jubilee and Metropolitan tube lines run through the western and eastern parts of the borough. In the centre, Harrow and Wealdstone are linked by overground trains to London Euston as well as being on the trans-Thames route to Clapham Junction and places south, while Harrow-on-the-Hill is linked to London Marylebone. Buses are good for local journeys but won't take you into central London. There are no major roads through Harrow but plenty of traffic, and there's controlled parking in most areas.

Facilities

Harrow has a below average selection of theatres, cinemas, museums and galleries, just one leisure centre, although it's the largest in north London, and few golf courses. There's plenty of open space, however, with more than 50 parks including Bentley Priory Nature Reserve and woodland at Stanmore and Harrow Weald on the edge of Hertfordshire, as well as one of London's few working farms at Pinner. Good views can be had from Harrow-on-the-Hill. There's a reasonable selection of restaurants in Harrow town, Harrow-on-the-Hill and Pinner.

Schools

Harrow has an unusual state school structure, secondary schooling starting at the age of 12 instead of 11 and pupils moving to one of two tertiary colleges (there's also a Roman Catholic sixth-form college) at the age of 16. The famous Harrow School caters for boys only (boys whose parents are **very** wealthy).

Shopping

The new shopping centre in Harrow town is claimed to be one of London's 'top ten'. Otherwise, Harrow-on-the-Hill and Pinner have attractive shops, but Wealdstone and Stanmore are a let-down.

Other Information

Council Offices: Civic Centre, Station Road, Harrow HA1 2XF
(☎ 020-8863 5611, ✉ info@harrow.gov.uk).
   Postcodes: HA1, HA2, HA3, HA5 (part), HA7 and HA8 (part).
   Population: 212,00. Harrow is 30 per cent 'ethnic', with a large Indian population and a Jewish community centred on Stanmore, although the majority of inhabitants are white-collar workers who commute into the city centre.
   Unemployment: The percentage of the working-age population that are unemployed is 7.1 – well below the London average of 7 per cent.
   Crime Rate: Harrow has some of the capital's lowest crime rates, including the lowest rate of violent crime and the third-lowest incidence of car stealing (see page 347).

HAVERING

London's easternmost borough and the only one with a border outside the M25 orbital motorway, Havering offers more space between its houses than any other borough. Havering Atte Bower in the far north is more or less in the country, and there are marshes in the south around industrial Rainham by the River Thames. The main towns are in the centre and west: Hornchurch and Upminster, which grew up around the District tube line, and Romford (on the border with Barking & Dagenham), which is Havering's commercial and administrative centre.

Property

Havering has the lowest percentage of flats of any borough (just 18 per cent – almost all purpose-built), 32 per cent terraces, 40 per cent semi-detached houses and 10 per cent detached. There's a mixture of Victorian and '30s terraces, converted and modern flats in Romford. Gidea Park to the east is one of London's garden suburbs, dating from the early years of the 20th century, and boasts some elegant Edwardian houses. The '50s council estate at Harold Hill in the north-east is now more than half privately owned and there are bargains to be found here. Hornchurch and Upminster offer attractive properties in a variety of styles. The southern part of Havering will be affected by the Thames Gateway housing scheme (see page 139).

Costs

Havering enjoys low average property prices in London (see pages 141 and 160) but council tax rates are the capital's fourth-highest (see page 210).

Communications

Elm Park, Hornchurch and Upminster are on the District tube line. Upminster is also served by overground trains into Liverpool Street and Fenchurch Street. Romford, Gidea Park and Harold Wood in the north are on the Liverpool Street Line and Rainham in the south is linked to Fenchurch Street. Elsewhere, cars are the order of the day, as few bus services reach the city centre. The A12 cuts through the northern part of the borough, the A13 through the southern part and the M25 makes a brief appearance in the east.

Facilities

There are two cinemas and two leisure centres in the borough but just one theatre and no public museums or galleries. Compensation is the amount of open space, including several parks and golf courses. The attractive River Ingrebourne virtually bisects the borough from north to south. From a culinary point of view, Havering is something of a desert.

Schools

Havering has 22 secondary schools, none of which are private. Since 1995, all pupils over 16 have been educated in one of two sixth-form colleges.

Shopping

There's nothing much in the way of shopping centres outside Romford, which isn't exactly in the premier league itself.

Other Information

Council Offices: Town Hall, Main Road, Romford RM1 3BD (☎ 01708-434343, ✉ info@havering.gov.uk).

Postcodes: CM14 (part), RM1, RM2, RM3, RM4 (part), RM5, RM7, RM9 (part), RM11, RM12, RM13, RM14 and RM15 (part).

Population: 225,000, with the lowest proportion of people between 20 and 35 of the 33 London boroughs and the highest proportion of people over 50. Havering has the lowest proportion of ethnic minorities of any London borough (a mere 3 per cent).

Unemployment: The percentage of the working-age population that are unemployed is 3.5 – among the lowest in London, where the average is 7 per cent.

Crime Rate: Havering has below-average crime rates for London, with the lowest rate of house burglary in the capital – along with Kingston and Sutton (see page 347).

HILLINGDON

London's second largest borough, Hillingdon covers the whole of the western end of the capital, but for the most part it's more like the Home Counties than London, with swathes of green belt (areas in which building is restricted) and expanses of suburbia. (Like the inhabitants of Harrow and Hounslow, most Hillingdon residents think they still live in Middlesex.) London's first airport, Heathrow, is entirely within the borough and is currently the site of one of the country's biggest construction projects, Terminal 5 (see page 106). Hillingdon also boasts a growing high-tech business centre at Stockley Park (between Uxbridge and Heathrow).

Property

Hillingdon's smartest areas are in the north-east: Eastcote, Ruislip, Northwood and Northwood Hills. This is Metroland, so-called because it grew up around the Metropolitan Line 'underground' (although it runs mostly above ground here) and memorably satirised by poet John Betjeman. The borough becomes progressively less salubrious as you move south, through Ickenham village, Uxbridge (the borough's administrative capital) to Hillingdon, Hayes and West Drayton. But government spending is revitalising these parts, particularly Uxbridge, where a massive new shopping and entertainment centre has recently been built (see below). Hillingdon boasts the second-highest proportion of detached houses (14 per cent) in London. Of the remainder, 35 per cent are semi-detached and 28 per cent terraced houses, with 24 per cent flats (almost all purpose-built). Much of the property is in the '30s suburban style – if it can be called a style. Victorian terraces can be found in Uxbridge to the west and Hayes in the south-east.

Costs

Average property prices and rents in Hillingdon are above the London average, although there are inexpensive houses to be found here (see pages 141 and 160). Council taxes are high (see page 210).

Communications

Hillingdon is well served by both underground and overground trains. The top half of the borough has three tube lines (Hammersmith & City /Metropolitan, Central and Piccadilly) as well as an overground line through Northolt Park and Ruislip. The bottom half has two train lines running into London Paddington, plus another branch of the Piccadilly tube line. Heathrow airport is also served by the non-stop link Heathrow Express from Paddington (see page 104). There are no regular bus services to central London. Three major roads cut across Hillingdon from east to west – the A4 and M4 in the south and the A40 in the centre – so in theory it's a good place to escape the city from (in theory, because all three roads are often jammed with traffic). For those that want to get away from it **all**, there's Heathrow airport itself!

Facilities

Hillingdon's new shopping centre houses a nine-screen cinema – the only cinema in the borough, as well as a number of restaurants. Elsewhere Hillingdon has a good supply of leisure centres and other sports facilities (Uxbridge even has a dry ski slope!) as well as several theatres, museums and galleries. Hillingdon is also well endowed with open space and borders the Chiltern hills to the west and Ruislip Woods, which is claimed to be the largest uninterrupted stretch of woodland in London. The Grand Union Canal, which runs across the borough

between the M4 and A40 through mostly industrial areas, isn't as picturesque as it might sound.

Schools

There are no selective state secondary schools in Hillingdon, where there are 17 comprehensives and two private schools, as well as colleges of languages, performing arts and technology.

Shopping

Uxbridge is the main shopping centre in Hillingdon, where a new shopping centre called The Chimes has recently opened. Windsor Road offers the most upmarket shopping in Hillingdon; the rest is fairly downmarket, as is Hayes. More interesting shops can be found in Ruislip and Northwood. The borough as a whole has recently been voted one of the ten best shopping areas in Greater London.

Other Information

Council Offices: Civic Centre, High Street, Uxbridge UB8 1UW (☎ 01895-250111).

Postcodes: HA4, HA5 (part), HA6 (part), TW6, UB3, UB4, UB7, UB8, UB9 (part), UB10, UB11 and WD3 (part).

Population: 249,000. Hillingdon is very much commuter-belt with a high proportion of white-collar workers and few non-whites.

Unemployment: The percentage of the working-age population that are unemployed is 3.8 – well below the London average of 7 per cent.

Crime Rate: Crime rates are around average for London (see page 347).

HOUNSLOW

Hounslow stretches all the way from Hammersmith & Fulham to Surrey. Like the people of Hillingdon and Harrow, most of Hounslow's inhabitants believe they live in Middlesex. Unfortunately, some of the borough lies directly under the path of planes landing at or (if the wind is from the east, as it occasionally is) taking off from Heathrow airport and much of the rest of it is affected by constant aircraft noise. Nevertheless, Hounslow has attractive areas, particularly at its eastern end (around Chiswick and Bedford Park), which borders the River Thames and boasts some of the most picturesque riverside views in London. Brentford in the north-east has recently experienced the second-fastest property price rises of any town in the UK as it undergoes a multi-million pound transformation from sleepy backwater to trendy enclave, complete with luxury riverside flats, hotels, restaurants, shops and offices. Other areas in line for development include Feltham High Street, where work on new flats, shops and leisure facilities began in March 2004, and Hounslow High Street, which is to undergo a major face-lift over the coming years.

Property

Hounslow has an even mix of property types with 33 per cent detached and semi-detached houses, 31 per cent terraces and 36 per cent flats (mostly purpose-built). Like neighbouring Hillingdon, Hounslow has more than its fair share of '30s developments, the worst of which are found around Feltham, Hanworth and Heston in the west. To the north, around Osterley Park, are more interesting properties. Chiswick in the east has Victorian and Edwardian terraces as well as Victorian semis and detached houses. The centre of Hounslow town also has Victorian terraces. Near the river in Isleworth are some interesting properties, some dating back to the 16th century.

Costs

Average property prices and rents are on the high side (see pages 141 and 160), as are council taxes (see page 210).

Communications

Only the north-east of the borough is served by the tube – the Piccadilly and

District lines. Other parts are well served by the South West Trains network. As in many other outer London boroughs, there are no regular bus services into central London. Running east/west through much of Hounslow are the A30, the A4 and (often directly above it) the M4.

Facilities

Hounslow is home to several stately homes including Chiswick, Gunnersbury, Osterley Park and Syon Houses with their accompanying parks and gardens. Bedfont Lakes Country Park and Cranford Countryside Park by the River Crane, both of which feature wetland, woodland and meadows, have recently won Civic Trust Green Flag awards. More open space is provided by Hounslow Heath between Hounslow town and Hanworth. The borough has no shortage of leisure centres, plus two cinemas and two theatres. Chiswick is the borough's restaurant capital.

Schools

Hounslow has 16 secondary schools, two of which are private, one voluntary-controlled and four voluntary-aided. The Local Education Authority has been awarded 'beacon' status, which means that education is a priority of the borough council, and Hounslow's schools were recently ranked fourth in the government's 'value added' tables.

Shopping

Hounslow town is the main shopping centre with an airy indoor mall and there are attractive and unusual shops in Chiswick. Brentford's transformation has greatly improved its shopping facilities, and Feltham High Street is next in line for revitalisation (see above).

Other Information

Council Offices: The Civic Centre, Lampton Road, Hounslow TW3 4DN (☎ 020-8583 2000, ✉ smpp@hounslow.gov.uk).
   Postcodes: W4, TW3, TW4, TW5, TW7, TW8, TW13 and TW14.
   Population: 213,000. Hounslow has a significant Indian population (25 per cent of the borough's residents belong to ethnic minorities) and is mostly a white-collar area.
   Unemployment: The percentage of the working-age population that are unemployed is 8.6 – above the London average of 7 per cent.
   Crime Rate: Hounslow's crime rates are generally around average for London, although the rate of violent crime is above average (see page 347).

ISLINGTON

Until 30 years ago Islington was run-down and undesirable. Today it's one of London's most trendy boroughs – and property prices have risen in proportion. There remain very poor areas, although the council is pouring money into revitalising the worst of them.

Property

Islington has the second-lowest proportion of detached and semi-detached houses in London (less than 1.5 per cent). Some 16 per cent of properties are terraced houses, the remaining 82 per cent being flats (more than a third conversions). In the extreme south of the borough, on the City border, are converted warehouses, council blocks and Georgian terraces in Clerkenwell and Finsbury (not to be confused with Finsbury Park a few miles further north in Haringey). Highbury and Islington in the centre are the smartest areas with attractive Georgian and Victorian terraces, although property becomes less desirable the further east you go. In the north of the borough, Tufnell Park and Upper Holloway offer a mixture of council property, Victorian terraces and grander detached houses.

Costs

Islington has high property prices and rents, although the range is wide (see pages 141 and 160), and council taxes are just below average (see page 210).

Communications

Islington is poorly served by trains: the Northern (tube) Line barely touches the south-west corner of the borough and the Piccadilly Line cuts across the north-west corner only. The main railway line from the north of England into Moorgate makes just three stops in the borough. Bus services, on the other hand, are good. The A1 cuts the borough in half vertically and traffic is particularly bad around Archway. At £95 a year, residents' parking permits are around average for central London.

Facilities

If you like open spaces, Islington isn't for you, as it has less than any other London borough. Only the Regent's Canal, which runs across the centre of the borough, and Highbury Fields in the north-east offer any escape from buildings. On the other hand, Islington is one of the best places in the capital for fringe theatre. It's also the home of Sadlers Wells, famous for opera and ballet, and the theatres and cinemas of London's West End are nearby. There are no fewer than seven leisure centres in Islington, as well as other sports facilities. There are plenty of restaurants, particularly in Clerkenwell, Holloway and Islington town, where Upper Street has almost nothing but eating places.

Schools

Islington's secondary schools have traditionally performed worse than those of any other London borough. However, since the school system was privatised in 2000 there has been considerable improvement. There's only one private school in the borough.

Shopping

Shopping facilities are generally no better than average, although Islington town has some unusual shops.

Other Information

Council Offices: Town Hall, Upper Street, London N1 2UD (☎ 020-7527 2000 ✉ contact@islington.gov.uk).
Postcodes: EC1, N1 (part), N5, N7 and N19.
Population: 180,000, with a high proportion of people between 20 and 35. Almost 20 per cent of Islington's population belong to ethnic minorities and there's a large Italian population around Clerkenwell. It's also known for its fashionable people, particularly left-wingers.
Unemployment: The percentage of the working-age population that are unemployed is 7.8 – about average for London, where the average is 7 per cent.
Crime Rate: Overall, Islington has the capital's highest crime rate, with violent crime and car theft figures more than double the national average (see page 347).

KENSINGTON & CHELSEA

Kensington & Chelsea is the most affluent borough not only of London but also of the UK, where 12.5 per cent of the population earns more than £60,000 per year. More than two-thirds of Kensington & Chelsea is a conservation area and the borough boasts some of the most attractive buildings in London. Not surprisingly, they're also some of the most expensive to buy. Kensington & Chelsea is also crowded, particularly in summer when tourists flock to its museums and galleries. Colville is London's most densely populated area with 20,000 residents per square kilometre. Development projects in the borough for 2004–07 include a major redesign of Exhibition Road, Sloane Square and the area around South Kensington tube station, and further tidying-up of Earls Court (where a drinking ban has been introduced in an effort to combat problems caused by alcoholics).

Property

Some 84 per cent of properties in Kensington and Chelsea are flats and it's the only borough in London where the number of conversions exceeds the number of purpose-built flats. Of the remaining 16 per cent, 14 per cent are terraced houses and just 2 per cent semi-detached or detached. Elegant properties in Chelsea (south), South Kensington (centre) and Knightsbridge (east) contrast with shabby Earls Court (west) and North Kensington (north). In between, Notting Hill has become one of London's trendiest areas and property prices have risen accordingly.

Costs

Not surprisingly, average house prices in Kensington & Chelsea are among the highest in London (see pages 141 and 160): if you want a large house in Holland Park, you'll need a cool £10 million or more; a three-bedroom Chelsea flat is a snip at a million or two! On the other hand, the borough has the third-lowest council tax rates in London (see page 210).

Communications

The Central, Circle, District and Piccadilly tube lines all run through the borough. Only Chelsea is a long way from a tube stop. Kensington/Olympia is also served by an overground rail route between Clapham Junction to the south and Willesden Junction to the north as well as by a second trans-Thames line linking the north and south of England. New stations on the West London line are planned. Bus connections to the city centre are good and both the A4 and M40 Westway run east/west through the borough. Parking, however, can be a problem, even outside your own home.

Facilities

If Westminster is London's 'theatreland', Kensington & Chelsea is its 'museumland'. The Science Museum, Natural History Museum and Victoria & Albert Museum are all crowded into a small area between Earls Court and Knightsbridge. There are also plenty of cinemas, although fewer theatres and leisure centres. Open space includes Kensington Gardens and Holland Park as well as numerous 'garden squares', to which access is usually for residents only. If there

1

isn't a restaurant to suit you in Kensington & Chelsea, you're extremely hard to please.

Schools

There are just five state secondary schools in the borough compared with 13 private schools, and over 50 per cent of children are educated privately. Several schools (particularly Holland Park) have pupils of a wide variety of nationalities. The construction of a new secondary school in Chelsea began in 2004.

Shopping

Kensington & Chelsea is also something of a shoppers' paradise, having the Kings Road, Kensington High Street (recently redesigned) and the Portobello Road within its boundaries, plus many interesting shops in Notting Hill and along the Fulham and Old Brompton Roads.

Other Information

Council Offices: Town Hall, Hornton Street, London W8 7NX (☎ 020-7361 3000, ✉ information@rbkc.gov.uk).

Postcodes: SW3, SW5, SW7, W8, W10, W11 and W14 (part).

Population: 185,000 – London's second-least populous borough, with a high proportion of people under 20 and between 50 and 65. The population of Kensington & Chelsea is among London's most affluent, although it has its share of deprived areas. There's a smaller proportion (16 per cent) of people from ethnic minorities than anywhere else in inner London, although there's a significant Afro-Caribbean community in North Kensington and Notting Hill, scene of an annual carnival over the August Bank Holiday weekend (if you choose to live there, you will either have to join in the fun or get out of town).

Unemployment: The percentage of the working-age population that are unemployed is 5.7 – below the London average of 7 per cent.

Crime Rate: Crime rates are around average for London (see page 347), although some figures are distorted by the influx of non-residents to the borough. Kensington & Chelsea recently became the first London borough to introduce Police Community Support Officers in an effort to improve public safety and reduce crime.

KINGSTON-UPON-THAMES

The borough of Kingston protrudes deep into Surrey along its southern border. Indeed to most people, Kingston is in Surrey rather than in London. Kingston town in the north-west dominates the borough. Once an attractive market town and still boasting the best-preserved medieval street plan in Greater London,

Kingston has been developed almost out of recognition – and more development are planned. New Malden has retained its 'village' atmosphere and Surbiton, once dubbed 'Queen of the suburbs' on account of its rail link with central London, is reasonably attractive.

Property

Kingston has the third-highest proportion of detached houses in London (13 per cent). A further 32 per cent are semi-detached, 21 per cent terraced and 34 per cent flats. The northern half of the borough is mostly a mass of '30s housing, with some Victorian and Edwardian properties by way of contrast. South of the A3 the housing thins out into fields as London gives way to Surrey. The most attractive properties are found in the north-east around Coombe, where large detached houses predominate. In Kingston town, there are some attractive (and very expensive) riverside properties. The least attractive areas are Tolworth and Chessington in the south.

Costs

Average house prices and rents in Kingston are around the London average (see pages 141 and 160), although there are some very expensive properties by the river (up to £20,000 per month to rent!) and council tax rates are the capital's third-highest (see page 210).

Communications

No tube lines reach as far as Kingston, the nearest tube stations being Richmond and Wimbledon (both a 15-minute bus ride from Kingston town). The borough is reasonably well served by the overground rail network (with ten stations), linking the south and south-west of England with London Waterloo. The A3 cuts across the middle of the borough on its way to Portsmouth on the south coast. As with most outer London boroughs, bus routes stop short of the city centre, although there are good services to Hampton, Kew, Richmond and parts of Surrey; services are also good within Kingston itself and there are coach links with both Heathrow and Gatwick airports.

Facilities

There's a fair amount of open space, particularly in the south, including Canbury Gardens on the river Thames, Fishponds, Queen's Promenade, Trapps Lane and the War Memorial Gardens; larger parks – Richmond, Bushy, Hampton Court and Wimbledon Common – are to be found in neighbouring boroughs. Kingston has just one cinema (a new 14-screen Odeon in Kingston town) and one theatre (part of a new complex, also in Kingston town). By way of compensation there are two ten-pin bowling centres, four leisure centres, as well as numerous sports clubs, and Chessington World of Adventures – Surrey's answer to Disneyland and the most popular theme park in the south of England. Thorpe Park (another theme park), The All England Tennis Club, Twickenham rugby stadium and Sandown Park racecourse are all nearby. Kingston town boasts several nightclubs and is the best place for eating out, although for the adventurous there are one or two Korean restaurants in New Malden. There are a number of art galleries and annual arts festivals in spring and autumn Kingston town. Kingston Parish Church is a popular venue for classical music concerts.

Schools

Kingston has some of the best-performing schools in the country (their GCSE results were the second-best in England in 2003), and many pupils live outside the borough. There are 14 secondary schools, of which four are private. Kingston College and Kingston University are near the centre of Kingston town.

Shopping

Kingston town is a mecca for shoppers and one of the major shopping centres outside central London (and the UK's seventh-largest) with its unique Bentalls department store and centre, containing branches of most leading chains. There are no fewer than ten car parks in the town (although at peak times it can still be impossible to find a space) and the council operates a 'Shopmobility' service for the disabled and people with limited mobility. More relaxed shopping experiences are offered by Chessington, Hook, New Malden and Surbiton. Tolworth, whose two shopping centres bestride the busy A3, has recently enjoyed a face-lift.

Other Information

Council Offices: Guildhall, High Street, Kingston-upon-Thames, Surrey KT1 1EU (☎ 020-8547 5757).
   Postcodes: KT1, KT2, KT3, KT5, KT6 and KT9.
   Population: 152,000 – London's least populous borough. Kingston is inhabited mostly by middle-class, white-collar workers and just 10 per cent of the population belongs to ethnic minority groups. The largest of these is Indian and there's a significant Korean population around New Malden. There's a large student population in Kingston town.
   Unemployment: The percentage of the working-age population that are unemployed is 5.8 – below the London average of 7 per cent.
   Crime Rate: Overall, crime rates in Kingston are the lowest in the capital, only violent crime spoiling its record of London's lowest rates of house burglary, stolen cars and theft from cars (see page 347).

LAMBETH

Lambeth is in the process of recovering from years of inefficient local government, and an ongoing regeneration programme has been successful in many parts of the borough, although there remain significant areas of poverty deprivation. Scene of rioting in 1981, Brixton (in the centre of the borough) is becoming one of the newly trendy areas of London, joining neighbouring Clapham to the west. Nearby Stockwell Park and Tulse Hill in the east are doing their best to catch up.

Property

Some 70 per cent of properties in Lambeth are flats (22 per cent conversions), 22 per cent are terraces, 6 per cent semi-detached and 1 per cent detached houses. The few properties along the River Thames in the north enjoy views of the Houses of Parliament. Most of the properties in Kennington in the northeast (where ex-council flats are to be found), Stockwell in the north-west, Brixton and Clapham are Victorian. Clapham – Lambeth's most expensive area – also boasts attractive Georgian houses. There are more Victorian terraces in West Norwood and Gipsy Hill in the south-east and typical '30s semis around Streatham in the south.

Costs

There are some cheap properties in Lambeth, although there's a huge variation in costs; overall prices and rents are average for London (see pages 141 and 160). Council tax rates are just above average (see page 210).

Communications

Only the north and west of the borough are served by the underground (Northern and Victoria lines). Other parts can be reached by various overground services: Brixton, Denmark Hill, Streatham, Tulse Hill and Norwood by services out of Victoria; Vauxhall and Clapham from Waterloo (which is in the far north-east of the borough). Clapham is also linked to Willesden Junction north of the River Thames, while Streatham and Tulse Hill are on the trans-Thames line running through Blackfriars to the north. (**Note that Clapham Junction station is in neighbouring Wandsworth.**) The Cross River Tram, due for completion in 2011, will link Brixton and Waterloo with Kings Cross, Euston and Camden in north London. Bus services are generally good, but roads are busy, particularly around Clapham (where the A3 Portsmouth road meets the A205 South Circular) and Vauxhall in the north-west.

Facilities

Lambeth is home to London's largest arts complex, now called the South Bank Centre, comprising three concert halls, three theatres, a gallery, the National Film Theatre and the Museum of the Moving Image. As if that weren't enough, there are cinemas in Waterloo, Clapham, Brixton and Streatham, the Imperial War Museum, the Old and Young Vic theatres, four leisure centres, four swimming pools, an ice rink and the Oval cricket ground. Brixton has a large number of excellent bars and clubs and, with Clapham, is increasingly a 24-hour entertainment venue. Clapham Common is one of the largest open spaces in London, but elsewhere a few small parks (Kennington Park, Brockwell Park and Streatham Common) are the best Lambeth can offer in the way of greenery, although West Norwood and Gipsy Hill in the south-east enjoy superb views. Clapham is the best place for eating out and the area around Waterloo station and the South Bank is improving. Brixton has a selection of Caribbean restaurants, Streatham has diverse range of eateries and Stockwell is becoming known for its Portuguese cafes and restaurants.

Schools

There are 11 secondary schools in Lambeth, only one of which is private, and standards are generally below the national average, although improving. There are no private primary schools.

Shopping

Shopping in the borough is generally unexciting. The biggest choice of and the most unusual shops are to be found in Brixton. Streatham High Road is Europe's longest shopping street and plans for a new shopping centre will transform the area. Clapham has a growing number of speciality shops.

Other Information

Council Offices: Town Hall, Brixton Hill, London SW2 1RW (☎ 020-7926 1000, ✉ infoservice@lambeth.gov.uk).

Postcodes: SE11, SE24 (part), SE27, SW1 (part), SW2, SW4, SW8 (part), SW9 and SW16 (part).

Population: 268,000, with the second-highest proportion of people (45 per cent) between 20 and 35 of all the London boroughs. Almost a third of its inhabitants belong to ethnic minorities, with a large Afro-Caribbean population centred on Brixton and a substantial Portuguese community in Stockwell and Vauxhall. Streatham has a growing Somali community.

Unemployment: The percentage of the working-age population that are unemployed is 9.7 – one of the highest rates in London, where the average is

7 per cent.

Crime Rate: Lambeth has generally the highest high crime rate, only second to the City, although its record has greatly improved in recent years thanks to concerted efforts by police and local authorities (a successful 'zero tolerance' policy has been implemented in Brixton) and the rate of theft from cars is only average for the capital (see page 347). The zero-tolerance policy is paying dividends in areas such as Brixton town centre.

LEWISHAM

Like Lambeth, Lewisham has only a short stretch of River Thames frontage, along its northern boundary. Many parts of the borough are somewhat down-at-heel, but it does have smart areas, particularly Blackheath in the north-east, and its worst parts (Deptford and Lewisham town centre) are being regenerated thanks to government money.

Property

Just 2 per cent of properties in Lewisham are detached houses, 9 per cent semi-detached, 37 per cent terraced and 52 per cent flats (a third conversions). Deptford, by the river, was once an industrial area and is overshadowed by ugly '60s tower blocks. However, there are inexpensive ex-council properties to be had as well as some attractive Victorian houses. Large (and affordable) Victorian properties are also to be found in Brockley, New Cross and Lewisham town just to the south, as well as around Forest Hill and Sydenham in the south-west corner of the borough. In the centre, Catford and Hither Green offer more modest Victorian and Edwardian terraces. By the time you reach Grove Park in the south-east, these have given way to the ubiquitous '30s semis of outer London.

Costs

Average house prices and rents are low in Lewisham, although the range of prices is greater than almost anywhere else in the capital (see pages 141 and 160). Council taxes are above average (see page 210).

Communications

The tube barely stretches into Lewisham, the East London Line reaching only as far south as New Cross, but the DLR extends as far as Lewisham town. The rest of the borough is served by overground trains only; a line running north/south through the extreme west of the borough links Sydenham, Forest Hill and Honor Oak Park to London Bridge and Charing Cross stations. A few buses reach into the city centre, while others link the borough with neighbouring Bromley.

Lewisham is criss-crossed by main roads: the A2 and A20 roads linking central London with Kent converge in the northern part of Lewisham, the A205 South Circular Road cuts across the southern part of the borough and the A21 splits it from north to south.

Facilities

Lewisham has at least 40 parks and gardens, although all except Blackheath are small; there are fine views to be had from the hills leading to Crystal Palace in the south-west corner of the borough. The borough has only one cinema and one museum, but boasts four leisure centres and several theatres. The widest selection of restaurants is found in Deptford and Blackheath.

Schools

There are 15 secondary schools in the borough, only one of which is private. Standards generally are above average for inner London but below the national average.

Shopping

In theory, Lewisham town is the best place for shopping, but the shops in Deptford and Blackheath are more interesting.

Other Information

Council Offices: Lewisham Town Hall, Catford Road, London SE6 4RU (☎ 020-8314 6000).

Postcodes: SE4, SE6, SE8, SE12 (part), SE13, SE14, SE23, SE26 and BR1 (part).

Population: 249,000. Just under 25 per cent of Lewisham's population belongs to ethnic minorities, the largest being Afro-Caribbean (around Deptford and Lewisham) and Turkish.

Unemployment: The percentage of the working-age population that are unemployed is 8.1 – above the London average of 8 per cent.

Crime Rate: Lewisham's crime rates are around the London average, except theft from cars, which is well below average (see page 347). Drug offences are also high in the area.

MERTON

Unusually, Merton's most sought-after areas (and most of its open spaces) are in the north of the borough, nearest central London. Wimbledon, famous for its annual tennis tournament in late June/early July, and Wimbledon Village are the smartest parts, and Merton Park to the south is also attractive.

Property

Merton has 4 per cent detached houses, 13 per cent semi-detached, 48 per cent terraced and 34 per cent flats. Wimbledon and South Wimbledon in the northern part of the borough are mainly Victorian. Raynes Park in the south-west offers Edwardian terraces, while Morden in the south is mostly '30s semis with some inexpensive houses on the St Helier Estate.

Costs

Average property prices and rental rates are on the high side (see pages 141 and 160), as are council tax rates (see page 210).

Communications

Surprisingly, two tube lines reach right down into Merton – the District line, which terminates at Wimbledon in the west of the borough, and the Northern line, ending at Morden in the south. Wimbledon and Raynes Park are on an overground line into Waterloo, while other parts of Merton are served by Thameslink trains (see page 115) serving the City and Hertfordshire. The new Tramlink service (see page 117) connects Wimbledon, Merton, Morden and Mitcham with various parts of the borough of Croydon. The A24 is the borough's major road, cutting through Merton on its way to Surrey.

Facilities

Most of Wimbledon Common is within the borough of Merton, as are Wimbledon Park, Merton Park and Mitcham Common, and there are pleasant walks along the river Wandle. The world-famous All England Lawn Tennis Club, home of the annual Wimbledon tournament, is in Merton, which has a reasonable selection of theatres (including the recently re-opened New Wimbledon Theatre), concert venues, museums and leisure centres, but the 12-screen cinema in Wimbledon is the borough's only cinema. There are plenty of restaurants throughout the borough, the widest choice being in Wimbledon Village, the 'in' place to eat out in Merton.

Schools

Until 2003, Merton had a three-tier state education system but this has now been changed to the usual primary/secondary structure. As a result, Rowan High School and Eastfields High School closed in 2002 and a new state secondary school, Mitcham Vale, was created to add to the existing four. There are also two voluntary-aided schools and three private schools. The latter, along with Merton's part-LEA-funded Roman Catholic schools, have excellent government performance reports. Merton boasts the best selection of nurseries, both state and private, in London.

Shopping

Outside Wimbledon, which has an attractive and up-market retail centre (appropriately named 'Centre Court') and exclusive boutiques in the Village, shopping in Merton is a pretty unexciting experience.

Other Information

Council Offices: Merton Civic Centre, London Road, Morden SM4 5DX (☎ 020-8543 2222, ✉ postroom@merton.gov.uk).
   Postcodes: SW19 (part), SW20, CR4 and SM4.
   Population: 193,000. Some 16 per cent of the population belongs to an ethnic minority, mostly Indian or Afro-Caribbean.
   Unemployment: The percentage of the working-age population that are unemployed is 7.1 – close to the London average of 7 per cent.
   Crime Rate: Merton has generally low crime rates for London (see page 347).

NEWHAM

Newham is one of London's fastest-changing boroughs: having been among the most deprived areas in England, it's now the centre of the capital's 2012 Olympic bid and the government is spending millions on regeneration schemes. Large-scale redevelopment of the Stratford and Royal Docks is now under way, incorporating a Channel Tunnel Rail Link station (see page 112) and a major exhibition centre (see **Facilities** below). Ten new hotels (eight of them in the Royal Docks) have recently brought the borough's total to 13, and the £500 million Royals Business Park is due to open in 2004. The borough is also home to the University of East London Docklands Campus, which opened in 1999 and accommodates some 7,500 students.

Property

Newham has the second-highest proportion of terraced houses in London (57 per cent), with 39 per cent flats, 3 per cent semi-detached and just 1 per cent detached houses. There's some unusual Victorian property between the docks and the river and new housing is being built around Beckton just to the north of the docks. Otherwise, it's rather a dull borough architecturally, with long rows of late 19th century/early 20th century terraces. Larger Victorian houses can be found in East Ham in the centre of the borough and Stratford in the north-west, as well as around Forest Gate in the north – probably the best part of Newham. Five residential developments have recently been completed in the Royal Docks, over 400 new homes are being built on Royal Quay (to be known as Furlong City), and imaginative warehouse conversions are being undertaken in Stratford. Further developments currently under consideration include Stratford City, to incorporate 4,500 homes, shopping, leisure and commercial developments, schools and hotels, and Silvertown Quays, 5,000 homes plus retail and entertainment facilities, including a National Aquarium.

Costs

Newham has average house prices and rents for London (see pages 141 and 160), although they're among the capital's fastest-rising. Council tax rates are below the London average (see page 210).

Communications

Unlikely as it may seem, Newham can boast an international airport – London City Airport, whose runway occupies a strip of land between two huge docks. The top part of the borough is served by the Hammersmith & City/Metropolitan and District lines, the lower part and Stratford by the DLR and the Jubilee Line, and Stratford by the Central Line. A further DLR extension is due to link City Airport and North Woolwich. Two overground lines run through Newham from east to west: one crossing the top of the borough en route to Liverpool Street station, the other running into Fenchurch Street station but stopping at West Ham only. A third overground service links London City Airport with Richmond via north London and the Stratford Channel Tunnel Rail Link station is due to open in 2007 (see page 112). A few bus services connect with central London. The main road through the borough is the A13, which cuts across it east to west; improvements are due to be completed in 2004.

Facilities

Newham has little open space, its 24 parks tending to be small, although there are attractive walks along the River Lea and Bow Creek in the west and the 22-acre Thames Barrier Park has recently opened. The borough has three cinemas, including the 14-screen Showcase Cinema in Beckton, and the Theatre Royal Stratford East reopened in 2001 after major restoration. Nearby Stratford Circus, a high-tech performing arts centre, opened in the same year. Newham also has unusually good sporting facilities, including four leisure centres, including a state-of-the art centre in East Ham, which opened in 2001, water sports in the Royal Docks. Beckton's former dry ski centre is due to re-open as a 'snowdome' in 2007. The borough is also home to West Ham United football club. A major new conference and exhibition centre, ExCeL, opened in 2000 and is the new home of the prestigious London International Boat Show. Traditional East End entertainment can be enjoyed at the Old Time Music Hall (formerly St Mark's Church) in Woolwich.

Schools

Newham has the country's highest proportion of children with special needs but since 2000 the borough has been one of the fastest-improving in terms of educational standards. There are 16 state secondary schools, none of which are private.

Shopping

Newham isn't known for its shopping, although Stratford's shopping centre was refurbished in 2001 and the New Gallions Reach development, completed in 2003, has brought the number of retail parks in the borough to three. Green Street in Upton Park, home to 400 retailers of Asian clothing, jewellery and food, was given a major facelift in 2003, and there are good street markets in Canning Town, East Ham and Stratford.

Other Information

Council Offices: Town Hall, Barking Road, East Ham, London E6 2RP (☎ 020-8430 2000, ✉ customer.services@newham.gov.uk).
   Postcodes: E3 (part), E6, E7, E13, E15 and E16.
   Population: 254,000, with the highest proportion of people under 20 and the lowest proportion of people over 65 of all the London boroughs. Newham has a higher proportion (nearly 50 per cent) of inhabitants from ethnic minorities than almost anywhere else in London, with particularly large Afro-Caribbean and Asian populations.
   Unemployment: The percentage of the working-age population that are unemployed is 9.4 – well above the London average of 3.5 per cent.
   Crime Rate: Newham has generally high crime rates, including the capital's highest rate of stolen cars, although the rate of house burglary is one of the lowest in London (see page 347). 'Safer Neighbourhood' initiatives hope to improve street safety.

REDBRIDGE

There's no town of Redbridge – the borough's 'capital' is Ilford in the south (curiously, IG postcodes derive from it) – and the borough takes its name from the brick bridge linking Ilford with Wanstead and Woodford. Redbridge is neither deprived nor particularly affluent, although it has plenty of smart areas. Generally, the eastern part of the borough is more working class and the west more middle class, with particularly well-to-do areas around Woodford and Wanstead. Ilford Council has initiated an ambitious regeneration programme that will create a new town square and high-quality housing and shopping facilities in the town centre.

Property

Property in Redbridge consists of 6 per cent detached houses, 27 per cent semi-detached, 40 per cent terraces and 27 per cent flats (a quarter conversions). In the south around Ilford there are mainly Victorian and Edwardian terraces, as in Goodmayes and Seven Kings to the east (where there are bargains to be found). Further north, around Gants Hill and Clayhall, are the usual '30s suburban semis, while the Hainault area in the north-east consists mainly of council estates (where good buys can also be had). The west boasts larger, semi-detached and detached properties.

Costs

Redbridge's property prices and rents are around the average for London (see pages 141 and 160) and its council taxes just-above-average (see page 210).

Communications

Redbridge is served by the Central tube line, which reaches as far as Epping in Essex. The only overground service runs across the south of the borough, through Goodmayes, Ilford and Seven Kings, linking them with London's Liverpool Street station. A few buses go as far as the city centre. The M11 (Redbridge's main escape route to the country) encroaches on the north-west corner of the borough. Other main roads are the A12, which cuts the borough in half from west to east, and the A406 North Circular in the west and south-west. Most of Redbridge still has 'permit free' parking.

Facilities

There are three leisure centres, two cinemas, a theatre and a museum (in Ilford). Known as the 'leafy suburb', Redbridge has plenty of open space (a third of the borough is Green Belt land), particularly in the north-east, where Hainault Forest offers wildlife and good views. Nearby are two golf courses and riding facilities as well as water sports on Fairlop Water. There's a vast choice of restaurants in Ilford but elsewhere it's rather limited.

Schools

Redbridge's 20 state secondary schools (including two grammar schools, Ilford County High and Woodford County High, and two private schools) rank fourth in England according to the percentage of high-grade GCSE passes in 2003 (over 65 per cent compared with the English average of under 53 per cent).

Shopping

The main shopping centre is Ilford, with smaller centres in Barkingside, Gants Hill, South Woodford, Wanstead and Woodford. although there are interesting shops in Woodford Green and Wanstead.

Other Information

Council Offices: Town Hall, High Road, Ilford IG1 1DD (☎ 020-8554 5000, ✉ customer.cc@redbridge.gov.uk).

Postcodes: E11 (part), E18, IG1, IG2, IG3, IG4, IG5, IG6, IG7, IG8, IG18 and RM6 (part).

Population: 238,500. More than 20 per cent of Redbridge's inhabitants belong to ethnic minorities, with a substantial Asian population, particularly in the east. There's also a considerable Jewish community in and around Gants Hill in the centre.

Unemployment: The percentage of the working-age population that are unemployed is 5.1 – well below the London average of 7 per cent.

Crime Rate: Redbridge's crime rates are generally low for London (see page 347).

RICHMOND-UPON-THAMES

Richmond is the only borough that's divided by the River Thames. One of London's greenest boroughs, it includes Hampton Court Park, Bushy Park, Old Deer Park, Kew Gardens and Richmond Park (the capital's largest, complete with herds of deer). Like neighbouring Hounslow, however, northern parts of Richmond suffer from the continual drone of aircraft landing at Heathrow.

Property

The mix of properties in Richmond is close to the outer London average, with 8 per cent detached houses, 23 per cent semi-detached, 31 per cent terraces and 38 per cent flats. A high proportion of buildings are Victorian, from Castlenau and Barnes in the north-east corner, past East Sheen and Richmond Hill (the borough's most desirable area) and across the river to Hampton Wick and Teddington. There are also many attractive Georgian properties; the inevitable '30s semis don't start until Hampton and Whitton (the cheapest part of Richmond) in the extreme south-west. Kew in the far north offers everything from turn-of-the-century to contemporary.

Costs

Richmond has high property prices (see pages 141 and 160) and London's highest council tax rates (see page 210).

Communications

As far as trains are concerned, Richmond is best served by the overground network. Richmond town itself is also at the end of both the rail route to the East End via north London and the District tube line. There are no bus services to the centre of London, but it's possible to get to Westminster by boat. The A205 South Circular Road cuts across the north-east part of the borough and the A316 (the extension of the M3) runs across the top to join it. Several parts of the borough have controlled parking.

Facilities

Richmond is richly endowed with parks (see above) and historic houses, most notably Hampton Court Palace on the Surrey border (one of the country's royal palaces, which is open to visitors except when the Queen is in residence), while Kew Gardens in the north-west incorporate the famous Royal Botanical Gardens. The borough also has three leisure centres and other sports facilities,including several golf courses, and there are three cinemas and two theatres in Richmond town.

Schools

Richmond's 13 secondary schools, which include two private schools, have generally high standards. There's also a German School and a Swedish School, which teach the curricula of those countries, and Richmond is home to the Royal Ballet School.

Shopping

Richmond has many interesting small shopping centres and plenty of restaurants (and Kingston is nearby).

Other Information

Council Offices: Civic Centre, 44 York Street, Twickenham TW1 3BZ (☎

020-8891 1411, ✉ press-pr@richmond.gov.uk).
Postcodes: SW14, KT8, TW1, TW2, TW10, TW11 and TW12.
Population: 183,000. Just 3 per cent of the population belongs to ethnic minorities in this largely white-collar borough.
Unemployment: The percentage of the working-age population that are unemployed is 4.6 – well below the London average of 7 per cent.
Crime Rate: Richmond enjoys the lowest crime rates in London, including its lowest rate of car violet and drugs-related crimes and second-lowest rate of violent crime (see page 347).

SOUTHWARK

Southwark is a borough of contrasts: in the north-east, the once industrial areas of Bermondsey and Rotherhithe have undergone a transformation in the last decade, including the construction of some 3,000 homes; in the west, formerly run-down Camberwell is fast becoming the borough's answer to Brixton and Notting Hill; in the centre, Peckham's grim tower blocks are being pulled down as part of a multi-million pound face-lift; and in the south there's the ultra-smart village of Dulwich. Despite redevelopment, however, multicultural Camberwell, Peckham and Newington are among the country's most deprived areas, albeit with oases of affluence, and even Dulwich has its pockets of deprivation.

Property

Some 76 per cent of properties in Southwark are flats and a further 19 per cent terraced houses, with just 4 per cent semi-detached and 1 per cent detached houses. Over half of Southwark's housing is publicly owned (compared with the London average of around 27 per cent). Bermondsey in the north consists mostly of council estates, but former warehouses are gradually being converted into flats (or 'lofts', as they're known). New houses are to be found in Rotherhithe in the north-east, while The Borough in the north-west and The Elephant & Castle, Camberwell, Peckham and Nunhead in the centre and Dulwich in the south offer Victorian, Edwardian and Georgian properties – varying enormously in price!

Costs

Like many other inner city boroughs, Southwark has a huge range of property prices and rents (see pages 141 and 160). Council tax rates are below average for London (see page 210).

Communications

Only the northern part of Southwark is served by the tube network, the Bakerloo and Northern lines reaching The Elephant & Castle and the Jubilee Line extension due to stop at Bermondsey. On the other hand, overground trains run from various parts of the borough into London Bridge, Blackfriars and Charing Cross. Bus services into central London are also good, although inevitably slow. The A205 South Circular passes through Dulwich, and The Elephant & Castle is effectively a huge roundabout.

Facilities

Government and National Lottery money has enabled Southwark to regenerate its stretch of River Thames frontage with the reconstruction of the Globe theatre, a modern art gallery (the Tate Modern) in the old Bankside power station and a new footbridge across the river linking its commercial and retail developments with the City. Elsewhere, there are two mainstream cinemas, five leisure centres and numerous museums and galleries (including the world's first wine museum!). Most of Southwark's open space is in the south, in and around Dulwich, and there are a few parks and gardens in the north. There's a variety of restaurants in Southwark, particularly in Dulwich and East Dulwich.

Schools

Southwark's schools have a high proportion (up to a third) of pupils for whom English is a second language. Nevertheless, educational standards are generally reasonable in the borough's 17 secondary schools, of which three are private (including the renowned Dulwich College).

Shopping

Southwark's main shopping centre is the unsightly complex at The Elephant & Castle. Elsewhere, shopping facilities are mostly uninspiring.

Other Information

Council Offices: Town Hall, Peckham Road, London SE5 8UB (☎ 020-7525 5000, ✉ customerfeedback@southwark.gov.uk).
   Postcodes: SE1, SE5, SE15, SE16, SE17, SE21, SE22 and SE24 (part).
   Population: 255,000, with a high proportion of people between 20 and 35. A third of Southwark's population belongs to ethnic minority groups, the largest being Afro-Caribbean, Turkish and Vietnamese. Camberwell, Peckham and Newington have a 40 per cent ethnic minority population, speaking over 100 languages. The borough tends to attract people dependent on state support, including asylum seekers and other needy immigrants.

Unemployment: The percentage of the working-age population that are unemployed is 11.2 – one of the highest rates in London, where the average is 7 per cent.

Crime Rate: Southwark's crime record has improved considerably in recent years. In 1999, it had the worst record of all the boroughs, but today its crime rates are lower than those of many other boroughs, although still above the London average (see page 347). The current focus is on tackling drugs and hate crimes such as racist and homophobic incidents.

SUTTON

Sutton calls itself the 'greener, cleaner borough' and is one of London's most affluent boroughs, having more in common with neighbouring Surrey than London 'proper'. The smartest areas are Carshalton Beeches (centre), North Cheam (north-west), South Sutton town (west) and Belmont (south-west). Cheaper parts include St Helier in the north and Beddington in the east.

Property

Sutton has 11 per cent detached houses, 27 per cent semi-detached, 29 per cent terraces and 33 per cent flats (the great majority purpose-built). Properties built in the '20s and '30s predominate the further south you go, although there are some Victorian and Edwardian houses in Sutton town as well as on a large council estate in St Helier to the north, where bargains can be found. Victorian terraces can also be found in Wallington and Beddington to the east and in the 'village' of Carshalton in the centre. Here and in North Cheam there are some 16th century properties, while Beddington and Sutton town offer modern homes.

Costs

Somewhat surprisingly, average property prices in Sutton are relatively low – even below those of neighbouring Croydon (see pages 141 and 160). Council tax rates are just above the London average (see page 210).

Communications

Sutton is beyond the reach of the tube network, but has good overground rail services. Buses will take you to the shopping centres of Kingston or Croydon but not to central London. Main roads include the A24 and A217, both running north/south, and traffic generally – as in most parts of London – is slow.

Facilities

Sutton's leisure facilities are limited to one cinema, two theatres, two leisure centres and a smattering of historic houses. But, as you might expect, there's plenty of open space including Beddington Park in the east and Cheam Park in the west, the latter adjoining Nonsuch Park just across the Surrey border. Croydon, Cheam and Carshalton are the best bet for eating out.

Schools

After Kingston, Sutton has the best-performing state secondary schools (there are 14) in London, although the highest performers are selective schools. There are also two private schools.

Shopping

The borough's main shopping centre is Sutton town, although it offers little competition to nearby Croydon. There are also some attractive shops in Cheam and Carshalton.

Other Information

Council Offices: Civic Offices, St Nicholas Way, Sutton SM1 1EA (☎ 020-8770 5000, ✉ customerservices@sutton.gov.uk).

Postcodes: CR0 (part), CR4, KT4, SM1, SM2 (part), SM3, SM5 and SM6.

Population: 179,000. Just 6 per cent of Sutton's inhabitants belong to ethnic minorities and most of the population is well-to-do.

Unemployment: Sutton (along with neighbouring Kingston and Richmond) has an unemployment percentage of 5.4, compared with the average of 7 per cent.

Crime Rate: Sutton has some of the lowest crime rates in the capital, including its lowest rate of house burglary (see page 347). A focus on controlling disorderley conduct in the town centre (usually fuelled by alcohol) is being reduced by a collaboration between the council and the police.

TOWER HAMLETS

Taking its name from the historical association between the Tower of London and the riverside hamlets that once surrounded it, Tower Hamlets claims to be 'the fastest-changing place in the UK'. Financial and media businesses are moving there from the City, the Jubilee Line extension is to link the East End to the West End, and the Spitalfields area (traditionally the centre of London's wholesale clothing industry) is fast establishing itself as an artistic quarter. It's estimated that 50,000 new jobs will be created within the borough by the year

2005. At the centre of this transformation is Docklands, previously an area of disused docks and derelict warehouses and now a thriving business centre.

Property

Tower Hamlets has the smallest proportion of detached and semi-detached houses outside the City of London (1 per cent). Some 14 per cent of properties are terraces and the remaining 85 per cent flats (almost all purpose-built), many council owned. This means that there are bargain ex-council properties to be found, particularly in Spitalfields and Whitechapel in the west and in Bethnal Green in the north-west. Stepney in the centre of the borough is almost all council property and there are some particularly unsightly council blocks in Bromley (not to be confused with Bromley town in the borough of Bromley) and Poplar in the east. In the north-east, Bow offers attractive Victorian and Georgian houses and the Spitalfields/ Whitechapel area is spawning 'loft' conversions, which are already prevalent in Wapping and Limehouse in the south-west. Here and on the Isle of Dogs (not an island at all, merely a bend in the river) construction is still going on so it can be rather like living on a building site.

Costs

Tower Hamlets has surprisingly high property prices and rents (see pages 141 and 160), but council tax rates are the fourth-lowest in London (see page 210).

Communications

Tower Hamlets has some of the best rail connections of any London borough. No fewer than six tube lines (Central, District, East London, Hammersmith & City/Metropolitan, Jubilee and the DLR) run in various directions through the borough. The overground line from Fenchurch Street station to parts of Essex also crosses the borough, and the service from Liverpool Street station to Cambridge cuts across its north-west corner. Bus services are better in the north than the south but Tower Hamlets is no place for car owners; there's nowhere to park without paying, even outside your own house.

Facilities

Good sports facilities (including five leisure centres) compensate for a shortage of cinemas (none) and theatres (one). The London Arena on the Isle of Dogs hosts pop concerts as well as exhibitions, and the capital's top tourist attraction, the Tower of London, is just within the borough's boundary (in the extreme west). Apart from Victoria Park in the north-east, Tower Hamlets has little green space to offer. What it does have in abundance is water – not only the River Thames, but the River Lea, the Regent's and Hertford Union Canals and, of course, the old docks. Tower Hamlets isn't noted for its restaurants, with the exception of some good ethnic eating places.

Schools

New LEA management appointed in 2000 has improved Tower Hamlets' previously poor education standards. Only one of its 16 secondary schools is private. Nowhere in London offers more state nurseries for the under-fives.

Shopping

Tower Hamlets' shopping facilities are rather patchy, but it has colourful markets such as Brick Lane (Shoreditch), Roman Road (Bow) and the famous Petticoat Lane (actually in Middlesex Street on the border with the City).

Other Information

Council Offices: Mulberry Place, 5 Clove Crescent, London E14 2BG (☎ 020-7364 5000, ✉ generalenquiries@towerhamlets.gov.uk).

Postcodes: E1, E2, E3 (part) and E14. **Population:** 211,000, with a high proportion of people between 20 and 35. Once the home of intrepid seafarers such as Walter Raleigh and Captain Cook, Tower Hamlets is now home to the UK's largest Bangladeshi community – almost 25 per cent of its inhabitants – as well as Vietnamese and Somali refugees.

Unemployment: Tower Hamlets has the highest unemployment rate in London at 13.2 compared with the London average of 7 per cent.

Crime Rate: Tower Hamlets has London's second-highest rate of violent crime and a high rate of theft from cars, but its rates of house burglary and car stealing are around average for the capital (see page 347).

WALTHAM FOREST

Waltham Forest is one of London's 'in-between' boroughs – neither affluent nor impoverished, neither fashionable nor conservative – but it has its attractions nevertheless, not least attractive woodland and parkland in historic Epping Forest. Its administrative and geographical centre is Walthamstow, which is undergoing a massive regeneration project promising to bring state-of-the-art shopping and leisure facilities, including a library, to the town centre, along with modern transport links. In the south of the borough are the former working-class areas of Leyton and Leytonstone, and to the north the smart suburb of Highams Park. Standard outer London suburbia takes over in the far north around Chingford before the border with Essex.

Property

Around 48 per cent of properties are terraced houses, 11 per cent semi-detached and 2 per cent detached. The remaining 39 per cent are flats. Leyton and Leytonstone in the south are mainly Victorian terraces, as is Walthamstow itself, where conversion flats are plentiful. In the north are the inevitable '30s semis of Chingford, mixed with some more attractive Victorian and Edwardian properties. A similar combination is found in Highams Park, which is nevertheless the borough's most sought-after area.

Costs

Waltham Forest offers some of the cheapest property in London (see pages 141 and 160), but its council tax rates are high (see page 210).

Communications

Tube services are limited here. The Central Line serves only Leyton and Leytonstone in the south, and the Victoria Line terminates at Walthamstow. The Barking to Richmond overground line also passes through Leyton and Walthamstow, northern parts of the borough only being reached by a line from Liverpool Street terminating at Chingford. The recently completed M11 link road provides quick access to Hackney. Other major roads through the borough include the A406 North Circular, which cuts across the centre, and the A11/A12 in the south-east corner. Residents' parking permits are in force in Walthamstow and Chingford.

Facilities

There's just one cinema in the borough, but live entertainment can be had at Chingford's and Walthamstow's Assembly Halls and there are five leisure centres to choose from. Walthamstow is also home to London's premier greyhound racing venue and the village is home to some good pubs and restaurants. Nearby Lloyd Park is home to the William Morris Gallery but is otherwise uninspiring. There are a number of attractive parks, the most attractive open space being what's left of Epping Forest in the east, the opposite side of the borough offering expanses of water in the shape of a chain of reservoirs. Highams Park has an attractive lake surrounded by woodland, and the Whipps Cross boating lake and park are popular. Outside Walthamstow Village, eating out is generally uninspiring.

Schools

Standards are improving in Waltham Forest's 19 secondary schools, two of which are private, although they're still below the national average.

Shopping

Walthamstow is the borough's shopping centre, with a shopping 'mall' and a daily High Street market (selling clothing and household goods as well as food) that claims to be the longest in Europe. The arcade being built at the top end of the High Street will provide more shopping facilities. Elsewhere in the borough, these are at best adequate.

Other Information

Council Offices: Town Hall, Forest Road, Walthamstow E17 4JF (☎ 020-8527 5544, ✉ wfdirect@lbwf.gov.uk).
   Postcodes: E4, E10, E11 (part) and E17.
   Population: 222,400. Unusually for an outer London borough, Waltham Forest has a high proportion (over 35 per cent) of residents belonging to ethnic minorities, particularly Black Caribbean and Pakistani.

   Unemployment: The percentage of the working-age population that are unemployed is 8.8 – just above the London average of 7 per cent.
   Crime Rate: Crime rates in Waltham Forest are around average for London and generally reducing due to a high level of police visibility on the street (see page 347).

WANDSWORTH

Wandsworth is one of the most 'upwardly mobile' of London's boroughs; once working class Battersea – where the council has spent millions on regeneration and developers have moved in – has recently become a trendy place to live. The borough council is one of the dozen best-performing in the country, according to the Audit Commission, and has won more awards for the quality of its services than any other UK local authority.

Property

Typically for an inner London borough, Wandsworth has 2 per cent detached houses, 5 per cent semi-detached, 30 per cent terraced and 63 per cent flats (almost a third of which are conversions). Most of the detached houses are to be found in Putney in the south-west, Southfields in the centre and Wandsworth Common in the north-east, while most semis are in Tooting in the south-east, where much of the property is Edwardian (as it is in Putney and Earlsfield in the south).

Costs

Average house prices and rents are on the high side, with some very expensive properties in smart areas (see pages 141 and 160), but Wandsworth boasts the second-lowest council tax rates in London – around half of those in most other boroughs (see page 210).

Communications

Two tube lines run through Wandsworth: the District line, slicing north/south through the centre of the borough, and the Northern line, cutting across its south-eastern corner. The UK's busiest railway station, Clapham Junction, is also in Wandsworth, providing overground rail links not only with the whole of the south of England but with the north as well. Wandsworth isn't the best place to live for car owners as the A3 and A205 South Circular merge in an almost constant traffic jam right in the centre of the borough and parking is restricted in many areas.

Facilities

Wandsworth is poorly supplied with entertainment facilities: one theatre, one cinema and a small museum, although a new 14-screen cinema is due to open in May 2004 in Wandsworth town centre as part of the Southside development (see **Shopping** below). The borough's impressively ugly landmark, Battersea Power Station (which ceased to be used decades ago) still stands empty despite several attempts to transform it into an entertainment centre. However, Wandsworth boasts over 70 parks, commons gardens and open spaces, which account for almost 20 per cent of its area – the largest proportion of any London borough. Most popular are Battersea Park, recently given an £11 million facelift, and Wandsworth Common in the north-east, Tooting Common in the south-east, and Putney Heath and Putney Common in the south-west as well as parts of Clapham and Wimbledon Commons (see **Lambeth** and **Merton**). Beautiful Richmond Park is just next door. When it comes to eating out, Wandsworth residents are spoilt for choice with umpteen ethnic restaurants in Battersea, Putney, Tooting and Wandsworth town.

Schools

Like Southwark, Wandsworth has a high proportion of schoolchildren for whom English is a second language. Nevertheless, exam results in Wandsworth's schools have improved faster than anywhere else in the country in recent years and its schools are now the most sought-after in London after those of Westminster. There are 15 secondary schools, of which three are private. There's also a good choice of nursery schools, both state and private.

Shopping

Shopping facilities are improving, thanks mainly to the £70 million refurbishment of the Arndale Centre (now called Southside) in Wandsworth town. with a new centre in Putney and another planned in Wandsworth town. Putney and Clapham Junction have good shops, and some unusual shops are to be found in Tooting.

Other Information

Council Offices: Town Hall, Wandsworth High Street, London SW18 2PU (☎ 020-8871 6000, ✉ enquiries@wandsworth.gov.uk).
   Postcodes: SW8 (part), SW11, SW12, SW15, SW17, SW18 and SW19 (part).
   Population: 278,000, with the highest proportion of people between 20 and 35 of all the London boroughs. Wandsworth has an increasingly middle-class population with a relatively large ethnic community.
   Unemployment: The percentage of the working-age population that are unemployed is 4.3 – just below the London average of 7 per cent.
   Crime Rate: Wandsworth's crime rates have improved considerably in recent years and are now around average for London (see page 347).

WESTMINSTER

The City of Westminster, as it's properly called (although it's a borough like any other), contains most of London's most frequently visited places: Buckingham Palace, the Houses of Parliament, Leicester Square, Piccadilly Circus and Trafalgar Square, to name but a few. Not surprisingly, these areas are among the most expensive in the capital, although Westminster also has less salubrious parts. These are mainly in the north-west around Paddington, where redevelopment is in the pipeline, but also (for different reasons) in Soho in the east – traditionally London's sleaze centre but also an 'in' place to live. In fact, Westminster is one of the country's most diverse boroughs and has an exceptionally wide disparity between rich and poor. The council's ambitious Civic Renewal programme aims to regenerate the more deprived areas. As the above places indicate, Westminster is the home of the monarchy and the seat of government.

Property

Some 90 per cent of properties in Westminster are flats (a third conversions), leaving just 9 per cent terraces and 1 per cent each of detached and semi-detached houses. There are flats of various styles (and prices) in Soho, Covent Garden (east), Marylebone (north-east), Pimlico (south) and Westminster itself (south-east). Maida Vale (north) and St John's Wood (north-east) offer some attractive properties near the Regent's Canal, but the crème de la crème is to be found in Mayfair (centre) and in Knightsbridge and Belgravia (south-west), where Eaton Square is reputed to be London's smartest address. Apart from Paddington, the cheapest properties are in Bayswater (west) and West Kilburn (north-west).

Costs

Not surprisingly, Westminster has the capital's most expensive property (see pages 141 and 160): a three-bedroom flat in Knightsbridge can set you back £2 million and a large house in St John's Wood can cost you £10 million! Small compensation is that its council tax rates are the lowest in the capital and around half of those in most other boroughs (see page 210).

Communications

Westminster is in the heart of tube-land, so getting around isn't a problem. With Paddington, Charing Cross and Victoria stations also in the borough, getting out of London (at least in a westerly or southerly direction) is also straightforward – the new Heathrow Express route out of Paddington is particularly handy for those wanting to escape the country! There are also plenty of bus routes to choose from (including open-top city tour buses), but not surprisingly, traffic is generally at a crawl and parking is a nightmare.

Facilities

Westminster is home to London Zoo, Madame Tussaud's, the Planetarium, the National and National Portrait Galleries, the Tate Gallery, the Royal Opera House, the Royal Albert Hall and the Wigmore Hall, not to mention over 40 theatres and more cinemas than you can shake a stick at (Leicester Square is the cinema-goer's 'mecca'). London's four most famous parks – Hyde Park, Regent's Park, Green Park and St James's Park – and the most attractive reaches of the Regent's Canal are also found within the borough. As if all that weren't enough to keep its residents (and millions of visitors) entertained, Westminster has four leisure centres and the best-used libraries in the capital. As with shops, Westminster is blessed with some of London's most exclusive eating places.

Schools

Westminster has 20 secondary schools, of which no fewer than 12 are private (including The American School in London, The International Community School, and a ballet and a theatre school). Standards vary and some state schools have suffered problems including violence. Over 120 languages are spoken by Westminster schoolchildren.

Shopping

When it comes to shops, Westminster has a veritable cornucopia of facilities, including Harrods, Covent Garden, Oxford Street and Regent Street.

Other Information

Council Offices: City Hall, 64 Victoria Street, London SW1E 6QP (☎ 020-7641 6000).

Postcodes: NW8, SW1, W1, W2 and W9.

Population: 230,000, with the lowest proportion of people under 20 outside the City of London and one of the highest proportions of people between 20 and 35 of all the boroughs. Almost 30 per cent of Westminster's population belongs to ethnic minority groups. There's also a large Jewish community in the north of the borough and London's greatest concentration of Chinese in Soho.

Unemployment: The percentage of the working-age population that are unemployed is 7.7 – just above the London average of 7 per cent.

Crime Rate: Westminster has easily the highest violent crime rate in London as well as a high rate of theft from cars (see page 347). However, these figures are highly distorted by the large number of non-residents (particularly foreign tourists) falling victim to petty crime while visiting the borough. Its rates of house burglary and car stealing are average for the capital.

2

ARRIVAL & SETTLING IN

2

If you're coming to London from overseas, your first task on arrival in the UK will be to negotiate immigration and customs, which fortunately presents no problems for most people. Non-EEA nationals must complete a landing card on arrival; these are distributed on international flights and are available from the information or purser's office on ferries. British customs and immigration officials are usually polite and efficient, although they may occasionally be a trifle 'over-zealous' in their attempts to deter smugglers and illegal immigrants.

The UK isn't a signatory to the 1995 Schengen agreement (named after a Luxembourg village on the Moselle River where the agreement was signed), which introduced an open-border policy between certain EU member countries. These now comprise Austria, Belgium, France, Germany, Greece, Italy, Luxembourg, the Netherlands, Portugal and Spain. The Scandinavian countries of Denmark, Finland, Iceland, Norway and Sweden have observer status. The UK has no plans to join, ostensibly because of fears of increased illegal immigration and cross-border crime such as drug smuggling. Therefore, anyone arriving in the UK from one of the above countries must go through the normal passport and immigration controls (the same applies when you enter a Schengen country from the UK).

Nationals of some non-Commonwealth and non-EEA countries who have been given permission to remain in the UK for more than six months, or who have been allowed to work for more than three months, are required to register with the police (see page 94). When applicable, this condition is stamped in your passport, either on entry or by the Immigration and Nationality Directorate (IND) of the Home Office when it grants an extension of stay. The Home Office has the final decision on all matters relating to immigration.

The latest information about immigration and permits can be obtained from the Immigration and Nationality Directorate (IND), Lunar House, 40 Wellesley Road, Croydon CR9 2BY, which publishes leaflets and booklets regarding all immigration categories, as well as from local law centres, Citizens' Advice Bureaux and community relations councils. The IND website (💻 www. ind. homeoffice.gov.uk) provides comprehensive coverage of these matters and enables you to download both application forms and related printed material in electronic form. Further information can also be found in *Living and Working in Britain* (Survival Books).

The Immigration and Nationality Enquiry Bureau (INEB) operates a telephone information service on ☎ 0870-606 7766 which deals both with general enquiries about immigration rules and procedures, and queries about specific cases. Its lines are open from 9am to 4.45pm on Mondays to Thursdays and from 9am until 4.30pm on Fridays, although you may have to wait a long time to speak to an official. The busiest days are Mondays, Tuesdays and Wednesdays; it's easier to get through towards the end of the week and in the afternoon. You can also use the following email address: ✉ indpublic enquiries@ind.homeoffice. qsi.gov.uk.

The organisation responsible for issuing visas and providing information about who needs one is UK Visas (a joint undertaking of the Foreign and Commonwealth Office and the Home Office). UK Visas is represented at British Embassies, High Commissions and other British Diplomatic Mission (collectively known as British Diplomatic Posts) abroad, a complete list of which can be found at ⌨ www.fco. gov.uk. You should apply to your nearest British Diplomatic Post for a visa. UK Visas can also be contacted by post at the Foreign and Commonwealth Office, King Charles Street, London SW1A 2AH, or by phone (☎ 020-7008 1500 between 9am and 5pm Mondays to Fridays) or via its website (⌨ www.ukvisas. gov.uk).

Immigration is a complex subject and the information in this chapter is intended only as a general guide. **You shouldn't base any decisions or actions on the information contained herein without confirming it with an official and reliable source, such as a British embassy.** Permit infringements are taken seriously by the authorities and there are penalties for breaches of regulations, including fines and even deportation for flagrant abuses. The police and immigration authorities have the right to arrest anyone 'reasonably suspected' of being an illegal alien and can obtain search warrants to enter homes or places of employment. **The penalties for harbouring illegal aliens are severe and prison sentences of up to seven years and heavy fines can be imposed on offenders.**

PERMITS & VISAS

Before making any plans to live or work in the UK, you must ensure that you have the appropriate entry documentation (e.g. a visa); without it, you won't be allowed into the country. If you're a national of a non-EEA country, you may need to obtain entry clearance (see page 88). **If you're in any doubt as to whether you require clearance to enter the UK, enquire at a British Diplomatic Post overseas before making plans to travel to the UK.** Note that applications for entry clearance made in some countries can take some time to be processed owing to the high number of applications received.

Visas & 'Visa Nationals'

Nationals of certain countries, officially called 'visa nationals', require a visa (an official stamp in their passport) to enter the UK, irrespective of the purpose of their visit, e.g. holiday, residence or employment. If you need a visa and arrive without one, you will be sent back to your home country at your own expense. Visitors' visas are issued for a maximum stay of six months and are never extended beyond this period. If you want to stay longer, you must leave and apply for a new visa. Visa nationals aren't permitted to change their status. Contact your nearest British Diplomatic Post for details.

The government plans to make a visa compulsory for everyone remaining in the UK for more than six months. Over the next few years, the visa requirement will be applied to all nationalities previously exempt. This will be done in stages. The first group of countries to be included in the visa requirement consists of Australia, Canada, Hong Kong, Japan, Malaysia, New Zealand, Singapore, South Africa, South Korea, and the US. Nationals of these countries travelling to the UK for a stay of more than six months now require a visa.

Entry Clearance

With the exception of EEA nationals, foreigners entering the UK may need entry clearance from the Home Office or a British Diplomatic Post in their country of residence, **before arrival in the UK**. Entry clearance in the form of a visa or entry certificate also applies to returning residents who have been abroad for over two years. Entry clearance is usually issued for a single entry but may also allow multiple entries over a number of years, e.g. two. A fee is payable depending on the type of entry clearance issued. Contact your nearest British Diplomatic Post for details.

An entry certificate, which, like a visa, consists of an official stamp in your passport, is required by non-visa nationals, such as Commonwealth citizens coming to work or settle in the UK. If you're refused entry to the UK for any reason, an entry certificate gives you the right to an immediate appeal in the same way as a visa. Contact your nearest British Diplomatic Post for details.

A letter of consent is required by non-visa, non-Commonwealth citizens wishing to enter the UK for certain reasons. Contact your nearest British Diplomatic Post for details.

Work Permits

If you're an EEA national, you can enter the UK in order to take up or seek employment, set up in business or become self-employed without a work permit.

It's difficult for non-EEA nationals to obtain entry clearance to work in the UK unless they don't qualify under a permit-free category, particularly if their prospective employer is located in an area of high unemployment. Normally a work permit must be obtained by an employer for a named worker and permits are always issued for a specific job and for a specified period. Permits are issued provided no other person who's already allowed to live and work in the UK can be found to do the job, which must be proven by providing copies of advertisements and explaining why any such applicants weren't suitable.

Applications for work permits are dealt with by Work Permits UK (☎ 0870 606 7766, ✉ customrel.workpermits@wpuk.gov.uk, 🖥 www.workpermits. gov.

uk). An employer must make an application no more than six months and no less than three months before the date of the proposed entry to the UK of the person he wants to employ. The necessary application form (WP1 for first applications) can be downloaded from the Work Permits UK website or ordered from its forms distribution centre (☎ 08705-210224).

Working Holidaymakers

The working holidaymaker scheme is an arrangement whereby (primarily) single people aged from 17 to 30 can come to the UK for a maximum of two years. To qualify you must be a Commonwealth, British Dependent Territories, British Overseas or British National (Overseas) citizen. During the two-year period the employment you take up is no longer hedged about with restrictions as formerly. It can be almost any sort of work and it can be full- or part-time. You can also now pursue a career or work as a professional. However, professional sport and entertaining are excluded areas; for these a activities you need a work permit. Whatever work you do, you will be expected to take a holiday for part of your stay. Entry clearance (see above) must be obtained from a British Diplomatic Post before travelling to the UK, as it isn't possible to arrive as a visitor and change your status to that of a working holidaymaker.

The Self-Employed

If you wish to enter the UK to set up in business or self-employment and aren't an EEA national, you must obtain entry clearance in the form of a letter of consent (see above) specifically for that purpose, before arrival. To set up in business, you must show that you will be investing a minimum of £200,000 of your own money and that your business will create new, paid, full-time employment for at least two people already resident in the UK. You must also show that there's a genuine need for your services and investmentm, that you will be occupied full-time in the running of the business, and that you will be able to support yourself and your dependants from the profits of the business without recourse to public funds. A business can take one of the following forms: sole trading, a partnership, or a UK registered company.

Training & Work Experience

Under the training and work experience scheme, foreign nationals can work in the UK as trainees or gain practical work experience in a subject they've been studying either in the UK or abroad. An employer must obtain a trainee or work experience permit and show how the training or work experience he offers will be useful. Trainee positions are for a predetermined period: although permits are usually initially issued for one year, they may be extended for a maximum of three years.

Students

Overseas students who are non-EEA nationals are permitted to enter the UK for the duration of a course, provided they've been accepted at a bona fide educational establishment and intend to leave the UK at the end of their course of study. Your course must occupy a minimum of 15 hours a week during the daytime (9am to 5pm). You cannot combine a variety of part-time courses in order to make up the required 15 hours study per week, and evening courses don't qualify. Your fees must have been paid in full and you must show that you can financially support yourself and, in the case of married students, your spouse and children under 18 (if accompanied by them) without recourse to public funds. You must prove that you're married by producing a marriage certificate. If your country of residence has strict foreign exchange controls, it's important to make arrangements for banking facilities in the UK or for money to be sent to you.

Au Pairs

Unmarried people of either sex, aged from 17 to 27, can be admitted as au pairs for a period (or aggregate period) of up to two years. (They can be 28 when their entry clearance is finalised as long as they were 27 when they applied for it.) They must have no dependants in the UK and must be nationals of an 'approved' country. Non-EEA nationals must produce a letter from a host family confirming their invitation to work in the UK as an au pair. Immigration require a medical certificate (including a chest x-ray) confirming that they're in good health and free from contagious diseases. EEA nationals staying for longer than six months may apply for a residence permit from the Home Office on form EEC1. Non-EEA nationals must register with the police (see page 94) within seven days if they've been instructed to do so by the entry stamp in their passport. Au pairs from non-EEA countries aren't permitted to take any other kind of work during their stay in the UK.

Permanent Residence

Settlement is the name given to the status of permanent residence in the UK, which means you can stay in the UK indefinitely, without any restrictions on working or the need for a work permit. A foreigner married to a UK citizen is granted settlement status after one year. Foreign nationals who have held a residence permit for four years and who have been in continuous employment, self-employment or business in the UK, can apply for settlement. If you've stain the UK legally for ten years and don't qualify under the normal rules, you can apply for settlement on the grounds of the length of your stay. In this case the granting of settlement status will depend on a number of factors, including whether you've established a way of life in the UK and have strong ties with the country and, on the other hand, whether you have been in trouble with the law or have a criminal record or have spent long periods abroad.

IMMIGRATION

When you arrive in the UK, the first thing you must do is go through Passport Control, which is usually divided into two areas: 'EU/EEA Nationals' and 'All Other Passports'. Make sure you join the right queue. Passport control is staffed by immigration officers who have the task of deciding whether you're subject to immigration control and, if so, whether or not you're entitled to enter the UK. You must satisfy the immigration officer that you're entitled to enter the UK under whatever category of the immigration rules you're applying to do so. Present your passport to the immigration officer with any other documentation required (see **Permits & Visas** on page 89).

The immigration officer may decide to send you for a routine (and random) health check, before allowing you to enter the UK. After the health check you must return to immigration to have your passport stamped. **Generally the onus is on anyone entering the UK to prove that he is who and what he claims to be and that he won't infringe the immigration laws. The immigration authorities aren't required to establish that you will violate the immigration laws and can refuse your entry on the grounds of suspicion only.**

CUSTOMS

The belongings you're allowed to bring into the UK duty and tax free depend on your status, where you've come from, where you purchased the goods, how long you've owned them, and whether duty and tax has already been paid in another country, as detailed below. There are no restrictions on the importation of goods purchased tax and duty paid in another EU country, although there are limits for certain goods, e.g. tobacco, beer and wine.

Visitors & Students Resident Abroad: If you're a visitor, you can bring your belongings to the UK free of duty and tax provided that:

● All belongings are brought in with you and are for your use alone;

● They're kept in the UK for no longer than 24 months;

● You don't sell, lend, hire out or otherwise dispose of them in the UK.

If you're unable to export your belongings when you leave the UK, you must apply to the nearest Customs and Excise Advice Centre for an extension.

Students attending a full-time course of study in the UK can permanently import their clothing and household linen, study articles and household effects for furnishing their accommodation.

People Moving Or Returning To The UK: If you're moving or returning to the UK from outside the EU (including British subjects), you can import your belongings free of duty and tax provided that:

- You've lived at least 12 months outside the EU;

- Your possessions have been used for at least six months outside the EU before being imported;

- Tax and duty have been paid on all items being imported (this isn't applicable to diplomats, members of officially recognised international organisations, members of NATO or British forces and their spouses, or any civilian staff accompanying them);

- Articles are for your personal use, are declared to customs, and aren't sold, lent, hired out or otherwise disposed of in the UK (or elsewhere in the EU) within 12 months, without customs authorisation.

People With Second Homes In The UK: If you're setting up a second home in the UK, you can bring normal household furnishings and equipment with you free of duty and tax if you usually live in another EU country. If you've lived outside the EU for at least 12 months, you can import household furnishings and equipment for setting up a second home free of duty but not free of value added tax (VAT), which is levied at 17.5 per cent.

To qualify, you must either own or be renting a home in the UK for a minimum of two years, and your household furnishings and equipment must have been owned and used for at least six months. Articles must be for your personal use, must be declared to customs, and mustn't be sold, lent out, hired out, or otherwise disposed of in the UK (or elsewhere in the EU) within 24 months without authorisation from Customs and Excise. If furnishings and effects for a second home in the EU are imported unaccompanied, customs form C33 must be completed (see below).

Procedure

If you need to pay duty or tax, it must be paid at the time the goods are brought into the country. Customs accept cash (sterling only), personal cheques supported by a cheque guarantee card, credit cards such as MasterCard and

Visa and, at some ports and airports, Switch debit cards. If you're unable to pay on the spot, customs will keep your belongings until you pay the sum due, which must be paid within the period noted on the back of your receipt. Postage or freight charges must be paid if you want the goods sent on to you.

All ports and airports in the UK use a system of red and green 'channels'. Red means you have something to declare and green that you have nothing to declare (i.e. no more than the customs allowances, no goods to sell and no prohibited or restricted goods). If you're **certain** that you have nothing to declare, go through the 'green channel'; otherwise go through the red channel. Customs officers make random checks on people going through the green channel and there are stiff penalties for smuggling. A list of all items you're bringing in is useful, although the customs officer may still want to examine your belongings. **If you're arriving by ferry with a motor vehicle, random checks can be rigorous – even to the point of dismantling the vehicle in search of undeclared or prohibited items!**

Your belongings may be imported up to six months in advance of your arrival in the UK, but no more than a year after your arrival, after transferring your residence. They mustn't be sold, lent, hired out, or otherwise disposed of in the UK (or elsewhere in the EU) within a year of their importation, without first obtaining customs authorisation.

If you're shipping your belongings (which includes anything for your family's use, such as clothing, cameras, television and stereo, furniture and other household goods) unaccompanied to the UK, you must complete (and sign) customs form C3, obtainable from your shipping agent, HM Customs and Excise (see address below) or 🖳 www.hmce.gov.uk, and attach a detailed packing list. If you employ an international removal company, they will handle the customs clearance and associated paperwork for you.

Further Information

Information about customs regulations is contained in a number of booklets, called Notices. They cover belongings, household effects, private motor vehicles and people moving to the UK after marriage (Notice 3); pleasure craft or boats (Notice 8); inherited goods and vehicles (Notice 368); antiques (Notice 362); and motor vehicles, boats or aircraft imported from elsewhere in the EU (Notice 728). Customs and Excise can also provide detailed information regarding the importation of special items.

Copies of the Notices listed above can be obtained from customs offices or downloaded from 🖳 www.hmce.gov.uk. The primary source of further information is the Customs and Excise national advice line (☎ 0845-010 9000 or, if phoning from abroad, ☎ +44 20-8929 0152). Email and postal enquiry addresses for your local area can be found on the website. The principal address for written enquiries in London is HM Customs and Excise, Thomas Paine House, Angel Square, Torrens Street, London EC1V 1TA.

RETIREMENT

Pensioners who are EEA nationals have the right of residence in any EEA country, provided they can prove that they have sufficient income not to become a burden on the host country and have private health insurance (if they're ineligible for cover under the National Health Service). An application for a residence permit must be made before an EEA national has spent six months in the UK. Non-EEA nationals who wish to live but not work in the UK require entry clearance in the form of a letter of consent (see page 88) before arrival in the UK.

To qualify you must be aged at least 60 and have under your control and disposal in the UK an income of not less than £25,000 a year. You must also be able to show that you're able to support and accommodate yourself and your dependants indefinitely without working and without recourse to public funds. Your presence must be 'in the best interests of the UK' (whatever that means!) or you must have close ties with the UK, e.g. close relatives, children attending school there or periods of previous residence in the UK. If you're prohibited from working in the UK, this also applies to members of your family and any dependants. People of independent means are usually admitted for an initial period of a year and qualify for settlement (permanent residence) after four years' continuous residence.

POLICE REGISTRATION

Foreigners over 16 are required to register at their local police station within seven days of arrival if they:

- Are nationals of Afghanistan, Algeria, Argentina, Armenia, Azerbaijan, Bahrain, Belarus, Bolivia, Brazil, China, Columbia, Cuba, Egypt, Georgia, Iran, Iraq, Israel, Jordan, Kazakhstan, Kuwait, Kyrgyzstan, Lebanon, Libya, Moldova, Morocco, North Korea, Oman, Palestine, Peru, Qatar, Russia, Saudi Arabia, Sudan, Syria, Tajikistan, Tunisia, Turkey, Turkmenistan, United Arab Emirates, Ukraine, Uzbekistan or Yemen or are stateless;

- Have limited leave to stay in the UK for longer than six months for employment, or as au pairs, students, businessmen, self-employed people, investors, people of independent means or creative artists;

- Being a national of one of the above countries, weren't originally required to register but have since been granted an extension of stay, which means that they will be in the UK for longer than six months;

- Are the spouse or child of a person who must register with the police;

- Are a national of any of the above countries given limited permission to remain (confusingly called 'leave to remain'), whom the immigration authorities suspect won't abide by their entry conditions.

Exceptions are seasonal workers at agricultural work camps, private servants of diplomatic households, clergymen, spouses of people settled in the UK, and those formally granted asylum.

When required, registration is indicated by the immigration stamp in your passport. You must report to the police station nearest to where you're staying within seven days, even when you're staying in temporary accommodation. You will require your passport, work permit if you have one, any letters from the Home Office or documents from the Overseas Visitors Record Office, two passport-size photographs (black and white or colour) and the fee, currently £34. In the Greater London area, all residents must register at the Overseas Visitors Record Office, Brandon House, 180 Borough High Street, London SE1 1LH. The nearest underground station is Borough and the information line is ☎ 020-7230 1208. Business hours are 9am to 4pm Mondays to Fridays and you should expect to wait for a long time (unless you're first in the queue).

Details, such as your name, address, occupation, nationality, marital status and the date your permission expires, are entered in a green booklet called a Police Registration Certificate. It's advisable to take a copy of your marriage and birth certificates with you. If the police registration certificate isn't given to you on the spot, you may need to surrender your passport, which will be returned to you later with your certificate. Make a photocopy or a note of the certificate's number, date, and place of issue, in case you lose it (in which case the fee must be paid again). You should inform the authorities here of any change in your situation within seven days, e.g. if you change your address or extend your permission to remain in the UK.

You're required to carry your Police Registration Certificate with you at all times, but not your passport. It's advisable to take your Police Registration Certificate with you when travelling abroad, as this will make re-entry into the UK easier. It should be surrendered to the Immigration Officer if you're travelling abroad for longer than two months. Unlike many other Europeans, Britons aren't legally required to prove their identity on demand by a policeman or other official, although identity cards are likely to be introduced in the near future.

COUNCIL TAX REGISTRATION

All residents or temporary residents of the UK are required to register with their local authority or council for council tax purposes soon after arrival in the UK or
after moving to a new home, either in the same council area or a new area. For information about council taxes see page 210.

EMBASSY REGISTRATION

Nationals of some countries are required to register with their local embassy or consulate as soon as possible after arrival in the UK. Registration isn't usually mandatory, although most embassies like to keep a record of their nationals resident in the UK and it may help to expedite passport renewal or replacement. For a list of embassies and consulates in London see **Appendix A**.

FINDING HELP

One of the biggest difficulties facing new arrivals in London is how and where to obtain help with day-to-day problems, e.g. finding a home, schools, insurance requirements and so on. This book was written in response to this need. However, in addition to the comprehensive information you will find here, you will also require detailed local information. How successful you are at finding help will depend on your employer, the borough or area where you live, your nationality and your English proficiency.

Obtaining information isn't a problem, as there's a wealth of data available in London on every conceivable subject. The problem is sorting the truth from the half-truths, comparing the options available and making the right decisions. Much information naturally isn't intended for foreigners and their particular needs. You may find that your friends, colleagues and acquaintances proffer advice based on their own experiences and mistakes. But beware! Although they mean well, you're likely to receive as much misleading and conflicting information as you are helpful (i.e. not necessarily wrong but invalid for your particular area or situation).

Your local council offices, library, tourist information centre and Citizens' Advice Bureau are excellent sources of reliable information on almost any subject. Some large employers may have a department or staff whose job is to help new arrivals, or they may contract this job out to a relocation consultant (see page 149). There are expatriate clubs and organisations for nationals of many countries in most areas, many of which provide detailed local information regarding all aspects of living in the UK, including housing costs, school details, names of doctors and dentists, shopping information and much more. Clubs produce data sheets, booklets and newsletters and organise a variety of social events, which may include day and evening classes ranging from local cooking to English-language classes. One of the best ways to get to know local people is to join a social club, of which there are hundreds in all areas of London (look under 'Clubs and Associations' in your local yellow pages).

Embassies and consulates usually provide information bulletin boards (jobs, accommodation, travel) and keep lists of social clubs for their nationals. Many businesses (e.g. banks and building societies) produce books and leaflets containing valuable information for newcomers. Local libraries and bookshops usually have books about their areas (see also **Appendix B**).

CHECKLISTS

Before Arrival

The following checklist contains a summary of the tasks that should (if possible) be completed before your arrival in London:

- Obtain a visa, if necessary, for all your family members. Obviously, this must be done before leaving for the UK.

- If possible, visit London in advance of your move to compare communities and schools and arrange schooling for your children.

- Find temporary or permanent accommodation and buy a car. If you purchase a car in the UK, register it and arrange insurance.

- Arrange for shipment of your personal effects to the UK.

- Obtain an international credit or charge card, which will be invaluable during your first few months in the UK.

- Arrange health insurance for your family. This is essential if you won't be covered by the National Health Service on your arrival in the UK.

- Open a bank account in the UK and transfer funds (you can open an account with many British banks overseas). It's best to obtain some British currency before your arrival in the UK, as this will save your having to change money on arrival.

- Obtain an international driving permit, if necessary.

- Collect and update your personal records, including those relating to your family's medical, dental, educational (schools), insurance (e.g. car insurance), professional and employment history (including job references) and take them with you to the UK. Don't forget birth certificates, driving licences, marriage certificate, divorce papers, death certificate (if a widow or widower), educational diplomas and professional certificates, student identity cards, medical and dental records, bank account and credit card details, insurance policies and receipts for any valuables you're bringing with you. You also need the documents necessary to obtain a residence or work permit, plus certified copies, official translations and numerous passport-size photographs.

After Arrival

The following checklist contains a summary of tasks to be completed after arrival in London (if not done before):

- On arrival at a UK airport or port, have your visa cancelled and passport stamped, as applicable.

- If you don't own a car, you may wish to rent one for a week or two until you buy one locally. It's difficult to get around in some suburban areas without a car.

- Register for council tax at your local town hall.

- Register with your local consulate.

- Register with your local social security office.

- Open an account at a local bank and give the details to your employer.

- Arrange schooling for your children.

- Find a local doctor and dentist.

- Arrange whatever insurance is necessary, including health insurance, car insurance, home contents insurance and personal liability insurance.

3

GETTING THERE & GETTING ABOUT

Getting to London from most countries is relatively easy as it's served by all the world's major airlines and by a direct rail connection from Brussels and Paris, and there's also a regular ferry service to the UK from a number of European countries. London has five international airports (City, Gatwick, Heathrow, Luton and Stansted), which between them provide services to all major domestic and international destinations. London is the hub of air, rail and road communications in the UK and, as you'd expect, has excellent connections with the rest of the country. London is also at the centre of a extensive network of motorways.

London has a comprehensive public transport system encompassing suburban trains, underground (tube) trains, trams, buses and river ferries. Getting around London by tube, train and tram (where it operates) is relatively fast and convenient, although travel by bus or car is slow due to interminable traffic jams. It's also easy to get around central London by bicycle (although you will need a smog mask!) or even on foot, particularly in the central area which is surprisingly compact. (The best way to get to know – and enjoy London – is to wander the streets at random.) However you plan to get around London, one of your first acts should be to buy a good street map, such as the excellent street plans produced by the Geographers A-Z Map Co.

It isn't essential to own a car if you live in central London, where a car is a liability and parking is prohibitively expensive if you don't have a private garage. If you commute into London from one of the outer boroughs or surrounding counties it will almost certainly be faster by public transport, although you may need a car to get to your local railway or tube station. In common with most major cities, London is plagued by chronic traffic problems and most roads are permanently jammed with traffic, making travel by car slow and frustrating. Parking in central London is at best difficult (and expensive) and at worst impossible. During rush hours, from around 7.30 to 9.30am and 4.30 to 6.30pm, Mondays to Fridays, traffic flow is painfully slow, particularly in central London, where the average traffic speed is around 10mph (it takes as long to cross London by car as it did 200 years ago in a horse and cart!). In an effort to improve traffic flow in central London, a 'congestion charge' was introduced in February 2003, which has proved successful, although unpopular with those unable or unwilling to forsake their cars, who must pay £8 per day to enter the restricted area (see page 129).

However, although public transport, both from a convenience and environmental point of view, is a better option than attempting to get around by car (Transport for London claims that 400,000 Londoners have abandoned their cars since the introduction of the congestion charge), services are often stretched to breaking point, particularly during peak hours and the summer tourist season. Most experts believe that the only long-term solution to the city's traffic problems, and that of urban Britain in general, is to impose stiff costs on people bringing cars into city centres or to 'pedestrianise' central areas completely, while simultaneously making a massive investment in public transport.

The umbrella organisation for London transport is Transport for London (💻 www.tfl.gov.uk). A wealth of information about public transport is published by borough councils, local transport authorities and transportcompanies, many of which you will find mentioned in the relevant section in this chapter.

Fares

Despite more people using public transport in London than in any other European city – London has the world's largest rail and tube network – it has the most expensive public transport of any capital city in Europe, with fares around four times higher than in Rome and some 15 times more expensive than Budapest. Public transport is, however, cheaper if you're able to take advantage of the wide range of discount, combination (e.g. rail, bus and underground), season and off-peak tickets available.

For the purposes of public transport, London is divided into six concentric fare zones stretching 12mi (19km) from the centre. The central area is designated zone 1, while the outer suburbs are in zone 6, and ticket prices depend on how many zones you travel through. You can buy a ticket for a single or day return trip, although a Travelcard, which is valid on the underground (tube), the Docklands Light Railway (DLR), buses and suburban trains and offers unlimited travel for one day, seven days, one month or one year, provides better value if you're planning to use public transport extensively.

A basic adult single fare in Zone 1 is £4 and in Zones 2-6 £3 (DLR only in Zones 2-3 is £1.50). A one-day Travelcard for zones 1 and 2 costs between £5.10 and £6.60 and for all six zones between £6.70 and £13.20 (depending on peak/off peak times). Seven-day, monthly and annual as well as family Travelcards are also available. You can limit a Travelcard to specific zones if your travelling won't cover the whole network.

If you're travelling into London by rail, your ticket can include a Travelcard supplement so that you can use it for onward travel on the tube and buses. If you need a Travelcard for seven days or more (called a Seasonal Travelcard) or a child rate ticket for someone under 17, you will require a free 'photocard', for which you need a passport-size photograph and proof of age for children.

A new public transport pass, introduced in 2003, is the Oyster card, offering discounts to families, students and regular travellers (eg, single adult tube fares within Zone 1 cost £4 but with Oyster costs just £1.50). From Easter 2007 travel for under 11s on the Tube and DLR is free all day and at all times with an Under-14 Oyster Photocard. Oyster cards must be registered for but can be used like a debit card ('Oyster Pre Pay') on the underground, buses, Tramlink and DLR.

Senior citizens who are permanent London residents may qualify for a Freedom Pass, issued by each borough and entitling them to free or discounted public transport. Enquire at your borough council offices or go to their website (see **Chapter 1**).

AIR

London is one of the busiest air transport hubs in the world and you can fly there from practically any country. Whether you're travelling to London from Dublin, Denver or Delhi, if you travel by air you will arrive at one of London's five international airports: Heathrow, Gatwick, Stansted, Luton and City (in order of size and passenger numbers). With the exception of the small City airport, all are situated some distance outside the city and entail a 20 to 60 minute journey into the centre (see the map of **Major Roads & Airports** on page 403). Some airlines flying into London have negotiated discount rates for onward travel by coach, so it's advisable to retain your airline ticket and ask for information when you arrive.

If you're part of a group and finances permit, you can charter a private helicopter to get to London. Contact Biggin Hill Helicopters (☎ 08704 430 555, 💻 www.bhh.co.uk) or Fast Helicopters Ltd. (☎ 01264-772508, 💻 www.fast-helicopters.com) for information and rates.

Heathrow

Heathrow airport (☎ 0870-000 0123, 💻 www.baa.co.uk/airports/heathrow) is located 15mi (24km) south-west of the city centre and is the world's busiest airport, handling over 60 million passengers a year. Over 90 airlines are based here, spread over its four sprawling terminals. Terminals 1, 2 and 3 are in the centre of the Heathrow complex, while terminal 4 is a few miles further south. An application to build a fifth terminal has recently been approved (despite strong opposition from environmental groups and local residents) and work started in 2004, although the terminal won't open until 2008 and won't be fully operational until 2016; this is expected to increase Heathrow's annual throughput to 35 million passengers. Demands from the airlines for a third runway (a take-off and landing slot at Heathrow currently costs them up to £10 million), on the other hand, have been met with objections on the grounds of pollution, which would exceed EU limits.

Access

Train: The high-speed Heathrow Express rail service is by far the quickest and easiest way to get to or from central London. The airport has two stations, one for Terminals 1, 2 and 3 and another for Terminal 4, operating direct trains to London's Paddington station. The single fare is £14, a return £28, and the journey takes around 15 minutes from Terminals 1–3 (23 minutes from Terminal 4), with trains running every 15 minutes between 5am and midnight. Alternatively, you can take the cheaper (and slower – 50 to 60 minutes to Piccadilly Circus) underground into central London for

£3.80 (adult single); trains run between 5.30am and 11.30pm. Information is available from London Transport Travel Centres at Heathrow's tube stations or by phone (☎ 0845-600 1515) or via the internet (💻 www. heathrowexpress. com).

Bus: Heathrow is also served by buses, operating from the Central Bus Station above the underground station. The A2 bus operates frequently between the four terminals and central London, but the journey takes over an hour and a half and an adult single ticket costs £11, so the tube is preferable. If you arrive in the dead of night, you can catch the hourly night bus (N9) to Trafalgar Square – a leisurely trip of around 75 minutes and a bargain at just £1 for a single fare.

Taxi: The journey by taxi costs between £45 and £50 and the journey time is from 45 minutes to well over an hour, depending on the traffic congestion.

Gatwick

Gatwick airport (☎ 0870-000 2468, 💻 www.baa.co.uk/airports/gatwick) is situated 30mi (50km) to the south of London and is the UK's second-busiest airport (and the busiest single-runway airport in the world), operating two terminals (North and South) linked by a monorail service. International flights are handled by both terminals, while most domestic flights are serviced by the South terminal only.

Access

Train: Gatwick Express (☎ 0845-850 1530, 💻 www.gatwickexpress. co.uk) operates a regular train service between 5.20am and 1.35am between the airport's South terminal and Victoria station in central London (trains normally run every 15 minutes but every hour before 6.50am and after 8.50pm). The journey takes 30 minutes and tickets, which you can buy on the train, cost £15 one way. South Central's slower trains cover the same route for a slightly lower fare and run every 15 minutes during the day and every hour at night. There are also Thameslink trains (☎ 0845-605 0600, 💻 www.thameslink.co.uk) running every 15 minutes from Gatwick to other London stations, including London Bridge, Blackfriars, City, Farringdon and King's Cross.

Bus: A cheaper but much slower option – the journey takes at least 80 minutes – is the National Express (☎ 020-8668 7261, 💻 www.nationalexpress. com) Shuttle No.025 which runs approximately every hour between 5.15am and 9.15pm to London's Victoria Coach Station. Single tickets cost £6.50 for adults.

Taxi: A taxi from Gatwick to central London costs at least £60 and takes as long as a bus.

Stansted

Stansted airport (☎ 0870-000 0303, 💻 www.baa.co.uk/airports/stansted) is located 34mi (60km) north-east of the capital. It's the newest of London's airports and the fourth largest in the UK in terms of passenger numbers, serving over 60 destinations. It has two terminals for domestic and international flights respectively and handles a range of flights within the UK, the Irish Republic and most European countries.

Access

Train: The fastest way to get to central London from Stansted is by train via the Stansted Express (☎ 0845-850 0150, 💻 www.stanstedexpress.com), which takes 45 minutes to Liverpool Street station in central London (single fare £25.50). Trains depart every 15 or 30 minutes from 8am to 8pm and hourly from 8pm to midnight and between 6 and 8am. Trains stop at Tottenham Hale on the Victoria underground line. A slower, stopping service is also available.

   Bus: Alternatively, you can catch one of three buses which link the airport with London: the A6 to Victoria Coach Station (stopping at Golders Green and Finchley Road underground station), which operates 24 hours a day, every 20 minutes at peak times, takes around an hour and 40 minutes and costs £12 (adult single); the A7 to Liverpool Street railway station and Victoria, which runs every half hour between midnight and 4.30am only; the Terravision Express Shuttle to Victoria Coach Station, which operates between 9am and 0.30am, every 45 minutes at peak times, and costs £8.00 (adult single). Further details of the A6 and A7 services are available from National Express (☎ 08705 808080, 💻 www.nationalexpress.com) and for information about the Terravision service, call ☎ 01279-680028, 💻 www.terravision.it).

   Taxi: Taking a taxi to central London costs over £60 for a journey of around an hour.

Luton

Luton airport (☎ 01582-405100, 💻 www.london-luton.com, ✉ info@ltn.aero), situated around 30mi (50km) north-west of central London, handles scheduled (around two-thirds of the total) and charter flights to a wide range of destinations in the UK and Europe. It opened the second of its two terminals in October 1999.

Access

Luton airport's promotional strapline is 'We're easier to get to than you think', suggesting that the airport is all but inaccessible. In fact, there are plenty of transport links.

Train: Trains operated by First Capital Connect (💻 www.firstcapitalconnect. co.uk for information, 💻 www. flybytrain.co.uk for booking – see also page 113) from Luton Airport Parkway offer a direct link (the 'Luton Express') every half hour or so, 24 hours a day, from the airport to King's Cross station taking between 25 and 50 minutes, depending on the number of stops, and costing £12.00. Trains also serve other London stations, including Hendon, Cricklewood, West Hampstead, Kentish Town, Farringdon, City, Blackfriars, London Bridge and East Croydon. A regular free shuttle bus runs between the airport and the station.

Bus: A cheaper (£9 for an adult single) and slower (70 minutes) journey is via a Green Line 757 coach (see page 122) to the Green Line Coach station near Victoria Coach Station. Coaches run approximately every half-hour throughout the day and night.

Taxi: A taxi to central London from Luton isn't recommended, as it takes over an hour and costs at least £80.

City

City airport (☎ 020-7646 0088, 💻 www.londoncityairport.com) is the smallest of London's five airports and is situated just 9mi (14km) east of London's centre in the old Docklands district. Only domestic and European flights operate from here (destinations include Amsterdam, Antwerp, Belfast, Bremen, Brussels, Cardiff, Cork, Dublin, Dundee, Edinburgh, Frankfurt, Geneva, Leipzig, Liverpool, Luxembourg, Manchester, Paris, Rotterdam, Swansea and Zurich) and the airport courts its largely business clientele by offering (supposedly) the fastest check-in and arrival times in Europe.

Access

Train: Silvertown & City Airport railway station (DLR – see page 117) is a ten minute walk from the airport and trains to the centre of London run every 20 minutes, linking with the tube system.

Bus: Shuttle bus services operate every ten minutes between 7am and 9pm weekdays, 7.30am and 1pm on Saturdays and from 11am to 9pm on Sundays between the airport and Canning Town (£3 adult single), Canary Wharf (£2) and Liverpool Street (£8) underground stations.

Taxi: Taxis to the City take up to 40 minutes and cost around £20.

SEA

Regular car and passenger ferry services to the south-east of England operate from ports in Belgium, France and the Netherlands. Some services operate year round, others only during the summer (usually May to September), and the frequency of services varies from dozens a day on the busiest Calais/Dover route during the summer to one a week on longer routes out of season. On the longer routes (i.e. from France to Portsmouth and Poole and Hook of Holland/Harwich), there are overnight services. Most ships have a restaurant, self-service cafeteria, a children's play area and shops, and some have 'executive' lounges, where for a few pounds extra you can enjoy superior facilities. Generally, the longer the route, the better and more comprehensive the facilities provided. Although Calais/Dover is the shortest route and offers the most crossings, ships on longer routes are generally less crowded and more relaxing. The following is a list of the services available in 2004, with an indication of the distance of each UK port from central London:

Belgium

- Ostend/Dover: Hoverspeed (💻 www.hoverspeed.com).

Denmark

- Dunkirk/Dover (60mi/100km): Norfolk Line (💻 www.norfolkline.com);

- Calais/Dover: Hoverspeed (💻 www.hoverspeed.com), P&O Ferries (💻 www.poferries.com) and Sea France (💻 www.seafrance.co.uk);

- Boulogne/Dover: Speed Ferries (💻 www.speedferries.com) – a new five-times daily fast ferry service;

- Dieppe/Newhaven: Hoverspeed and Transmanche Ferries (💻 www.transmancheferries.com);

- Le Havre/Portsmouth (60mi/100km): P&O Ferries;

- Caen/Portsmouth: Brittany Ferries (💻 www.brittany-ferries.co.uk);

- Cherbourg/Portsmouth: P&O Ferries;

- Saint-Malo/Portsmouth: Brittany Ferries;

- Cherbourg/Poole (100mi/160km): Brittany Ferries;

- Saint-Malo/Poole via Guernsey and Jersey: Condor Ferries (💻 www.condorferries.co.uk).

Netherlands

- Hook of Holland/Harwich (80mi/130km): Stena Line (💻 www.stenaline.co.uk).

Fares

Ferry companies offer a range of fares, including standard single and return fares, and three and five-day returns. Fares vary enormously, and whenever you travel, always check for special offers. If you're able to book several months in advance, you can often earn up to 50 per cent discounts. It's worthwhile shopping around for the best deal, which is probably best done by a travel agent who has access to fares from all companies or by using a company specialising in discount Channel crossings. There are a number of online ferry booking sites, including the following:

- www.channelcrossings.net;
- www.channel-travel.com;
- www.ferrybooker.com;
- www.ferrybookings.com;
- www.ferry-tickets-online.co.uk;
- www.ferry-tickets.uk.com;
- www.intoferries.co.uk;
- www.cross-channel-ferry-tickets.co.uk.

Note that it's difficult to consult ferry company fares online, as you don't have access to the full range of fares and can only find the price by using the (time-consuming) booking form or quote facility. Brochures rarely include the range of fares.

RAIL

Since the opening of the Channel Tunnel in 1994, London has had a direct rail connection with the continent of Europe. There are two ways of travelling through the tunnel: by train (see **Eurostar** below) and by car (see **Eurotunnel** below).

Eurostar

Eurostar is an international train service linking London, Brussels, Lille and Paris. (There are also excursion trains to Disneyland Paris and, during the ski season, to La Plagne in the French Alps.) Since the opening of the high-speed rail link between Folkestone and London Waterloo in October 2003, it's possible to reach London from Paris (Gare du Nord) in under 2 hours and 50 minutes and from Brussels in two-and-a-half hours. By the end of 2007, it will be possible to travel to London's St Pancras station in less time than it takes to reach Waterloo (see **Channel Tunnel Rail Link** below).

Fares vary widely according to the class (there are three: standard, first and 'premium'), the date and time of travel and the duration of the stay (in the case of return tickets). For example, it's possible to travel from Paris to London for as little as £50, but you can pay £275 for a premium class single fare. For details, timetables and booking, contact Eurostar (☎ 08705-186186, 🖳 www.eurostar.com). **Note that bookings made over the telephone attract a £5 surcharge.**

Channel Tunnel Rail Link

The Channel Tunnel Rail Link (CTRL), which is under construction and expected to be completed later this year, is a new line extending the existing high-speed link from Folkestone to St Pancras station via Stratford (which will be called Stratford International Station). The Eurostar will take just 2 hours and 20 minutes to travel from Paris to St Pancras, where most trains will terminate, although Waterloo will retain some services. At St Pancras, passengers will be able to join the Thameslink service (see page 113); at Stratford, there will be connections with other London services and trains to the north-east of England; connections with other parts of south and south-east England will be available from a new station, Ebbsfleet International (foreigners should have fun pronouncing that) near Junction 2 of the M25.

Eurotunnel

If you want to travel to London through the Channel Tunnel by car, you must drive to Coquelles, near Calais and board a special train, which takes you to Folkestone near Dover. This service is operated by Eurotunnel, which recently won approval from a Paris court to reduce it's debt of. Eurotunnel trains run every 20 minutes and cross the Channel (the tunnels actually run through the rock beneath the sea) in just 35 minutes. There are no services, other than toilets, on trains and you can remain in your car or walk up and down the carriages.

Fares are higher than those for the Calais/Dover ferry crossing (e.g. £150 one way for an average vehicle and up to four passengers), although off-peak and short break reductions are available. For details and bookings, contact Eurotunnel (🖳 www.eurotunnel.com, ☎ 08705-353535). **Note that booking doesn't guarantee you a particular time, and you may have to wait for the next train at peak times.** On the other hand, if you arrive early, you may be able to take an earlier train; this doesn't always apply, however! Trains carry all vehicles, including cycles, motorcycles, cars, trucks, buses, caravans and motorhomes. **Fares are higher for vehicles exceeding around 6ft (1.83m) in height.**

Travelling time to central London from the Folkestone terminal is around an hour, via the M20 motorway.

The Rail Network

The world's oldest, the UK's railway system has been the subject of controversy, scandal and tragedy in recent years. Privatised in 1996, the service went from boom (two years later) to bust (in 2001, when the operating company, Railtrack, went into liquidation with debts of £700 million) and suffered several fatal crashes resulting from poor maintenance and management. The new not-for-profit operator, Network Rail, has inherited something of a poisoned chalice, with unreliable services and an infrastructure badly in need of renovation.

Network Rail owns the infrastructure but the trains themselves are operated by a number of regional companies. Those that serve London stations include those listed below. Note, however, that the Strategic Rail Authority, which oversees the operation of the rail network, recently proposed handing over 1,300mi (2,000km) of rural lines (12.5 per cent of the network) to local authorities, for them to be staffed by volunteers!

- Anglia Railways – serves East Anglia via Stratford and Romford from Liverpool Street;

- Arriva Trains Wales – serves Wales from Paddington (no other stops in London);

- c2c – serves southern Essex via Stratford and Romford from Fenchurch Street;

- Chiltern Railways – serves the north-west via Harrow-on-the-Hill from Marylebone;

- Eurostar (see page 111);

- First Great Eastern – serves Essex and Suffolk via Stratford and Romford from Liverpool Street;

- First Great Western – serves the west from Paddington (no other London stops);

- Gatwick Express (see page 107);

- Great North Eastern Railways (GNER) – serves the north-east from King's Cross (no other London stops);

- Heathrow Express (see page 106);

- Midland Mainline – serves the north via Luton airport from St Pancras;

- Silverlink – serves the north-west via Harrow & Wealdstone from Euston;

- South Central Trains – serves the south and south-east via West and East Croydon and Sutton from Waterloo; also a cross-Thames service to Watford (see page 113);

- South Eastern Trains – serves the south-east via Bromley South, East Croydon and Dartford from Cannon Street, Charing Cross, London Bridge, Victoria and Waterloo;

- South West Trains – serves the south-west via Clapham Junction, Richmond and Wimbledon from Waterloo;

- Thameslink (see page 115);

- Thames Trains – serves the west via Ealing Broadway from Paddington;

- Virgin Trains – serves the north via Harrow & Wealdstone from Euston;

- Wagn – serves the north-east via Finsbury Park and Highbury & Islington from Ming's Cross and Moorgate and via Seven Sisters and Tottenham Hale from Liverpool Street.

Links to the websites of these and all the other regional rail operators can be found on the Network Rail website (⌨ www.networkrail.co.uk), where there are also timetables for all main services nationwide. For a map of London showing the main stations, see page 404.

Although a number of companies may be involved, you can buy 'through' tickets to stations on a different company's network; the price shouldn't vary, irrespective of where you purchase your ticket, although individual train companies sometimes offer reduced fares on their own routes. Depending on the special offers available, you may obtain a better deal by purchasing separate tickets for different 'legs' of a long journey.

There's no a clear distinction between 'mainline' rail services between major cities and local services. A company may offer either or both services on its routes. Suburban or local trains stop at most stations along their route, while long distance trains are express services that stop at major towns only and often include first or 'executive' class carriages.

While it's usually possible to buy a meal on long-distance trains, either in a restaurant car or from a buffet, suburban trains usually offer just a snack trolley service or nothing at all. Toilets are provided on trains on all but the shortest services. **Toilets shouldn't be used when a train is in a station and smoking is forbidden on all British trains.**

There's a bewildering array of different-priced tickets available, including child and youth discounts (up to 25-year-olds), family and group tickets, and discounts for the over 60s (known as 'seniors') and disabled people, as well as special holiday and advance purchase excursion (Apex) tickets. Some tickets require the purchase of an annual 'railcard', which entitles you to discounts each time you buy a ticket. If you're a regular train traveller, you can buy a weekly, monthly or annual point-to-point season ticket, for which you need a passport-size photo. **If you're taking a long journey by train, bear in mind that buying a ticket doesn't guarantee you a seat on any particular train unless it's specifically reserved.** If you know what time you plan to travel, it's advisable to reserve a seat, particularly during holi-day periods and at weekends.

Information about tickets is available from information and ticket offices at stations. To check timetables, book tickets and obtain other information, you can consult the Network Rail website (⌨ www.networkrail.co.uk) or go to ⌨ www.nationalrail.co.uk, 'the gateway to the UK's national rail network' operated by the Association of the Train Operating Companies, or ⌨ www.thetrainline.com, run by the Trainline Rail Enquiry Service and Trainline.com – wholly owned subsidiaries of Trainline Holdings, which is owned by travel groups, Virgin Group Investments and Stagecoach Group.

London is the hub of most long-distance railway travel in the UK, although there are only two trans-capital services (see below) and in most cases if you want to cross London by rail, you must make your way between stations by underground, bus or taxi.

Travel in peak periods is to be avoided, when packed trains (often standing room only) cause considerable discomfort for those commuting into central London from the suburbs and outlying country areas. Londoners call it 'the rush hour', but it actually extends to over two hours both morning and evening. If you're fortunate enough not to be tied to the nine-to-five routine, you should avoid using London's transport system between 7.30 and 9.30am and from 4.30 to 6.30pm at the very least.

Cross-London Trains

There are currently only two overground railway lines that connect north and south London: Thameslink in the east and a South Central line in the west. Three more lines have recently been proposed (see **City Tram** and **Cross River Transit** below and **East London Line Project** on page 118).

Thameslink: This service, which dates from 1989 when the Snow Hill Tunnel under central London was re-opened, has two lines. One runs from Bedford in Bedfordshire to Brighton on the south coast via Luton and Gatwick airports and serves King's Cross, Farringdon, City, Blackfriars and London Bridge in central London and East Croydon in the borough of Croydon. The other line runs from Luton and Luton Airport to Sutton, serving the same London stations (except London Bridge) plus Mill Hill, Hendon, Cricklewood, West Hampstead and Kentish Town north of the river, and numerous stations including Elephant & Castle, Streatham, Wimbledon, South Merton, Morden, Sutton and Mitcham south of the river.

South Central Line: One of South Central's lines runs from Watford in Hertfordshire just north of London to Brighton and other towns in the south-east via Harrow & Wealdstone and Kensington north of the river, and Clapham Junction and Croydon south of the river.

Suburban Trains

London's suburban rail network is concentrated to the south of the city, where the underground service peters out. Travelcards (see page 105) are valid on this network and you can purchase a Network Railcard for £20 that provides discounts on most fares in the south-east of England for a year. Most lines are used by commuters in south-east England, living in what's known as the 'stock-brocker belt' (from where hundreds of thousands of workers travel into London each day). There are also suburban services to the east, north and west of the city (see above).

Trams & Light Rail Systems

The most recent development of London's transport system has been the intro-duction of 'light rail' systems, sometimes comprising trams, which are making a comeback in the UK (as elsewhere in Europe) in the 21st century after the original pre-war systems were abandoned in the century before. Familiar to Americans as 'transits' or 'streetcars', these systems are different from tradi-tional railways. Short trains or 'trams' run as single or articulated units on tracks laid along streets, in cuttings or on elevated platforms. They usually stop more frequently than conventional trains, even where there's no driver. Fuel-efficient (they're electrically powered), quiet and non-polluting, they also help to reduce traffic congestion on London's busy roads. There's a fascinating website (⌨ www.lrta.org) that offers everything you could ever want to know about light rail systems. London's two main light rail systems are the DLR, serving east Lon-don, and Tramlink, serving south London (see below), but others are planned, including the following:

- **City Tram** – A light rail system possibly running from Hackney to Battersea via Shoreditch, Bishopsgate, Elephant & Castle and Vauxhall;

- **Cross River Transit** – A light rail system running from King's Cross and Camden via Euston and Waterloo to Peckham and Brixton and expected to be completed by 2011;

- **Hounslow Tram Project** – A tram system aimed at relieving increased traffic congestion caused by Heathrow's Terminal 5 (see page 104), running from the airport to Hammersmith and possibly to Kingston; the scheme is at an early planning stage;

- **West London Rapid Transit** – A tram system running from Uxbridge to Shepherd's Bush due to start construction in 2005 and be completed by 2009.

Docklands Light Railway: The Docklands Light Railway (DLR) was one of the first success stories of the light rail revival. Treated as part of the underground network (see below) with regard to fares, the DLR covers the whole Docklands area and beyond, from Tower Gateway to Beckton, Stratford to the Isle of Dogs, Greenwich and Lewisham. It's also an excellent way to see some of the most interesting parts of London, where old meets new in a redeveloped and regenerated landscape. London's docks were once the busiest port in the world; now they're home to many of London's workers and to industries such as the UK's major newspapers, which moved from Fleet Street to the Canary Wharf development in the '80s.

The DLR has three lines: the Red line running north-south, the Green line running from east to west, and the Beckton line starting at Poplar station and running 5mi (8km) to the east. It links with both the main overground railway system and the tube. The network is being extended to south-east London and north Kent.

Unusually for light rail systems, the DLR uses modern station designs with high level platforms. The trains are driver-less and remotely operated from the permanently staffed control centre located at Poplar. Facilities for disabled passengers are excellent, all stations having wheelchair access. Most stations are also unmanned, although they're equipped with closed-circuit TV for security reasons. Like underground stations, all DLR platforms have train indicators which show the destination of trains and their estimated arrival times.

Information about the DLR is available from DLR Customer Service (☎ 020-7363 9700 and the internet (🖳 www.dlr.co.uk), where a map of the system is also available.

Tramlink: Tramlink (formerly called Croydon Tramlink) is a light rail system connecting New Addington and Addington Village (on one line) and Beckenham Junction, Birbeck and Elmers End (on another) in the east of the borough of Croydon with Wimbledon in the borough of Merton via East and West Croydon and Mitcham Junction. Further details and a map of the system can be found on 🖳 www.tramlink.net.

Station Facilities

Most main railway stations have restaurants, buffets and snack outlets. The standard of food has improved since privatisation, although prices can be high. Smaller stations sometimes have vending machines for snacks, sweets and drinks. Only large London stations have wash and brush-up facilities, although most provide basic toilet facilities (sometimes for a fee) and many have baby changing rooms. All stations have payphones, most accepting phonecards and coins, and most larger stations provide instant 'passport' photo machines. **Car parking is provided at most country and suburban stations, although there's a high level of theft of (and from) cars parked at railway stations, so don't leave your CD collection on the back seat!**

Many stations and airports have luggage lockers or 'left luggage' offices and you can usually find a trolley to wheel your bags around, although porters are rare these days. Disabled passengers can use the wheelchairs available at major railway stations and most trains have special facilities for their storage. Shops are provided at most central London stations and some large termini, e.g. Liverpool Street, have full-size shopping centres with banking facilities.

UNDERGROUND

In most European countries, an underground train system is called a metro system, while in the US it's the subway. In London the vernacular is the 'tube' – a term derived from the tube-shaped tunnels through which the trains run under the city. Outside the central areas (and even within some of them) trains actually run above ground -- something which, not surprisingly, many first-time visitors to the city find confusing! The London underground system is the oldest (parts of it have been around since the 1860s) and largest in the world, with almost 500 trains and over 270 stations and handling some 2.5 million passenger journeys a day. Given the congestion above ground, London without its tube would be unthinkable and it's easily the fastest and most convenient way to get around the city and its suburbs.

Although few Londoners have much good to say about it, the tube is nowhere near as bad as some people would have you believe. Despite hot, sticky and airless conditions in some older parts of the network, there are other areas, such as the recently opened Jubilee Line extension to Greenwich, which are clean, efficient and air-conditioned. Nevertheless, like most of the UK's rail network, the tube desperately needs a huge investment to overcome the backlog of neglect and to modernise it, and privatisation (or a public-private partnership) has been suggested as a means of providing the necessary funds.

East London Line Project

The East London Line Project (formerly known as the East London Line Extension/ELLX) aims to upgrade and extend the East London underground line and make it part of the (overground) rail network. The northern extension will run from a new Shoreditch station as far as Highbury & Islington via Hoxton, Haggerston, Dalston Junction and Canonbury, while the southern extension (south of the river) will link with existing overground lines to provide services to Clapham Junction and West Croydon. Further details of the scheme can be found on the Transport for London website 🖳 www.tfl.co.uk.

The Tube Network

Free maps of the tube network are available at stations, London Transport Information Centres and from Transport for London (☎ 020-7222 1234, 🖳 www.tfl.gov.uk/tube). The network has 11 separate lines (strictly speaking the DLR – see above – is classed as part of the tube network), each of which is colour-coded on the tube map, e.g. yellow for the Circle Line, green for the District Line, red for the Central Line and so on. This makes it easy to follow your route and find your way to the correct platform (**although you need to know whether you're travelling north, south, east or west in order not to catch a train going in the opposite direction**). Some larger stations have electronic route planners where you input the name of your destination station and the shortest route is displayed.

Although the tube is most widely used in the centre of the city, where it provides a useful alternative to fighting your way through the gridlocked London traffic, it also includes extensive coverage of the suburbs to the north, east and west of the city. There are fewer lines and stops south of the River Thames, where commuters tend to use the main rail network. The tube operates for some 20 hours a day, until around 00.30am – it varies with the day of the week, the station and the line. If you miss the last tube, you can take a taxi or a night bus (see page 125).

Stations & Tickets

A typical tube station has an entrance above ground, indicated by the London Transport 'bull's eye' logo of a red circle with a horizontal line through the middle. **Smoking isn't permitted anywhere on the network. Neither are you allowed to drop litter or take flash photographs. Security is tight, so don't leave your bags unattended or staff might treat them as 'suspicious packages' or suspected bombs.**

On entering a station you must buy a ticket before starting your journey – **there's a £10 fine if you're caught travelling without one!** You can buy tickets from machines and from ticket windows at most stations. Most machines provide change and if a machine runs out of change it will display a message telling you to deposit the exact fare. It's advisable to carry some change when travelling on the tube, as queues at ticket windows in central London can be long.

Like all London's public transport, the tube network is divided into (six) fare zones. The city centre is designated zone 1, while the outer suburbs such as High Barnet in the north or Upminster in the east are in zone 6. The price of your ticket depends on how many zones you travel through: they range from £1.10 for a single-zone journey (excluding zone 1, which costs £2) to £3.80 for a journey across all six zones. You can buy a ticket for a single or day return trip, although a Travelcard (also valid on London's buses and many over-ground trains) offers better value if you're going to be using the system more extensively (see page 105).

If you're exploring the central area and expect to be making a lot of short journeys, buy a carnet of ten tickets for £10, but bear in mind that you cannot travel outside zone 1 without buying another ticket.

Most central London stations have automatic ticket barriers that speed up the flow of passengers from the concourse to the platforms. Once you have your ticket, insert it into the slot on the front of the machine. It will pop out at the top and as you take it the gates will open to let you through. If you have problems, there's usually a member of staff nearby to help; special gates are provided for wheelchair users, those with children in pushchairs or bulky luggage. Once through the barrier, access to platforms is via escalators (moving staircases) or lifts, although some stations have stairs only. **Escalators can be tricky if you have young children with you, so fold pushchairs before you start and take extra care. Stand on the right** – those in a hurry (half of London) like to stampede past you on the left – **and hold the moving handrail at the side.** If you have young children, you may need to help them to jump on and off at the right moment. One last fashion note – stiletto heels and long skirts can be a menace on escalators.

Once safely at the bottom of the shaft, make sure you're following the signs to the right line in the right direction, e.g. Northern Line southbound or Piccadilly Line westbound. There are electronic displays on platforms that tell you the time until the next train and its destination. **On many lines, trains can have more than one destination on the same line (i.e. a number of branches) and some trains terminate before the end of the line.** Train doors open and shut automatically or you may be required to press a button near the door to open them.

Travelling By Tube

The tube system can become **very** crowded, particularly at peak hours (around 8 to 9.30am and 5 to 6.30pm, Mondays to Fridays**). It's advisable to avoid these times if you can.** Standing in a train that's packed to the doors can be an uncomfortable and claustrophobic experience, and packed platforms and trains are a haven for pickpockets (and gropers). **Keep a tight hold on your valuables.** The District Line is the busiest, although the shorter Victoria Line carries more passengers per mile, with Victoria and Oxford Circus the two busiest stations on the network.

At quiet times, tube travel can be moderately relaxing, provided you keep an eye on the frequent stops and don't miss your destination or interchange point! Each carriage has seats, although priority should be given to the elderly, pregnant, disabled or those laden with children or heavy bags. If you don't get a seat it's wise to hang on tight, as trains can hurtle through twisting tunnels at an alarming rate and it's easy to find yourself tumbling into the lap of a surprised stranger. There are plenty of rails to hold on to, as well as handles or 'straps' that dangle from the ceiling for support.

If you have children with you keep a firm grip of them, as it's easy to become separated in the crush on a train or platform. You should also stand well back from the platform edge. If you stand too close to the edge, it' possible to fall or be pushed onto the live rail or under the wheels of an approaching train (the wind in the stations can be surprisingly strong as trains force pockets of air along the tunnels). When you arrive at your destination, follow the directions to the exit. In central London you will probably have to negotiate more escalators or lifts and another set of automatic barriers. If your ticket has expired the machine will 'swallow' it so that it cannot be used again.

Information

There are Transport for London (TfL) centres throughout central London at Euston, King's Cross, Liverpool Street, Oxford Circus, Piccadilly Circus, Victoria and St James's Park rail/tube stations and at Hammersmith Bus Station (plus Heathrow Airport). TfL centres provide extensive information about the tube network plus bus services and the DLR. Business hours vary, but there's also a 24-hour hotline (☎ 020-7222 1234) and a recorded information line (☎ 020-7222 1200). London Transport publishes a booklet about facilities for disabled passengers, called *Access to the Underground*, available free from ticket offices or from TfL's special Unit for Disabled Passengers (☎ 020-7941 4600, ✉ access&mobility@tfl.gov.uk). *Access in London* by Gordon Couch, William Forrester and Justin Irwin (Quiller Press, 1996) also provides details of the most accessible tube stations and step-free routes for wheelchairs.

The internet positively pulsates with tube-related websites, both official and enthusiastically amateur. One of the best is Carter's Unofficial Guide to the London Underground (💻 www.geocities.com/CollegePark/3812).

BUSES

When you mention a London bus, most people immediately conjure up the image of the old Routemaster: post-box red double-deckers with a roving conductor or 'clippie' and a rear platform you can hop on and off. Sadly, the days of the traditional London bus are numbered. The youngest are now 30 years old, they've been criticised for being inaccessible to disabled people, and they're gradually being replaced with cheaper-to-run, one-man buses. The newest of these are 18m long 'bendy' (single-deck) buses, so far operating only on Route 18 but (if London's Mayor, Ken Livingstone has his way) soon to be introduced on other routes.

With conductor-less buses, you board at the front and pay the driver, so the new buses also tend to be slower – **it's advisable to have the correct change ready, which on some buses is mandatory.** New buses are also trickier to negotiate if you have heavy bags or pushchairs to manage, as the entrance is narrow and there's no helpful conductor to give you a hand.

Old or new, double-deck buses can be one of the most pleasurable and scenic ways to get around the capital (or out to the suburbs), provided you don't try to do it during the rush hour when progress can be painfully slow and it may be quicker to walk! Fares are low: any journey costs just £2 – or £1 using an Oyster card (see page 105) or if you buy a carnet of six tickets. Most bus routes accept Travelcards (see page 105) or you can buy a daily, weekly or monthly pass that's valid for all six travel zones. A one-day adult pass costs £6.60.

To catch a bus, first find a bus stop on the right side of the road for the direction you want to go. Bus stops are roadside poles with a red sign at the top. Many are request stops, which means you need to put your arm out to hail the bus as it approaches or it won't stop. There are many different routes serving the same stops, so look at the front of the bus for an indication of its destination or study the bus routes in advance by picking up a free bus map and timetable from a London Transport centre (see page 119). Alternatively, have a look at the Greater London Bus Map (🖳 www.busmap.co.uk or 🖳 www.busmap.org).

The regular red bus service runs between 6am and midnight, after which a restricted night bus service comes into operation. These buses have numbers prefixed with the letter 'N' and all routes radiate from Trafalgar Square. Night buses run approximately every hour and charge a flat fare of £1 irrespective of the distance travelled. You can use Travelcards (see page 105) on night buses.

Further information about London's bus services can be obtained from Transport for London (☎ 020-7918 4300, 🖳 www.tfl.gov.uk/buses).

Green Line

The outer suburbs of London within a 40mi (64km) radius are served by Green Line buses (☎ 0870-608 7261, 🖳 www.greenline.co.uk), most of which leave from Victoria Coach Station in Eccleston Street. Travelcards can be used on some Green Line bus services.

International Services

International bus services to and from the UK are provided principally by Eurolines, which operates through National Express (☎ 0870-580 8080, 🖳 www.nationalexpress.com), with regular services to around 200 destinations in Europe and Ireland. Other operators provide services to Eastern European countries, such as Bulgaria, the Czech Republic, Latvia, Lithuania and Poland, including Capital Express, Ecolines, ETAP, Karolina, Kingscourt Express, Nordbecker and Orbis Transport. Most international services operate to and from Victoria Coach Station in Buckingham Palace Road, near Victoria Station (☎ 020-7730 3466, bookings

020-7730 3499, ⌨ www.tfl.gov.uk/vcs), although some operate directly from the provinces.

RIVER FERRIES

One method of getting around London that's often overlooked is river transport. If your daily route to and from work follows the line of the River Thames, this is a pleasant (but expensive) 'alternative' way to travel, although most services don't operate in winter.

London River Transport Services

London River Services/LRS (☎ 020-7941 2400, ⌨ www.tfl.gov.uk/river) is a subsidiary of Transport for London, which aims to develop river passenger transport by providing new river piers and boat services. To this end, LRS has recently acquired seven piers: Bankside, Blackfriars, Embankment, Greenwich, Temple, Tower, Waterloo (formerly Festival) and Westminster. Other piers on the river are in private or local government ownership. Its river taxi services include those listed below. Travelcard (see page 105) holders qualify for a 33 per cent discount on most fares and Freedom Pass holders for a 50 per cent discount.

Embankment-Greenwich

Daily service between mid-April and late October stopping at Waterloo, Bankside and Tower. An adult return ticket for the whole route costs £8; a single costs £6.60. For further details and bookings, contact Bateaux London and Catamaran Cruisers (☎ 020-7987 1185 or 2062, ⌨ www.bateauxlondon).

Hampton Court-Westminster

Daily service between early April and late September, stopping at Richmond and Kew. An adult return ticket for the whole route costs £18; a single costs £12. For further details and bookings, contact Westminster Passenger Services Association (Upriver) Ltd (☎ 020-7930 2062, ⌨ www.wpsa.co.uk).

Savoy-Masthouse Terrace

Daily service all year round, stopping at Blackfriars, Bankside, London Bridge, St Katharine's, Canary Wharf and Hilton Docklands. An adult return ticket for the whole route costs £5; a single costs £3. For further details and bookings, contact Thames Clippers (☎ 0870 781 5049, ⌨ www.thamesclippers.com).

Westminster-St Katharine's

Daily service between early April and late October, stopping at Festival Pier, Embankment, Bankside and London Bridge. An adult return ticket for the whole route costs £6.30; a single costs £5. For further details and bookings, contact Crown River Cruises (☎ 020-7936 2033, 💻 www.crownriver.com).

Westminster-Greenwich

Daily service between late March and early November, stopping at Waterloo and Tower. An adult return ticket for the whole route costs £6.30; a single costs £5.20. For further details and bookings, contact City Cruises (☎ 020-7740 0400, 💻 www.citycruises.com).

Westminster-Barrier Gardens

Daily service between early April and late October, stopping at St Katharine's and Greenwich. An adult return ticket for the whole route costs £9; a single costs £7.50. For further details and bookings, contact Thames River Services (☎ 020-7930 4097, 💻 www.westminsterpier.co.uk).

Other Services

Other river taxi services run by independent operators include those listed below. There are also a number of other services intended for tourists.

Chelsea Harbour-Embankment

A service Mondays to Fridays between early April and late October, stopping at Cadogan. An adult return ticket for the whole route costs £8; a single costs £4. For further details and bookings, contact Riverside Launches (☎ 020-7352 5888).

Richmond-Hampton Court

Daily service between mid-May and late September (Mondays only late July to late August), stopping at Kingston. An adult return ticket for the whole route costs £7; a single costs £5.50. For further details and bookings, contact Turks Launches (☎ 020-8546 2434, 💻 www.turks.co.uk).

Woolwich Ferry

Daily free ferry across the Thames operated by the London Borough of Greenwich (☎ 020-8312 5576).

TAXIS

London is famous for its purpose-built black taxi cabs but there are other taxi services available in the capital.

Black Cabs

Although most of London's purpose-built cabs are black, they also come in other colours, including *Financial Times* pink and *Evening Standard* 'newsprint' pattern. Nevertheless, they all have a yellow 'For Hire' sign at the front and a white numbered licence plate on the back. Black cabs, officially called Hackney Carriages (a term that has no connection with the name of the London borough but derives from an old French word *haquenée*, meaning a type of horse that could be hired) are licensed by the Metropolitan Police and each cab has a licence number plate and the driver (known as a cabby) wears a badge bearing his driver number.

Black cabs cover a vast area of around $610mi^2$ ($1,580km^2$) stretching well into the outer suburbs and are obliged to undertake journeys of up to 12 miles from anywhere in Greater London (20 miles from Heathrow Airport). Further information about London taxis is available from Transport for London (💻 www.tfl.gov.uk/pco).

Fares

Taxis are quite expensive in the UK, although they're cheaper than in some other European countries. They have a strictly regulated scale of fares and charges (which can be viewed on 💻 www.tfl.gov.uk/pco – click on 'Taxi fares & tariffs'), to which it's customary to add a tip of around 10 per cent. Fares vary according to the day and time. From Mondays to Fridays between 6am and 8pm, there's a minimum charge of £2.20 for the first 361m (around 450 yards) or 77.6 seconds and 20p for each additional 180.5m or 38.8 seconds up to a total of £12.40 and thereafter a further 20p for each 128.9m or 27.7 seconds (take a stop watch and an inch-tape if you want to check the fare!). At other times, the charges are the same but the distance or time covered for the basic £2.20 and for each additional 20p is less. **This means that taxis are less good value for longer journeys and that, even if you're stuck in a traffic jam, the meter will continue to notch up the pennies.** There are extra charges for journeys at Christmas and New Year and sometimes a fee of up to £2 for booking by telephone.

Although they aren't a cheap mode of transport (unless three or four people share a fare), a licensed cab driver won't usually take anything but the shortest route between two points (unless he does so to avoid traffic congestion). You can be sure that you won't be cheated by a London cabbie.

There are also business-class cabs with luxurious seats, soundproofing and a telephone (and higher rates than standard cabs).

If you want to book a cab, call Radio Taxicabs (☎ 020-7272 0272) or Dial-a-Cab (☎ 020-7253 5000), email the Licensed London Taxi Booking Service (✉ sttaxi@aol.com) or go to the London Black Taxis site (🖥 www.london blacktaxis.com).

Drivers

Before obtaining his licence, a cab driver must undergo a long training period and pass a stiff exam on what's known as 'The Knowledge' – an encyclopaedic test of London's geography. Cabbies vary from grimly silent to cheerfully loquacious, and many won't hesitate to tell you their opinions on every topic under the sun. Just nod and smile. Most drivers are more than pleased to help disabled passengers and wheelchairs can usually be stored inside the cab along with any luggage. If you have a complaint about a taxi driver, contact the Public Carriage Office (☎ 020-7941 7941, 🖥 www.tfl.gov.uk/pco) with the number of the offending cab and the driver's badge number.

Minicabs & Other Taxis

As an alternative to a black cab, you can take a minicab, which, unlike a black cab, cannot be hailed in the street and must be booked by phone. (**It's illegal for minicabs to ply for hire in the street like licensed taxis, although some do.**) Minicabs are cheaper than licensed taxis, but you have no guarantee that the driver will be reliable, honest or know his way around. There's no official training scheme for minicab drivers and there are dozens of companies available, so the best way to find a good one is to ask someone you trust. Phone for a minicab in advance and agree the price to your destination before starting your journey, as few have meters.

If you're female and worried about your safety late at night, you might want to consider Ladycabs (☎ 020-7272 3019), which employ women only.

In addition to taxi services, many taxi and minicab companies operate private hire (e.g. weddings or sightseeing), chauffeur and courier services, and provide contract and account services, e.g. to take children to and from school.

DRIVING IN LONDON

You need nerves of steel and the patience of Job to drive in central London – and it also helps to be a little crazy. Not only will it cost you dearly in terms of time, petrol (among the most expensive in Europe), insurance and headache pills, it's also virtually impossible to find affordable parking (see below) in the central area. Few central London properties have garages or off-road parking, although you may be fortunate enough to find a house or apartment with a residents' parking scheme (see page 133). Very few employers provide workplace parking in central London and when they do it's usually for an elite few only. Parking meters are for temporary stays of up to two hours and private car parks are for the seriously rich only.

An additional hazard is having your car stolen. The number of cars stolen in London is the highest (per capita) in Western Europe and if you work or live in London and park your car there, you have a one in four chance of having it stolen or broken into (see crime statistics for each borough on page 348).

Congestion on London's roads and the resulting air pollution has reached nightmare proportions in recent years. Getting anywhere by private car takes eons, and an accident at a busy intersection can cause long tailbacks or even gridlock throughout the city. There has been a widespread debate about traffic congestion in recent years and various measures have been introduced to limit its effects, ranging from special bus and cycle lanes to help speed traffic, and punitive parking fees to discourage driving in the city. However, these measures have, so far, had little impact.

If you think you cannot live without a car in London, you can gain some first-hand experience of the nightmare by hiring one for a week or two. Many people soon realise that they're better off without one and use public transport to get around; over 50 per cent of those living in central London don't own a car, along with some 40 per cent of Greater London's residents.

If you aren't used to driving in the UK, you'd also be advised to buy a copy of the *Highway Code*, available from any bookshop. **Finally, bear in mind that UK speed limits are 30mph (48kph) in urban areas, 60mph (96kph) on unrestricted single-carriageway roads (outside towns), and 70mph/ 113kph on motorways and dual-carriageways unless otherwise indicated. It's also useful to remember that traffic drives on the left-hand side of the road!** Valuable advice and assistance about driving in the UK is available on the internet at Driving Online (💻 www.driving.co.uk).

Car Hire

To hire a car you need at least one year's driving experience and must be aged at least 21 or 25, depending on the rental company. European Union driving licences are valid indefinitely in the UK, while most other licences are valid for one year, after which the nationals of many countries must pass a British driving test. The major car hire companies in London include Avis (☎ 0870-010 0287, 💻 www.avis.co.uk), British Car Rental (☎ 0845-225 084539, 💻 www. carrentals.co.uk), Europcar BCR (☎ 0870-607 5000, 💻 www.europcar.co.uk) and Hertz (☎ 0870-844 8844, 💻 www.hertz.co.uk). Shop around, as hire charges vary considerably. Disabled drivers can hire vehicles with hand controls from Hertz and other national car hire companies and specialist companies such as

Wheelchair Travel (☎ 01483-233640) based in Guildford (Surrey), 32mi (51km) south of London.

Travelling To London By Road

The web of motorways leading into London intersects with the M25, London's orbital motorway, and some of them continue towards the city centre (see the map of **Major Roads & Airports** on page 416). The M25 (nicknamed 'the world's largest car park') was intended to consolidate the motorway system around the capital, drawing long-distance traffic away from the centre. However, it attracted a huge volume of local traffic, as a result of which long stretches have had extra lanes added, increasing the number of carriageways from three to four (mainly in the south-western section between the intersections with the M4 and M23) and further widening work is planned or in progress. There are also controversial plans to charge lorries and even cars for using it.

M40: The M40 from Birmingham to the north-west becomes the A40 inside the M25 and is dual-carriageway all the way to Regent's Park, although there are some dreadful bottlenecks along the way.

M1: Further to the north the M1 pushes some way into London ending at an intersection with the North Circular, the original (and now inner) London ring road. From here, follow either the A41 for Regent's Park and the West End, or peel off the M1 one exit before it ends and merge with the A1, which takes you further east to Islington and the City.

A41: The A41 is one of the better roads leading into the city centre but, because it brings you into the heart of London's leisure and shopping areas, it can get clogged at unexpected times, for example, going **into** London in the early evening.

A10: The A10 is a good road from the north until it hits the North Circular, after which traffic speeds fall considerably.

M11 & A12: The M11 enters London from the north-east, also terminating at the North Circular at the same point as the A12 from the east. However, there's no fast road on which to continue, leaving several miles of congested East End high streets before you reach the City.

M2 & M20: South of the river, road access to the centre is frustratingly complicated. There are almost no fast roads in from the south-east, the best being the M2/A2 and M20/A20. Both of these leave you with Hobson's choice of either entering the Blackwall Tunnel under the river, from which you will emerge still some way from the City and even further from the West End, or heading further west up the Old Kent Road before crossing the River Thames. Either way is likely to consist of a lengthy crawl through congested urban streets.

M23: The M23 arrives from the south and finishes soon after its intersection with the M25, becoming dual carriageway for a few miles but soon degenerating into another crawl through a mass of crowded suburban high streets towards the centre.

Christmas lights, Oxford Street ▲

▲ Portobello Road Market

▼ Bank of England

Richmond waterfront ▲

▼ Thames flood barrier

▲ *Chapel Market, Islington*

▲ *Notting Hill Carnival*

▶ *The York pub, Islington*

▼ *Westminster Abbey*

▲ *St. James's Park & Buckingham Palace*

▲ *Thames River Bus*

► *British Museum*

▲ *Tower of London and Tower Bridge*

▲ *Palace Theatre*

► *Antique 'stall', Camden Passage*

◀ Greenwich Park

▼ Christmas tree, Trafalgar Square

◀ BA
London
Eye

▲ Oxford Street

 ◀ St. Katherine's Dock

All photographs
© *www.visitlondon.com*

A3 & M3: From the south-west, the A3 and M3 are completely separate roads, both of which continue as dual-carriageways some distance towards the centre of London after reaching the M25 (the M3 becomes the A316).

M4: Entry to London from the west is via the M4, which runs to Chiswick in west London before merging with London's urban sprawl. The M4 is one of the UK's busiest and most dangerous motorways, carrying London's traffic from prosperous industrial towns such as Slough and Reading, the tourist traffic for Windsor and the West Country, and swarms of taxis and coaches going to and from Heathrow airport.

Congestion Charge

In an effort to improve traffic flow in central London, a 'congestion charge' was introduced in February 2003, whereby most vehicles must pay £8 per day to enter an area roughly bounded by the railway stations of Marylebone, Euston, St Pancras, King's Cross, Fenchurch Street and Victoria, although this has recently (February 2007) been slightly extended westward – the exact area is shown on a map available from Congestion Charging, PO Box 2985, Coventry CV7 8ZR (☎ 0845-900 1234) or downloadable from its website (🖳 www.cclondon.com) – between 7am and 6.30pm Mondays to Fridays. The area is marked by signs showing a white C in a red circle and you can pay on the spot or in advance of your journey (by phoning the above number). CCTV cameras check whether your car remains in the charging area for longer than the period paid for, in which case you're liable for fines.

Certain vehicles and drivers are exempt from the congestion charge, including the disabled, residents of the charging area, vehicles using 'alternative' fuel (including electrically-powered vehicles) and vehicles with nine or more seats. Details of exemptions and how to apply for them are available from Congestion Charging.

Congestion charging has been successful in reducing traffic in central London (and in earning money for the government!)..

Breakdown Assistance

If you break down anywhere in the UK, you can obtain roadside assistance if you're a member of a motoring organisation such as the Automobile Association/AA (☎ 0870 085 2721, 🖳 www.theaa.com), the Royal Automobile Club/RAC (☎ 08705 722 722, (🖳 www.rac.co.uk) and Green Flag National Breakdown (☎ 0845-246 1557, 🖳 www.greenflag.com). Membership costs between £40 and £150 per year, depending on the level of cover required.

Parking

Parking in central London is expensive, prohibitively so if you drive into the city every day. On-road parking (waiting) restrictions in the UK are indicated by yellow lines at the edge of roads, usually accompanied by a sign indicating when parking is prohibited, e.g. 'Mon–Sat 8am–6.30pm' or 'At any time'. If no days are indicated on the sign, restrictions are in force every day including public holidays and Sundays. **Note that, unlike many other European countries, the UK doesn't have a cavalier attitude towards illegal parking and the authorities rarely (if ever) turn a blind eye to it.** Yellow signs indicate a continuous waiting prohibition and also detail times when parking is illegal, while blue signs indicate limited waiting periods. Yellow lines provide a guide to the restrictions in force, but the signs must always be consulted. The following road markings are in use in London and its suburbs:

Road Marking	Prohibitions
White zigzag line or studded	No parking or stopping at any time (e.g. next to a zebra crossing)
Double yellow lines	No parking at most or all times (it may be possible to park on double yellow lines during some periods, but if in doubt, don't)
Single yellow line	No parking for at least eight hours between 7am and 7pm (e.g. from 8.30am to 6.30pm) on four or more days a week
Broken yellow	Restricted parking shown by a sign

Loading restrictions for loading and unloading goods may be shown by one, two or three short yellow lines marked diagonally on the kerb and a sign. Red lines along the side of a road mean that you aren't permitted to stop between the hours of 7am and 7pm (or as indicated by a sign) from Mondays to Fridays, except for loading or unloading. Parking bays marked in red have similar restrictions. A double red line indicates no stopping, loading or parking at any time. If you park illegally on a red route, your car will be towed away in the blink of an eye and minimum charges of £60 will be levied on the spot. For more information consult the *Highway Code*.

In most towns there are public and private off-road car parks, indicated by a sign showing a white 'P' on a blue background. Parking in local authority (council) car parks usually costs from around 20p for half an hour. Parking in short-term (local authority) car parks may become progressively more expensive the longer you stay and can cost as much as £5 for over five hours' parking. However, parking is generally cheaper (per hour) the longer you park, up to a maximum of around nine hours.

Private Car Parks

Parking in a private central London car park costs as much as £5 an hour or £50 per day (monthly and annual season tickets are usually available for commuters). National Car Parks (NCP, 🖳 www.ncp.co.uk), the UK's largest car park operator, has a number of 24-hour car parks in central London. A free map of NCP car parks can be requested by telephone (☎ 0870-606 7050) or an area can be searched using the Car Park Finder function on the website. In many areas there are short-stay and long-stay car parks. Fees may be the same for short stays of up to two or three hours, beyond which rates at short-stay car parks are much more expensive. If you commute into London, it's cheaper to drive to a convenient railway station, where parking costs around £3 to £4 a day, and take a train into central London. Weekly, monthly and annual season tickets are usually available at rail and underground stations. Parking in public car parks and at meters may be free on Sundays and public holidays, so check the notice **before** buying a ticket.

Parking Meters

The maximum permitted parking period at meters varies from 30 minutes to two hours. **Meter-feeding (i.e. returning to a meter to insert more money) is illegal.** You must vacate the parking space when the meter time expires, even if it was under the maximum time allowed, and you may not move to another meter in the same group.

Meters normally accept a combination of 20p to £1 coins and are usually in force from 7am until 7pm, Mondays to Fridays, and from 7am to 6pm on Saturdays (check the sign on a meter). Sundays are usually free. Meters at railway stations and airports may be in use 24-hours a day. **Don't park at meters that are out of use, as you can be towed away.**

If you remain at a meter beyond the excess charge period, you will be liable for a fixed penalty handed out by a police officer or by London's infamous and much reviled traffic wardens. Parking meters are being phased out and replaced by pay-and-display parking areas.

Pay-And-Display

These are parking areas where you must buy a ticket from a machine and display it behind your windscreen. It may have an adhesive backing which you can peel off and use to stick the ticket to the inside of your windscreen or a car window. Parking costs at least 50p an hour in most areas and machines usually accept all coins from 5p to £1. When you've inserted sufficient coins for the period required, press the button to receive your ticket. Pay-and-display parking areas usually operate from 7am until 7pm, excluding Sundays and public holidays.

Parking Fines & Penalties

The fine for illegal parking depends on where you park. There's usually a fixed penalty ticket of £40 or £60 (50 per cent discount if you pay within 14 days) for parking illegally on a yellow line. Parking in a dangerous position or on the zigzag lines or studded area near a pedestrian crossing results in a higher fine, plus three penalty points on your driving licence. Penalties for non-payment or overstaying your time in a permitted parking area (e.g. at a parking meter or in a pay-and-display area) are set by the local authorities who issue parking tickets. **In Westminster, which operates a 'reign of terror' against motorists, you may be hit with an £80 fine for over-staying your time at a £4 an hour parking meter!**

You shouldn't even **think** about parking illegally, e.g. in a residents' only area, on a double yellow line or at an expired meter. Illegal parking can result in your car being 'clamped', where a large metal device (a clamp) is fixed to one of its wheels, thus preventing you driving it away. Over 3,000 cars are clamped each week in London and 2,000 are towed away. (In one notorious case a woman's car was seized by bailiffs and sold at auction to pay a £30 fine while she was on holiday. Of the auction proceeds of £3,500 – £1,500 below its market value – she eventually received £1,700.)

If your car is clamped, there will be a sticker on the windscreen -- partly to prevent you inadvertently attempting to drive off and damaging your car and partly to instruct you how to get the clamp removed. You will have to pay a substantial fee (e.g. over £100) before your car is released, plus the parking fine. If you've been clamped, you will have a lengthy wait even after you've paid the fine (some boroughs allow you to pay over the phone by credit card, while others insist that you pay in person). Companies say they will unclamp your car within four hours of receiving your payment, but they won't give you a precise time. If they do unclamp it and you don't remove the car quickly, e.g. within an hour, they're within their rights to re-clamp it and the process starts all over again.

If you find that your car isn't where you left it, it has been either stolen or towed away. To find out which, call Trace Information (☎ 020-7747 4747), who will tell you whether it has been towed away and, if so, what to do in order to recover it. You will have to pay around £200, and a car pound won't release your car until you've paid (in cash or by guaranteed cheque only). All car pounds charge a daily storage fee after the first 24 hours of around £12 a day.

Cars parked at meters aren't usually clamped unless a parking bay is suspended, the meter was 'fed' with coins, or a car has stayed two hours beyond the period paid. You cannot be towed away from a pay-and-display area or a parking meter (unless the parking bay is out of use). If you believe that you've been treated unfairly there's a Parking Appeals Service (PO Box 1010, Sutton

SM1 4SW, ☎ 020-7747 4700, 💻 www.tcfl.gov.uk). If you're in the habit of parking illegally, you can join the London Motoring Club (☎ 020-8777 2287, 💻 www.londonmotoringclub.com), who will recover your car for you for an annual fee of £100 and also offer a congestion charge payment scheme (see page 126) and a 'car-sitting' service to look after your precious vehicle while you're away!

Note also that the owners of private car parks or private land can also clamp a car parked illegally and can set their own charge to remove clamps (e.g. £100 or more). It's inadvisable to park on private land, particularly where there's a 'clamping' sign, as private clamping is widespread throughout the UK, although it's often illegal. Many 'cowboy' clamping companies clamp and tow away cars that are legally parked and charge up to £250 a time to free them. You will be pleased to note that most clampers and towers **really** enjoy their work, despite the universal abuse they attract!

Whether parking restrictions exist or not, when parking on a road, be careful where you park, as you can be prosecuted for parking in a dangerous position and could also cause an accident. If your car contributes to an accident you may need to pay damages. Take care in car parks, as accidents often occur there and they may not be covered by your car insurance. Parking on pedestrian footpaths is illegal everywhere. **Note that parking in towns with your hazard warning lights on makes no difference if you're parked illegally.** Wherever you drive in the UK, keep a supply of coins handy for parking meters.

Residents' Parking

Most central London residents (those whose postcode lies within a controlled parking zone) can obtain a residents' parking permit that provides inexpensive local (on-street) parking in designated spaces. Any resident whose postcode lies within a controlled zone can apply for a permit from his local council by providing proof of identity and residence (usually a council tax bill). Charges vary, as they're set by local borough councils, but are generally between around £80 and £120. There are also special permits for disabled drivers who are permitted to park in reserved spaces, park free at meters and in car parks, and to ignore many on-road parking restrictions.

Information about parking regulations throughout London (including how to appeal against parking tickets) is available from the Parking Committee for London (New Zealand House, 80 Haymarket, London SW1Y 4TE, ☎ 020-7747 4700, 💻 www.alg.gov.uk) or you can obtain a copy of the *London Parking Atlas* (Pathmedia) showing parking areas throughout central London.

CYCLING

Short of walking, cycling is the cheapest way to get around in central London and one of the fastest. **It's also the most dangerous!** If the traffic doesn't flatten you first, any positive effect on your physical fitness may be offset by the adverse effects of air pollution. **Always wear a smog mask with a proper air filter as well as a safety helmet, and don't try this mode of transport at all unless you're an experienced cyclist.** Carrying children on the back of a bike in London's heavy traffic isn't advisable, but if you must do it, ensure that they're also fitted with helmet and mask and are securely strapped into an approved child seat. When you park your bicycle, make sure that you lock both the frame and the wheels to an immovable object or it's unlikely to be there when you return.

All this is discouraging for cycling enthusiasts in London, who need to head out to the suburbs to enjoy it in relative safety. Unfortunately, many modes of public transport won't carry bicycles. Restrictions on suburban railways vary, so phone to check before attempting to take your bike on the train. The DLR has a blanket ban on bikes and only four tube lines (the District, Circle, Metropolitan and Hammersmith & City) allow them, but only outside peak hours. Other tube lines allow them on overground sections only, i.e. those in the outer suburbs.

For over 25 years the London Cycling Campaign (LCC, Unit 228, 30 Great Guildford Street, London SE1 0HS, ☎ 020-7234 9310, 💻 www.lcc.org.uk) has been trying to promote the rights of cyclists in London. The crisis in London's transport system is widely acknowledged and the London boroughs are setting up a network of 1,200mi (1,931km) of cycle routes throughout the capital, with the help of government funding. Routes (marked by blue signs showing a bicycle) bypass the major thoroughfares, usually taking fairly direct routes through residential areas that are unsuitable for heavy traffic. Companies are beginning to encourage their employees to cycle to work and there are increased facilities for cycle parking at workplaces and elsewhere. Annual membership of the LCC costs £32 (£14 for students, youths, the unemployed and senior citizens) and includes a subscription to the bi-monthly magazine, *London Cyclist*. The London Cycling Campaign publishes a number of information booklets, much of the information in which is downloadable from the website.

If you want to get a taste of what cycling in London is like, you can hire a bike for around £12 a day or £36 per week from a number of sites in central London (a deposit is necessary). Try the London Bicycle Tour Company at 1a Gabriel's Wharf on the South Bank (☎ 020-7928 6838, 💻   www.londonbicycle.com), which also organises cycle tours. Alternatively, you can hire a motorbike for £20 to £80 per day, £130 to £400 per week, depending on its size and power. This is usually inclusive of insurance, breakdown cover, tax, helmet and unlimited mileage. One company you can try is Two Wheels in King's Cross (☎ 020-7833 4607), which also sells bikes and accessories.

4

SOMEWHERE TO LIVE

There are over three million dwellings in London and some 20,000 new homes are built each year, which makes choosing where to live a difficult task, particularly as in most areas there's a wealth of accommodation to rent and buy, in every price range. However, prices in central London are astronomical and finding property at an affordable price is difficult. Unless you're wealthy, you will invariably find that you will need to compromise to find a home you like. For example, you will probably need to pay more than you had planned, buy or rent a smaller home than you'd like or live in a less desirable area. You may also need to live further from the centre and possibly further away from public transport and other amenities than you'd wish. Before choosing somewhere to live it's advisable to check the present and planned public transport services, particularly if you will be commuting to a job in central London or one of its suburbs. If you're buying you will find that a planned improvement in local public transport – such as a new tube or rail extension – offering a fast journey time into central London will have a dramatic effect on property values.

Renting isn't as common in the UK as it is in many other European countries, and some 70 per cent of Britons own their own homes – one of the highest figures in Europe. The average age of first-time buyers is around 27, one of the lowest in the world, due mainly to easy access to mortgages and the large loans (as a percentage of a property's value) offered by lenders. Four out of five people in the UK live in houses rather than flats (apartments) and most Britons aren't keen on apartment living or townhouses and want their own detached houses with a garden and garage. Nevertheless, the vast majority of Londoners live in flats!

Most Londoners don't live in central London but in the numerous suburbs, where life's still largely community based. Many people who work in London commute into the city from the surrounding (home) counties, with thousands travelling from even further afield. Wherever you are in the suburbs, you're never far from a traditional 'parade' of shops selling the essentials of life, and all areas provide amenities such as schools, health and leisure facilities. Much of London's suburbia is characterised by row upon row of brick terraced houses, mainly built in Victorian times to provide housing for the rapidly growing population, or tree-lined avenues of endless semi-detached properties dating from the '20s and '30s. The price of this kind of typical suburban architecture varies considerably with the area, although prices in London are generally much higher than in other parts of the UK. As with all large cities, there's a huge variation in housing quality and price (see page 141).

Most property in the UK is owned freehold, where the owner acquires complete legal ownership of the property and land and his rights over it, which can be modified only by the law or specific conditions in the contract of sale. Most houses, whether detached, semi-detached, terraced or townhouses, are sold freehold. However, unlike most other countries, flats in London aren't usually owned outright under a system of co-ownership, but are 'leasehold', with a lease of, for example, 99 to 999 years (see page 145).

A number of books are published specifically for house hunters in London, including *Where to Live in London* by Sara McConnell (Simon & Schuster) and *The New London Property Guide* by Carrie Segrave (Mitchell Beazley).

HOUSING MARKET

The UK generally has a fairly buoyant property market in most regions, although in recent decades it has been prone to boom and bust cycles. For example, the boom years of the late '80s (when property values were doubling every few years in some areas) ended in a disastrous collapse during the recession of the early '90s, when many people lost their homes when mortgage interest rates soared to over 15 per cent, leaving almost 2 million owners with negative equity (where the amount owed on the mortgage exceeds the value of a property). Negative equity was widespread in London and the south-east, where over 25 per cent of owners were affected in some areas. The shock of falling home values hit the British particularly hard, as they traditionally view buying a house as an investment rather than a home for life (as is normal in most of the rest of Europe).

It took almost ten years for house prices to return to what they were at the end of the '80s. In recent years there has been a strong recovery in property values in most regions. In 2006 prices continued to rise in all parts of London. The cost of buying in Kensington & Chelsea shot up by 16% and in Barking & Dagenham by 4.1%. Current prices are almost seven times what they were 20 years ago. Predictions for 2007 see a rise in interest rates slowing the market value considerably.

The recent unexpected reverse in London's decade-long population growth has cast doubts on the need for new housing schemes such as the Thames Gateway (see below) and may well lead to a similar reverse in house price rises. Another factor affecting the availability and cost of housing may be the conversion of office buildings. During the '90s, many new homes were created when unused office buildings were converted to housing. This trend stopped in 2000, when office space became more valuable than accommodation, but there are signs that office conversions could again become common.

Housing Schemes

When London's population was growing at a rate of over 40,000 per year, the government planned to create four new 'cities' in the south-east of England: one near Milton Keynes to the north, one near Ashford to the south-east, one along the Thames Estuary (see **Thames Gateway** below) and one along the M11 corridor. Parts of these developments are already under way, principally (as far as Greater London is concerned) in the Royal Docks, which is within both the M11 and Thames Gateway areas, and at Stratford (see **Newham** on page 68).

Such schemes involve, and require, additions or extensions to London's transport network and, once these are in place (which is by no means a foregone conclusion), property prices tend to rise dramatically, as has happened in the case of the recent Jubilee Line and DLR extensions.

Like all plans, housing schemes are subject to change and even cancellation, so beware of buying a property on the assumption that a scheme will go ahead and cause its price to rise.

Thames Gateway

Thames Gateway is the name given to an ambitious East London regeneration and development programme – the largest such scheme in Europe – which aims to create some 200,000 new 'affordable' homes and 150,000 jobs by 2015 along either side of the Thames between Docklands and Thurrock (north of the river) and Dartford (south of the river). The scheme is being co-ordinated by the Thames Gateway London Partnership, an alliance of 13 local authorities, the Universities of East London and Greenwich and the London Development Agency. An integral part of the project is the improvement of transport links in the area, including three new river crossings and stops on the new Channel Tunnel Rail Link to St Pancras.

Property Prices

Property prices in London are the highest in the UK and among the highest in Europe. For the price of a two-bedroom flat in London you can buy a substantial three or four-bedroom detached house almost anywhere else in the country. Nevertheless, buyers have had to move fast in recent years, as good properties at realistic prices were being snapped up (for cash) as soon as they came onto the market. Not surprisingly, first-time buyers are finding it hard to get their foot on the property ladder. **If you're anxious to climb onto the bandwagon, bear in mind that while many analysts expect the current boom to last a number of years, others fear a crash is imminent.** You need to take what the 'experts' say with a pinch of salt, as virtually nobody saw the last boom or crash coming!

As with most things, higher-priced houses generally provide much better value for money than cheaper houses, with a proportionately larger built area and plot of land, better build quality, and superior fixtures and fittings. Most semi-detached and detached houses have single or double garages included in the price. When property is advertised in the UK, the number of bedrooms and bathrooms is given and possibly other rooms such as a dining room, lounge (living/sitting room), study, breakfast room, drawing room, library, playroom, utility, pantry, cloakroom, cellar and conservatory. More expensive properties often simply list the number of reception rooms (e.g. lounge, dining room, study, drawing room, etc.).

The total living area in square feet or square metres is almost never stated in advertisements, although knowing the size of house you want saves a lot of house-hunting time. For most people the size (total area) is much more important than the number of bedrooms. The average size of new homes in inner London is: one-bedroom flat (650ft²/60m²), two-bedroom flat (850ft²/80m²), three-bedroom flat (1,300ft²/120m²), four-bedroom house (2,000–2,500ft²/185–230m²) and five-bedroom house (3,000–3,500ft²/280–325m²).

The table below gives an indication of house prices in late 2006 in the 33 London boroughs. As can be seen, prices vary considerably in some boroughs; the cost per square foot can vary by up to 400 per cent according to the location.

| Borough | Price (£'000) | | | | |
| | Flats | | | Houses | |
	S–1 Bed	2–3 Bed	4–5 Bed	2–3 Bed	4–5 Bed
Barking & Dag.	90-130	140-190	-	160-400	320-550
Barnet	115-210	230-260	300-420	280-390	450-650
Bexley	150-240	170-300	-	150-400	280-880
Brent	125-230	150-370	-	240-600	300-880
Bromley	70-100	70-130	-	110-275	200-910
Camden	180-300	370-600	450-670	690-800	870-1m
City Of London	150-300	190-680	300-1m+	350-800	600-3.5m
Croydon	95-160	150-330	-	180-300	230-2.4m
Ealing	140-340	160-400	-	220-600	280-2.5m
Enfield	100-420	150-480	-	200-590	260-4m
Greenwich	90-450	120-460	-	140-700	170-1.5m
Hackney	100-265	170-310	-	210-440	250-1.3m
Hamm. & Ful.	170–260	140–700	185–1m	200–600	380–1.3m
Haringey	100–350	125–600	400–750	150–750	190–1.7m
Harrow	120–180	120–350	-	180–400	250–3m
Havering	90–150	140–400	-	200–400	300–650
Hillingdon	100–250	175–400	-	150–350	250–2m
Hounslow	130–275	200–500	375–500	275–600	350–3m
Islington	180–290	180–500	500+	250–850	350–2m

Ken. & Chelsea	185–600	240–2m	550–3m	400–2m	550–10m
Kingston	120–175	125–475	-	180–650	255–3m
Lambeth	110–250	105–440	150–450	150–500	200–1m
Lewisham	140–200	90–300	155–300	170–350	200–900
Merton	115–325	115–500	320–525	145–700	180–6m
Newham	105–300	120–350	-	130–300	180–500
Redbridge	125–175	150–400	-	135–350	200–800
Richmond	130–300	170–750	350–600	220–800	325–4m
Southwark	115–300	105–800	150–350	150–650	200–1m
Sutton	100-185	150-225	-	215–440	265-1.5m
Tower Hamlets	170–200	130–350	160–320	150–450	240–800
Waltham Forest	90–140	125–175	-	160–300	250–1m
Wandsworth	120–270	150–480	400–500	160–600	240–3.5m
Westminster	200–650	225–2m	350–5m	300–4m	450–8m

Note: S = Studio flat or bedsit

BRITISH HOMES

British homes are usually built to high structural standards and whether you buy a new or an old home, it will usually be extremely sturdy. There are stringent planning regulations in most areas regarding the style and design of new homes and the restoration of old (listed) buildings. The UK offers a vast choice of properties (few countries have such a variety of housing), including some of the most luxurious and expensive homes in the world. At the bottom end of the market they're likely to be terraced or semi-detached houses, whereas more expensive homes are detached and are built on a half or one acre (2,000 to 4,000m^2) plot. In recent years Britons have taken to apartment living in London and other cities (often more out of necessity than choice), many of which are tasteful conversions of old buildings that have been converted into luxurious loft apartments. Many single people live in huge flats or large houses and generally people live in as much space as they can afford.

The British usually prefer older homes with 'charm and character' to modern homes, although you often find pseudo period features such as wooden beams and open fireplaces in new homes. Some new luxury homes are built to modern standards using reclaimed materials, thus offering the best of both worlds.

Although new properties may be lacking in character, they're usually well endowed with modern conveniences and services, which cannot be taken for granted in older properties. Standard fixtures and fittings in modern houses are more comprehensive and generally of better quality than those found in old houses. For example, central heating, double or triple-glazing and efficient insulation are standard in new houses and are essential in the UK's climate. Central heating may be gas (the most common) or oil-fired, or a home may have electric night-storage heaters. Air-conditioning is rare in the UK, although many luxury flats and houses have what's called comfort cooling, air cooling, or a climate controlled refrigerated air system. Swimming pools are rare in the UK, although indoor pools are becoming more popular in large luxury homes.

In the last decade or so, flat and townhouse conversions have been common throughout the country and include former stately homes, hospitals, schools, churches, mills, warehouses, offices and factories. Barn conversions are also popular (and **very** expensive), although rare due to the lack of barns (you can also have a 'barn' home built from new). Loft conversions are popular due to their high (cathedral) ceilings and general spaciousness.

Information

Home and property magazines (see **Appendix B**) contain a wealth of information about new homes, including a list of new developments throughout the country, and numerous advertisements from builders and developers. Daily newspapers are a good source of information, particularly the quality Saturday and Sunday newspapers such as *The Times* and *The Telegraph* (Saturday editions) and *The Sunday Times* and *The Sunday Telegraph*. Many home and property exhibitions are held throughout the UK, including the 'Daily Mail Ideal Home Show', staged in March at the Earls Court Exhibition Centre (London), the 'House & Garden Fair' (held in June at the Olympia Exhibition Centre, London) and the 'Evening Standard Homebuyer Show' (🖳 www.homebuyer.co.uk). You can also search for a new home on the internet with Your New Home (🖳 www.yournewhome.co.uk), new-homes.co.uk (🖳 www.new-homes.co.uk), and Smart New Homes (🖳 www.smartnewhomes.co.uk). See also **Appendix C**.

Types Of Home

The most common kinds of home in the UK are the described below. Most of these can obviously be either 'old' or 'new' (see above).

Bedsit: Short for 'bedsitter', which is itself an abbreviation of 'bed-sitting room', a studio flat with one room for living and sleeping.

Bungalow: A single-storey detached or semi-detached house. Popular with the elderly as they have no stairs.

Cottage: Traditionally a pretty, quaint house in the country, perhaps with a thatched roof (although the name is often stretched nowadays to encompass almost anything except a flat). May be detached or terraced.

Detached House: A house that stands alone, usually with its own garden (possibly front and rear) and garage.

Flat: An apartment or condominium, usually on one floor. A block of flats is an apartment building, high-rise tower block, or possibly a large house that has been converted into flats.

Houseboat: These are popular in some cities (with waterways!) and modern houseboats are luxurious and spacious. One of the drawbacks is finding a suitable mooring, which costs over £2,000 a year in London.

Maisonette: Part of a house or apartment block forming separate living accommodation, usually on two floors with its own outside entrance.

Mews House: A house that's converted from old stables or servants' lodgings (usually 17th to 19th century) which is the town equivalent of a genuine cottage. These are common in London, although expensive.

Mobile (Park) Home: A pre-fabricated timber-framed home that can be moved to a new site, although most are permanently located on a 'home park'.

Period Property: A property built before 1900 and named after the period in which it was built, e.g. Elizabethan, Georgian or Victorian.

Semi-Detached House: A detached building containing two separate homes joined in the middle by a common wall.

Stately Home: A grand country mansion or estate, usually a few centuries old, many owned by the UK's oldest titled families and open to the public.

Terraced House: Houses built in a row of three or more, usually two to five storeys high.

Townhouse: Similar to a terraced house but more modern and larger, often with an integral garage.

BUYING PROPERTY

Buying a house or flat in the UK has traditionally been an excellent investment, although this was severely tested in the '90s during much of which a property investment was anything but as safe as houses! However, most people still find buying preferable to renting, depending, of course, on how long you're planning to stay in London and where you're planning to live. If you're staying for a short term only, say less than two years, then you may be better off renting (see page 155). If you're planning to stay for longer than two years, have a secure job and can afford to buy, then you should probably do so, particularly as buying a house or flat is generally no more expensive than renting and you could make a sizeable profit. For information about mortgages, see page 202.

Most property in the UK is owned freehold where the owner acquires complete legal ownership of the property and land and his rights over it, which can be modified only by the law or specific conditions in the contract of sale.

Most houses, whether detached, semi-detached, terraced or townhouses, are sold freehold. However, this doesn't apply to flats, which are usually sold leasehold where 'ownership' is limited to the life of the lease, for example, 80 to 100 years for an old building and up to 999 years for a new building (unlike in most other countries, where apartments or condominiums are owned outright under a system of co-ownership). See **Flats** below.

Flats

Flats are common in London. In recent years many old properties, including stately homes, hospitals, warehouses, offices and factories have been converted into luxury flats, which have proved extremely popular in London, where houses are rare and prohibitively expensive. Although there's often little choice if you want to live in a city, many young professionals prefer to live in flats rather than houses. So called 'mega-apartments', i.e. huge open plan flats, and loft apartments with double or triple height 'cathedral' ceilings are popular in London as are penthouses, some of which sell for £5 million (£1,000 per ft^2) or more in London. They're often an emotive purchase, where you pay dearly for the panoramic views.

Most flats in London are sold leasehold and a property can change hands several times during the life of a lease, although when the lease expires, the property reverts to the original owner (the freeholder). When buying a leasehold property, the most important consideration is the length of the lease, particularly if it has less than around 50 years to run, in which case you will have difficulty obtaining a mortgage. Most experts consider 75 years to be the minimum lease you should consider. Leases often contain special terms and conditions which should also be taken into account.

New flats (particularly in London) are invariably lavishly appointed, which is essential nowadays if they're to sell well. The best flats are beautifully designed and fitted, with developers vying with each other to design the most alluring interiors. These include designer kitchens complete with top quality appliances; en suite bathrooms with separate showers; fitted carpets; built-in wardrobes; ceramic floors in kitchens and bathrooms; and telephone and TV points (including cable) in all rooms. Luxury flats often have a discreet system that allows you to control the temperature, lighting, security, music and TVs. Many luxury flats and houses also have air-conditioning or what's called comfort cooling, air cooling or a climate controlled refrigerated air system.

Modern developments often have a leisure complex with swimming pool and gymnasium, sauna, Jacuzzi, tennis courts, plus secure parking and landscaped gardens. Sports facilities are often the clincher in an inner-city development. Some developments also have an in-house medical centre, business centre, private meeting rooms for residents' exclusive use, a restaurant and a bar. Security is a key feature of most developments, which may have a 24-hour caretaker/concierge, CCTV surveillance and a security entry system with entry phones (some even have a video entry system that takes a picture of callers who press your door button when you aren't at home!). Bear in mind, however, that amenities such as a health club or gymnasium don't come cheap and there are often high service charges (see below), which may, however, include hot water and heating. The price of luxury flats often includes a year's free membership of a health club.

In an older development, you should check whether access to private grounds and a parking space are included in the lease. Garages and parking spaces may need to be purchased separately. If you're buying a resale property, check the price paid for similar properties in the same area or development in recent months, but bear in mind that the price you pay may have more to do with the seller's circumstances than the price fetched by other properties. Find out how many properties are for sale in an old development; if there are many on offer you should investigate why, as there could be management or structural problems. If you're still keen to buy, you can use any negative aspects to drive a hard bargain. **Note that flats aren't universally popular, particularly one-bedroom flats, and can be difficult to sell.**

Before buying a flat, it's advisable to ask the current owners about a development. For example, do they like living there, what are the charges and restrictions, how noisy are other residents, are the recreational facilities easy to access, would they buy there again (why or why not?), and, most importantly, is the development well managed? You may also wish to check on your prospective neighbours. A flat that has other flats above and below it is generally more noisy than a ground or top floor flat. If you're planning to buy a flat above the ground floor, you may wish to ensure that the building has a lift. Ground or garden level flats (along with the penthouse) are more prone to theft and an insurance company may insist on extra security before they will insure a property. **Note that upper floor flats are both colder in winter and warmer in summer, and may incur extra charges for the use of lifts.** Flats under the roof may also have temperature control problems (hot in summer, cold in winter), although they enjoy better views.

Apartment prices in London, where many flats are purchased by investors, have risen considerably in recent years (see table on page 141). Nevertheless, London flats are a good long-term investment and have excellent letting potential, always assuming that the rental market doesn't become saturated. Penthouses sell like hot cakes, although few people can afford the astronomical prices (often millions of pounds). **Note that in popular developments you must usually buy off plan long before a development is completed – but don't expect it to be completed on time or even to be given a completion date!**

Service Charges

Flat owners pay service charges for the upkeep of communal areas and for communal services. Charges are calculated according to each owner's share of the development and a proportion of the common elements is usually assigned to each flat owner depending on the number and size of flats in a development. Ground floor owners don't usually pay for lifts and the amount that other owners pay depends on the floor (those on the top floors generally pay the most because they use the lifts most). Service charges include such things as road and pathway cleaning; garden maintenance; cleaning, decoration and maintenance of buildings; caretaker; communal lighting in buildings and grounds; water supply (e.g. swimming pool, gardens); insurance; administration; and fees for communal facilities such as a health club or gymnasium. Service charges may also include heating and hot water. Buildings insurance is provided by the freeholder, but you're usually required to have third party insurance for damage you may cause to other flats, e.g. through a flood or fire.

Always check the level of service charges and any special charges before buying a community property. Fees are usually billed monthly or bi-annually and adjusted at the end of the year (which can be a nasty shock) when the actual expenditure is known and the annual accounts have been finalised. If you're buying a flat from a previous owner, ask to see a copy of the service charges for previous years, as owners may be 'economical with the truth' when stating service charges, particularly if they're high. Fees vary considerably and can be high (e.g. £4,000 a year or more) for luxury developments with a high level of amenities such as a health club and swimming pool. They may also increase annually. An apartment block with a resident caretaker will have higher community fees than one without, although it's preferable to buy in a block with a caretaker. If a management company is employed to manage and maintain an apartment block, the service fees will be higher but the building will also usually be maintained better. High fees aren't necessarily a negative point (assuming you can afford them), provided you receive value for money and the development is well managed and maintained. The value of a leasehold flat depends to a large extent on how well it's maintained and managed.

Disputes over service charges can be acrimonious, although they're usually confined to old buildings. Under the 1996 Housing Act, leaseholders can take disputes over service charges or bad management to a Leasehold Valuation Tribunal (LVT), with a panel comprising a solicitor, a valuer and a third experienced person, as these disputes are no longer decided by the courts. In the past landlords used threats of expensive court action to intimidate owners into paying higher fees. Many landlords have increased their service charges significantly in recent years, which often bear little or no relationship to actual costs, and many people have been hit by high charges for major repairs (see below). **It's essential when buying a leasehold property to take legal advice and have the lease checked by a solicitor.**

Maintenance & Repairs

If necessary, owners can be charged an additional service fee to make up for any shortfall of funds for maintenance or repairs. You should check the condition of the common areas (including all amenities) in an old development and whether any major maintenance or capital expense is planned for which you could be assessed. Beware of bargain flats in buildings requiring a lot of maintenance work or refurbishment. Most developments have a sink or reserve fund to pay for major expenses, which is funded from general service charges.

Ground Rent

Ground rent is a nominal rent for the land on which an apartment block is built and is usually around £100 a year. The lease should indicate whether the ground rent is fixed or whether it can be reviewed after a certain period.

Covenants & Restrictions

Covenants are legally binding obligations of the freeholder and leaseholder to do or refrain from doing certain things, while restrictions are regulations governing how leaseholders are required to behave. Restrictions usually include such things as noise levels; the keeping of pets; renting; exterior decoration and plants (e.g. the placement of shrubs); rubbish disposal; the use of health clubs and other recreational facilities; parking; business or professional use and the hanging of laundry. Check the regulations and discuss any restrictions that you're unsure about with other residents. Permanent residents should avoid buying in a development with a high percentage of rental units, i.e. units that aren't owner-occupied, although you may have little choice in London.

Buying The Freehold

It's sometimes possible for lessees to buy the freehold of their flats and they may have a statutory right of first refusal if the landlord plans to sell. A lease may also be renewable, which must usually be contained in the leasehold agreement. In 1993 the Leasehold Reform, Housing and Urban Development Act gave certain lessees the right to acquire the freehold or a lease for a further 90 years. This right is available to tenants who have lived in a property for the preceding three years or three of the previous ten years, when the original lease was for 21 years or longer and the ground rent is above a certain threshold. For information contact the Leasehold Advisory Service (LEASE), 31 Worship Street, London EC2A 2DXJ (☎ 020-7374 5380, 🖥 www.lease-advice.org), which provides free advice and maintains lists of valuers and solicitors specialising in leasehold properties. If you sell a lease that was drawn up prior to 1996, you must ensure that your solicitor includes an indemnity in the contract that allows you to pass liability for any debts on to the new leaseholder, otherwise you could be held liable – this anomaly was abolished in the Landlord and Tenants (Covenants) Act of 1995.

Houses

The vast majority (over 80 per cent) of people in the UK live in houses rather than flats, although these are obviously less common the nearer you are to the centre of London. Houses are also generally better value than flats and may be a better investment. If you decide to buy a house, your next decision will be whether to buy a new or an old home.

New Houses

The quality of new buildings in the UK is strictly regulated and they must conform to stringent building regulations and energy efficiency standards. Nevertheless, the quality of new houses is extremely variable and some developments in London suffer from poor quality, as they're built for the investment (letting) market and aren't suitable for owner-occupiers. Your best insurance when buying a new house is the reputation of the builder and it pays to buy from a long-established builder with a reputation for quality.

New houses often contain a high level of 'luxury' features, depending on individual developments and (of course) the price. You can also have a variety of 'custom' extras included at additional cost. An added advantage is that the cost of extras can be included in your mortgage, although it's important to check that they offer good value (many developers overcharge on extras, which is a common cause of complaints).

Most new homes are made of brick but some employ steel-framed panels, a recent introduction to the UK. Frames are pre-fabricated with foam insulation board ready for bolting together, which increases fuel efficiency and sound insulation. Although rare, stone (usually from a local source) is again in vogue as a building material for new homes. In some areas, new homes must be styled to blend in with existing homes and many builders offer a number of 'mock' period styles, possibly using recycled materials (e.g. bricks, tiles, oak timber beams, fireplaces, doors, etc.) from old properties, thus offering the best of both worlds for those who cannot decide between a period home and a maintenance-free new home. Some developers even create new houses in the style of barn conversions to keep up with demand. Homes with thatched roofs have always been popular and specialist builders offer thatched homes of almost any size – at a price! Many new houses are part of purpose-built developments, which offer a range of sports facilities such as a golf course, swimming pool, tennis and squash courts, a gymnasium or fitness club, and even a bar and restaurant. Some properties built on private estates have a resident's association or management committee to manage the upkeep of roads, landscaping, trees, plants, lighting, etc., for which owners pay an annual fee. There are usually also a number of restrictive covenants that owners must adhere to (see page 146). The cost of land is usually included when buying a detached house on its own plot, unless you agree a separate contract for the land and the house.

Warranty: Most new properties are covered by the National House Building Council's (NHBC, ☎ 01494 735363, 🖳 www.nhbc.co.uk) Buildmark ten-year warranty or the Zurich Municipal Building Guarantee (☎ 01252 377 474, ☎ 01252-522000). Most lenders will refuse to lend against a new house without a warranty. The NHBC warranty covers the owner for claims of up to £10,000 against the builder's failure to complete the house, for the loss of a deposit (up to 10 per cent of the agreed price) or any expenses incurred in completing building work.

Buying Off Plan: When buying a new property in a development, you're usually obliged to buy it 'off plan', i.e. before it's built. In fact, if a development is finished and largely unsold, particularly in a popular area, you should beware as it usually means that there's something wrong with it that the locals know about! In recent years people have queued overnight to buy properties in many new developments. In a rising market it's possible to make a good profit buying off plan, between the period when you pay the deposit and when the property is completed a year or two later.

Some analysts advise buyers against buying off plan, which is undoubtedly risky. It may be better to wait until a property is almost complete before buying, or you could end up paying more than a property is worth or the developer could even go bust. You must put down at least 10 per cent of the price as a deposit and pay over £500 in legal fees to exchange contracts, which legally obliges you to go through with the purchase. If the developer goes bust, you may have to wait years for a property to be completed and there's no guarantee that it will be finished to the original specifications. Added to which you could lose your loan if bad publicity has an adverse effect on the market value of the property. In 2003, many buyers pulled out of off-plan purchases (and lost their deposits), particularly in London, amid fears that the property wouldn't be worth what they had agreed to pay and that the rent wouldn't cover their mortgage payments. When buying off plan, choose a large developer or one who's selling different types of property in different areas, as he is better placed to weather a storm.

Old Houses

In the UK, the term 'old house' usually refers to a building that's pre-1940, while homes built before 1914 are generally referred to as 'period homes' and their age identified by reference to the monarch reigning at the time they were built, e.g. Georgian (1910–35), Edwardian (1901–10) and Victorian (1837–1901). In the case of Victorian properties, these are sometimes qualified as 'early', 'mid-' or 'late Victorian'. If you want a property with abundant charm and character, a building for renovation or conversion, outbuildings or a large plot, you must usually buy an old property. When buying an old building you aren't just buying a home, but a piece of history, part of the UK's cultural heritage, and a unique building that represents the architects' and artisans' skills of a bygone age.

Old houses can provide better value than new houses, although you must check their quality and condition carefully. As with most things in life, you generally get what you pay for, so you shouldn't expect a fully renovated property for a knock-down price. Many people are lulled into a false sense of security and believe they are getting a wonderful bargain, without fully investigating the renovation costs, which are invariably higher than you imagined or planned! Some properties even lack basic services such as electricity, a reliable water supply and sanitation. If you're planning to buy a property that needs renovation, have a full structural survey and obtain an **accurate** estimate of the costs **before** buying it! While you may get more for your money when buying an old home, the downside is that they require much more maintenance and upkeep than new homes, and heating costs can be high unless a property has good insulation.

For those who can afford them, at the top end of the scale there's a wealth of beautiful mansions, castles and stately homes available with extensive grounds (some country homes even come with their own golf course!). Substantial period homes certainly don't come cheap, although this segment of the market has suffered in recent years and larger homes costing in excess of £750,000 are generally excellent value. If you aspire to live the life of the landed gentry in your own stately home, bear in mind that the cost of their upkeep is usually **astronomical**. As a consequence many mansions have been converted into luxury apartments and townhouses in recent years.

Council Tax

Council tax is a local tax levied by local councils on residents to pay for such things as education, police, roads, waste disposal, libraries and community services. Each council fixes its own tax rate, based on the number of residents and how much money they need to finance their services, and charges vary considerably (by over 100 per cent) from borough to borough, although affluent boroughs don't necessarily charge higher taxes than relatively poor boroughs; in fact, the opposite is often the case. In most boroughs you can expect to pay between £2,000 and £2,500 per year for a property worth over £320,000 – around £400 less for a property worth between £160,000 and £320,000. For exact council tax charges in each borough and details of what they include and how to pay, see page 210.

Relocation Consultants

If you know what sort of property you want, how much you wish to pay and where you want to buy or rent, but don't have the time to spend looking, e.g. you live abroad, you can engage a relocation agent or property search company to find a home for you. This can save you considerable time, trouble and money, particularly if you have special or unusual requirements. Many relocation consultants act as buying agents, particularly for overseas buyers, and claim they can negotiate a better deal than private buyers (which, if true, could save you the cost of their fees). Some specialise in finding exceptional residences costing upwards of £500,000.

Agents can usually help and advise with all aspects of house purchase and may conduct negotiations on your behalf, organise finance (including bridging loans), arrange surveys and insurance, organise your removal to the UK and even arrange quarantine for your pets (see page 355). Most agents can also provide a comprehensive information package for a chosen area, including information about employment prospects, health services (e.g. local hospitals), local schools (state and private), shopping facilities, public transport, sports and social facilities, communications, and amenities and services.

Agents charge a fee of 1.25 to 1.5 per cent of the purchase price (or up to 2 per cent in London) and a retainer of between £300 and £1,000 payable in advance. The retainer is deducted from the fee when a property is purchased, but if no deal is done it's usually non-returnable. To find an agent contact the Association of Relocation Professionals (ARP), PO Box 189, Diss IP22 1PE (☎ 0870-073 7475, ▭ www.relocationagents.com) or look in the yellow pages under 'Relocation Agents'.

If you just wish to look at properties for sale in a particular area, you can make appointments to view properties through estate agents (see below) in that area and arrange a viewing visit. However, you must make **absolutely certain** that agents know exactly what you're looking for and obtain property lists in advance.

Estate Agents

Most property in the UK is bought and sold through estate agents (they aren't called real estate agents, realtors or brokers in the UK) who sell property on commission for owners, although an increasing number of people are selling their own homes. Property sold by estate agents is said to be sold by private treaty, a method of selling a property by agreement between the vendor and the buyer, either directly or through an estate agent. Although there are nation-wide chains of estate agents in the UK, e.g. covering England and Wales, most agents are local and don't have a nationwide listing of properties in other regions. There's no multi-listing system in the UK, as there is, for example, in North America, and agents jealously guard their list of properties from competitors. If you wish to find an agent in a particular town or area, look under estate agents in the local yellow pages (available at main libraries in many countries), check the internet (see below) or hire a relocation consultant (see page 151) to find you a home. Many estate agents are also letting and management agents.

Internet

You can search for an estate agent or property on the internet, which has come a long way in recent years and is expected to dominate the market in the next decade (in the US some 70 per cent of homes are advertised on the internet). It's particularly useful when you're looking for a property from abroad, when the internet can be a good place to start and allows you to peruse property lists at your leisure. Some agents offer virtual viewing whereby you can take a guided tour around a property via your computer.

The websites listed below are some of the many offering properties for sale on behalf of one or more estate agents and allowing you to search for homes and agents throughout the UK, e.g. by location and price; a directory of London agents' websites (there are hundreds of them) can be found on the Find a Property's site.

- Faron Sutaria (💻 www.faronsutaria.co.uk);

- Find a Property (💻 www.findaproperty.com) – The site includes a list of London estate agencies;

- Fish4Homes (💻 www.fish4homes.co.uk);

- Half A Percent (💻 www.halfapercent.com);

- Hamptons International (💻 www.hamptons. co.uk) – Specialises in the top end of the property market;

- Home.co.uk (💻 www.home.co.uk);

- Homesonline (💻 www.homes-on-line.com);

- Houseweb (💻 www.houseweb.co.uk) – A property search portal.

- The Move Channel (💻 www.themovechannel.com) – Property search portal (in conjunction with Partake – see below)

- Property.Finder.com (💻 www.propertyfinder.co.uk);

- Prime Location (💻 www.primelocation.com);

- Property Live (💻 www.propertylive.co.uk) – Site run by the National Association of Estate Agents;

- Property Mart Online (💻 www.propertymartonline.com) – Specialises in properties in East London;

- Real Estate (💻 www.realestate.com) – A division of LendingTree, Inc.;

- Smart Media Services (💻 www.smartestates.com and 💻 www.smartnew homes.com) – The latter service specialises in brand new homes;

- Spicerhaart (💻 www.spicerhaart.com);

Many estate agents produce free newspapers and magazines containing details of both old and new houses, and colour prospectuses for new property developments.

Always choose an estate agent who's a member of a professional organisation, such as the National Association of Estate Agents (NAEA, ☎ 01926-496800, 🖥 www.naea.co.uk). You should also check whether an agent is a member of the Ombudsman Scheme for Estate Agents (☎ 01722-333306, 🖥 www.oea.co.uk), whose members must abide by a code of practice and to whom you can complain if you have a problem.

Contracts

When buying property in England, prospective buyers make an offer subject to survey and contract. Either side can amend or withdraw from a sale at any time before the exchange of contracts (when a sale is legally binding). In a seller's market, gazumping, where a seller agrees to an offer from one prospective buyer and then sells to another for a higher amount, is rampant and **isn't illegal**. There are proposals to speed up the home buying process (see below), which would reduce the risk of gazumping, although many people believe that following the example of Scotland and many other countries, where a contract is legally binding once an offer has been made and accepted, is the only way to stamp it out altogether. On the other hand, in a buyer's market a buyer may threaten to pull out at the last minute unless the seller reduces the price (called 'gazundering').

Home Information Pack

The conveyancing process in the UK is among the slowest in the world, with the average time required to complete a sale twice as long as in many other countries. To reduce the average time it requires (to around six weeks in trials) and lessen the risk of gazumping, the government has recently introduced a new law requiring vendors to produce a 'home information pack' (HIP) at a cost of between £600 and £1,000 before putting a property on the market. This includes:

● Ownership details;
● Home energy performance certificate;
● Details of guarantee and warranties in force;
● Details of any relevant planning or listed building regulations;
● A survey report (possibly a full structural survey);
● Local authority searches;
● A draft sales contract.

Leasehold properties would also require details of the lease, service charge details, a building insurance policy and any regulations made by the landlord.

However, among the reservations voiced are fears that buyers and lenders wouldn't trust a survey commissioned by the vendor, who could bribe a surveyor to overlook certain matters (of course, no surveyor would ever accept a bribe!), and most people may still commission their own survey. Another problem is that surveyors are currently responsible only to the person who commissions a survey, and the buyer would have no come back if a major fault was discovered, which would be disastrous and could lead to costly legal disputes. **Now that trials have been successfully carried out, the date the home information pack's become mandatory is June 1st 2007.**

Information

There are numerous books on the subject of buying a home, including ***Buying a Home in Britain*** and ***Buying, Selling and Letting Property*** by David Hampshire (Survival Books – see page 414). There are also many magazines published in the UK for homebuyers, including *What Mortgage*, *Mortgage Magazine*, *What House* and *House Buyer*, which contain the latest information about mortgages and house prices throughout the UK. Up-market properties are advertised in glossy magazines and national broadsheet newspapers such as *The Sunday Times*. Homebuyer Events, Mantle House, Broomhill Road, London SW18 4JQ (☎ 020-8877 3636, ⌨ www.homebuyer.co.uk) organises the Homebuyer Show, the UK's leading property show, in early March at the ExCeL exhibition centre in Docklands. Most building societies and banks publish free booklets for homebuyers, most of which contain excellent (usually unbiased) advice.

RENTED ACCOMMODATION

Renting accommodation is advisable for people who will be staying in London for one or two years only (when buying isn't usually practical) or those who don't want the trouble, expense and restrictions involved in buying a home. Unlike in most other European countries, there isn't a strong rental market in the UK (less than 10 per cent of private properties are rented in the UK, compared with around 20 per cent on the continent), where families traditionally prefer to buy rather than rent. There's a chronic shortage of good rental properties in London and properties with three or more bedrooms located in good areas are in short supply everywhere. Furthermore, rental accommodation can be prohibitively expensive and the quality of properties often leaves a lot to be desired, particularly at the lower end of the market. **You should be aware that renting accommodation is a jungle in the UK, which has one of the most unregulated letting markets in Western Europe and there's little consumer protection against unscrupulous agents and landlords.**

One of the reasons for the unpopularity of renting in the UK is that it has traditionally been relatively easy to obtain a 95 or even 100 per cent mortgage with repayments over 25 or 30 years. This means that it's usually cheaper or no more expensive to buy a home in the UK than it is to rent. According to research done by the Abbey National Bank, renting is around 35 per cent more expensive than buying a home over the long term and people who rent a house 'waste' an average of £85,000 over 25 years! Owners can also make a tax-free profit (or a tax-free loss!) in a relatively short period, as no capital gains tax is paid on the profits from the sale of your principal home. Many people who cannot afford to pay a high mortgage often let a room (or rooms) to reduce the cost.

The 1988 Housing Act deregulated new lettings in the private sector. Since January 1989 new lettings were generally of two kinds: an assured tenancy (abolished in 1996) with a long-term security of tenure or an assured shorthold tenancy for a fixed period of at least six months (see **Rental Contracts** on page 158). These changes were intended to encourage greater choice and competition in the rental market. Unlike many other countries, 95 per cent of rental properties in the UK are let furnished. The reason is historical: until January 1989 landlords had much greater protection under the law if properties were let furnished, although this is no longer the case. The furniture and furnishings in many rental properties vary from fair to terrible, except for the rare luxury property that's let for a fixed term by owners spending a period abroad.

Rental property can usually be found in two to four weeks in most areas, with the possible exception of large houses (four or more bedrooms), which are rare and **very** expensive. Family accommodation in particular is in short supply in London, with the possible exception of luxury homes with astronomical rents. Most people settle for something in the suburbs or country and commute to work. **Note that if you need to travel into London each day, you should be prepared to spend at least an hour or more travelling each way**.

Most rented property is let through letting agencies or estate agents, who charge between £25 and £150 for 'administration', taking up references, drawing up tenancy agreements and making an inventory. You must usually pay one month's rent in advance, depending on the type of property and the rental agreement, plus a deposit against damages equal to one to two months rent. When you agree to rent a property you're usually asked for a holding deposit of between £50 and £200 before an agreement is signed (this should go towards your rent but is often simply an additional fee). Some letting agents charge an up-front fee of around £100 to house hunters with the promise of finding them accommodation, in return for which they simply supply a list of 'vacant' properties often just taken from newspapers. You shouldn't pay a letting agent an up-front fee to find you a property, which is, in any case, illegal.

Agents usually have a number of properties available for immediate occupancy and lists are normally updated weekly. You should have no problem finding something suitable in most areas if you start looking at least four weeks prior to the date when you wish to take occupancy. Most letting agents require a reference from your employer (or previous employer if you've been less than one year with your current employer) and bank, and possibly a credit reference. Copies of audited accounts and status are required for company lets. Agents may ask to see a foreign resident's police registration certificate.

Your deposit should be put into a savings account in your name and the name of the agent or landlord, although this is rare (if it isn't and the letting agent goes bankrupt, you will lose your deposit). If possible, you should deal only with a member of the Association of Residential Letting Agents (ARLA) or the National Association of Estate Agents (NAEA), both of which insist that members have a bonding scheme or professional indemnity cover to safeguard rental income and deposits. However, agents are totally unregulated in the UK and you may have no option but to deal with a 'cowboy'.

Note that you must be over 18 to hold a tenancy agreement and young people usually find it harder to find a rental property than more mature people, due to the usual arguments that the young are unreliable, noisy, poor, itinerant and untidy, and so on. If you're seeking cheap accommodation, you may find it more difficult in September when the new term starts and students are looking for accommodation. Before taking on long-term accommodation, you may wish to check the council tax rate in the borough (see page 210).

Local Housing Aid or Advice Centres offer advice concerning finding somewhere to live and usually handle both private and council house problems. Contact your local council for information. A Citizens' Advice Bureau can also offer advice regarding the legal aspects of letting and a tenant's rights. In some towns and cities there are council-run housing aid centres where you can obtain free advice on housing problems. There are also a number of useful books published detailing the legal rights and duties of both landlords and tenants including the *Which? Guide to Renting and Letting* (Which? Books).

Shared Accommodation

Finding accommodation in London that doesn't break the bank is a huge problem for young people and students (and anyone not earning a fortune). For many the solution is sharing accommodation with others, officially termed 'houses in multiple occupation' (HMOs). Sharing usually involves sharing the kitchen, bathroom, living room, dining room and possibly even a bedroom. Sharing also usually involves sharing all bills (in addition to the rent) including electricity, gas and telephone, and may also include sharing food bills and cooking. Some landlords include electricity and gas (plus heating) in the rent. The cleaning and the general upkeep of a house or flat is also usually shared. As always when living with others there are advantages and disadvantages, and success depends on the participants' ability to live together in harmony.

Shared accommodation in many areas is in old, run-down houses where even the living and dining rooms have been converted into bedrooms. You may also be sharing with the owner, which can be a bit inhibiting. In an English

House Conditions Survey in 1996 it was estimated that around 20 per cent (much higher in London and other major cities) of all privately rented homes were unfit for human habitation. In fact, at the bottom end of the market the UK has among the worst rental accommodation in Western Europe which may include faulty plumbing, poor sanitation, decrepit furniture, insect and rodent infestations, dangerous wiring and unsafe gas appliances. There's little or no control over landlords who get away with almost anything, although legislation has been proposed that will lay down minimum standards and include a registration scheme. **If you rent a property with the intention of sharing, you should ensure that it's permitted in your contract.**

The cost of sharing a furnished flat varies considerably depending on the size, location and amenities. Costs start from around £60 per week (single) or £85 per week (double).

Many newspapers and magazines contain advertisements for flat-sharers, such as the *Evening Standard, Loot* and *Time Out,* the free *Midweek* magazine available from tube stations on Thursdays and a multitude of free expatriate publications such as *TNT* magazine (also available from tube stations). Capital FM (formerly Capital Radio) publishes a weekly flat-share list, available from the foyer of its offices at 30 Leicester Square, WC2 on Fridays after 6pm.

An alternative for those on a tight budget is to find lodgings (also called digs) in a private home, which is becoming increasingly common as many people are forced to take in lodgers to pay their mortgages. This is similar to bed and breakfast accommodation, except that you're usually treated as a member of the family and your rent normally includes half-board (breakfast and an evening meal). In lodgings you have less freedom than in shared accommodation and are required to eat at fixed times, but you will at least have some company. Lodgings are often arranged by English-language schools for foreign students. A boarding house is similar to lodgings where the owner takes in a number of lodgers and may provide half-board or cooking facilities. Lodgings or a room in a boarding house cost from around £95 per week in London, for a room with breakfast. With breakfast and an evening meal, the cost starts at around £140 per week.

Other options include hostels (including student and youth hostels), guesthouses, bed and breakfast, and cheap hotels, although these usually provide relatively expensive short-term accommodation only.

Bedsits

If you prefer to live on your own, but don't want to pay a lot of rent (who does?), the solution may be a bedsit (also called a studio). A bedsit usually consists of a furnished room in an old house, where you live, eat, sleep and sometimes cook. If separate cooking facilities are provided, you must usually share them with someone else (or a number of people). You must also normally share a bathroom and toilet, provide your own linen (sheets, blankets and towels), and do your own laundry and cleaning. Bedsits offer privacy but can be lonely and depressing. A single bedsit costs from around £85 per week in London. Double bedsits are also available costing from around £120 per week. Slightly up-market from a bedsit is a flatlet or studio flat, which may have its own bath or shower and toilet, and sometimes a separate kitchen or kitchenette (a tiny kitchen). The rent for a studio flat is around 50 per cent higher than for a bedsit.

Rental Costs & Standards

Rental costs vary considerably depending on the size (number of bedrooms) and quality of a property, its age and the facilities provided. Not least, rents depend on the neighbourhood and the suburb or county, and are generally lower the further you are from the centre of London. Rents are high in London, particularly when you consider that renting can cost more than buying a home in many areas. Rents vary from under £300 per month for a tiny bedsit (studio flat) in a run-down area of central London to £3,000 or more for a three or four-bedroom detached house or luxury flat in a desirable area. (If you fancy renting a large house in Kensington, you'll need to have up to £40,000 to spare – per month!) It may be possible to find cheaper, older flats and houses for rent, but they're rare, generally small and don't usually contain the conveniences that are standard in a modern home, e.g. no central heating or double glazing (heating in old houses can be highly 'eccentric'). If you like a property but think the rent is too high, you should try to negotiate a reduction or ask an agent to put an offer to the owner. In addition to the rent, tenants must pay for utilities such as gas, electricity and phone, and also water if it's metered.

Kitchens normally contain an oven with a grill, refrigerator (usually small), fitted kitchen units, and occasionally a dishwasher and a separate freezer. Many houses don't have basements or utility rooms, so washing machines (usually provided) and dryers are located in the kitchen. Many houses have lofts and garages that are often used for storage. Most have baths (but not enough hot water to fill them!) and may have a separate shower or an *en suite* shower or bathroom. Often shower attachments are run from a bath and don't have a separate power pump, which means that the water trickles out. Bathrooms occasionally contain a bidet. In general, British plumbing is better than that found in many countries, although Americans won't be impressed. All modern houses have central heating (see page 165), although it's rare at the bottom end of the market. An airing cupboard (linen closet) is common and usually contains the hot water boiler. Unfurnished flats and houses usually have light fittings in all rooms, although there may be no bulbs or lampshades. Fitted wardrobes in bedrooms are rare in older homes and curtain rails aren't provided unless they're built-in. Most houses, whether furnished or unfurnished, are fully or partly carpeted.

Many flats are parts of old houses that have been modernised and converted into apartments. At the bottom end of the market, many properties have dreadful furnishings, e.g. flowery wallpaper which may 'match' the equally awful three-piece suite, with sickly green carpets and brown bathroom suites (or vice versa). Upmarket (i.e. expensive) property may, however, be furnished to a high standard. In furnished accommodation you usually need to provide your own bedding and linen, although crockery, kitchen utensils and most household appliances are usually provided. It may be possible to 'throw out' the owner's or landlord's tatty furniture and replace it with your own (but you may have to pay to store it).

The table below shows the approximate range of monthly rents in early 2004 in each London borough, listed in alphabetical order.

Borough	Monthly Rent (£)					
	Flats			Houses		
	S–1 Bed	2–3 Be	4–5 Bed	2–3 Bed	4–5 Bed	6–8 Bed
Barking	600–800	600–1,000	-	700–1,200	1,250+	-
Barnet	540–1,300	680–3,000	1,200–8,000	800–2,800	1,000–16,000	2,400–8,000
Bexley	400–750	500–900	-	600–1,000	900–2,000	-
Brent	550–950	720–1,600	1,200–1,700	720–2,200	1,320–2,400	1,800–3,000
Bromley	300–800	700–1,100	-	750–1,200	1,000–2,000	-
Camden	720–2,000	920–3,200	1,800–8,000	1,000–4,000	1,680–12,000	3,000–20,000
City	700–1,400	1,200–2,200	-	1,600–2,600	3,000+	-
Croydon	470–680	700–1,120	-	680–1,200	920–1,600	1,400–1,650
Ealing	520–1,200	680–1,800	1,400–2,400	800–3,200	880–12,000	2,400–20,000
Enfield	650–900	700–1,300	-	750–1,300	1,000–2,000	-
Green'ch	450–1,000	750–1,600	-	800–1,800	1,400–2,600	-
Hackney	420–800	680–920	800–2,000	700–1,400	1,000–2,000	1,800–2,200
H&F	600–1,600	880–3,200	1,200–5,200	880–3,400	1,600–6,000	3,200–6,000
Haringey	560–1,320	740–3,200	1,600–4,000	720–2,600	960–4,000	2,400–12,000
Harrow	520–950	750–1,200	-	800–1,400	1,000–2,000	-
Havering	450–800	600–1,100	-	650–1,200	900–2,000	-
H'don	550–900	700–1,100	-	700–1,200	1,000–2,000	-
H'slow	640–1,200	920–2,000	2,000–3,200	1,200–2,200	1,600–6,400	4,000–8,000
Islington	740–1,400	920–4,000	1,400+	720–3,000	1,280–10,000	3,000–30,000
K&C	670–2,600	1,120–8,00	12,800–12000	1,800–6,400	3,200–12,000	8,000–40,000

Kingston	500–4,000	2,000–13,000	-	300–6,000	4,000–20,000	7,500–20,000
Lambeth	440–1,200	600–1,920	920–2,800	640–1,440	920–3,200	1,600–3,200
Lewish'm	500–920	600–1,600	880–2,400	640–1,440	920–3,200	1,600–3,200
Merton	550–1,200	580–2,550	800–2,800	700–1,680	720–5,600	-
Newham	600–1,000	640–1,400	-	680–1,200	940–1,400	-
Redb'ge	330–750	500–2,000	-	500–1,200	800–3,000	3,000+
R'mond	570–1,200	680–3,600	1,200–2,400	620–2,400	1,400–5,600	3,400–10,000
S'wark	450–1,900	600–4,000	920–8,000	640–2,000	880–2,000	1,640–2,400
Sutton	500–1,000	500–1,500	-	750–2,000	1,500–4,000	-
T. Ham.	680–940	800–1,600	-	880–1,800	720–2,000	-
W. Forst	400–640	640–920	920–1,080	680–920	880–1,040	-
W'worth	560–1,200	720–2,400	1,600–2,120	800–2,400	1,200–4,000	2,000–8,000
Westmin.	850–2,200	1,000–8,000	2,200–12,000	1,500–6,400	2,600–16,000	4,000–36,000

Note: S = Studio flat or bedsit

4

Rental Contracts

When you find a suitable house or flat to rent, you should insist on a written contract with the owner or agent, which is called a tenancy or rental agreement. Make sure that you obtain a rent book, which is used to record all payments made. If you don't have a rent book, always pay by cheque and insist on a receipt. Your contract may include details of when your rent will be reviewed or increased, if applicable. When you wish to leave rented accommodation you must give at least one month's notice in writing, unless it's within the first six months of an assured shorthold tenancy (see below), in which case you must pay the rent to the end of the period. If your landlord wants you to leave, the notice he must give you depends on your agreement with him and whether your tenancy is covered by the law. **It's a criminal offence for your landlord to harass you in any way in an attempt to drive you out.** Under the Housing Act (1988) the following kinds of rental agreements and tenancies were created, which provide tenants with fewer rights than previously and make evictions easier for landlords.

Assured Tenancy

An assured tenancy is a tenancy for an indefinite period and doesn't need to be in writing. The landlord cannot live on the premises and, provided you pay the rent and take care of a property, you cannot be asked to leave.

Your landlord must apply to a county court and must have a good reason to evict you, e.g. unpaid rent, damage to the property or its contents, or you must have otherwise broken your contract with him. However, if he offers you similar accommodation, needs the property for himself, or a mortgage lender requires vacant possession in order to sell it, a court may serve you with written notice to leave. The rent cannot be increased until one year after you've signed a contract and if you don't agree with the increase you can ask the council's Rent Assessment Committee to set a fair rent.

Note that under the Housing Act (1996), assured tenancies are no longer legal for new lettings.

Assured Shorthold Tenancy

An assured shorthold tenancy is a tenancy with a fixed time limit, for which a written rental agreement is necessary, clearly stating that it's an assured shorthold tenancy. There was previously an initial minimum let of six months, although a shorter term can now be agreed between the landlord and tenant. You cannot terminate your agreement (or be evicted) during the initial period and thereafter, you or your landlord must give two months notice in writing to terminate the agreement. Under an assured shorthold tenancy you have the right in certain cases to ask the Rent Assessment Committee to set a fair rent, but only during the first six months of the tenancy. Under the Housing Act (1996), all new tenancies have automatically been short-hold tenancies unless rents are over £25,000 a year or other arrangements (such as company lets) are agreed in writing.

A tenant in an assured shorthold tenancy can ask the local Rent Assessment Committee for help in ensuring that his rent isn't too high. Your complaint will be investigated and your rent could be lowered or raised (if it's decided the rent is too low). If you've been overcharged, the landlord can be ordered to repay the excess as far back as two years. Information concerning rent allowances, rent rebates, fair rents and housing benefits is contained in a series of free housing booklets published by the Department of the Environment and available from rent (registration) offices, local authorities, Citizens Advice Bureaux and housing advice centres.

No Agreement

If you don't have an agreement with your landlord, you're protected under the law and have the same rights as an assured shorthold tenancy (see above) if your landlord doesn't live on the premises. Always try to obtain a tenancy agreement and retain evidence of all payments to your landlord. If, after taking up residence, you're offered a holiday let, licence agreement or tenancy with board and service, you should refuse and contact a Citizens Advice Bureau for advice. **These agreements provide you with no security and few legal rights as a tenant.**

Flat-Sharers

The law regarding flat-sharing is more complicated and it's simpler when one person is the tenant and sub-lets to the others, which must be permitted by the tenant's agreement. It's possible for all sharers to be joint tenants with one tenancy agreement (in which case they're jointly and severally responsible) or individual tenants with individual tenancy agreements. Whatever the agreement, you should have just one rent book and pay the rent in a lump sum. It's usually the occupants' responsibility to replace flatmates who leave during the tenancy.

Deposits

Usually a deposit equal to one or two months' rent (the maximum permitted by law) must be paid for an assured shorthold tenancy. This should be repaid when you leave, provided there are no outstanding claims for rent, unpaid bills, damages or cleaning. **Always check a contract to find out who holds the deposit and under what circumstances it will be returned, and obtain a receipt.** Note than many agents and landlords will go to almost any lengths to avoid repaying a deposit and tenants in the UK lose millions of pounds to landlords and letting agents who refuse to repay deposits when a lease expires. Often a landlord will make a claim for 'professional' cleaning running into hundreds of pounds, even when you leave a property spotless. If the landlord fails to return your deposit you should threaten legal action and if this has no affect you should take him to the small claims court.

Don't sign a contract unless you're sure you fully understand all the small print. Ask one of your colleagues or friends for help or obtain legal advice. English law usually prevents you from signing away your rights; nevertheless, it pays to be careful. **Note that most rental agreements forbid the keeping of pets.** In order to avoid disputes, the agreement should spell out in detail who's responsible for maintenance, e.g. appliances, building, decoration and garden. If you have any questions regarding your rental agreement or problems with your landlord, you can ask your local Citizens Advice Bureau for advice. They will check your rental agreement and advise you of your rights under the law.

Inventory

One of the most important tasks after moving into a new home is to make an inventory of the fixtures and fittings and, if applicable, the furniture and furnishings. When you've purchased a property, you should check that the previous owner hasn't absconded with any fixtures and fittings that were included in the price or anything which you specifically paid for, e.g. carpets, light fittings, curtains, furniture, kitchen cupboards and appliances, garden ornaments, plants or doors.

It's common to do a final check or inventory when buying a new property, which is usually done a few weeks before completion. **Note the reading on your utility meters (e.g. electricity, gas and water) and check that you aren't overcharged on your first bill.** The meters should be read by utility companies before or soon after you move into a resale property, although you usually need to organise this yourself.

It's advisable to obtain written instructions from the previous owner concerning the operation of appliances and heating and air-conditioning systems; maintenance of grounds, gardens and lawns; care of special surfaces such as wooden or tiled floors; and the names of reliable local maintenance men who know a property and are familiar with its quirks. Check with your local town hall regarding local regulations about such things as rubbish collection, recycling and on-road parking.

GARAGES & PARKING

A garage or private parking space isn't usually included in the price when you buy a flat in the UK, although private parking may be available at an additional cost, possibly in an underground garage. Modern townhouses, semi-detached and detached homes usually have a garage or car port. Smaller homes usually have a single garage, while larger 'executive' homes often have integral double garages or garaging for up to four cars. Parking isn't usually a problem when buying an old home in a rural area, although there may not be a purpose-built garage.

When buying a flat or townhouse in a modern development, a garage or parking space may be available as an extra, although the price can be high, e.g. £20,000 for a space in an underground garage. Note that the cost of an optional garage or parking space isn't always recouped when selling, although it makes a property more attractive to buyers and may clinch a sale. In suburban and rural areas, a garage is essential and a double garage is even better. The cost of parking is an important consideration when buying a property in London or its suburbs, particularly if you have a number of cars. It may be possible to rent a garage or parking space, although this can be prohibitively expensive in London. Bear in mind that in a large development, the nearest parking area may be some distance from your home. This may be an important factor, particularly if you aren't up to carrying heavy shopping hundreds of metres to your home and possibly up several flights of stairs.

Without a private garage or parking space, parking can be a nightmare, particularly in central London. In many areas of London it's necessary to obtain a resident parking permit from the local council to park on public streets, although this doesn't guarantee you will be able to find a parking space! Free on-street parking can be difficult or impossible to find in London and is inadvisable for anything but a wreck. A lock-up garage is important in London, where there's a high incidence of car theft and thefts from cars, and it's also useful to protect your car from climatic extremes such as ice, snow and extreme heat.

UTILITIES

Utilities is the collective name given to electricity, gas and water supplies (and usually also includes telephone services). All the UK's utility companies have been privatised in the last decade or so, which was quickly followed by increased prices and worse service. However, in the last few years, most people have been able to choose their electricity and gas supplier and the increased competition has led to lower prices, with many companies promising savings of around 10 per cent to switch companies. Many companies now provide both electricity and gas and offer contracts for the supply of both fuels, often called 'dual fuel', which may result in a discount (although you may be better off buying from separate companies). You can find the cheapest supplier of electricity, gas and water on the internet (⌨ www.buy.co.uk), although you should carefully compare rates, standing charges and services before changing your supplier.

Electricity

The electricity supply in the UK is 240 volts AC, with a frequency of 50 hertz (cycles). This is suitable for all electrical equipment with a rated power consumption of up to 3,000 watts. For equipment with a higher power consumption, a single 240V or 3-phase, 380 volts AC, 20 amp supply must be used (in the UK, this is installed only in large houses with six to eight bedrooms or industrial premises). Power cuts are rare in most parts of the UK, although some areas experience many a year. Electricity companies pay compensation for a power cut lasting longer than 24 hours, but nothing for cuts of less than 24 hours (which includes 99.9 per cent of cuts).

If you move into an old home in the UK, the electricity supply may have been disconnected by the previous electricity company and in a brand new home you will also need to have the electricity connected. In the last few years householders have been able to choose their electricity company from among British Gas, Eastern Energy, Eastern Electricity, East Midlands Electricity, Independent Energy, London Electricity, Manweb, MEB, Northern Electric & Gas, Norweb, Scottish Hydro-Electric, Scottish Power, SEEBOARD, Southern Electric, SWALEC, South Western Electricity and Yorkshire Electricity. Most companies cover the whole country, while a few cover certain regions only.

You should allow at least two days to have the electricity reconnected and the meter read after signing a contract with an electricity company. There's usually a charge for connection. If you're in the UK for a short stay only, you may be asked for a security deposit or to obtain a guarantor (e.g. your employer). **You must contact your electricity company to get a final reading when you vacate a property.**

Complaints

If you have any complaints about your electricity bill or service, contact your local electricity company. If after ten days you don't receive satisfaction, contact The Gas & Electricity Consumer Council, known as EnergyWatch (☎ 0845-906 0708 or 0800-451451 for the address of your local office, 💻 www.energy watch. org.uk).

Gas

Mains gas is available in all but the remotest areas of the UK. However, you may find that some modern houses aren't connected to the mains gas supply. If you're looking for a rental property and want to cook by gas, make sure it already has a gas supply (some houses have an unused gas service pipe). If you move into a brand new home you must have a meter installed in order to be connected to mains gas (there may be a charge for this, depending on the gas company). In some remote areas without piped gas, homes may have a 'bottled gas' (e.g. Calor Gas) cooker. If you buy a house without a gas supply, you can usually arrange to have a gas pipeline installed from a nearby gas main. You're usually connected free if your home is within 25 metres of a gas main, otherwise a quotation is provided for the cost of the work involved. A higher standing charge is made for properties in remote areas. See also **Heating** on page 165.

Gas was previously supplied by British Gas throughout the UK, which was the monopoly supplier to some 19 million homes. However, since May 1998, everyone in England, Scotland and Wales has been able to choose from up to 26 gas supply companies. Depending on where you live, up to 17 companies may compete for your business including Amerada, Beacon Gas, British Fuels, British Gas, Calortex, Eastern Natural Gas, Energi from Norweb, Independent Energy, London Electricity, Midlands Gas, North Wales Gas, Northern Electric & Gas, ScottishPower, Southern Electric Gas, SWALEC Gas, York Gas and Yorkshire Electricity. Among the cheapest suppliers in London are Independent Energy and London Electricity.

If your new home already has a gas supply but you don't know who the supplier is, call National Grid (formerly Transco), the gas supply watchdog (☎0845 070 0203). If you wish to use a different supplier, simply contact the company of your choice to have the gas supply reconnected or transferred to your name (there's a connection fee) and the meter read. You must contact your gas company to get a final meter reading when you vacate a property.

For further information and a wide range of gas brochures, contact your local gas company. If you have a complaint about your gas bill or service and you don't receive satisfaction from your gas company within ten days, you can contact The Gas & Electricity Consumer Council, known as EnergyWatch (☎ 0845-906 0708 or 0800-451451 for the address of your local office, 💻 www. energywatch.org.uk).

Water

The water industry in England and Wales was privatised in 1989, when ten regional water companies were created to provide water and sewerage services (there are also a further 18 local water-only companies). You're unable to choose your water company (as you are your electricity and gas companies), which have a monopoly in their area. Less than 10 per cent of households in England and Wales have water meters, where you're billed for the actual water used (plus a standing charge). For all other households, water and sewerage rates are based on the rateable value of a property (although rates were abolished in April 1990 and have been replaced by the council tax).

Water companies include an annual standing charge of around £50 (for both water and sewerage), which is the same for all properties, plus a variable charge based on the rateable value of your property if you don't have a water meter. If you have a water meter installed, water is charged by the cubic metre. Bills, which usually include sewerage, are sent out annually and can usually be paid in full, in two six-monthly payments or in ten instalments. In some areas, water and sewage are handled by separate companies and homeowners receive bills from each company. Since water privatisation in 1989, water bills have increased by some 47 per cent in real terms. The cost of water varies widely according to the local water authority concerned, but the average unmetered annual water and sewerage bill in 2007 as projected by WaterVoice, the industry's official consumer watchdog, will be £336.

If you have a complaint that you cannot resolve with your water company, you should contact WaterVoice, the industry watchdog. The London area is covered by three different offices: north-east London by WaterVoice Eastern (☎ 01223-323889); south-east London by WaterVoice Southern (☎ 020-7831 4790); the rest of the capital by WaterVoice Thames (also on ☎ 020-7831 4790). Alternatively, complaints can be registered by email via the WaterVoice website (🖥 www.watervoice.org.uk).

HEATING & AIR-CONDITIONING

Central heating, double or triple-glazing and good insulation are standard in new houses and are essential in the UK's climate. Around 80 per cent of British homes have central heating (including all new homes) or storage heater systems, most of which also provide hot water. Central heating systems may be powered by oil, gas (the most common), electricity (night-storage heaters) or solid fuel (e.g. coal or wood). Whatever form of heating you use, you should ensure that your home has good insulation including double glazing, cavity-wall insulation, external-wall insulation, floor insulation, draught-proofing, pipe lagging, and loft and hot water tank insulation, without which up to 60 per cent of heat goes straight through the walls and roof.

Many companies advise and carry out home insulation, including gas and electricity companies, who produce a range of leaflets designed to help you reduce your heating and other energy bills.

The cheapest method of central heating is gas (indicated in advertisements as GCH or GFCH), which is estimated to be up to 50 per cent cheaper than other forms of central heating and hot water systems, particularly if you have a high-efficiency, condensing boiler. Many homes have storage heaters that store heat from electricity supplied at the cheaper off-peak rate overnight and release it to heat your home during the day. If an apartment block is heated from a central system, radiators may be individually metered so you pay only for the heating used, or the cost of heating (and hot water) may be included in your service charges. If you wish to install heating in your home, you should use a company that's a member of the Heating and Ventilating Contractor's Association (HVCA), 34 Palace Court, London W2 4JG (☎ 020-7313 4900, 🖳 www.hvca.org.uk), which operates a guarantee scheme for domestic heating.

You can reduce your heating and other energy bills by saving energy. For information contact your gas or electricity company (see above), EnergyWatch EnergyWatch (☎ 0845-906 0708 or 0800-451451 for the address of your local office, 🖳 www.energywatch.org.uk), the Energy Saving Trust (☎ 0845-727 7200, 🖳 www.est.org.uk) or the Energy Efficiency Advice Centre (☎ 0800-512012). The National Energy Foundation (☎ 01908-672787, 🖳 www.natenergy.org.uk) will provide the names of energy surveyors in your area who will perform an energy survey for around £100.

Air-Conditioning

Although summer temperatures can be above 30°C/86°F (a few parts of southern England experienced temperatures of over 38°C/100°F for the first time in recorded history in August 2003), British homes rarely have air-conditioning and aren't usually built to withstand the heat. However, in recent years many luxury flats and houses have been built with cooling systems such as comfort cooling, air cooling or a climate controlled refrigerated air system. If you want to install air-conditioning you can choose between a huge variety of systems including fixed or moveable units, indoor or outdoor installation, and high or low power. An air-conditioning system with a heat pump provides cooling in summer and economical heating in winter. **Note, however, that there can be negative effects if you suffer from asthma or respiratory problems.**

HOME SECURITY

When moving into a new home it's often wise to replace the locks (or lock barrels) as soon as possible, as you have no idea how many keys are in circulation for the existing locks. This is true even for brand new homes, as builders often give keys to sub-contractors. In any case, it's advisable to change the external locks or lock barrels periodically, particularly if you let a home. If they aren't already fitted, it's advisable to fit high security (double cylinder or dead bolt) locks. **It pays to look at your home through the eyes of a burglar and remedy any weak points.** Many modern developments have intercom systems, CCTV, alarms, security gates and 24-hour caretakers. In areas with a high risk of theft (e.g. most areas of London), your insurance company may insist on extra security measures and the policy may specify that all forms of protection must be employed when a property is unoccupied. If security precautions aren't adhered to, a claim can be reduced or even dismissed. It's usually necessary to have a safe for insured valuables, which must be approved by your insurance company.

You may wish to have a security alarm fitted, which is usually the best way to deter thieves and may also reduce your contents insurance (see page 211). It should include all external doors and windows, internal infra-red security beams (movement detectors), activate external and internal lights, and may also include a coded entry keypad (which can be frequently changed and is useful for clients if you let a home) and 24-hour monitoring – with some systems it's even possible to monitor properties remotely from another country via a computer.

New high-tech alarms can be purchased that broadcast a personal message, e.g. "there's an intruder in the house at number XX, please call the police". With a monitored system, when a sensor (e.g. smoke or forced entry) detects an emergency or a panic button is pushed, a signal is automatically sent to a 24-hour monitoring station. The duty monitor will telephone to check whether it's a genuine alarm (a password must be given) and if he cannot contact you, someone will be sent to investigate. Alarms should be approved by the National Security Inspectorate/NSI (☎ 0845 006 3003, 🖥 www.nsi.org.uk).

You can deter thieves by ensuring that your home is well lit and not conspicuously unoccupied. External security 'motion detector' lights (that switch on automatically when someone approaches); random timed switches for internal lights, radios and televisions; dummy security cameras; and tapes that play barking dogs (etc.) triggered by a light or heat detector may all help deter burglars. In remote areas it's common for owners to fit two or three locks on external doors, alarm systems, grills on doors and windows, window locks, security shutters and a safe for valuables. You can fit UPVC (toughened clear plastic) security windows and doors, which can survive an attack with a sledge-hammer without damage, and external steel security blinds (which can be electrically operated), although these are expensive. A dog can be useful to deter intruders, although he should be kept inside where he cannot be given poisoned food. Irrespective of whether you actually have a dog, a warning sign with a picture of a fierce dog may act as a deterrent. If not already present, you should have the front door of a flat fitted with a spy-hole and chain so that you can check the identity of visitors before opening the door. **Bear in mind that prevention is better than cure, as stolen property is rarely recovered.**

If you vacate your home for an extended period, it may be obligatory to notify your caretaker, landlord or insurance company, and to leave a key with the caretaker or landlord in case of emergencies. One way to avoid burglaries when you're away is to employ house sitters. Home insurance companies usually offer discounts for owners who employ house-sitters – you should, in any case, tell your insurance company if you employ a sitter. There are a number of companies including Absentia (☎ 01279-777412, 💻 www.home-and-pets. co.uk), Home and Pet Care (☎ 01697-478515,💻 www.homeandpetcare. co.uk) and Homesitters (☎ 01926-630730, 💻 www.homesitters.co.uk). Check that house-sitters are experienced and have been vetted. Companies charge a daily fee (e.g. £20 or £25) plus travelling expenses, a daily food allowance (e.g. £5 per day), and extras for looking after pets such as dogs and cats.

If you have a robbery, you should report it immediately to your local police station, where you must make a statement. You will receive a copy, which is required by your insurance company when you make a claim. When closing up a property for an extended period, you should ensure that everything is switched off and that it's secure.

Another important aspect of home security is ensuring that you have early warning of a fire, which is easily accomplished by installing smoke detectors. Battery-operated smoke detectors can be purchased for around £5 or less (they should be tested periodically to ensure that the batteries aren't exhausted). You can also fit an electric-powered gas detector that activates an alarm when a gas leak is detected. See also **Crime** on page 339.

For information about home insurance, see **Buildings Insurance** on page 214 and **Home Contents Insurance** on page 216.

MOVING HOUSE

After finding a home in the UK it usually takes just a few weeks to have your belongings shipped from within continental Europe. From anywhere else it varies considerably, e.g. around four weeks from the east coast of America, six weeks from the US west coast and the Far East, and around eight weeks from Australasia. Customs clearance is no longer necessary when shipping your household effects from one European Union (EU) country to another. However, when shipping your effects from a non-EU country to the UK, you should enquire about customs formalities in advance. If you're moving to the UK from a non-EU country, you must provide an inventory of the things that you're planning to import. If you fail to follow the correct procedure you can encounter problems and delays and may be charged duty or even fined. The relevant forms to be completed by non-EU citizens depend on whether your British home will be your main residence or a second home. Removal companies usually take care of the paperwork and ensure that the correct documents are provided and properly completed (see **Customs** on page 93).

It's advisable to use a major shipping company with a good reputation, e.g. a member of the British Association of Removers (BAR). For international moves it's best to use a company that's a member of the International Federation of Furniture Removers (FIDI) or the Overseas Moving Network International (OMNI), with experience in the UK. Members of FIDI and OMNI usually subscribe to an advance payment scheme providing a guarantee. If a member company fails to fulfil its commitments to a client, the removal is completed at the agreed cost by another company or your money is refunded. Some removal companies have subsidiaries or affiliates in the UK, which may be more convenient if you encounter problems or need to make an insurance claim.

You should obtain at least three written quotations before choosing a company, as costs can vary considerably. Moving companies should send a representative to provide a detailed quotation. Most companies will pack your belongings and provide packing cases and special containers, although this is naturally more expensive than packing them yourself. Ask a company how they pack fragile and valuable items, and whether the cost of packing cases, materials and insurance (see below) are included in a quotation. If you plan to do your own packing, most shipping companies will provide packing crates and boxes. Shipments are charged by volume, e.g. the square metre in Europe and the square foot in the US. If you're flexible about the delivery date, shipping companies will quote a lower fee based on a 'part load', where the cost is shared with other deliveries. This can result in savings of 50 per cent or more compared with an individual delivery. **Whether you have an individual or shared delivery, obtain a delivery date in writing, otherwise you may need to wait weeks or months for delivery!**

Be sure to fully insure your belongings during removal with a well-established insurance company. Don't insure with a shipping company that carries its own insurance, as they will usually fight every penny of a claim. Insurance premiums are usually 1 to 2 per cent of the declared value of your goods, depending on the type of cover chosen. It's prudent to make a photographic or video record of valuables for insurance purposes. Most insurance policies cover for 'all-risks' on a replacement value basis. **Note that china, glass and other breakables can usually be included in an 'all-risks' policy only when they're packed by the removal company.** Insurance usually covers total loss or loss of a particular crate only, rather than individual items, unless they were packed by the shipping company. If there are any breakages or damaged items, they should be noted and listed before you sign the delivery bill (although it's obviously impractical to check everything on delivery). If you need to make a claim, be sure to read the small print, as some companies require clients to make a claim within a few days, although seven is usual. Send a claim by registered post. Some insurance companies apply an 'excess' of around 1 per cent of the total shipment value when assessing claims. This means that if your shipment is valued at £25,000, a claim must be for over £250.

If you're unable to ship your belongings directly to the UK, most shipping companies will put them into storage and some allow a limited free storage period prior to shipment, e.g. 14 days. **If you need to put your household effects into storage, it's important to have them fully insured as warehouses have been known to burn down!** Make a complete list of everything to be shipped and give a copy to the removal company. Don't include anything illegal (e.g. guns, bombs, drugs or pornographic videos) with your belongings as customs checks can be rigorous and penalties severe. Provide the shipping company with **detailed** instructions how to find your British home from the nearest motorway or trunk road and a telephone number where you can be contacted.

After considering the shipping costs, you may decide to ship only selected items of furniture and personal effects and buy new furniture in the UK. If you're importing household goods from another European country, it's possible to rent a self-drive van or truck. **Note, however, that if you rent a vehicle outside the UK you usually need to return it to the country where it was hired.** If you plan to transport your belongings to the UK personally, check the customs requirements in the countries you must pass through. Most people find it isn't advisable to do their own move unless it's a simple job, e.g. a few items of furniture and personal effects only. It's no fun heaving beds and wardrobes up stairs and squeezing them into impossible spaces. If you're taking pets with you, you may need to get your vet to tranquillise them as many pets are frightened (even more than people) by the chaos and stress of moving house.

Bear in mind when moving home that everything that can go wrong often does, therefore you should allow plenty of time and try not to arrange your move from your old home on the same day as the new owner is moving in. That's just asking for fate to intervene! If your British home has poor or impossible access for a large truck you must inform the shipping company. **Note also that if furniture needs to be taken in through an upstairs window you will usually need to pay extra.** See also **Customs** on page 93 and the **Checklists** on page 96.

5

EARNING A LIVING

There are over 250,000 businesses in London employing some 3.5 million people (2 million men and 1.5 million women). The vast majority of businesses are small, with almost 90 per cent employing less than 25 people and just 10 per cent with a turnover of over £1 million. Compared with the UK as a whole, London has a high proportion of self-employed people, which has risen sharply in recent years, and there are now almost 50 per cent more self-employed women in London than there were a decade ago. This trend looks set to continue, with large companies 'downsizing' and 'outsourcing', and an increasing number of small businesses being set up to provide services for them.

Despite a vast labour market and inflated salaries, London has higher unemployment than the UK as a whole (7 per cent in late 2006). The percentage of people unemployed in each borough is shown in **Chapter 1**. As in other countries, the majority of unemployed people are unskilled or young (or both). Many Europeans find that job opportunities in London (and the UK in general) far outweigh those in their home countries. **Note, however, that if you don't automatically qualify to live in the UK, for example as a national of a European Economic Area (EEA) country, obtaining a work permit may probably be more difficult than finding a job.**

Average earnings in London have always been significantly higher than the UK average, although the cost of living is also higher (see page 204). Men in manual (blue-collar) jobs earn around 12 per cent more than the UK average, while those in non-manual (white-collar) occupations earn almost 30 per cent more (the figures for women are 15 and 27 per cent respectively). This is largely a reflection of the high earnings in the financial and business services sectors, and the high salaries paid to managers and administrators generally. The highest-paid workers in London earn over 35 per cent more than their counterparts elsewhere in the UK, and earnings in professional and technical occupations are 45 per cent higher than the UK average.

Over the past few decades there has also been a shift (throughout the UK, but more marked in the capital) away from manufacturing towards service industries. Today, London's job market is dominated by financial and business services (40 per cent) followed by other services industries such as education, social work and health (15 per cent), distribution, hotels and catering (15 per cent), transport, storage and communications (10 per cent), public administration and defence (5 per cent), and other industries (5 per cent).

Manufacturing now makes up just 10 per cent of London's GDP, most of it confined to the boroughs of Hackney and Barking & Dagenham, the latter being the only London borough to have a higher proportion (30 per cent) of employees in manufacturing than the UK average (18 per cent), thanks largely to the Ford car plant at Dagenham. Other boroughs with a significant manufacturing industry include Brent (mainly food and drink), Haringey (footwear, printing and publishing, drink, food and tobacco, metal goods, motor vehicles, rubber and plastic products, timber and wooden goods), Tower Hamlets (mainly clothing and printing), Merton and Waltham Forest.

The highest concentration of service industries is to be found in a 'corridor' across north and central London incorporating the boroughs of Barnet, Camden, City, Westminster, Kensington & Chelsea, Hammersmith & Fulham, and Wandsworth, where over 90 per cent of jobs are in the service sector. Certain areas also concentrate on specific business sectors: for example, the City of London is (of course) mostly finance and insurance, a sector which is also on the increase in neighbouring Tower Hamlets. Docklands (in Tower Hamlets) is still being developed and will comprise over half a million square metres of office and retail space by the time building is completed. The workforce of Canary Wharf alone is expected to total around 100,000 by the year 2006. On the other side of central London, Hammersmith & Fulham has recently become the focus of the media and entertainment industries, and in Kensington & Chelsea there are opportunities in the pharmaceutical and cosmetics industry, creative and media work, leisure and tourism. Cultural and media jobs are also available in Lambeth.

The UK is a nation of commuters (it's considered nothing for people to travel 160km/100mi or more to work and back each day) and nowhere is this more true than in and around London. Tele-working is gaining momentum, with annual increases averaging 12 per cent over the past six years. Over 2.2 million Britons now work from home on at least one day a week according to the latest data from the Office for National Statistics. This is 7.4 per cent of the total labour force. Of these, 44 per cent do their main job at home. Expansion is expected to continue and some experts estimate that up to 23 per cent of workers will be involved in tele-working within ten years.

There are numerous books written for those seeking a job in the UK, including *The Job Search Manual* by Lina Aspey (Management Books 2000), *How to Find the Perfect Job* by Tom Jackson (Piatkus), *The Job Application Handbook* by Judith Johnstone (How To Books), and *London Jobhunter's Guide* (Pearson Books). There are numerous work-related magazines and newspapers, many of which are dedicated to particular professions, industries or trades. Further information is also contained in **Living and Working in Britain** by David Hampshire (Survival Books).

QUALIFICATIONS

The most important qualification for working in London is the ability to speak fluent English. Once you've overcome this hurdle you should establish whether your trade or professional qualifications and experience are recognised in the UK. If you aren't experienced, British employers usually expect studies to be in a relevant discipline and to have included work experience. Professional or trade qualifications are necessary to work in many fields in the UK, although these aren't as stringent as in many other European Union (EU) countries.

Theoretically, any qualifications recognised by professional and trade bodies in one EU country should be recognised in the UK. In practice, recognition varies from country to country, and in some cases foreign qualifications aren't recognised by British employers or professional and trade associations. All academic qualifications should also be recognised, although they may be less acceptable than equivalent British qualifications, depending on the country and the educational establishment concerned. A ruling by the European Court declared that when examinations are of a similar standard and differences are not extensive, then individuals ought to be required to take additional examinations only in those particular subject areas which don't overlap in order for their qualification to be acceptable.

All EU member states issue information sheets about occupations each of which contains a common job description together with a table of qualifications which permit you to practise that occupation anywhere in the Union. They're intended to help someone with the relevant qualifications look for a job in another EU country and numerous trades and professions are covered. To obtain a comparison of British vocational qualifications and those recognised in other EU countries, particularly with regard to the Certificate of Experience scheme, contact Carol Rowlands, Department for Education and Skills, Room E3b, Moorfoot, Sheffield S1 4PQ (☎ 0114-259 4151, ✉ carol.rowlands@ dfes.gsi.gov.uk). For a comparison of academic qualifications contact UK NARIC, Oriel House, Oriel Road, Cheltenham, Gloucestershire, GL50 1XP (☎ 0870-990 4088, 💻 www.naric.org.uk).

JOB HUNTING

When looking for a job in London, it's wise not to put all your eggs in one basket and to spread your net far and wide – the more job applications you make, the better your chances of finding the right job. Contact as many prospective employers as possible, either by writing, telephoning, or calling on them in person. Whatever job you're looking for, it's important to market yourself correctly and appropriately, which depends on the type of job you're after. For example, the recruitment of executives and senior managers is handled almost exclusively by consultants, who advertise in the British quality national press (and also abroad) and interview all applicants prior to presenting clients with a shortlist. At the other end of the scale, manual or part-time jobs requiring no previous experience may be advertised at Jobcentres, in local newspapers and in shop windows, and the first suitable, able-bodied applicant may be offered the job on the spot.

Your method of job hunting will depend on your particular circumstances, qualifications and experience and the sort of job you're looking for, and may include the following:

● Contacting the government employment service and visiting local Jobcentres (see below);

● Registering with private employment agencies and recruitment consultants (see page 180);

● Obtaining copies of British daily and weekly newspapers, most of which have 'positions vacant' sections on certain days (see page 182);

● Surfing the internet, where there are literally hundreds of sites for jobseekers, including corporate websites, recruitment companies and newspaper job advertisements (see page 182);

● Checking TV teletext job services (on BBC, ITV and Sky);

● Making applications directly to companies in London. You can obtain a list of companies operating in a particular field from trade directories, such as *Kelly's* and *Kompass*, copies of which are available at reference libraries in London and British Chambers of Commerce overseas. Most medium to large companies also advertise job vacancies on the internet.

● 'Networking', which is basically getting together with like-minded people to discuss business, which is a popular way of making business and professional contacts in the UK. It can be particularly successful for executives, managers and professionals when job hunting.

● Asking relatives, friends or acquaintances working in London whether they know of an employer looking for someone with your experience and qualifications.

If you're already in London, you can contact or join expatriate social clubs, churches, societies and professional organisations, or your country's chamber of commerce. Many good business contacts can also be made among expatriate groups.

Government Employment Service

Jobcentre Plus is the new name for the government employment service, which is an executive agency of the Department of Work and Pensions. Its task is to provide help for the unemployed, but particularly those who have been jobless for over six months, or who are disabled or disadvantaged. It's responsible for paying them the Jobseeker's allowance through its network of offices, helping them with other relevant benefits, and otherwise assisting them in two ways: by placing people directly in jobs, or by offering guidance and counselling so that they can find the best way to return eventually to employment, e.g. through education or training. Jobcentre Plus offices – currently co-existing with 'Jobcentres' which have yet to be re-named and which perform a similar function – advertise jobs and training courses, operate a number of programmes and training initiatives, and provide a wide range of publications about help available.

Their activities include Employment on Trial, Jobclubs, Jobfinder's Grant, Jobmatch and the New Deal scheme introduced in 1998. The New Deal programme provides advice, support, training and direct work experience for young people aged between 18 and 24 and those aged 25 or over who have been claiming Jobseeker's Allowance for two years or more. It's also open to EU nationals. Information can be obtained from Jobcentre Plus offices or the website 🖥 www.newdeal.gov.uk.

The vast majority of jobs advertised in Jobcentre Plus offices and Jobcentres are manual or low paid and don't usually include managerial or professional positions (or jobs for 16 to 18-year-olds which are advertised in careers centres). Jobs are displayed on boards under headings such as building, clerical, domestic, drivers, engineering, factory, hairdressing, hotel and catering, industrial, motor trade, nursing, office, receptionists, shops, temporary and latest vacancies (where new vacancies are initially posted).

Such offices are generally self-service, although staff are on hand to provide advice and help when required. If you find a job which is of interest, write down the reference number and take it to one of the staff who will tell you more about the job and arrange an interview if required. You can register with a Jobcentre Plus office by completing a card and providing details of the kind of job you're looking for. If the office doesn't deal with your profession or industry, they should at least be able to tell you about other sources of information. When a job comes in that matches your requirements, you will be informed. But don't rely on this method. **Check the boards regularly, as new jobs are displayed each morning and good jobs don't remain vacant for long.** You can usually check on new vacancies by telephone. Many cities and boroughs have their own employment centres or 'job shops' where jobs with the local council are advertised.

European Employment Service

Jobcentre Plus is also responsible for EURES operations in the UK. EURES is the European system for exchanging job applications and vacancies between member states, which participating employment services carry out on a monthly basis. Members are the EEA countries. Details are available in all Employment Service offices in each member country, as is advice on how to apply for such jobs. Local offices have access to overseas vacancies held on the National Vacancy Computer System (NATVACS). Applicants are required to complete two ES13 application forms, either in response to advertised vacancies or to make a general application, which is valid for six months.

Employment Agencies & Consultants

In London, private recruitment consultants and employment agencies even outnumber pubs and are big business. Most large companies are happy to engage consultants to recruit staff, but this is particularly true if they're seeking executives, managers and professional employees. Head-hunters, as they're known, account for around two-thirds of all top level executive appointments in the UK. Some rather less grand agencies cover a wide range of occupations but most specialise in particular fields, e.g. computer or nursing personnel; accounting, sales, secretarial and office staff; engineering and technical specialists; catering, industrial and construction workers. Many more deal exclusively with 'temps: temporary office staff, baby-sitters, home carers, nannies and mothers' helps, housekeepers, cooks, gardeners, chauffeurs, hairdressers, security guards, cleaners, labourers and factory hands. Specialist nursing agencies, which are fairly common, also cover related occupations like physiotherapy, occupational and speech therapy, and dentistry.

Employment agencies make a lot of money from finding people jobs so, provided you have something to offer, they will be keen to help you (if you're a computer expert, you may get trampled in the rush to find you a job). If they cannot help you, they will usually tell you immediately and won't waste your time.

Agencies, which must be licensed by local councils, don't usually charge empioyees, but receive a fee from employers equivalent to one to four months of the salary you will be receiving , plus a fixed amount in many cases. Some agencies act as employers themselves, hiring workers and contracting them out to companies at a higher hourly rate than they themselves are paying. As a result of recent EU legislation, hourly rates paid should include an additional amount in lieu of holiday pay after a qualifying period, if employees don't take a paid annual holiday. Agencies must deduct PAYE income tax and National Insurance contributions if employees don't operate their own limited company. Many agencies also employ freelance staff on a contract basis, e.g. accountants, computer personnel, nurses, technical authors, draughtspersons and engineers (see **Contract Jobs** below).

The Recruitment and Employment Confederation (REC), 15 Wellbeck Street, London W1G 9XT (☎ 020-7009 2100, 🖥 www.rec.uk.com) is the trade association for recruitment agencies in the UK; a list of its members can be found on the website. To find those in your own area look both in the yellow pages under 'Employment Agencies', and in local newspapers, where their advertising is usually prominent. Agency jobs are also advertised on TV teletext and via the internet. If you're using agencies to look for work you will find an outline of your relevant legal rights on 🖥 www.rec.uk.com/legal-rights-jobseekers.htm.

Newspapers & Magazines

The national newspapers all have 'situations vacant' or 'appointment' sections, some of which specialise in particular fields or industries on certain days, e.g. Monday's *Guardian* for sales, marketing, PR and secretarial, Wednesday's *Times* for secretarial, and Thursday's *Daily Telegraph* for technical and managerial, sales and marketing. The Sunday broadsheet newspapers such as the *Observer*, *Sunday Telegraph* and *Sunday Times* also have 'appointments' sections for management staff and professionals. The *Evening Standard*, which is London's own newspaper, has a job section in all weekday issues, each one featuring vacancies in an particular field. The *London Job Supplement* is free with the *Standard* on Mondays and *Classified Week*, containing recruitment and property adverts, is published on Mondays (price £1.30). Details can be found on the *Standard*'s website (🖳 www.standard.co.uk). Most newspapers also list all jobs advertised on the internet, e.g. 🖳 www. jobsunlimited.co.uk (*Guardian*), 🖳 www.careerlink.co.uk (*Daily Mail*) and 🖳 www.thisislondon.co.uk (*Evening Standard*).

Each area of London has local (free) newspapers and magazines, most of which also contain recruitment sections, and many London boroughs have business magazines or newsletters, For example, Croydon Marketing and Development publishes an information sheet, *Croydon – The Facts* (☎ 020-8686 2233, 🖳 www.croydon.gov.uk).

A number of free newspapers and supplements for jobseekers aged 21 to 45 are also published in London, including *Girl About Town*, *Midweek* (men), *Ms London* and *Nine to Five* (men), all of which are published on Mondays by Independent Magazines (UK), 191 Marsh Wall, London, E14 9RS (☎ 020-7005 2000, 🖳 www.londoncareers.net). Others Associated Newspapers include *Metro London* (☎ 020-7651 5200, 🖳 www.metro.co.uk), a free daily (Mondays to Fridays) newspaper aimed at commuters travelling into London, and *TNT* and *TNT Midweek* (☎ 020-7373 3377, 🖳 www.tntmagazine.com), free magazines published weekly, on Mondays and Wednesdays respectively and targeted at Australians and New Zealanders living in London; they contain a wealth of advertisements from employment agencies. Most of these free newspapers and magazines are distributed at train and tube stations and other outlets such as newsagents, pubs, and newspaper dispensing machines in central London.

Placing an advertisement in the 'Situations Wanted' section of a local newspaper in London may prove fruitful and, if you're a member of a recognised profession or trade, you could place an advertisement in a newspaper or magazine dedicated to your profession or industry.

The Internet

The internet is fast becoming one of the most important resources for both job hunters and employers. In addition to those listed below, don't neglect newspaper websites (where jobs advertisements are usually listed) and company websites – many companies receive as many as half of all their job applications via advertisements placed on their websites. Listed below are some of the many websites for those seeking a job in London:

🖥 http://cafe.sdc.uwo.ca/joblistings – The site of the Student Development Centre, which lists jobs for students;

🖥 www.badenochandclark.com – Badenoch and Clark, a recruitment consultant specialising in accountancy, banking/financial services, law and IT jobs;

🖥 www.dotjobs.co.uk – Dotjobs, for jobs throughout the UK in the printing packaging sectors;

🖥 www.easynet.net – Easynet, a general job search site;

🖥 www.gradunet.co.uk – Gradunet, for graduate jobs throughout the UK and abroad;

🖥 www.jobs-by-email.co.uk – Jobs-by-email, listing up to 3,500 jobs in various categories in the UK and abroad;

🖥 www.jobserve.com – Jobserve, offering jobs in all areas;

🖥 www.jobsite.co.uk – Jobsite, listing vacancies in all sectors;

🖥 www.londoncareers.net – The site of Independent Magazines (UK), publishers of *Girl About Town*, *Midweek*, *Ms London* and *Nine to Five* (see **Newspapers & Magazines** above), listing selected jobs advertised in those publications, including information for overseas applicants;

🖥 www.manpower.co.uk – Manpower, which claims to be 'the UK's leading employment company';

🖥 www.monster.co.uk – Monster UK, a search engine for both job seekers and employers, which claims to be 'the world's leading career network';

🖥 www.peoplebank.com – PeopleBank, a database of vacancies and CVs which matches jobseekers with employers;

🖥 www.prospects.csu.ac.uk – Prospects.ac.uk, which claims to be 'the UK's official graduate careers website';

🖥 www.reed.co.uk – Reed Recruitment's site, on which you can post your CV and search for suitable jobs or careers;

🖥 www.stepstone.co.uk – StepStone, which claims to be 'Europe's leader in online career services and recruitment solutions';

🖥 www.topjobs.co.uk – Top Jobs, offering jobs in all areas.

5

Each London borough also has its own website containing information on jobs, all of which can be accessed via 🖥 www.bubl.ac.uk/uk/england/london.htm; the addresses of individual sites are www.[borough name].gov.uk, e.g. 🖥 www. brent.gov.uk, except those of Barking & Dagenham (🖥 www.lbbd.gov.uk), City of London (🖥 www.corpoflondon.gov.uk), Hammersmith & Fulham (🖥 www. lbhf.gov.uk), Kensington & Chelsea (🖥 www.rbkc.gov.uk) and Waltham Forest (🖥 www.lbsf.gov.uk).

SELF-EMPLOYMENT & DOING BUSINESS

Anyone who's a British citizen, an EEA-national, or a permanent resident can work as self-employed in the UK, which includes partnerships, co-operatives, franchise and commission-only jobs, or a private business. There have traditionally been fewer restrictions and red tape for anyone wanting to start a business or work as self-employed in the UK, although this has changed in recent years with a veritable tidal wave of employment legislation emanating from both the British government and the European Union. Many experts believe that red tape is strangling enterprise, so much so that many companies pay consultants a retainer just to be kept informed of new legislation! **You must be particularly wary of employment legislation, which can be very expensive if you fire an employee and are subsequently sued for unfair dismissal.**

However, this doesn't deter most people and the UK is traditionally a country of enterprise and entrepreneurs, where the business climate positively encourages self-employment and business creation. The key to starting and running a successful business is exhaustive research, research and yet more research. If you want to join London's growing legions of self-employed, you need to carefully select the area in which to establish your business. Each borough, naturally, claims special advantages and is keen to attract entrepreneurs who will stimulate the local economy. Consequently there's no shortage of information and advice (most of it free) on all aspects of starting and developing a business, either in London as a whole, a particular region, or individual boroughs.

Information & Support

The organisations listed below provide general information about doing business in London (and in some cases other parts of the UK) and various support services.

- **Awards For All – London** (☎ 0845 600 20 40, 🖥 www. awardsforall.org.uk) provides Lottery-funded grants for projects enabling people to participate in community activities.

- **Business Link for London** (☎ 020-7010 1000 or 0845-600 0787, 💻 www. bl4london.com), part of the national Business Link network, provides independent advice, information and support services for small businesses, including benchmarking, market research, consultancy subsidies, seminars and training courses.

- The **Department of Trade and Industry** (☎ 020-7215 5000, 💻 www. dti.gov.uk) provides a wealth of information and publications for budding entrepreneurs.

- **Greater London Enterprise** (☎ 020-7403 0300, 💻 www.gle.co.uk) provides support for smaller companies through loans, advice and training.

- **InBiz** (💻 www.inbizonline.co.uk) helps the long-term unemployed to set up their own businesses. There are three London offices: Central (☎ 020-7290 0130), North (☎ 020-7561 5550) and West (☎ 020-7610 5373).

- **Lambeth Small Business Growth Initiative** in Brixton (☎ 020-7924 9078) offers support and advice to those wanting to set up a small business anywhere in London.

- The **London Development Agency** (☎ 020-7593 9001, 💻 www.lda.gov.uk) is the agency with overall responsibility for the development of business in London.

- The **London First Centre** (☎ 020-7718 5400, 💻 www.lfc.co.uk) is the inward investment agency for London, providing a free and confidential service to companies considering London as a business location. It provides a general introduction to London and a complete relocation service, from assistance with company registration to identifying the best location and finding premises. It can also introduce companies to potential partners and investors.

- **PRIME** (☎ 020-8765 7833, 💻 www.primeinitiative.org.uk) is a national organisation that helps people over 50 to set up in business.

- The **Prince's Youth Business Trust** (☎ 020-7543 1234 or 0800-842 842, 💻 www.princes-trust.org.uk) provides financial and other assistance to those aged 18–30 starting a business.

- **TNG**, formerly The Training Network Group (☎ 020-8367 0647, 💻 www. tnguk.com) is a national private training company, whose head office is in London.

5

Organisations that can help you once your business is established include the following:

- **Acas – London** (☎ 020-7396 0022 or 0845-747 4747, 🖥 www.acas.co.uk) provides information, advice and training aimed at improving business performance.

- **Business In The Community** (☎ 0870 600 2482, 🖥 bitc.org.uk) provides advice and organises events for businesses.

- **Corporate Venturing UK** (☎ 020-7246 0751, 🖥 www.corporateventuringuk. org) is a DTI-sponsored programme designed to encourage business growth through entrepreneurship.

- The **London Chamber of Commerce and Industry** (☎ 020-7248 4444, 🖥 www.londonchamber.co.uk) is the largest business organisation in London, whose members range from small retailers to large 'blue chip' companies. It seeks to help businesses succeed by representing and promoting their interests and expanding their opportunities, through providing members with business information, co-ordinating trade missions, and organising training and networking events.

- The **London Growth Fund** provides low interest loans to companies that have been trading for at least a year and wish to expand but have been unable to obtain a conventional loan (e.g. from a bank). For information contact **Greater London Enterprise** (see above).

- The **North London Chamber of Commerce** (☎ 020-8443 4464, 🖥 www. nlcc. co.uk) provides support and advice to existing businesses in north London.

Area Organisations

Organisations that cover only a part of London include the following:

- **Central** – The Portobello Business Centre (PBC) in North Kensington (☎ 020-7460 5050, 🖥 www.pbc.co.uk) is central London's leading enterprise agency, specialising in providing advice to new businesses in various sectors, including media, fashion, catering, design, building and craft manufacturing. PBC also provides information on sources of funding and runs training programmes.

- **North** – Prevista (☎ 020-7609 4198, 🖥 www.prevista.co.uk) is a government-funded agency providing information and advice to those wishing to start a business in northern central London. Prevista works in partnership with Business Link for London (see above).

- **South** – The South London Partnership fosters economic development in the boroughs of Croydon, Merton, Sutton and Wandsworth through training, courses, consultations and a recruitment service. For details, contact the council offices of the relevant borough (see **Chapter 1**).

- **South-East** – The Business Information Service (☎ 020-8461 7897, 🖥 www. thebis.org.uk) serves Bromley and south-east London, providing information to help businesses with planning and marketing, although this isn't a free service.

- **South-West** – The Other Media (☎ 020-7089 5959, 🖥 www.othermedia. com) provides impartial advice and help with all IT-related matters.

  Connections (☎ 020-8254 3300, 🖥 www.prospects.co.uk) is a small company with centres in Battersea (Wandsworth), New Malden (Kingston) and Wimbledon (Merton) offering careers information and guidance to people of all ages.

- **West** – West London Business (☎ 020-8607 2500, 🖥 www.westlondon.com) is a Chamber of Commerce initiative aimed at maintaining the commercial competitiveness of west London (principally the borough of Hounslow), one of its goals being to attract new business to the area.

  The West London Enterprise Agency/Richmond In Business (☎ 020-8666 0221, 🖥 www.richmondinbusiness.co.uk) assists business starters in the Richmond borough and helps existing businesses to obtain training.

Boroughs

London's boroughs compete vigorously for business investment and most have an Economic Development Unit (or something similar) that can provide local demographic and other statistical information and an industrial profile of the borough, including local market information and wage rates. It can also provide information about the local property market, house prices and availability; vacant office and industrial premises, development sites and managed workspaces; information about renting council premises; help in identifying local suppliers; recruitment advice; a list of key local contacts and business support services;

details of grants, loans and funds for which you may be eligible; and information about the regulations concerning your business. Borough councils also issue licences for certain types of businesses. Your local Chamber of Commerce may organise free, impartial business advice sessions, such as explaining the loans and grants available.

Most councils have established Local Business Partnerships (e.g. with Chambers of Commerce and local businesses) to enable new businesses and local authorities to work together to streamline the various regulatory processes (e.g. consumer, health and safety, and standards). The aim is to make it easier for businesses to understand and comply with regulations, and consequently save money and become more competitive. Councils provide information about legal requirements and good business practice, inform you how to apply for registration or approval, and act as the co-ordinator with the relevant regulatory bodies to smooth your path. Councils may also have a Business Support Unit that will put you in touch with people and organisations who can provide the help and advice you need, and a Business Network providing links between businesses.

There are also numerous local organisations offering help and information, some of which are listed below:

- **Brent** – Brent Business Venture (☎ 020-3110 2300, 🖳 www.bbv.co.uk), a member of the Business Link for London partnership (see page 182) provides information and advice for people starting businesses in the borough.

- **Bromley** – Business Focus (☎ 0845 466 4700, 🖳 www.business-focus. co.uk) is run by Bromley's Chamber of Commerce and is dedicated to support local businesses.

  The Bromley Business Help Line (☎ 020-8313 4100, 🖳 www. bromley.gov. uk and click on 'Business') helps businesses wanting to move to the borough by providing details of vacant commercial property and relevant local support services.

- **Camden** – The Camden Enterprise Agency (CENTA) Business Services (☎ 020-7278 5757, 🖳 www.centa.co.uk) provides a complete support service for people starting a business in the borough.

- **Enfield** – The London Business Innovation Centre (☎ 020-8350 1350, 🖳 www.londonbic.com) provides low-cost office space to start-up business in high-tech fields.

  The Enfield Enterprise Agency (☎ 020-8443 5457, 🖳 www. enfieldenterpriseagency.co.uk) aims to help both new and established businesses.

- **Greenwich** – The Greenwich Business Support Service (☎ 020-8858 8850, 🖥 www.greenwich.gov.uk/greenwich/working/businesssupportservice) maintains a database of available commercial property, information on grants and other forms of financial assistance, and links to business support agencies in the borough.

- **Hackney** – HBV Enterprise (☎ 020-7254 9595, 🖥 www.hbv.org.uk) provides help, including loans, grants and training, to those wishing to become self-employed.

  Hackney Co-operation Developments (☎ 020-7254 4829, 🖥 www.hced. co.uk) is a non-profit organisation that helps women and people from ethnic minority groups to establish businesses and co-operatives.

  Social & Environmental Analysis (☎ 020-7923 9230, 🖥 www. wiseowls. co.uk) provides business start-up and self-employment training, including 'e-learning' courses, and information about sources of funding. The parent organisation, Wise Owls Employment Agency, offers business support services for the over 45s and e-learning programmes for all, and its website (🖥 www.wiseowlslearn.org) includes a database of training providers in east and central London.

- **Hammersmith & Fulham** – Business Enterprise Centre (☎ 020-8746 0355, 🖥 www.bectek.co.uk) is a resource centre for small to medium-size companies.

  The Community & Enterprise Opportunities Centre (☎ 020-8746 2120) concentrates on projects in media and IT.

  The Park Royal Partnership (☎ 020-8961 9696, 🖥 www.parkroyal.org) provides advice and assistance for businesses on the Park Royal estate (see also **Regeneration** on page 187).

- **Haringey** – The Haringey Business Development Agency (☎ 020-8376 6262) assists in the creation of new businesses and helps existing businesses to survive and expand. It also manages a loan fund.

  The Haringey Education Business Partnership (☎ 020-8375 3500, 🖥 www.hebp.co.uk) provides work experience and training for young people in the borough.

- **Harrow** – Harrow In Business (☎ 020-8427 6188, 🖥 www.hib.org.uk) provides advice, information and support for new and existing businesses.

- **Islington** – The Islington Enterprise Agency (☎ 020-7226 2783, 🖥 www. islingtonenterprise.co.uk) provides training and small business support and encourages management development and the setting-up of co-operatives.

- **Sutton** – Sutton Business Federation (☎ 020-8773 8555, 💻 www. suttonbusinessfederation.org.uk), which is soon to become the borough's Chamber of Commerce, provides support mainly for existing businesses.

- **Wandsworth** – The One London Business Advice Service Wandsworth (☎ 020-8870 1451) is a division of One London.

  The Economic Development Office (☎ 020-8871 7031) offers up to 25 per cent support towards the cost of refurbishing shop fronts and business interiors in the borough as part of its Town Centre Improvement Scheme. It also co-ordinates the Wandsworth Business Support Network, a bi-monthly forum for borough business matters.

The Internet

The following websites are just a few of those providing help and advice to people planning to establish a business in London. See also **Appendix C**.

💻 http://bubl.ac.uk/uk/england/london.htm – Has links to all borough sites, many of which have search pages where you can look up businesses of a particular type in the area;

💻 http://seirc.org.uk – The site of the south-east England Innovation Relay Centre, serving small and medium-size businesses by helping them to find European partners);

💻 www.brint.com/interest.html – Provides the text of business management and IT journals;

💻 www.bl4london.com – the site of Business Link for London – see page 182;

💻 www.govgrants.com – The site of the private Enterprise Advisory Service for information on financial support available from the UK government and the EU;

💻 www.tsnn.co.uk – provides information and help arranging an exhibition stand for your business;

💻 www.netaccountants.com – The site of the Dyer Partnership, which provides accounting and tax information for small and medium-size businesses;

💻 www.inlandrevenue.gov.uk – The Inland Revenue's site, containing information on self-assessment, etc.;

💻 www.reedinfo.co.uk – The site of Reed Business Information, which provides publications and 'marketing solutions' for businesses.

REGENERATION

Many parts of London are either undergoing or are planned for regeneration, thanks to large injections of government, local council or private money. The most high-profile scheme is the transformation of London's former docks into the now thriving business area known as Docklands. Whether you're thinking of setting up your own business or looking for a position as an employee, there are many projects worth investigating, some of which are listed below. For the latest information, contact the relevant borough councils (see **Chapter 1**).

- **Cityside** (the western part of Tower Hamlets, bordering the City) is being revitalised through the Cityside Regeneration Company (☎ 020-7377 5277, 🖳 www.cityside.org.uk), which has won £11.5 million of government funding.

- The **Cray Valley** in the eastern part of Bromley is being regenerated by the Cray Valley Partnership (☎ 020-8313 4880 or 020-8461 7890, 🖳 www.bromley.gov.uk/content/council/partnerships_and_initiatives/Cray_Valley_Partnership.jsp).

- **Crystal Palace Park** and the surrounding area (in the boroughs of Bromley, Croydon, Lambeth, Lewisham and Southwark) has been the focus of a £150 million regeneration scheme by the Crystal Palace Partnership (🖳 www. bromley.gov.uk/content/council/partnerships_and_initiatives/Crystal_Palace_Partnership.jsp) which officially ended in March 2004 but which will no doubt have knock-on effects in terms of business development.

- **East Battersea** (Wandsworth) has received £2.6 million from the government to transform the former Battersea Power Station into a leisure facility. The site's website (🖳 www.thepowerstation.co.uk) contains details of current vacancies.

- **Haringey** has over 30 development sites centred on Tottenham and Wood Green. Details can be found on the borough's website (🖳 www.haringey.gov.uk).

- **Leaside** is the name given to the area on the eastern edge of Tower Hamlets with the River Lea as its boundary and its long-term regeneration scheme offers some of the best business opportunities in London; details can be obtained from the Leaside Regeneration company (☎ 020-7364 4639, 🖳 www.leasideregeration.com). The Upper Lea Valley Partnership is one of the largest partnerships in the UK, investing £120 million in the area over seven years; details can be obtained from the North London Learning Skills Council (☎ 020-8929 1797, 🖥 www.lsc.gov.uk)

- **Park Royal** is a huge industrial estate in Brent (home of Guinness, among 800 other companies), on which the Park Royal Partnership (☎ 020-8961 9696, 🖥 www.parkroyal.org) aims to create an additional 20,000 jobs.

- **Peckham** (Southwark) is the site of a recent £250 million regeneration scheme. Other nearby areas due for redevelopment are the Aylesbury Estate, Elephant & Castle, Old Kent Road and Burgess Park. Details are available from Southwark council (☎ 020-7525 5000, 🖥 www.southwark. gov.uk).

- The **Thames Gateway** project (see page 139) is an ambitious scheme to develop east London and is the largest urban regeneration project in Europe. Details are available from the Thames Gateway London Partnership (☎ 020-8221 2880, 🖥 www.thames-gateway.org.uk).

- **Wandsworth** is the site of a recent £20 million regeneration programme co-ordinated by the Wandsworth Challenge Partnership (☎ 020-8871 7806, 🖥 www.wandsworth.gov.uk).

- The **White City** (Lambeth) development scheme (which has been on the cards for 20 years) aims to develop a 40-acre site into a vast shopping and leisure centre. Details are available from Lambeth council (☎ 020-7926 1000, 🖥 www.lambeth.gov.uk).

5

6

MONEY MATTERS & INSURANCE

Competition for your money in the UK has never been fiercer and, in addition to many British and foreign banks, financial services are provided by building societies, investment brokers, insurance companies, the post office and even large chain stores, supermarkets and service organisations. London is the most important financial market in Europe and the third most important in the world after Tokyo and New York (although there are fears that it could lose its position if the UK continues to remain outside the Euro group of countries). Deductions from gross salary, including income tax, social security and other benefit contributions, total an average of around 30 per cent (overall the tax burden has increased in recent years when direct and indirect taxes are taken into account). However, taxes (particularly income tax) are still lower in the UK than in many other European countries. (Among the many British eccentricities is the government's financial tax 'year', that runs from 6th April to 5th April of the following year.) The cost of living has been steadily rising in recent years and the UK is now one of the most expensive countries in Europe in which to live and London one of the most expensive cities in the world.

Britain is a credit-financed society (in recent years, debt has doubled, while savings have halved) and companies queue up to lend you money or give you credit. Credit and assorted other plastic cards have largely replaced 'real' money and now account for over 75 per cent of all retail purchases. Britons owe over £55.5 billion on credit cards and almost 5 per cent of cardholders owe £5,000 or more. Your financial standing in the UK is usually determined by the number of cards you have, which include credit cards, cash cards, debit cards, cheque guarantee cards, charge cards, store cards and affinity cards.

Britain has been one of the least regulated financial service industries in the western world, in the sense that there are few controls over interest rates and charges, although recently-created regulatory bodies should tighten things up. Currently, however, anyone can set himself up as an investment expert and charge whatever fees and interest he wishes. The UK has been described as the financial rip-off centre of Europe and it's estimated that finance companies overcharge small investors by over £500 million per year. Personal finance is a jungle and there are plenty of predators about just waiting to get their hands on your loot. Always shop around for financial services and never sign a contract unless you know exactly what the costs and implications are.

When you arrive in London to take up residence or employment, make sure you have sufficient cash, travellers' cheques, credit cards, luncheon vouchers, coffee machine tokens, silver dollars, gold sovereigns and diamonds to last at least until your first pay day, which may be some time after your arrival. Don't, however, carry a lot of cash. During this period you will find that a credit card or two is useful.

There are numerous books and magazines published to help you manage your finances, including *The Penguin Personal Financial Guide* by Alison Michell (Penguin) and the *Moneywise Family Finance Guide* (Clark Publishing).

The Consumers' Association publishes a number of excellent financial books, including *450 Money Questions Answered, Getting the Best Deal for Your Money, Which? Way to Save and Invest, Finance Your Future* and *How to Buy, Sell and Own Shares*. Personal finance magazines include *Personal Finance, Money Observer, What Investment* and *Moneywise*. Personal finance information (including the best loan and mortgage interest rates) is published in the financial pages of the Saturday and Sunday editions of national newspapers, and is also available via the television teletext information service and on the internet. Further general information about finance and insurance can be found in *Living and Working in Britain* (Survival Books).

The figures and information contained in this chapter are based on current law and Inland Revenue practice, which in the UK are subject to change (frequently).

BANKS & BUILDING SOCIETIES

The major British banks with branches throughout London (termed 'high street' banks) include the Abbey (⌨ www.abbey.com), Barclays (⌨ www.barclays.co.uk), HSBC (⌨ www.hsbc.co.uk), Lloyds TSB (⌨ www.lloydstsb.com) and National Westminster (⌨ www.natwest.com). Other major banks with branches in London are the Co-operative Bank (⌨ www.co-operativebank.co.uk), the Bank of Scotland (part of HBOS Group, ⌨ www.bankofscotland.co.uk) and the Royal Bank of Scotland (⌨ www.rbs.co.uk) – the last two being completely separate organisations despite the similarity of their names.

There are also telephone banks (including First Direct, ⌨ www.firstdirect.com) that don't have branches and are 'open' 24 hours per day. For the wealthy, there are many private banks (mainly offering 'portfolio management' services) and foreign banks in London (there are over 500 foreign banks in the City of London alone). Most banks have websites and many offer online banking, a rapidly growing area. In recent years there has been a flood of new-style 'banks' such as Virgin Direct, supermarkets and stores such as Marks & Spencer, which have shaken up the traditional high street banks with their innovative accounts and services.

British banks provide free banking for personal customers who remain in credit, pay interest on account balances and offer a range of financial services (although they usually **aren't** the best place to buy insurance or pensions). If you do a lot of travelling abroad, you may find the comprehensive range of services offered by the high street banks advantageous. Many services provided by British banks are also provided by building societies (see below).

The relationship between the major UK banks and their customers has deteriorated in the last decade. During the recession, banks dramatically increased their charges to personal and business customers to recoup their losses on bad loans to developing countries. Few people in the UK have a good word to say about their banks, which are widely perceived to be profit-hungry and impersonal. Complaints against banks have risen greatly in recent years. British banks made record profits (running into billions of pounds) in the 1990s and early 2000s, which has served only further to annoy customers. Many think their banks are ripping them off: for example, it can take four days to transfer cash from one account to another via the internet, a transaction that should be instantaneous. Often the worst place to buy financial products is from a major high street bank; building societies usually offer better deals.

To be fair, most banks have been busy trying to improve customer relations by introducing codes of conduct and payments for mistakes or poor service. Many people could save money by changing their banks. You shouldn't allow loyalty to prevent you from switching banks as, when times are hard, your bank won't hesitate to withdraw your safety net (during the recession banks were directly responsible for the failure of hundreds of small businesses through arbitrarily withdrawing or refusing overdrafts and loans).

Building Societies

Building societies date back to 1775 and were originally established to cater for people saving to buy a home. Savers would deposit 5 or 10 per cent of the cost of a home with the building society, which then lent them the balance. A building society would rarely lend to anyone who wasn't a regular saver, although this changed many years ago. In 1987, the regulations governing institutions offering financial services were changed and, as a result, banks and building societies now compete head-on for customers. There has been a wave of mergers and take-overs in recent years, and the number of societies has fallen dramatically. Many building societies have converted to banks (called de-mutualisation) in recent years, offering account holders large cash incentives as an inducement to vote in favour of such moves. Many people (known as carpetbaggers) have taken advantage of these pay-outs by opening accounts at a number of building societies.

Nowadays, building societies offer practically all the services provided by banks, including current and savings accounts, cheque guarantee cards, cash cards, personal loans, credit cards, insurance and travel services. In an effort to woo customers away from banks, many building societies produce special brochures and 'transfer packs' (even containing pre-printed 'letters') detailing exactly how to transfer your account. Building societies don't always all offer the same services, types of accounts or rates of interest (those offering the best interest rates are often the smaller ones). If you're looking for a long-term investment, the number of branches may not be of importance and members of all building societies can use cash dispensers at other building society branches via the Link system.

Deposit Protection

All banks, including branches and subsidiaries of foreign banks accepting sterling deposits in the UK, must be licensed by the Bank of England and contribute to the Deposit Protection Fund (DPF), which guarantees that 90 per cent of deposits up to £20,000 will be repaid if a bank goes bust. Because of the limit, it's worthwhile spreading your investments around several banks and financial institutions (see also **Building Societies** above).

Complaints

British banks are very slow to rectify mistakes or to resolve disputes and rarely accept responsibility, even when clearly in the wrong. It has been estimated (based on proven cases) that banks routinely overcharge small business customers by hundreds of millions of pounds every year. If your bank makes a mess of your account and causes you to lose money and spend time resolving it, you're within your rights to claim financial compensation for your time and trouble in addition to any financial loss. However, banks typically stall complaints for up to six years and simply use their financial muscle to wear down customers (some banks fight every case in the courts). If you have a complaint against a British bank and have exhausted the bank's complaints procedure, you can apply for independent arbitration to the Office of the Banking Ombudsman, 70 Grays Inn Road, London WC1X 8NB (☎ 020-7404 9944).

Business Hours

Normal bank (and building society) opening hours are from 9 or 9.30am until 3.30 or 4pm (some are open until 5.30pm) Mondays to Fridays, with no shutdown over the lunch period in most parts of London. Most branches are open late one day per week until between 5.30 or 6pm (it varies according to the bank and its location) and many open on Saturdays, e.g. from 9.30am until 12.30pm (some are open until 3.30pm). *Bureaux de change* have longer opening hours, including Saturdays and Sundays in tourist areas, but should be used in dire circumstances only, owing to their high commission and/or poor exchange rates. When banks are closed, you can change money at post offices, which are usually open from 9am to 5.30pm, Mondays to Fridays and from 9am to 12.30pm on Saturdays. All banks are closed on public holidays which, for this reason, are generally called 'bank holidays'.

Most banks at major airports are open from 6.30 or 7am to 11 or 11.30pm, seven days per week, and some airports, e.g. London's Gatwick and Heathrow airports, have 24-hour banks. Some banks at London railway stations also have extended opening hours (e.g. those at Victoria). Most banks, building societies and main post offices in the UK have 24-hour cash dispensers/machines (officially called Automatic Teller Machines/ATMs) at branches for cash withdrawals, deposits and account balance enquiries. Cash machines are also located in some supermarkets and other large stores.

Opening An Account

If you're planning to work in London and will be paid monthly, one of your first acts should be to open a current (or cheque) account with a bank, building society or the Girobank (post office), like over 80 per cent of the British working population. Your salary will usually be paid directly into your account by your employer (many will insist that your salary is paid into an account) and your salary statement will either be sent to your home address or be given to you at work.

You may need to wait up to two months for your first pay cheque. Although this is unusual, you should check with your employer, who may (if necessary) give you a salary advance. Employees who are paid weekly are often paid in cash, in which case it's up to you whether you open a bank or building society account (although it's difficult to survive without one). Many people have at least two accounts, a current account for their out-of-pocket expenses and day-to-day transactions, and a savings account for long-term savings (or money put aside for a 'rainy day'). Many people have both bank and building society accounts. Before opening an account, compare bank charges, interest rates (e.g. on credit cards) and other services offered by a number of banks. **If you're planning to buy a home with a mortgage, one of the best accounts is a an all-in-one account or mortgage current account** (see **Mortgages** on page 202).

To open an account, you simply go to the bank or building society of your choice and tell them you're living in London and wish to open an account. You will be asked for proof of identity, e.g. a passport or driving licence, plus proof of address in the form of a utility bill. Foreign residents may be required to provide a reference from their employer or a foreign bank. Many banks provide new account holders with a free cash card wallet, cheque book cover and statement file. After opening an account, don't forget to give the details to your employer (if you want to get paid).

Current Accounts

The facilities you should expect from a current account include a cheque book, a paying-in book, a cheque guarantee card (preferably £100 or £250), interest paid on credit balances, no charges or fees when in credit, a free cash card and lots of cash machines, a free debit card, monthly statements, an automatic authorised overdraft facility, and the availability of credit cards.

A cheque book usually contains 30 cheques and paying-in slips (at the back), with which you can make payments into your account. Most businesses won't accept a cheque without a guarantee card, which (for that reason) should be kept separately from your cheque book in case of theft.

Most people pay their bills from their current account, either by standing order or by cheque. Bank statements are usually issued monthly (optionally quarterly). Interest may be paid on deposits (usually quarterly) and an overdraft facility may be provided. Most banks don't levy charges on a current account, provided that you stay in credit. However, if you overdraw your account without a prior arrangement with your bank, you may be billed for bank charges on all transactions for the accounting period (usually three months).

High-Interest Cheque Accounts

Most banks and building societies offer high-interest cheque accounts for customers who maintain a certain minimum balance, e.g. £1,000. These accounts offer a range of benefits, including a cheap overdraft facility and a £250 cheque guarantee card. Some current accounts pay variable rates of interest according to the account balance. Interest on high-interest accounts may be paid monthly and there's usually no transaction or monthly fees. If you don't need instant access to large sums of cash, you're better off with a **Savings Account** (see below) than a high-interest cheque account. **It's never wise to keep a lot of cash in an account with a cash card, as fraudulent withdrawals aren't unknown!**

If you never overdraw on your current account and aren't being paid interest, you're making a free loan to your bank (something they most certainly **won't** do for you).

Savings Accounts

All banks and building societies provide a wide range of savings accounts, also called deposit, term deposit or high-interest accounts, most of which are intended for short or medium-term savings rather than long-term growth. When opening an account, the most important considerations are how much money you wish to save (which may be a lump sum or a monthly amount), how quickly you might need access to it and whether you're a taxpayer.

Before committing your money to a long-term savings account or investment, shop around, not just among banks and building societies but also among other financial institutions. Interest rates, conditions and fees vary, so take them into account. Banks and building societies often introduce new types of account paying increased rates of interest, **but they don't usually notify existing customers of this (some even forbid staff to tell customers about accounts paying higher interest).**

The best savings interest rates are published in Saturday and Sunday newspapers such as *The Times* and *The Sunday Times*, and in financial magazines like *Personal Finance, Money Observer, What Investment* and *Moneywise*. Information is also available via the television teletext information service and the internet. *Which?* magazine (see **Appendix B**) also offers invaluable advice and surveys.

MORTGAGES

Mortgages are available from a huge number of lenders, including building societies, high street and foreign banks (including offshore banks), direct lenders, finance houses and credit companies, insurance companies, developers, local authorities and even employers. The UK has a fiercely competitive mortgage business with around 150 lenders offering over 3,000 different mortgage products vying for your business. There are over 11 million mortgages in the UK, worth a staggering £750 billion in 2003 – equal to the annual take-home pay of the entire country! The average loan of a first-time buyer is over £90,000 and for someone moving up the property ladder is over £100,000.

However, in 2003, mortgage rates were the lowest for 50 years and you could easily obtain a low-start mortgage at 2 per cent below the standard interest rate, pay off some of your loan without charge or switch to another lender for a better deal. In fact, there had never been a better time to change your mortgage. **A survey by Clear Cut Mortgages in autumn 2003 showed that homeowners were losing out on potential savings of £7.5 billion per year by failing to switch to more competitive home loans.** Overpaying on your mortgage in order to pay it off early will save you tens of thousands of pounds in interest and is recommended when the interest paid on savings is low.

A voluntary Mortgage Code for lenders was introduced in the 1990s, which sets standards of good mortgage advisory practice and provides safeguards for clients. Details are contained in a booklet (published in large print, audio and Braille formats), available from lenders or from the Council of Mortgage Lenders, 3 Savile Row, London W1S 3PB (☎ 020-7440 2255 for recorded information, 🖥 www.cml.org.uk). However, the code has been criticised as too vague and is broken by many lenders.

Three factors determine whether you can obtain a mortgage and its size: your income, your credit history, the size of the deposit you can make and the type and condition of the property itself (lenders won't lend on a ruin). If you're an employee in steady employment, you should have no problem obtaining a mortgage, although whether it will be enough to buy the home you want is another matter entirely.

Lenders cannot require you to buy expensive buildings and contents insurance from them, but will insist that you have buildings insurance and will require evidence.

Income

You can usually borrow up to 3.75 times your gross (pre-tax) salary or 2.75 times the joint income of a couple. For example, if you earn £25,000 per year and your wife earns £30,000, you would qualify for a £151,250 mortgage (2.75 x £55,000). A single person would need to be earning over £40,000 to obtain a similar mortgage. However, lenders are flexible and some will lend 3.25 times your salary plus the salary of a partner, while others will lend much more to those with good career prospects (e.g. graduates). Some lenders will lend professionals up to five times their annual salary, although you should be extremely wary of taking out too large a mortgage. Up to four people can legally share the ownership of a property (although most lenders allow a maximum of three co-owners), when the incomes of all co-owners are taken into account.

Most lenders will give you a conditional decision over the phone and will provide a written 'mortgage promise' that you can show sellers to prove that you're a serious buyer. If you're refused a mortgage, you can ask the Council of Mortgage Lenders (see above) for advice. In England, Wales and Northern Ireland, you can apply for a mortgage after an offer on a property is accepted.

Self-Certification Mortgages

Self-certification mortgages are targeted at the self-employed (a huge market, which includes some 3 million people) and allow borrowers to estimate their earnings rather than provide proof of income. Borrowers can obtain a mortgage of between 75 and 85 per cent of the value of a property. The rates offered to high-risk borrowers are typically around 2 per cent above the standard rates for new customers. Brokers may push self-certification mortgages to the self-employed, as they earn higher commission, but you should treat them as a last resort.

Size Of Mortgage

The larger the deposit you can pay (as a percentage of the value), the larger the mortgage you can obtain and the wider the choice of mortgages and deals available. In the UK, most borrowers can obtain 90 to 95 per cent mortgages and some lenders offer 100 per cent mortgages (a few even offer up to 125 per cent mortgages!). The size of the mortgage as a percentage of the price or value of a property is known as the 'loan-to-value' (LTV) ratio. For example, a £180,000 mortgage on a house worth £200,000 is an LTV ratio of 90 per cent.

Mortgage Indemnity Guarantee

If you borrow more than a certain percentage of a property's value, which varies according to the lender but is usually 90 per cent, you must usually have a mortgage indemnity guarantee (MIG) – also called a high lending fee, mortgage risk fee or maximum advance premium. This is to protect the lender in the event that you're unable to repay the loan and the lender is forced to repossess a property. However, a number of lenders don't levy an MIG, including HSBC, the Nationwide Building Society, the Co-Operative Bank and Northern Rock, although they may charge a higher interest rate when the loan-to-value ratio is over 90 per cent.

Where applicable, the difference between the LTV and the MIG threshold is the amount on which you must pay MIG, which typically costs around £2,000 on a £100,000 loan. The interest rate charged for an MIG varies and it can be paid up-front or added to the mortgage (some lenders allow you to pay it over a few years without interest). If you add it to the mortgage, the MIG premium is likely to cost you three times as much over 25 years and if you pay off the mortgage early you don't receive a refund of a portion of the MIG.

Term

The usual home loan period in the UK is 25 years on repayment mortgages and 40 years for interest-only mortgages (see below). Reducing the term, say from 25 to 20 years, will save you a lot of money, e.g. £12,000 in interest on a £50,000 repayment mortgage. Most mortgages allow you to pay off lump sums at any time, which can also save you thousands of pounds in interest and reduce the term of your loan. For example, a lump sum payment of £5,000 results in a saving of £17,948 on a 20-year mortgage at 7.7 per cent and a payment of £10,000 a saving of £32,551. There are usually minimum lump sum payments, e.g. £500 or £1,000, and lenders may credit lump sum payments immediately, monthly or annually. There are usually penalties with fixed rate loans.

Types Of Mortgage

Once you've calculated how much you wish to pay for a home, how much you need to or can afford to borrow and the term of the loan, you must decide what kind of mortgage is best for you. The most common types of mortgage currently offered in the UK are described below.

Repayment Mortgages

Repayment mortgages account for some 80 per cent of all mortgages in the UK. They're so called because you repay the original loan and interest over the period of the mortgage, as with most personal loans. Your monthly payment includes both interest and capital payments – mostly interest at the start and mostly capital towards the end of the term.

One advantage of a repayment mortgage is that the term of the loan can be extended if you have trouble meeting your monthly repayments. A Disadvantage is that you must take out a form of life insurance called a 'mortgage protection policy' to ensure that your loan is paid off if you die. This policy isn't expensive, as it pays off the mortgage only if you die before the term of the loan is completed (and both the term and amount owed decrease over time). For the majority of people, a repayment mortgage together with adequate life insurance is the best choice, as it's the only loan that guarantees to pay off your mortgage by the end of the term (provided you maintain the stipulated payments).

Interest-Only Mortgages

Interest-only mortgages account for around one in five of all mortgages – you take out a mortgage loan in the normal way and pay interest as usual. However, instead of the payments being calculated to repay the loan at a fixed date in the future, the loan simply stays in existence until you decide to repay it, which could be any time from six months to 60 years. Interest-only loans are good for single people with no dependants, heavily-mortgaged families, those whose earnings fluctuate, people who expect to receive an inheritance and those whose salary is likely to rise substantially in the future.

It isn't necessary to have an insurance policy to repay the loan should you die, but it's recommended if others are dependent on your income. The major disadvantage of interest-only mortgages is that most lenders will lend only from 50 to 75 per cent of a property's value. For most people, it's essential to make provision for repaying the capital sum at the end of the original mortgage term, which can be done with an investment (such as an ISA), endowment or pension mortgage (see below). An Individual Savings Account (ISA) can be invested in cash, stocks or life insurance, and the pay-out is tax-free.

However, owing to the high charges and poor performance of these products in recent years, particularly endowments, interest-only mortgages are no longer so popular. They're favoured by the majority of buy-to-let investors and are a good way to get onto the housing ladder, as your repayments are lower, although you can store up problems for the future.

Endowment Mortgages

With an endowment mortgage you pay interest over the length of the loan. You also take out an endowment policy, which should provide a large enough lump sum to pay off the mortgage at the end of the term, usually 25 years. Your monthly mortgage payments are made up of an interest payment and an insurance (endowment) payment. The policy also carries life insurance, which ensures that, if you die, the mortgage is paid off in full and any money left over is paid to your estate. The loan and endowment are separate and you can obtain them from different sources. You should obtain independent advice and try to find a lender with a low interest rate and an insurance company with a good track record.

Like all endowment policies, you could be left with a tax-free sum at the end of the term after your loan has been paid off, although there are no guarantees. Investments depend on the stock market, which has performed very badly in recent years. **In 2003, over 75 per cent of endowment policies were facing a shortfall amounting to thousands of pounds, which means that some 7.5 million endowments could fail to repay mortgages.** Some endowments are worth less than the holders have paid in, even after ten years! **Consequently, in recent years mortgage advisers have advised most borrowers to avoid endowment mortgages like the plague!**

Interest Rates

An important aspect of a mortgage is how interest is calculated, which may be daily, monthly or annually. Daily is the best method for borrowers as, when you make payments (or overpayments), they take effect immediately. With a repayment mortgage, payments include part interest and part capital repayments, and when interest is calculated annually the outstanding debt doesn't decrease daily or even monthly, but once per year. This results in your paying interest on money you have already repaid! You can generally also choose between fixed and variable rate mortgages.

Fixed rate loans, where the interest rate is fixed for a number of years (e.g. from one year to the whole mortgage term) no matter what happens to the base rate in the meantime, are rare in the UK and aren't popular with borrowers or lenders. In recent years (with falling rates) they have been at a record low, although in 2003 many market analysts were recommending fixed rate loans to avoid being caught out by future interest rate rises. Those on tight budgets who cannot afford an increase in their mortgage repayments are better off with a fixed rate mortgage. The longer the fixed rate period, the lower the interest rate offered. If interest rates go down, you may find yourself paying more than the current rate, but at least you will know exactly what you must pay each month.

Most property buyers choose a variable rate mortgage, where the interest rate goes up and down in accordance with the base rate. Theoretically, when the base rate changes, the variable rate should rise or fall by the same percentage. However, when the base rate falls, many lenders don't pass on cuts (or the whole amount) to borrowers, ostensibly to protect savers, because when mortgage rates are cut the interest paid to savers must also be reduced. More recently the Bank of England has raised UK interest rates to 5.25% from 5% in an effort to curb inflation with these rates expected to rise.

To judge which type of mortgage is better for you, you must estimate in which direction interest rates are heading – a difficult feat that even the so-called experts cannot manage. The standard variable rate is usually around 1.5 per cent above the base rate (set by the Bank of England). Building societies typically offer standard variable rate mortgages that are around half a percentage point below high street banks. If you have a fixed rate for a pre-set period, there are high penalties for switching lenders during this period. The interest rate returns to the standard variable rate (SVR) after the fixed rate period.

You can be locked into a fixed rate deal that costs much more than the current variable interest rate and there may also be other restrictions such as early repayment penalties and no capital repayments during the period of a limited fixed, discounted or capped rate of interest. The best deals are offered to new borrowers and often have a maximum loan of £200,000 or £250,000, which excludes 'wealthy' buyers and existing borrowers.

Fees

There are various fees associated with mortgages. All lenders charge an arrangement fee (also called a completion, booking or reservation fee) for establishing a loan, which is either a fixed amount or a percentage of the loan. This is usually from £150 to £400 and is paid when you apply for a loan or when you accept a mortgage. This has been branded a rip-off by mortgage brokers and others in the loan business, particularly as some 20 per cent of purchases fall through and lenders keep the fee. Some lenders charge an up-front application fee and a completion fee when you accept the mortgage. Mortgage brokers may also levy a fee, e.g. 1 per cent of the value of the loan or a fee starting at around £300 to find you a deal. **Always check whether fees are refundable if the purchase falls through.** There's usually a valuation fee of around £200 and the lender's legal fees, although many lenders now waive these.

Foreign Currency Mortgages

It's possible for some lenders to obtain a foreign currency mortgage, e.g. in Euro, Swiss francs, US dollars or Japanese yen. All these currencies have historically low interest rates and have provided huge savings for borrowers in recent decades. However, you should be cautious about taking out a foreign currency mortgage, as interest rate gains can be wiped out overnight by currency swings. **Most lenders advise against taking out a foreign currency loan unless you're paid in a foreign currency, and some lenders will make this a condition of a loan.** Euro loans are available for expatriates paid in Euro. These may offer lower interest rates than sterling but usually require a higher deposit (e.g. 30 per cent) and a high booking fee, e.g. £500.

The lending conditions for foreign currency home loans for UK residents are stricter than for sterling loans and are generally granted only to high-rollers (those earning a minimum of £40,000 or £50,000 a year) and may be for a minimum sum of £100,000 and a maximum of 60 per cent of a property's value.

If you take out a foreign currency loan with an offshore bank, switching between major currencies is usually permitted. **When choosing between a sterling loan and a foreign currency loan, make sure that you take into account all charges, fees, interest rates and possible currency fluctuations.**

Advice & Information

Whatever kind of mortgage you want, you should shop around and take the time to investigate all the options available. One way to find the best deal is to contact an independent mortgage broker. Mortgage advice offered by lenders is often misleading and biased and not to be trusted (surveys have found that the mis-selling of mortgages is widespread among high street lenders). The best independent advice is found in surveys carried out by publications such as *Which?* magazine (see **Appendix B**), which accepts no advertisements, and daily newspapers. The best variable, fixed-rate and discount mortgage rates are published in Sunday newspapers such as *The Sunday Times*, *The Sunday Telegraph*, *The Observer* and *The Independent on Sunday*, and in monthly mortgage magazines such as *What Mortgage* and *Mortgage Magazine*. You can also make comparisons on the internet (e.g. 💻 www.hot-property.com/mortgages, www.moneyextra.co.uk and www.moneynet.co.uk).

However you finance the purchase of a home in the UK, you should obtain professional advice from your bank manager and accountant.

6   COST OF LIVING

No doubt you would like to know how far your pounds will stretch and how much money (if any) you will have left after paying your bills. In 2003, the UK had one of the highest costs of living in the world according to figures from Employment Conditions Abroad. High rates of duty, on everything from petrol to tobacco and alcohol to cars, help (?) to make it one of the world's most expensive places to live – and London is one of the world's most expensive cities with a cost of living ranking seventh in a 2003 survey of the world's 50 most expensive cities by Mercer Human Resources Consulting, the top six being (from first to sixth), Tokyo, Moscow, Osaka, Hong Kong, Beijing and Geneva. British consumers pay more for food and most consumer goods than people in most other western countries. While direct taxes are relatively low, indirect taxes are high.

The UK also has a relatively high rate of inflation, at least compared with other European countries. The UK's inflation rate is based on the Retail Prices Index (RPI), which gives an indication of how prices have risen (or fallen) over the past year. The prices of around 600 'indicator' items are collected on a single day in the middle of the month (a total of around 130,000 prices are collected for the 600 items in the RPI 'basket'). On this basis, the UK's inflation rate in early 2007 averaged around 3.9 per cent.

On the plus side, the UK's standard of living has soared in recent years and, compared with most other European Union countries, British workers take home a larger proportion of their pay after tax and social security. The middle classes have never been better off and the super rich go on spending sprees buying holiday homes, cruises, yachts, power boats, luxury cars and private aircraft. On the other hand, the gap between rich and poor in the UK is the largest since records began in 1886, and state pensioners are unable to afford basic comforts such as a healthy diet, a car and an annual holiday.

It's difficult to calculate an average cost of living, as it depends on each individual's circumstances and lifestyle. What is important to most people is how much money they can save (or spend) each month. Your food bill will naturally depend on what you eat and is usually around 50 per cent higher in London than in the US and up to 25 per cent higher than in other Western European countries. Approximately £250 should be sufficient to feed two adults for a month in most areas (excluding alcohol, fillet steak and caviar). Even in London, however, the cost of living needn't be astronomical. If you shop wisely, compare prices and services before buying and don't live too extravagantly, you may be pleasantly surprised at how little you can live on. It's also possible to save a considerable sum by shopping for alcohol and other products in France, buying your car in Europe, and shopping overseas by mail and via the internet (see **Buying Overseas** on page 335).

A list of the approximate **minimum** monthly major expenses for an average person or family in London are shown in the table below. When calculating your cost of living, deduct the appropriate percentage for taxes, National Insurance and pensions from your gross salary. The figures in brackets relate to the notes below the table.

MONTHLY COSTS (£)			
ITEM	Single	Couple	Family Of Four
Housing (1)	370	495	765
Food	145	260	395
Utilities (2)	60	85	110
Leisure (3)	125	150	200
Car/travel (4)	135	1240	165
Insurance (5)	40	550	70
Clothing	95	170	220
Council Tax (6)	50	60	80
TOTAL	**£920**	**£1,330**	**£1,880**

NOTES

1. Rent or mortgage on a modern flat or semi-detached house in an 'average' London suburb. The amount for a single person is for a bedsit or shared accommodation. Other costs are for a two- or three-bedroom property. They don't include council or other subsidised housing.

2. Includes electricity, gas, water and telephone, plus heating bills.

3. Includes all entertainment, sports and holiday expenses, plus TV licence, newspapers and magazines (which could of course be much higher than the figures given).

4. Includes running costs for an average family car, plus third party insurance, road tax, petrol and servicing, but not depreciation or credit costs.

5. Includes all 'voluntary' insurance, excluding car insurance.

6. This is a guesstimate only, as council tax is based on a property's value.

COUNCIL TAX

Council tax (until 1990 it was referred to as 'rates' and until 1993 as the 'poll tax') is a tax levied by local councils on residents to pay for such things as education, police, roads, waste disposal, libraries and community services. The tax includes payments for the county, borough or district council (borough council in the case of London), the local police, fire and civil defence authorities, and possibly a 'special expenses' payment in certain areas.

Each council fixes its own tax rates, based on the number of residents and how much money they need to finance their services. The amount payable depends on the value of your home, as rated by your local council (not necessarily the market value). Properties in England are divided into the following bands:

Band	Property Value (£)
A	Up to 40,000
B	40,001 – 52,000
C	52,001 – 68,000

D	68,001 – 88,000
E	88,001 – 120,000
F	120,001 – 160,000
G	160,001 – 320,000
H	Over 320,000

Cynically, the government hasn't changed these bands since their introduction in 1993, so vast the majority of London properties now fall into bands D to H. Not only that, but councils have announced 6 per cent rate increases for 2004/05 – more than twice the rate of inflation. The 2003/04 rates for bands D to H in each borough are given in the table below. If you're fortunate enough to find a property valued at less than £68,000, simply multiply the band H rate by the following figures to arrive at the tax rate for bands A to C: 0.333 (A), 0.387 (B), 0.444 (C).

Borough	Council Tax Rates				
	Band D	Band E	Band F	Band G	Band H
Average	1,063	1,299	1,535	1,772	2,126
Barking & Dagenham	1,220	1,500	1,760	2,030	2,440
Barnet	1,300	1,590	1,880	2,170	2,600
Bexley	1,316	1,608	1,900	2,193	2,631
Brent	1,239	1,514	1,789	2,065	2,477
Bromley	1,160	1,418	1,676	1,935	2,321
Camden	1,285	1,571	1,856	2,142	2,570
City Of London	861	1,055	1,243	1,434	1,721
Croydon	1,302	1,591	1,881	2,170	2,604
Ealing	1,310	1,600	1,891	2,182	2,619
Enfield	1,287	1,573	1,859	2,145	2,574
Greenwich	1,222	1,484	1,766	2,037	2,445
Hackney	1,287	1,573	1,859	2,145	2,574

Hammersmith & Fulham	1,206	1,473	1,741	2,009	2,411
Haringey	1,384	1,691	1,999	2,306	2,767
Harrow	1,356	1,657	1,958	2,260	2,712
Havering	1,380	1,687	1,993	2,300	2,760
Hillingdon	1,330	1,626	1,921	2,217	2,660
Hounslow	1,379	1,686	1,993	2,299	2,759
Islington	1,191	1,455	1,720	1,984	2,381
Kensington & Chelsea	1,016	1,242	1,467	1,693	2,032
Kingston	1,149	1,491	2,093	2,415	2,898
Lambeth	1,130	1,381	1,632	1,883	2,260
Lewisham	1,256	1,535	1,815	2,094	2,512
Merton	1,303	1,592	1,882	2,171	2,605
Newham	1,163	1,421	1,679	1,938	2,325
Redbridge	1,267	1,549	1,831	2,112	2,535
Richmond	1,419	1,735	2,051	2,367	2,840
Southwark	1,138	1,384	1,636	1,888	2266
Sutton	1,311	1,602	1,893	2,185	2,622
Tower Hamlets	1,086	1,327	1,569	1,810	2,172
Waltham Forest	1,365	1,688	1,971	2,275	2,730
Wandsworth	643	786	929	1,072	1,287
Westminster	659	805	952	1,098	1,318

Council tax can usually be paid by direct debit from a bank or building society account, by post with a personal cheque, in person at council offices, by credit card, or at a bank or post office. Payment can be made in a lump sum (for which a reduction may be offered) or in ten instalments a year, from April to January.

The full council tax assumes that two adults are living permanently in the dwelling. If only one adult lives in a dwelling (as their main home), the bill is reduced by 25 per cent. If a dwelling isn't a main home, e.g. it's unoccupied or is a second home, the bill is reduced by 50 per cent.

Exempt dwellings include those that are unfurnished (exempt for up to six months) or undergoing structural alteration or major repair (exempt for up to six months after completion), and those that are left empty for specific reasons (e.g. the occupier is in hospital, a nursing home or prison, or is a student) or are occupied only by people under 18 years of age.

Certain people aren't counted when calculating the number of adults resident in a dwelling, e.g. full-time students and 18 and 19-year-olds who have just left school. If you or someone who lives with you has special needs arising from a disability, you may be entitled to a reduction in your council tax bill. Those receiving Income Support usually pay no council tax and others on low incomes have their bills reduced. You can appeal against the assessed value of your property and any errors due to exemption, benefits or discounts.

All those who are liable for council tax must register with their local council when they take up residence in a new area, and are liable to pay council tax from their first day of residence. A register is maintained by councils, containing the names and addresses of all people registered for council tax, which is open to public examination. If you don't want your name and address to appear on the register, e.g. for fear of physical violence, you can apply for anonymous registration. New arrivals in the UK must register with their local council after taking up residence or after moving house. When moving to a new county or borough, you may be entitled to a refund of a portion of your council tax.

INSURANCE

In the UK you can insure practically anything from your car to your camera, the loss of your livelihood to your life. You can also insure against most eventualities, such as rain on your parade or village fête, or the possibility of twins (or sextuplets) or missing your holiday. If your livelihood depends on a particular part of your anatomy, e.g. your voice, legs, teeth or posterior, you can also insure it against damage or decline. For particularly unusual requests you may be required to obtain a quote from Lloyd's of London, the last resort for unusual insurance needs (not only within the UK, but also internationally). Note, however, that if an insurance requirement is particularly unusual or risky, you may find the premiums prohibitively high and restrictions may be placed on what you can and cannot do.

The UK is renowned as a nation of gamblers, which is reflected in the relatively low cost of insurance, not only for such basic requirements as loss of income or car accidents but also for homes and their contents. When it comes to health, many people tend to rely on state 'insurance' benefits, which come under the heading of 'social security'. These include sickness and unemployment pay, income support (for families on low incomes) and state pensions. Note, however, that social security usually provides for the most basic needs only and those who are reduced to relying on it often exist below the poverty line.

It isn't necessary to spend half your income insuring yourself against every eventuality from the common cold to a day off work, but it's important to be covered against any event which could precipitate a major financial disaster (like telling your boss what you think of him when you've had a few drinks too many). There are just two cases in the UK when insurance for individuals is compulsory: buildings insurance if you have a mortgage (because your lender will insist on it) and third party motor insurance, which is required by law. You may also need compulsory third party and accident insurance for high-risk sports. Voluntary insurance includes pensions, accident, income protection, health, home contents, personal liability, legal expenses, dental, travel, motor breakdown and life insurance.

As with everything to do with finance, it's important to shop around when buying insurance. It bears repeating – always shop around when buying or renewing insurance! Simply picking up a few brochures from insurance brokers or making a few phone calls can save you a lot of money (enough to pay for this book many times over).

If you're coming to the UK from abroad, you'd be wise to ensure that your family has full health insurance during the period between leaving your last country of residence until your arrival in the UK. This is particularly important if you're covered by a company health insurance policy terminating on the day you leave your present employment. If possible, it's better to continue with your present health insurance policy, particularly if you have existing health problems that may not be covered by a new policy. If you aren't covered by the National Health Service it's important to have private health insurance.

If you want to make a claim against a third party or a third party is claiming against you, you'd be wise to seek legal advice for anything other than a minor claim. **Note that British law is likely to be different from that in your home country or your previous country of residence and you should never assume that it's the same.**

Buildings Insurance

For most people, buying a home is the biggest financial investment they will ever make. When buying a home, you're usually responsible for insuring it before you even move in. If you take out a mortgage to buy a property, your lender will usually insist that your home (including most permanent structures on your property) has buildings insurance from the time you exchange contracts and are legally the owner. If you buy the leasehold of an apartment, your buildings insurance will be arranged by the owner of the freehold. Even when it isn't required by a lender, you'd be extremely unwise not to have buildings insurance.

Buildings insurance usually includes cover for loss or damage caused by fire, theft, riot or malicious acts, water leakage from pipes or tanks, oil leakage from central heating systems, floods, storms and lightning, explosions or aircraft impact, vehicles or animals, earthquakes, subsidence or landslides, and falling trees or aerials, as well as cover for temporary homelessness, e.g. up to £5,000. Some insurance companies also offer optional cover to include trees and shrubs damaged maliciously or by storms. There may be an excess (see below), which is intended to deter people from making small claims. Buildings insurance should be renewed each year and insurance companies are continually updating their policies, so you must take care that a policy still provides the cover required when you receive a renewal notice.

Lenders fix the initial level of cover when you first apply for a mortgage and usually offer to arrange the insurance for you, but you're normally free to make your own arrangements. If you arrange your own buildings insurance, your lender will insist that the level of cover is sufficient. Most people take the easy option and arrange insurance through their mortgage lender. This is generally the most expensive option and, if you change your buildings insurance from your lender to another insurer, you may be charged a transfer fee (e.g. £25) and an 'administration' fee (i.e. another transfer fee!).

The amount for which your home must be insured isn't the current market value but the cost of rebuilding it, should it be totally destroyed. This varies according to the type of property and the area. There's generally no deduction for wear and tear and the cost of redecoration is usually met in full. Buildings insurance doesn't cover structural faults that existed when you took out the policy, which is why it's important to have a full structural survey done before buying a property. Many people pay far too much for their buildings insurance, as many insurance companies have greatly over-estimated the cost of rebuilding. In many cases, building costs were calculated using the Royal Institute of Chartered Surveyors (RICS, 🖳 www.ricsfirms.com) Rebuilding Costs Index rather than the correct Tender Price Index, which takes into account actual building prices. If you're in doubt, check how the rebuilding cost of your home was calculated and whether it's correct.

Most lenders provide index-linked buildings insurance, where premiums are linked to inflation and increases in building costs (premiums are usually added to your monthly mortgage payments). **It is, however, your responsibility to ensure that your level of cover is adequate, particularly if you carry out improvements or extensions which substantially increase the value of your home.** All lenders provide information and free advice. If your level of cover is too low, an insurance company is within its rights to reduce the amount it pays out when a claim is made, in which case you may find you cannot afford to have your house rebuilt or repaired, should disaster strike.

The cost of buildings insurance varies according to the insurer, the type of building and the area, and is calculated per £1,000 of insurance. In London, insurance rates are generally over £4 per £1,000. Therefore, insurance on a property costing £100,000 to rebuild usually costs around £400 to £500 per year. In recent years, increased competition, particularly from direct insurers, has helped to moderate premium increases. Shop around, as many people can reduce their premiums by half. (But don't believe the advertising blurb, as some companies that claim to save you money actually charge more). Insurance for 'non-standard' homes, such as those with thatched roofs, timber construction, holiday homes, period properties and listed buildings, is usually much higher. The highest level of cover usually includes damage to glass (e.g. windows and patio doors) and porcelain (e.g. baths, washbasins and WCs), although you may have to pay extra for accidental damage, e.g. when your son blasts a cricket ball through the patio window. **Always ask your insurer what isn't covered and what it will cost to include it (if required).**

Premiums can usually be paid monthly (although there may be an extra charge) or annually. Some home insurance policies charge an excess (deductible), e.g. £50 or £100, for each claim, while others have an excess for certain claims only, e.g. subsidence or landslide, which is usually £1,000 or £2,000. Owners of houses vulnerable to subsidence (e.g. those built on clay) and those living in flood-prone areas (whose numbers are increasing, as more residential housing is built on flood plains and weather changes increase the risk of flooding) are likely to pay much higher premiums. However, it's estimated that over a million people pay too much for their insurance cover, because their insurers have wrongly assumed that they're at risk from subsidence. Subsidence is a risk primarily in east and south England, exacerbated by a series of warm, dry years beginning in the 1990s. (Even when your home isn't at risk from subsidence, it's difficult to find a policy that excludes it).

Many insurance companies provide emergency telephone numbers for policyholders requiring urgent advice. Should you need to make emergency repairs, e.g. to weather-proof a roof after a storm or other natural disaster, most insurance companies allow work up to a certain limit (e.g. £1,000) to be carried out without an estimate or approval from the insurance company, but check first. If you let your house (or part of it) or you intend leaving it unoccupied for a period of 30 days or longer, you must usually inform your insurance company. A booklet entitled *Buildings Insurance for Home Owners*, including a valuation table, is available from the Association of British Insurers (51 Gresham Street, London EC2V 7HQ, ☎ 020-7600 3333, 🖳 www.abi.org.uk).

Buildings insurance is often combined with home contents insurance (see below), when it may be termed household insurance, although it's often cheaper to buy buildings and home contents insurance separately.

Home Contents Insurance

Home contents insurance (also called contents insurance) is recommended for anyone who doesn't live in an empty house. Domestic burglary is a major problem in parts of London; statistics for each of the London boroughs (except the City) are included in the table on page 348.

Although there's a lot you can do to prevent someone breaking into your home, it's often impossible or prohibitively expensive to make your home burglar-proof. However, you can ensure you have adequate contents insurance and that your most precious possessions are locked in a safe or safety deposit box.

Combining your home contents insurance with your buildings insurance (see above) may save you money, although it's often cheaper to buy separate insurance. On the other hand, it can be advantageous to have your buildings and contents insurance with the same insurer, as this avoids disputes over which company should pay for which item, which can arise if you have a fire or flood affecting both your home and its contents.

Take care that you don't under-insure your house contents (including anything rented such as a TV or video recorder) and that you periodically reassess their value and adjust your premium accordingly (half of all homeowners are thought to underestimate the value of their home contents). Your contents should include everything that isn't part of the fixtures and fittings and which you could take with you if you were moving house. If you under-insure your contents, your claim may be reduced by the percentage by which you're under-insured.

Types Of Policy

There are two types of contents insurance policy: 'sum-insured' (where you calculate the cover you need and the insurer works out the premium based on the cover required) and 'bedroom-rated' (where you pay a set premium based on the number of bedrooms in your home).

With a bedroom-rated policy, the insurance company cannot scale down a claim because of under-insurance; however, you're usually better off calculating the value of the contents to be insured. Some companies have economy, standard and deluxe rates for contents valued, for example, from £10,000 to £40,000. You can take out a special policy if you have high-value contents, which may be cheaper than a standard contents policy. However, this usually requires a valuation costing around £300 and therefore isn't worthwhile unless your home contents are worth over £50,000. **Always list all previous burglaries on the proposal form, even if nothing was stolen.**

A standard home contents policy (of either type) covers your belongings against the same sort of 'natural disasters' as buildings insurance (see page 214). You can optionally insure against accidental damage and all risks. A basic contents policy doesn't usually include such items as credit cards (and their fraudulent use), cash, musical instruments, jewellery (and other valuables), antiques, paintings, sports equipment and bicycles, for which you normally need to take out extra cover. You can usually insure your property for its second-hand value (known as indemnity insurance) or its full replacement value (new or old insurance). This covers everything except clothes and linen (for which wear and tear is assessed) at the new cost price. Replacement value is the most popular form of contents insurance in the UK. It's best to take out an index-linked policy, where the level of cover is automatically increased by a percentage or fixed amount each year.

A basic policy doesn't usually include accidental damage caused by you or members of your family to your own property) or your home freezer contents (in the event of a breakdown or power failure). A basic policy may include replacement locks, garden contents, personal liability insurance (see below), loss of oil and metered water, and temporary accommodation. If not included, these can usually be covered optionally. Some policies include legal expenses cover (e.g. up to £50,000) for disputes with neighbours, shops, suppliers, employers and anyone who provides you with a service (e.g. a plumber or builder). Most contents policies include public liability cover up to £1 million. Items such as computers and mobile phones may need to be listed as named items on your policy, and equipment used for business isn't usually covered (or may be covered only for a prohibitive extra payment). If you have friends or lodgers in your home, their property won't usually be covered by your policy.

Premiums

Premiums depend largely on where you live and your insurer. All insurance companies assess the risk by location based on your postcode. **Check before buying a home, as the difference between low and high-risk areas can be as much as 500 per cent!** The difference between premiums charged by companies for the same property can also vary by as much as 200 per cent. Annual premiums are usually calculated per £1,000 of cover and range from around £3 to £4 in a low-risk area to between £12 and £20 in a high-risk area, sometimes more. Although many homeowners in high-risk areas would be willing to forego theft insurance, insurance companies are unwilling to offer this, because premiums would be substantially reduced if theft was omitted (theft is a convenient excuse to load premiums). Your premiums will also be higher if you live in a flood-prone area.

If you're already insured, you may find that you can save money by changing insurers, particularly if you're insured through a bank or building society, which are usually the most expensive. However, watch out for penalties when switching insurers.

Those aged over 50 or 55 (and possibly first-time homeowners) are offered discounts or special rates by some companies (e.g. Saga, 🖳 www.saga.co.uk, who specialise in insurance for people over 50). Some companies also provide special policies for students in college accommodation or lodgings (ask an insurance broker).

Most insurers offer no-claims discounts or discounts for homes with burglar alarms, high security locks, neighbourhood watch schemes or smoke detectors.

In high-risk areas, good security is a condition of insurance. Beware of the small print in policies, particularly those regarding security, which insurers often use to avoid paying claims. You will forfeit all rights under your policy if you leave doors or windows open (or the keys under a mat or flower pot), particularly if you've claimed a discount due to your 'Fort Knox' security. If there are no signs of forced entry, e.g. a broken window, you may be unable to claim for a theft. You should inform your insurer of any changes that may affect your policy, e.g. a loft conversion or extension. If you're going to leave your house empty for a long period, e.g. a month or longer, you should inform your insurer.

Worldwide Cover: Worldwide or extra cover is offered by most insurance companies as an extension to a home contents policy. With this type of policy, your possessions are covered against accidental loss or damage outside your home, anywhere in the world. Usually each item valued above a minimum sum, e.g. £250 to £1,000, must be declared in writing (it's wise to take photographs of your valuables and to keep a record of the make and serial numbers of valuable items). The cost is between £12 and £35 per year for each £1,000 covered, depending on the insurer.

6

7

GETTING AN EDUCATION

Like all major capital cities, London comprises a wide social, economic and cultural mix, which is reflected in its education system. In few other places in the world can you find such a diversity of educational options at all levels, from pre-school to university postgraduate, nor such a variety of ethnic and linguistic backgrounds. (It's reckoned that some 200 different languages are spoken in London.) Most establishments cater for overseas students, many of whom are attracted by London's reputation as a centre of educational excellence.

However, the range of choices may not be quite as wide as it appears at first glance. Some of the best establishments may be closed to you because they're too expensive, too exclusive or too popular, or they cater for a religious group or nationality to which you don't belong, or because you cannot meet the entry criteria, or simply because you don't live within a particular catchment area. Although London has some of the best schools in the country, within both the state and private (fee-paying) sectors, it also has some of the worst. These include a number of relatively poor private schools that do little to justify their fees and many under-performing state schools, some of which have failed official inspections and face closure if their standards don't improve.

GENERAL INFORMATION

Each London borough is also a Local Education Authority (LEA), which can provide information about its state schools. Telephone numbers for each London borough are listed in **Chapter 1** and a list of LEA addresses can be found on 🖥 www.dfes.gov.uk/leagateway – click on 'LEA Addresses'.

The weekly *Times Educational Supplement* (available from newsagents) contains up-to-the-minute news and opinion about education and schools in England, including management, governors, research and teaching posts. There are numerous books for parents faced with choosing a suitable state or private school, one of the best being *The London Schools Guide* (Mitchell Beazley), which is updated annually.

You can consult an independent adviser such as Gabbitas Educational Consultants (Carrington House, 126–130 Regent Street, London W1B 5EE, (020-7734 0161, 🖥 www.gabbitas.co.uk), which claims to be the UK's leading independent educational consultancy and can provide advice and information on any aspect of education in the UK. An annual guide to full-time courses in Greater London, *Full-Time Floodlight*, is published by Floodlight Publishing and available direct from them (☎ 020-7878 2309, 🖥 www.floodlight.co.uk) or from book shops in London. The website features a 'course finder' service.

There are many other useful education-related websites, including Schoolsnet (🖥 www.schoolsnet.com), 'the world's No.1 education website'; the National Grid for Learning (🖥 www.ngfl.gov.uk), a government site run in conjunction with the DfES; BBC Education (🖥 www.bbc.co.uk/education), the BBC's guide to online learning; and TSL Education (🖥 www.learnfree.co.uk), which claims to be the UK's leading educational publisher. Learn Direct, part of the University for Industry (☎ 0800-100900, 💻 www.learndirect-advice.co.uk), is a government-funded charitable organisation providing free information and advice on learning courses and career paths.

The Advisory Centre for Education (ACE), 1C Aberdeen Studios, 22 Highbury Grove, London N5 2DQ (☎ 020-7704 3370, 💻 www.ace-ed.org.uk), provides information on all matters related to state education and operates a telephone advice line from 2pm to 5pm Mondays to Fridays (☎ 0808-800 5793 in the UK and +44 20-7354 8321 from overseas).

An invaluable organisation for overseas students is the UK Council for Overseas Student Affairs (UKCOSA, 9–17 St Alban's Place, London N1 0NX, ☎ 020-7288 4330, 💻 www.ukcosa.org.uk), which is a registered charity established in 1968 to promote the interests and meet the needs of overseas students in the UK and those working with them as teachers, advisors or in other capacities. The British Council (☎ 020-7930 8466, 💻 www.british council.org) provides foreign students with information concerning all aspects of education in the UK.

PRE-SCHOOL

Pre-school is for children aged two to five and takes place in nursery schools or nursery classes attached to a primary school, and may be private or state-maintained. In practice, however, there's little state provision for pre-school education in London (or, indeed, in the UK as a whole). Workplace nurseries and crèches are often greatly over-subscribed, private nannies are expensive and places at private nurseries, pre-preps and prep schools in inner London are so rare that many people register their children at birth (or even before). Finding reliable childcare for babies and toddlers under the age of four can be one of the biggest headaches for working parents. However, the government is now offering four-year-olds a free place in a private or community nursery school, playgroup, or special nursery class, and it has also begun to extend the provision to three-year-olds.

There are too many nursery schools in London to list here, but there are some useful resources to help you find those in your area. The British Association for Early Childhood Education (111 City View House, 463 Bethnal Green Road, London E2 9QY, ☎ 020-7539 5400, 💻 www.earlyeducation.org) is a voluntary organisation providing information about childcare and education facilities for under eight-year-olds. The Pre-School Learning Alliance (69 King's Cross Road, London WC1X 9LL, ☎ 020-7697 2500, 💻 www.pre-school.org.uk) was

established in 1963 when parents, frustrated by the lack of nursery provision, decided to take matters into their own hands and created their own self-help nursery schools. Today it's a registered charity and the single largest provider of education and care for under-fives in England.

PRIMARY & SECONDARY SCHOOLS

London schools vary enormously in their facilities, the type and 'quality' of their pupils and the exam results those pupils achieve – which are among the many factors you need to take into account when choosing a school for your children. Of course, it's a moot point whether a child will get better grades at a high-achieving school than at a low-achieving one. Rightly, the DfES no longer publishes league tables of schools by Local Education Authority (LEA), which gave an unhelpful average picture of each area. Instead, it produces performance reports for each school, which are assessed according to a variety of criteria, including absentee rates as well as exam results. These can be viewed on the DFES website (🖥 www.dfes.gov.uk/performancetables) or hard copies obtained via the 'Performance Tables' order line (☎ 0845-602 2260). The same reports can be viewed on the website of the Office for Standards in Education (Ofsted), a non-ministerial government department that regularly inspects schools (🖥 www.ofsted.gov.uk).

The UK is currently suffering a chronic shortage of teachers, which means that average class sizes are increasing. A recent survey by the *Guardian* newspaper indicated that there were around 3,000 teachers too few in secondary schools.

Schooling in the UK is divided into four 'key stages', which help parents to know what their children are learning at various ages. Parents receive a report containing the results of Standard Assessment Tests (SATs) at the end of each key stage (at ages 7, 11, 14 and 16), based on national attainment targets. The key stages are:

Key Stage	Age	Year Groups (Classes)
1	5 – 7	1 & 2
2	7 – 11	3 – 6
3	12 – 14	7 – 9
4	14 – 16	10 & 11

Unhelpfully, the government's performance reports are divided into the following categories:

● Primary School (Key Stage 2)

● Secondary School (Key Stage 3)

● Secondary School (GCSE/GNVQ)

- Post-16

- Key Stage 2 to GCSE/GNVQ

When choosing a school (or indeed a place to live on the basis of local schools), take care not to rely on out-of-date information: London is in a constant state of flux and an area that was firmly downmarket five years ago may have suddenly become fashionable, driving up house prices and over-subscribing the local state schools. An inspired new head teacher or a glowing Ofsted report can have much the same effect. Competition for places at the best and most popular London schools – whether fee-paying or state-funded – is fierce.

In many areas, getting your children into a particular state school may be dependent on how close you live to it, so before buying or renting a home check the current position as regards school catchment areas.

Obtain local authority information leaflets and visit and talk to the teachers to form your own impression of a school's atmosphere and the staff's attitude. How big are class sizes? How well qualified and experienced are the teaching staff? Are there regular parents' evenings and opportunities for consultation? Are there problems with maintaining discipline or with drugs? Is there a uniform? What extra-curricular activities are offered, such as sports and after-school clubs and societies? Talk to playgroup leaders, nursery teachers, school secretaries or parent governors, all of whom can keep you up-to-date and pass on the kind of information the school may not care to reveal.

STATE SCHOOLS

The National Curriculum, introduced in 1989 and revised in 1993, is compulsory in all state schools in England and Wales and affects most pupils between the ages of 5 and 16. It's designed to ensure that all children have a broad and balanced education up to the age of 16, as well as standardising education in state schools throughout the country. So if you decide at a later date to move from London to Manchester or Bristol, the disruption to your child's education should be minimal. Bear in mind though, that Scotland operates an entirely different educational system.

Generally, schools in inner London achieve worse results than those in the outer boroughs, although there are notable exceptions. Pupils living in inner London boroughs such as Lambeth, Southwark, Hackney or Tower Hamlets frequently come from poorer families where the parents may be unemployed and living in poor housing. There's also a much higher percentage of children who don't speak English as their first language. Because of the difficulties associated with teaching children in these areas, there's often a high turnover of teaching staff and a consequent lack of commitment and continuity.

Ofsted reports have spotlighted low teacher expectations in some inner London schools and poor teaching of basic literacy and numeracy skills at the primary school level. The London borough of Hackney recently became the first education authority to be stripped of its powers and to have its education services put out to private tender. Islington and Southwark are under threat of similar treatment. Those who can afford to pay their way out of this situation do so and the professional middle classes in inner London have largely deserted the state sector, most parents preferring to pay for independent education, with the result that London now has the highest proportion of schoolchildren in private schools (10 per cent). Nevertheless, the Higher Education Funding Council for England recently reported that state-school students achieve better degree results than private school students.

The present government has implemented several new measures to help improve standards in the worst inner London state schools, encouraging them to form 'Education Action Zones' (EAZs) run by partnerships of local authorities, private businesses and community groups. If you're going to be living in a 'bad' London borough (education-wise) then the best thing to do is to live near the border so that you can try to get your child into a school in the neighbouring borough. It's illegal for a state school to select a resident child for a place over a non-resident child if the non-resident lives nearer. Most migrations are from inner to outer London, but not always, for example, many families living in Islington try to get their children into a Camden school, replacing the children who scramble over the border from Camden into Westminster!

The National Curriculum determines what children must study and what they're expected to know at 'key stages' of their school career (see above). National tests are set to check whether children are meeting these targets. The 'core subjects' of the National Curriculum are English, maths and science. So-called 'foundation' subjects include technology (incorporating design as well as computer-based information technology), history, geography, music, art and physical education. A modern foreign language is no longer compulsory after the age of 14. Religious and sex education must also be provided, but parents have a right to withdraw children from these subjects if they wish. In 2002, the government added 'citizenship' to the curriculum, a subject that covers social and moral responsibility, community involvement and politics, and is compulsory between the ages of 11 and 16. You can find further information about the curriculum on the National Curriculum website (🖳 www.nc.uk.net).

Types Of School

State schools (which aren't called 'public schools' – a term that confusingly refers to private schools) don't charge fees and are run by LEAs. State schools in London are usually classified as follows:

Type Of School	Age Group
Nursery	Up to 5
Infant Or First School	5 – 7 or 5 – 8
Junior Or Middle	7 – 11 or 8 – 12/13
Primary	5 – 11
Secondary	11 – 18 or 12/13 – 18
Secondary Plus	11 – 16
Sixth Form College	16 – 19

Note that in the borough of Harrow, secondary schooling starts at the age of 12 instead of 11 and pupils move to one of two tertiary colleges when they reach the age of 16.

There are three kinds of state school in the UK: grant-maintained schools, county schools, and voluntary-aided or voluntary-controlled schools, which are described below. LEAs also provide schools for children with special educational needs (see **Specialist Schools** on page 232).

Grant-Maintained Schools

The 1988 Education Reform Act allowed primary and secondary state schools to opt out of LEA control and adopt grant-maintained status, provided that a majority of their governors and parents voted in favour. Grant-maintained schools receive funding directly from central government, based on the number of pupils. Schools must manage their own budgets and employ their own support staff, including caterers and cleaners. The previous government heavily promoted grant-maintained schools and offered inducements, such as increased funding, to persuade schools to opt out.

County Schools

County Schools are owned by LEAs and wholly funded by them. They're non-denominational (not church-aided or supported) and provide both primary and secondary education.

Voluntary-Aided & Voluntary Controlled Schools

Voluntary-aided and voluntary-controlled schools provide both primary and secondary education and are financially maintained by LEAs. The difference between them is that voluntary-aided school buildings are in many cases the responsibility of voluntary bodies (e.g. a church or a foundation). Schools with 'CofE' (Church of England) or 'Catholic' in their name may be aided schools.

Primary Schools

State primary schools are obliged to take local children from the term in which their fifth birthday falls, although some will accept younger children into nursery or reception classes. Many schools admit new pupils at just one point in the year (usually September), which means that they accept all children who will be five within the coming school year (September to August). Therefore, children born in the summer start school not long after their fourth birthdays, which is an advantage or a disadvantage depending on how you view it. Primary schools consist mainly of infant departments for children aged five to seven and junior departments for those aged 7 to 11. Primary schools tend to operate their admissions policies purely on catchment area, unless they're voluntary-aided and stipulate parental religious observance.

Secondary Schools

In the state sector, most children transfer from primary school to secondary school at the age of 11. Most secondary schools are comprehensives (almost 90 per cent of English children attend them), which cater for children of all abilities, but there are still some selective or 'grammar' schools, mainly in the wealthier suburbs of south London, which are always vastly oversubscribed. These schools select pupils on the basis of academic attainment. The government has pledged that there will be no new grammar schools but will allow existing schools to continue, provided they have the support of local parents. Opinion polls have indicated that there's strong parental support for selection by ability, so their future – although by no means certain – seems relatively safe, at least in the short to medium term.

Single-sex schools are also increasingly popular within the state system, particularly for girls. Many parents believe that girls do better without boys around to distract them and there are several good girls' schools in the capital. However, bear in mind that, if there are a lot of girls' schools in a particular area, local mixed schools may be male-dominated.

PRIVATE SCHOOLS

Parents seeking private (fee-paying) education for their children will find many excellent schools in London (over 400). These are sometimes referred to as independent schools, referring to the fact that they're independent of the state system, although this is a misleading term, as not all independent schools are fee-paying.

Most private secondary schools are single-sex, at least until the sixth form, and most are day rather than boarding schools. Almost all of them are located in north, west and south London, rather than in the east. The best schools are very expensive and exclusive with long waiting lists, although it's generally easier to find places at short notice in outer London private schools. Fees for private schools vary from around £4,000 per annum in the least expensive day schools up to £15,000 or more for a boarding school place. It's worth bearing in mind that, although you may be living and working in London, your children can be educated further afield (for example, if you wish your children to attend a special school due to your religious beliefs or because they have a particular gift that you wish to foster). This may allow you to spread your net wider in search of the right school.

Children pass through several stages within the private school system. Preparatory schools take pupils from as young as two if they have a nursery or pre-prep department, or more usually from six or seven up to the age of 14. After prep school they progress to a senior school (sometimes confusingly called a 'public' school) where they take GCSE examinations at the age of around 16 and A-levels two years later, going to university at the age of 17 or 18.

Entry to some private schools involves a tough selection process, whereas others achieve good results from a wider ability range. Most day schools still use the '11 Plus' examination as an academic filter, while senior boarding schools tend to favour the Common Entrance Examination (CEE), usually taken two years later at the age of 13. Details and past papers of both tests are available from the Independent Schools Examinations Board (☎ 01425-621111, 🖥 www. iseb.co.uk).

Many private senior schools have associated junior, preparatory, pre-prep or even nursery schools. If you're likely to be staying in London for the majority of your children's education, this is a good way of ensuring continuity as they grow up.

The internet is a valuable resource when researching private schools in London, where the website of publisher John Catt Educational (☎ 01728-663666, 🖥 www.johncatt.co.uk) is an excellent starting point. It provides a free search facility via email, where you enter details about your child and your requirements for their education and they will search their database and suggest suitable schools. It also offers links to schools' own websites. Most private (and many state) schools have their own websites, which should be examined in conjunction with their printed prospectuses.

John Catt publishes a number of annually updated books about private schools, including *Boarding Schools & Colleges*, *Education at 16*, *International Schools*, *Preparatory Schools* and *Which London School?*.

Other useful resources for those interested in private education include the following:

- The **Independent Schools Council/ISC** (💻 www.iscis.co.uk) is the central body that co-ordinates and represents the interests of the various organisations concerned with private education in the UK, the most significant of which are listed below. Some 80 per cent of privately-educated children in the UK attend ISC schools.

- The **Girls' Day School Trust** (100 Rochester Row, London SW1P 1JP, ☎ 020-7393 6666, 💻 www.gdst.net) was founded in 1872 and was the pioneer of quality education for girls.

- The **Girls' Schools Association/GSA** (130 Regent Road, Leicester LE1 7PG, ☎ 0116-254 1619, 💻 www.gsa.uk.com) represents around 220 independent girls' schools throughout the UK.

- The **Headmasters' & Headmistresses' Conference/HMC** (12, The Point, Rockingham Road, Leicestershire, LE16 7QU, ☎ 0116-255 1567, 💻 www. hmc.org.uk) represents a membership of 250 heads of boys' and co-educational independent schools. The HMC is proud of the fact that their pupils come from a wide variety of backgrounds and that, although the assisted places scheme (whereby pupils receive government grants to attend private schools) is now being phased out, many schools still provide bursaries and scholarships for over a third of their pupils. Over 90 per cent of pupils go on to higher education.

- The **Independent Association Of Preparatory Schools/IAPS** (☎ 01926-887833, 💻 www.iaps.org.uk) is a professional body representing prep school heads throughout the UK and overseas. As well as completely independent prep schools, the association also represents schools affiliated to senior schools and offers day, boarding and, in some cases, flexible (e.g. weekday) boarding places. Schools range from rural to urban and single-sex to co-ed.

- The **Independent Schools Association of the Central States/ISACS** (☎ 01926 887833, 💻 www.isacs.org) has a membership of around 300 schools covering a wide variety of establishments, including nursery, prep, junior, senior, single-sex, co-ed, day and boarding schools.

- The **Society of Heads of Independent Schools/SHIS** (☎ 01858 433760, 💻 www.shmis.org.uk) represents a range of smaller independent schools, which include those catering for pupils with a specific religious orientation, pupils gifted in one of the performing arts and those with special needs. Most schools have around 300 pupils or fewer and are co-educational.

RELIGIOUS SCHOOLS

Schools linked to a particular church or religion include both state (e.g. many voluntary-aided schools) and private schools. The former often have wider catchment areas than other state schools, taking pupils from all over London who satisfy their entry requirements and whose families are devout. These include the Roman Catholic London Oratory School (favoured by the current Prime Minister) and Sacred Heart High School (both in Hammersmith), the Anglican girls' comprehensive Lady Margaret in Parson's Green and Hasmonean in Hendon, which serves the Jewish community.

Many private schools cater for particular religious beliefs. If you're looking for a fee-paying school with a particular religious affiliation, you should contact one of the organisations listed below:

● The **Catholic Education Service** (☎ 020-7901 4880, 🖳 www.cesew.org. uk) represents Catholic education interests in England and Wales with government and national agencies, advises teachers and supports the work of Catholic schools and colleges.

● The **British Sikh Education Council** (☎   0208 544 8037, 🖳 www.nsouk. co.uk) supports the religious and educational needs of Sikhs in the UK and assists parents, teachers and LEAs.

● The **Methodist Colleges & Schools Organisation** (☎   020 7935 3723, 🖳 www.methodisteducation.co.uk) takes administrative responsibility for Methodist colleges and schools and provides advice to the church on the formulation of educational policy.

● The **Muslim Educational Trust/MET** (☎ 020-7272 8502, 🖳 www.muslim-ed-trust.org.uk) is the UK's oldest national Muslim educational organisation dealing with the concerns of Muslim parents and children. The MET arranges for teachers to give lessons in Islamic Studies in English to Muslim children in state schools and publishes a range of internationally-orientated books and posters on Islam for use by pupils and teachers.

● The **United Synagogue Agency for Jewish Education** (☎ 020-8457 9700, 🖳 www.brijnet.org/aje) provides training for teachers, runs an educational resource centre and acts as a liaison between secular institutions and the Anglo-Jewish community. It also acts as the examination board and internal inspectorate for Jewish educational institutions.

SPECIALIST SCHOOLS

Specialist schools include those that develop particular skills, e.g. in technology, languages, sports or the arts, as well as those that provide for special educational needs. There are almost 2,000 schools (both day and boarding) in the UK for pupils with special educational needs (sometimes known as special schools), some of which are contained within hospitals. The typical pupil-teacher ratio in special schools is around 6:1 compared to 20:1 in mainstream state schools. However, the government wishes to see more special needs children entering mainstream schools.

All state secondary schools are eligible to apply for specialist school status if they can raise at least £100,000 in private sector sponsorship, prepare a three-year development plan and demonstrate provision to involve other schools and the wider community. If they succeed they receive an annual government grant of £100,000, plus £100 per pupil (up to a maximum of £100,000 a year) for three years.

State Specialist Schools

Specialist state schools in London include the following:

- **BRIT School For Performing Arts & Technology** (☎ 020-8665 5242, 💻 www.brit.croydon.sch.uk) in the borough of Croydon, which is the UK's only free performing arts school;

- **Archbishop Michael Ramsey Technology College** (☎ 020-7701 4166, 💻 www.amrtc.southwark.sch.uk) in Southwark, a Church of England school specialising in technology subjects;

- **Bethnal Green Technology College** (☎ 020-7920 7900) in Tower Hamlets, specialising in IT;

- **Islington Arts & Media School** (☎ 020-7281 5511, 💻 www.iamschool. co.uk) in the borough of Islington, specialising in dance, drama, music and the performing arts;

- **The London Nautical School** (☎ 020-7928 6801, 💻 www.lns.org.uk) in Lambeth, which 'prepares its pupils to meet the requirements of society, either at sea or in any other occupation';

- **Loxford School Of Science & Technology** (☎ 020-8514 4666) in Redbridge, specialising in maths, science and information and other technologies.

Private Specialist Schools

Some private schools provide education wholly or mainly for children with special educational needs or learning difficulties such as dyslexia. They're required to meet similar standards to those for maintained special schools and their pupils should have access to as much of the National Curriculum (see page 221) as possible. For example, the Dyslexia Institute, 2 Grosvenor Gardens, London SW1W 0DH is one of 27 UK centres under the auspices of the Dyslexia Institute (☎ 01784-222300, 💻 www.dyslexiaaction.org.uk), a charitable body responsible for setting up a range of institutes providing instruction and support for pupils and teachers dealing with dyslexia.

Other private schools provide a special education for gifted or talented children and include the following:

- **Choir Or Cathedral Schools** – If your son or daughter is blessed with an angelic voice, entering them for voice trials can be a wonderful way of ensuring that they receive a superior education for which you're usually required to pay only a portion of the fees. There isn't always a stipulation regarding religion, and musical talent is generally deemed more important than religious beliefs. For further information contact the Choir Schools' Association (☎ 01962 890530, 💻 www.choirschools.org.uk), which represents all cathedral and choir schools in England, of which three are in London: St Paul's Cathedral School, the Westminster Abbey Choir School and the Westminster Cathedral Choir School.

- **The Arts Educational School** (☎ 020-8987 6600, 💻 www.artsed.co.uk) in the borough of Hounslow, which specialises in all the arts, including dance, music, drama and literature;

- **BLA Theatre School** (☎ 020-8850 9888) in the borough of Greenwich, a small school specialising in the performing arts generally;

- **Italia Conti Academy Of Theatre Arts** (☎ 020-7608 0047, 💻 www.italiaconti.com) in the borough of Islington, Britain's first school of performing arts (founded in 1911 by the actress Italia Conti), specialising in dance, acting and singing;

- **The Royal Ballet School** (☎ 020-8392 8000, 💻 www.royal-ballet-school.org.uk) in the borough of Richmond, with separate locations for the lower and upper schools; admits pupils on the basis of their ability to dance rather than academic standard;

- **Sylvia Young Theatre School** (☎ 020-7402 0673, 🖳   www. sylviayoungtheatreschool.co.uk) in Westminster, specialising in music and dance as well as drama;

- **The Urdang Academy of Ballet** (☎ 020-7836 5709, 🖳 www. theurdangacademy.com) in Westminster.

The world-famous Italian teaching system, Montessori, is popular in London, mainly in the pre-school age range. Information is available from the Maria Montessori Training Organisation (26 Lyndhurst Gardens, Hampstead, London NW3 5NW, ☎ 020-7435 3646, 🖳   www.mariamontessori.org).

Further Information

The Advisory Centre for Education (ACE, ☎ 020-7354 8318, 🖳 www.ace-ed.org.uk) can answer questions and give advice on specialist education. Contact your local LEA for information about specialist schools in your area or write to the Department for Education and Skills (Sanctuary Buildings, Great Smith Street, London, SW1P 3BT), which publishes numerous booklets about special education. These are also downloadable from the DfES website (🖳 www.dfes.gov.uk/sen), where you can find a list of specialist schools throughout the UK. There are several books available for parents of children with special needs, including *Which? School for Special Needs* by Derek Bingham (John Catt Education).

INTERNATIONAL & FOREIGN

International schools teach foreign pupils in their home language but are also used by native Londoners who have family or working links with other countries or who simply want their children to be bilingual. London's international schools, as well as some of those teaching the curriculum of particular countries, are listed below.

- **American Community Schools** – There's one ACS in London, in Uxbridge in the borough of Hillingdon (☎ 01895-259771), and two just outside London, in Cobham (☎ 01932-867251) and Egham (☎ 01784-430800) in Surrey. Details of all three schools can be found on the ACS website (🖳 www.acs-england.co.uk).

- **American School in London** (☎ 020-7449 1200, 🖳 www.asl.org) in Westminster;

- **Centre Academy** (☎ 020-7738 2344, ▭ www.centreacademy.com) in Westminster, which offers both the US and the UK curriculum;

- **Hellenic College of London** (☎ 020-7581 5044, ▭ www.hellenic.org.uk) in Westminster, serving the Greek community;

- **International Community School** (☎ 020-7935 1206, ▭ www.ics.uk.net) in Westminster, part of the Skola Group of schools;

- **International School of London** (☎ 020-8992 5823, ▭ www.islondon. com) in the borough of Ealing, catering for all nationalities;

- **King Fahad Academy** (☎ 020-8743 0131, ▭ www.thekfa.org.uk) in the borough of Ealing, which serves the Arab community;

- **Lycée Français Charles de Gaulle** in Kensington & Chelsea (☎ 020-7584 6322, ▭ www.lyceefrancais.org.uk);

- **Marymount International School** (☎ 020-8949 0571, ▭ www. marymountlondon.com) in Kingston, which is part of a worldwide system of schools and colleges directed by the Sacred Heart of Mary, a Roman Catholic order;

- **Schiller International School** (☎ 020-7928 8484, ▭ www.schillerlondon. ac.uk) in Lambeth;

- **Southbank International School** (☎ 020-7229 8230, ▭ www.southbank. org) in Kensington & Chelsea (it was originally on the south bank!), which accepts pupils from the age of three and teaches the IB curriculum;

- **Woodside Park International School** (☎ 020-8920 0600, ▭ www.wpis. org) in Kingston.

For further information about schools teaching in a specific language contact your country's embassy in London (see **Appendix A**) or one of the organisations below.

- The **Council Of International Schools** (☎ 01730 263131, ▭ www.cois.org), a non-profit association of schools and higher education establishments;

- The **European Council Of International Schools** (☎ 01730 268244 ▭ www.ecis.org), a non-profit organisation with 436 member schools, including three in London.

UNIVERSITIES & COLLEGES

London has the largest student population of any city in the world, totalling some 250,000 students, many of whom are from overseas. EEA nationals can freely enter the UK but if you're a non-EEA national it's important to check whether you need a student visa (see **Permits & Visas** on page 89). If you require a visa, you will need to prove that you've been accepted for a full-time course of study, that you can meet the cost of your fees and maintenance (plus those of any dependants you bring with you) without recourse to public funds, and that you intend to leave the UK at the end of your course. London's universities and colleges are listed below.

Note that universities insist that students possess a reasonable command of English, which may be tested, before they're enrolled on a course. If your mother-tongue isn't English, you should check a college's prospectus or website for specific requirements.

- **The American University in London** (☎ 020-7263 2986, 🖥 www.aul.edu) in Islington;

- **American Intercontinental University London** (☎ 020-7486 1772, 🖥 www. aiulondon.ac.uk) in Westminster;

- **Brunel University** (☎ 01895-274000, 🖥 www.brunel.ac.uk) in Hillingdon;

- **City University** (☎ 020-7040 5060, 🖥 www.city.ac.uk) in Islington;

- **Huron University USA In London** (☎ 020-7584 9696, 🖥 www.huron.ac.uk) in Kensington & Chelsea;

- **Guildhall School Of Music & Drama** (☎ 020-7628 2571, 🖥 www. gsmd. ac.uk) in the City of London, specialising in all the performing arts;

- **Kingston University** (☎ 020-8547 2000, 🖥 www.kingston.ac.uk) in Kingston;

- **London Metropolitan University**, 2 Goulston Street, E1 (☎ university 020-7320 1000, students union ☎ 020-7247 1441, 🖥 www.lgu.ac.uk);

- **London South Bank University** (☎ 020-7928 8989, 🖥 www.lsbu.ac.uk) in Southwark;

- **Middlesex University** (☎ 020-8411 5000, 🖥 www.mdx.ac.uk) on the borders between Barnet, Enfield and Haringey;

- **Richmond American International University In London** (☎ 020-8332 9000, 🖥 www.richmond.ac.uk) in Richmond;

- **Roehampton University Of Surrey** (☎ 020-8392 3000, ⌨ www. roehampton.ac.uk) in Wandsworth ('Surrey' is presumably thought to sound better!);

- **Royal Academy Of Dramatic Art** (RADA, ☎ 020-7636 7076, ⌨ www. rada. org) in Camden, specialising in the performing arts;

- **Royal Academy Of Music** (RAM, ☎ 020-7873 7373, ⌨ www.ram.ac.uk) in Westminster, one of the foremost colleges for classical musicians in the UK;

- **Royal College Of Art** (RCA, ☎ 020-7590 4444, ⌨ www.rca.ac.uk) in Kensington & Chelsea, London's foremost art school;

- **Royal College Of Music** (RCM, ☎ 020-7589 3643, ⌨ www.rcm.ac.uk) in Kensington & Chelsea, one of the foremost colleges for classical musicians in the UK;

- **The Slade School Of Fine Art** (☎ 020-7504 2313, ⌨ www.ucl.ac.uk/slade). The Slade is a department of University College (part of the University of London – see below) and one of London's premier art schools;

- **Thames Valley University** (⌨ www.tvu.ac.uk), which has five campuses: three in Ealing – Ealing campus (☎ 020-8579 5000), the London College of Music, Media & Creative Technologies (☎ 020-8231 2304) and the Wolfson Institute of Health & Human Studies (☎ 020-8280 5252) – and two outside London, in Berkshire;

- **University Of East London** (☎ 020-8223 3000, ⌨ www.uel.ac.uk), which has a campus in Barking & Dagenham and three in Newham;

- **University Of Greenwich** (☎ 020-8331 8000, ⌨ www.greenwich.ac.uk) in Greenwich;

- **University Of London** (☎ 020-7862 8000, ⌨ www.lon.ac.uk), which has its heart in Bloomsbury but comprises around 30 colleges scattered across London: Birkbeck, Charing Cross, Goldsmiths, Heythrop, King's, Queen Mary, Royal Holloway (which is outside London, in Egham, Surrey), St Bartholomew's, University and Wye Colleges, plus the Westminster Medical School, Courtauld Institute of Art (see above), Eastman Dental Institute for Oral Health Care Sciences, Imperial College of Science, Technology and Medicine, the Institutes of Cancer Research, Child Health, Education and Psychiatry, the London Business School, London School of Economics & Political Science (LSE) and London School of Hygiene & Tropical Medicine, the Royal Free Hospital School of Medicine, Royal London Medical & Dental School, Royal Postgraduate Medical School and Royal Veterinary College, the School of Advanced Study, School of Oriental & African Studies and

School of Pharmacy, St George's hospital Medical School, the United Medical & Dental Schools, and the University of London Computer Centre;

- **University Of Westminster** (☎ 020-7911 5000, 💻 www.wmin.ac.uk) in Westminster.

Further Information

Links to the websites of all the above and other UK universities and colleges can be found on 💻 www.scit.wlv.ac.uk/ukinfo/alpha.html and 💻 www.web master. bham.ac.uk/ukuwww.html.

The Learning Skills Council (LSC, ☎ 0870-900 6800, 💻 www.lsc.gov.uk) is responsible for funding and planning education and training for over 16-year-olds in England and is a useful source of general information.

An invaluable organisation for overseas students is the Council for International Education (☎ 020-7107 9922, 💻 www.ukcosa.org.uk), which is a registered charity established in 1968 to promote the interests and meet the needs of overseas students in the UK and those working with them as teachers, advisors or in other capacities. Another important organisation is the British Council (☎ 020-7930 8466, 💻 www.britishcouncil.org), which has over 250 offices in some 110 countries and provides foreign students with information concerning all aspects of education in the UK.

For information about American universities in London, contact the Educational Advisory Service of The Fulbright Commission (☎ 020-7404 6880, 💻 www.fulbright.co.uk).

Courses

The UK offers the widest choice of university courses in Europe. The main categories of course are as follows:

- Three or four-year degree courses leading to qualifications such as Bachelor of Arts (BA) and Bachelor of Science (BSc). These tend to be taken by those who want a recognised academic qualification in a specific subject area, although there's scope to combine different subjects in a modular degree (see below).

- Two-year Higher National Diploma (HND) or Diploma of Higher Education (DHE) courses. These vocational courses are generally related to particular career areas such as agriculture, art and design, business studies, and hotel and catering. HNDs are made up of units of study and are usually taken over two years on a full-time basis. Courses may be longer if they include work experience or are taken part-time. HND students can sometimes subsequently transfer to the second (or occasionally third) year of a degree course, although the HND qualification is fully recognised by employers in its own right.

- The Higher National Certificate (HNC), which is usually taken part time by those in employment.

Part-time degree courses are normally taken over a longer period, which may vary according to the individual institution. As a general rule, you should allow at least five years for a part-time degree course. The distinction between part- and full-time study is becoming increasingly blurred and some institutions offer flexible arrangements to suit individual needs.

Many higher education establishments have adopted a modular structure for their courses which allows students to build a personalised degree by choosing modules or units of study from different subject areas. Modularity provides a high degree of flexibility and enables students to design personalised programmes to match their needs.

To check whether a university course and qualifications are accredited and internationally recognised, visit 💻 www.dfes.gov.uk/recognisedukdegrees/annex4.shtml or 💻 www.naric.org.uk or www.britishcouncil.org.

Tuition Fees

Students ordinarily resident in the UK or another EU country qualify as 'home' students. Overseas students ordinarily resident in the UK for a period of three years immediately prior to the start of a course are also treated as 'home' students, except where residence was wholly or mainly for educational purposes.

EU students enrolled on undergraduate courses must pay up to £1,025 per year. The exact amount payable is means-tested and dependent upon parental or individual income. Overseas undergraduate students should expect to pay up to £8,000 per year for an arts course, with annual fees increasing to £8,500 for engineering, £9,000 for computing and £10,000 for optometry. Overseas postgraduates fees range from £7,000 to £17,000. All fees are payable at the time of registration.

EU students are normally eligible to apply to the DfES for help with the payment of tuition fees. Further details can be obtained from the Department for Education & Skills, European Team, Student Support Division 1, 2F Area B Mowden Hall, Staindrop Road, Darlington DL3 9BG (☎ 01325-391199 or 0870-000 2288, 💻 www.dfes.gov.uk/studentsupport).

Living Expenses

As a student in London you will obviously need sufficient funds to support yourself on a day-to-day basis, i.e. to cover accommodation, food, clothing, travel, equipment, books and other incidental expenses. Under immigration regulations, you aren't usually permitted to work and study at the same time, so you cannot rely on topping up your wallet with casual wages from temporary work such as waiting or bartending. As a guide, you should have an income of around £8,000 to £10,000 per year if you're single and some £12,000 per year if you're married. You should also bear in mind that you could incur extra expenses when you first arrive in the UK, such as temporary hotel accommodation.

London can be expensive (see **Cost Of Living** on page 208), although many shops and companies provide student concessions. In order to qualify for them you must obtain a National Union of Students (NUS) card or an International Student Identity Card (ISIC), available from student union offices. Discounts are often available by showing your student card at theatres, cinemas, travel bureaux, driving schools, clothes shops and so on. Information about the discounts obtainable in London with an ISIC Card are available on the internet (🖥 www.nuscard.com) and students' unions also have information about the local discounts available.

Accommodation

General information about student accommodation is provided in university and college prospectuses. If you're a mature student or will have a family living with you, you will need to check the facilities offered and whether family accommodation is available. Many institutions have halls of residence, with or without catering facilities, some single-sex and some mixed. While a number of educational establishments guarantee accommodation for the first year, it's common for students in later years to rent accommodation. The staff at university accommodation offices can advise you about the costs and availability and may be able to help you find accommodation.

An increasing number of universities and colleges make specific housing provision for mature students and their families. You should, however, make enquiries with accommodation offices well in advance, particularly if you require family accommodation. The availability and cost of childcare facilities is also an important factor for families. If you're going to need support of this kind, you should contact the student services office of your chosen institution as far in advance as possible to check what childcare provision is available, what it costs and whether it will allow you sufficient time to study. Facilities vary considerably and there's stiff competition for places at a nursery or crèche; therefore, it's advisable to apply as early as possible. Facilities and costs vary considerably from one institution to another, which may be a key factor in determining where you study. Unless you're in a favourable financial position, you will probably have to make sacrifices as a student and shouldn't expect your accommodation and general standard of living to match what you've been used to.

International Students House/ISH (229 Great Portland Street, W1, ☎ 020-7631 8300, 🖥 www.ish,org.uk, Great Portland Street tube) is a useful meeting place for foreign students, where you can compare notes and share impressions of the life and studying in London. It also has single, twin and dormitory rooms available for visiting students as well as sports facilities, a bar and restaurant. ISH also operates an excellent travel club with cheap rates for students.

Student Entertainment

London provides a wealth of entertainment (see **Chapter 9**), in addition to which most universities have student unions, which are a valuable source of local information and support. Unions also provide excellent entertainment such as live music, often featuring world-class bands. Because student bars and entertainment are subsidised, most student unions admit only those with a student ID, so make sure that you have your NUS or ISIC card with you (see page 234). The best student unions in London include the following:

- **University Of London** (Malet Street, WC1, ☎ 020-7862 8000, ⌨ www.lon. ac.uk, Russell Square/Goodge Street tube), affectionately known as ULU. With two bars, this is probably London's trendiest student union, frequently offering the hottest up-and-coming bands. See them here first!

- **King's College** (Macadam Building, Surrey Street, WC2, ☎ 020-7836 5454, ⌨ www.kcl.ac.uk, Temple tube) vies with the ULU as the best student union in town. Following recent renovation it now boasts a great venue for live music as well as a bar serving meals.

- **University Of Westminster** (35 Marylebone Road, W1, ☎ 020-7911 5000, ⌨ www.wmin.ac.uk, Baker Street tube), as you might expect given its location, is the swankiest union in town.

- **Imperial College** (Beit Quad, Prince Consort Road, SW7, ☎ 020-7589 5111, ⌨ www3.imperial.ac.uk, South Kensington tube) is big, basic and friendly, with cheap beer.

Applications & Information

All applicants for entry to full-time first degree (undergraduate) courses at British universities must be made to the Universities and Colleges Admissions Service (UCAS, New Barn Lane or PO Box 28, Cheltenham GL52 3LZ, ☎ 0870-1122 211, ⌨ www.ucas.co.uk). Information will be sent as an automated response to an email enquiry (✉ enquiries@ucas.ac.uk). UCAS publishes the *UCAS University and College Entrance: The Official Guide* (updated annually, price £27) and *What Do Graduates Do?* (£10). A more detailed book, *The Complete Parent's Guide to Higher Education* (UCAS/Trotman and Co), is available from book shops. The British Council publishes *Studying and Living in the United Kingdom*, a guide for foreign students and visitors.

The NUS website (☎ 0845 045 1069, ⌨ www.nusonline.co.uk) is an invaluable source of information and advice on the courses available, your rights and what you can expect as a student in London. The free fortnightly newspaper, *London Student*, available in most student unions, is a mine of local information and the weekly *Time Out* entertainment magazine contains a student section. Time Out publishers also produce an annual *Student Guide*.

VOCATIONAL COURSES

In addition to establishments offering traditional academic courses, London offers a wealth of vocational courses, including those detailed below.

Childcare

If you're seeking a childcare qualification in preparation for working as a nanny or a nursery nurse, you will need to find a college providing training for a recognised childcare qualification. The National Nursery Examination Board's (NNEB) diploma is the best known and most widely recognised qualification in this field, covering care of children from birth to eight years of age. It's a full-time, two-year course comprising around 60 per cent theory and 40 per cent work experience on placements with families, nursery schools and hospital maternity units. If required, there's usually an opportunity for students to undertake a placement within a special needs environment.

The Business and Technical Education Council (BTEC) National Diploma in Nursery Nursing/Childcare and Education course covers many practical placements and can involve care of those in early education as well as very young children. The course covers care of sick children, growth and development, and community assignments. This is often a more flexible option than the NNEB course but involves up to 800 hours' work experience.

Alternatively, you can undertake the National Association of Maternal and Child Welfare (NAMCW) diploma, which also lasts two years and involves both practical experience and attendance at college, or the shorter one-year NAMCW certificate course. However, the NAMCW alone isn't generally recognised as a suitable qualification for a position in a day nursery and, if you're planning to work in this field, the NNEB or BTEC are preferable.

For more information about qualifications in childcare contact the Council for Awards in Children's Care and Education (CACHE), 8 Chequer Street, St Albans, Herts, AL1 3XZ (☎ 01727-818616, ⌨ www.cache.org.uk).

Cookery

Many people planning to enter the restaurant trade or train as chefs do so by taking catering courses at higher education establishments or by training 'on-the-job' as assistants or sous-chefs at one of London's better restaurants. However, Leith's School of Food and Wine (☎ 020-7229 0177, 💻 www. leiths. com) in Kensington & Chelsea is one of several establishments in the capital offering professional training for career cooks and qualification for those wishing to enter the highly competitive food and wine business. (Leith's also provides short courses and evening classes for 'amateurs'.)

ENGLISH-LANGUAGE SCHOOLS

Teaching English as a second language is big business in the UK, particularly in London, where there are dozens of English-language schools. However, the cost and quality of teaching can vary considerably and it's advisable to enrol with a reputable school such as one that is a member of the Association of Recognised English Language Services (ARELS) which has around 90 schools in the capital. For further details of these and other schools contact ARELS (56 Buckingham Gate, London SW1E 6AG, ☎ 020-7802 9200, 💻 www.arels.org.uk).

EVENING CLASSES & DISTANCE LEARNING

Evening classes in London range from spare-time interests such as flower-arranging and painting to academic and vocational courses leading to recognised qualifications in subjects such as information technology and accounting. Classes are usually provided by local education authorities. The bible for part-time courses in London is *Floodlight Part-Time*, a guide to part-time day and evening classes. *Summertime Floodlight* is a guide to summer courses in Greater London. Both are published by Floodlight Publishing and available direct from them (💻 www.floodlight.co.uk) and from book shops and newsagents in London.

Those who need (or prefer) to study at home or whose job frequently takes them away from home can enrol in a distance learning course. The Open University (OU), established in 1969, is the best known provider of such courses and offers everything from vocational qualifications to undergraduate and research degrees. Although jokes are often made about course programmes going out on TV at 5am, the widespread ownership of video recorders means that programmes can be viewed at a more 'civilised' hour. There are also courses that can be done via the internet. For information contact the London branch of the OU at 1–11 Hawley Crescent, Camden Town, London NW1 8NP (☎ 020-7485 6597, 💻 www3.open.ac.uk).

The UK's largest provider of distance learning courses, the National Extension College (NEC), offers written home study courses and, depending on circumstances, the support of a local college should you need it. Qualifications offered primarily focus on GCSEs, A-levels and National Vocational Qualifications (NVQs). For information contact the National Extension College (☎ 01223-400200, 💻 www.nec.ac.uk).

The London School of Journalism (126 Shirland Road, Maida Vale, London W9 2BT, ☎ 020-7289 7777, 💻 www.lsj.org) is the longest-established writing school in Europe (founded in 1920) and runs summer schools for prospective journalists and writers as well as offering correspondence courses.

8

STAYING HEALTHY

One of the most important aspects of living in London (or anywhere else for that matter) is maintaining good health. The UK is famous for its National Health Service (NHS), which provides 'free' healthcare to all British citizens and most foreign residents. The standard of training, dedication and medical skills of British doctors and nursing staff is among the highest in the world, and British medical science is in the vanguard of many of the world's major medical advances (many pioneering operations are performed in the UK). Many foreigners visit the UK for private medical treatment, and Harley Street in London is internationally recognised as having some of the world's pre-eminent (and most expensive) specialists, encompassing every conceivable ailment.

If you don't qualify for healthcare under the public health service, it's essential to have private health insurance (in fact, you may not qualify for a residence permit without it). This is often advisable in any case if you can afford it, owing to the inadequacy of public health services in many areas and long waiting lists for specialist appointments and non-urgent operations. Visitors to the UK should have holiday health insurance if they aren't covered by a reciprocal arrangement.

If you're taking regular medication, you should bear in mind that the brand names of medicines vary from country to country, and should ask your doctor for the generic name. If you wish to match medication prescribed abroad, you will need a prescription with the medication's trade name, the manufacturer's name, the chemical name and the dosage. Most medicines have an equivalent in other countries, although particular brands may be difficult or impossible to obtain in the UK. It's also advisable to take some of your favourite non-prescription medicines (e.g. aspirins, cold and flu remedies and lotions) with you, as they may be difficult to find or much more expensive. If applicable, you should also take a spare pair of spectacles, contact lenses, dentures or a hearing aid.

If you're planning to take up residence in London, even for part of the year only, you may wish to have a health check before your arrival, particularly if you have a record of poor health or are elderly. There are no special health risks in the UK and no immunisations are required unless you arrive from an area infected with yellow fever. You can safely drink the water (unless there's a sign to the contrary), although it sometimes tastes awful, and many people prefer bottled water (when not drinking tea, wine or beer!).

EMERGENCIES

If you're unlucky enough to be involved in an accident or suffer a sudden serious illness in the UK, you will be pleased to know that emergency transport by ambulance and treatment at a hospital Accident & Emergency (A&E) department is free to everyone. In a medical emergency, simply dial 999 from any telephone (calls are free) and ask for the ambulance service. State your name and location and describe your injuries or symptoms (or those of the patient) and an ambulance with paramedics will be despatched immediately to take you to hospital (the time you must wait will depend on your location and how busy the ambulance service is at that time). **Calls to 999 must be made in emergencies only and health authorities can levy a fee if an emergency ambulance is called unnecessarily.** The UK doesn't have a national air ambulance service, although there are emergency helicopter services in London for critical cases.

In minor 'emergencies' or for medical advice, you should phone your family doctor if you have one. Failing this you can ring a directory enquiries service, such as ☎ 118 118 or 11 88 88, for the telephone number of a local doctor or hospital (or consult your phone book). Police stations keep a list of doctors' and chemists' private telephone numbers, in case of emergency. There are private 24-hour doctors' and dental services in London that make house calls, but check the cost before using them (see the yellow pages).

If you're able, you can go to the A&E department of an NHS general hospital, many of which provide a 24-hour service. Check in advance which local hospitals are equipped to deal with emergencies and the fastest route from your home. This information may be of vital importance in the event of an emergency, when a delay could mean the difference between life and death. Not all London hospitals have A&E departments and, of those that do, not all are open round the clock. Hospitals in inner London (there are more in the outer suburbs) with 24-hour emergency facilities include the following:

- **Central** – St Mary's Hospital, Praed Street, W2 1NY (☎ 020-7886 6666, 🖳 www.st-marys.nhs.uk, Paddington tube) and University College Hospital, Cecil Flemming House, Grafton Way, WC1E 6DB (☎ 020-7387 9300, 🖳 www.uclh.org, Euston Square/Warren Street tube);

- **East** – Hackney & Homerton Hospital, Homerton Row, E9 6SR (☎ 020-8510 5555, 🖳 www.homerton.nhs.uk, Homerton rail) and Royal London Hospital, Whitechapel Road, E1 1BB (☎ 020-7377 7000, 🖳 www.bartsandthe london. org.uk, Whitechapel tube/Liverpool Street rail);

- **North** – Royal Free Hospital, Pond Street, NW3 2QG (☎ 020-7794 0500, 🖳 www.royalfree.org.uk, Belsize Park tube) and Whittington Hospital, St Mary's Wing, Highgate Hill, N19 5NF (☎ 020-7272 3070, 🖳 www. whittington.nhs.uk, Archway tube);

- **South** – St Thomas's Hospital, Lambeth Palace Road, SE1 7EH (☎ 020-7188 7188, 🖳 www.hospital.org.uk, Waterloo/Westminster tube), Guy's Hospital, St Thomas Street, SE1 9RT (☎ 020-7188 7188, 🖳 www.hospital.org.uk, London Bridge tube) and St George's Hospital, Blackshaw Road, SW17 0QT (☎ 020-8672 1255, 🖳 www.st-georges.org.uk, Tooting Broadway tube);

8

- **West** – Charing Cross Hospital, Fulham Palace Road, London, W6 8RF (☎ 020-8846 1234/1799, Barons Court/Hammersmith tube) and Chelsea & Westminster Hospital, 369 Fulham Road, SW10 9NH (☎ 020-8746 8000/8484, 💻 www.chelwest.nhs.uk, bus Nos 14, 73, 211).

It's advisable to keep a record of the telephone numbers of your doctor, local hospitals and clinics, ambulance service, first aid, poison control, dentist, and other emergency services next to your telephone.

Medic-Alert

If you have a rare blood group or a medical problem that cannot easily be seen or recognised, e.g. a heart condition, diabetes, epilepsy, haemophilia or a severe allergy, you should join Medic-Alert. Medic-Alert members wear a necklace or bracelet containing an internationally recognised symbol and engraved with their medical problem, membership number and a telephone number. When you're unable to speak for yourself, doctors, police or anyone providing aid can immediately obtain vital medical information from anywhere in the world by phoning a 24-hour emergency number. Medic-Alert is a non-profit registered charity and life membership is included in the cost of the bracelet or necklace (costing from £19.95) plus an annual £19.95 fee. For more information contact the Medic-Alert Foundation, 1 Bridge Wharf, 156 Caledonian Road, London N1 9UU (☎ 020-7833 3034, 💻 www.medicalert.co.uk).

NATIONAL HEALTH SERVICE

The National Health Service (NHS) was established in 1948 to ensure that everyone had equal access to medical care. NHS services include family doctors, specialists, hospitals, dentists, chemists, opticians, community health services (e.g. the district nursing and health visitor services), the ambulance service, and maternity and child health care. Originally, all NHS medical treatment was free, the service being funded entirely from general taxation and National Insurance contributions. However, as the cost of treatment and medicines has increased, part of the cost has been passed onto patients via supplementary charges. While hospital treatment, the ambulance service and consultations with doctors remain free, most patients must now pay fixed charges for prescriptions, dental treatment, sight tests and NHS glasses, although charges are usually well below the actual cost. Family doctors, called General Practitioners (GPs), still make free house calls and community health workers and district nurses visit people at home who are convalescent or bedridden or have newborn babies.

The quality of service you receive from the NHS depends very much on where you live, as waiting lists for specialist appointments and hospital beds vary from area to area. In fact, even the treatment you receive varies according to your local health authority, some of which don't provide certain expensive treatment (e.g. for cancer), as they simply cannot afford it.

The NHS provides free or subsidised medical treatment to all British nationals and foreigners with the right of abode in the UK and to anyone who, at the time of treatment, has been a resident for the previous year. Exceptions to the one-year qualifying rule include European Union (EU) nationals (with a form E111), refugees or those with 'exceptional leave to remain' in the UK, students on a course of over six months, foreign nationals coming to take up permanent residence in the UK, certain groups of sailors and offshore workers, non-EU recipients of British war disablement pensions, overseas crown servants, British pensioners living abroad, NATO personnel stationed in the UK, prisoners, anyone with a permit to work in the UK, and the spouse and children of the above.

Nationals of countries with reciprocal health agreements with the UK also receive free or subsidised medical treatment, including all EU nationals and citizens of Anguilla, Australia, the Balkan States, Barbados, British Virgin Islands, Bulgaria, Channel Islands, the Czech Republic, Falkland Islands, Gibraltar, Hong Kong, Hungary, Iceland, Isle of Man, Malta, Montserrat, New Zealand, Norway, Poland, Romania, Russia (and other former Soviet states excluding Latvia, Lithuania and Estonia), the Slovak Republic, St Helena, and the Turks & Caicos Islands. Exemption from charges for nationals of the above countries is generally limited to emergency or urgent treatment (e.g. for a communicable disease) required during a visit to the UK.

Anyone who doesn't qualify under one of the above categories must pay for all medical treatment received, although minor medical and dental emergencies may be treated free of charge, e.g. emergency treatment at a hospital outpatients department as a result of an accident or admission to hospital for no longer than one night.

In the last few decades, there have been sweeping NHS reforms, which have included self-governing hospitals, practice and prescribing budgets for GPs, funding and contracts for hospital services, and the creation of an NHS internal market. The NHS has traditionally been a political football and some of the reforms introduced by the Conservative government in the '80s and '90s are now being reversed by the Labour government. The services provided by the NHS have come under increasing pressure in recent years, largely as a result of a lack of funding by central government and the increasing demands on the NHS from an ageing population.

In April 2002, England's 95 existing Health Authorities were replaced by 28 larger Strategic Health Authorities (StHAs). London's 14 Health Authorities merged to create five StHAs. These are the North Central London StHA (☎ 020-7756 2500) the North East London StHA (☎ 020-7655 6600), the North West London StHA (☎ 020-7756 2500), the South East London StHA (☎ 020-7716 7000) and South West London StHA (☎ 020-8545 6000). The StHAs are responsible for health services within their areas. They also manage the performance of Primary Care Trusts (PCTs) and NHS Trusts.

One of the most serious problems facing the NHS is a chronic shortage of staff, particularly nurses (especially specialist-trained nurses), midwives, and health visitors, who have been leaving the NHS at a rate of up to 50,000 a year. The main problem is low salaries (one in five nurses is forced to take a second job to survive), although poor working conditions, long hours (the hours worked by junior doctors in NHS hospitals is a national scandal), a lack of resources and stress also take their toll. It's undeniable that NHS health services aren't as universally available as they once were. The best GPs and dentists in London have waiting lists.

A lack of doctors has meant that many hospitals and deputising services are forced to recruit an increasing number of doctors from abroad. Foreign doctors have flooded into the UK in recent years. It's estimated that over 25 per cent of NHS doctors have qualified overseas; among junior doctors the proportion is almost 40 per cent. One-fifth of all GPs practising in the UK are now from overseas, and some of them speak poor English or lack sufficient experience. The bulk of supply or locum doctors (who fill shortages when doctors are on holiday or sick) are also foreign. Although the UK doesn't train enough doctors, it also loses many doctors to other countries. Lack of funds have also resulted in hospital ward closures, long waiting lists for specialist appointments and hospital beds (patients are often left on trolleys in hospital corridors because no beds are available), cancelled operations, and long queues in doctors' surgeries and hospital waiting rooms.

Although funding has been increasing (in real terms) for a number of years, demand is rising at an ever-faster rate. Lack of resources has meant that NHS health services have to be rationed and decided on the basis of a patient's chances of recovery or life expectancy. This means the elderly and obese, heavy smokers and alcoholics have little chance of receiving expensive life-saving operations such as heart surgery and transplants on the NHS. There are long waiting lists for non-vital procedures such as hip replacements, varicose vein surgery, hernia operations and even sterilisation. The present government is attempting to address the NHS problems by injecting extra funds and resources, although it will take many years to resolve the problems of under-staffing and eradicate the waiting lists (if it's ever possible). Under current targets, the NHS plans to have no one waiting more than six months for treatment and are hoping to challenge this commitment to deliver a maximum of 18 weeks.

Another problem that requires addressing is how to tackle the long-term needs of an ageing population. Many people believe that more resources should be channelled into preventive medicine rather than cure, in particular the promotion of regular exercise and a healthy diet.

PRIVATE HEALTH INSURANCE

If you are not covered by the NHS, you should take out private health insurance, as medical treatment in the UK can be very expensive, the cost of an operation and hospitalisation running into thousands of pounds. The number of people with private health insurance in the UK increased from around 1.5 million in 1966 to some 8 million at the end of 2006, half of whose premiums are paid by their employers. The remainder is spilt between those who pay their own premiums and those who share them with their employers. Private health care is restricted mainly to the middle to upper income brackets. The main advantage of private health insurance is the reduced waiting time for non-emergency operations. One in five operations in the UK is performed privately.

Most patients who receive private health treatment in the UK are insured with provident associations such as BUPA and PPP, which pay for specialist and hospital treatment only and don't include routine visits to doctors and dentists (which are covered by the NHS). Private patients are free to choose their own specialists and hospitals and are usually accommodated in a private, hotel-style room with a radio, telephone, colour TV, en-suite bathroom and room service. Although some health checks and scans are available on demand under the NHS or with private health insurance, many aren't (including the most expensive). Private policies don't, for example, include a comprehensive health check-up or screening, which can be performed at private clinics throughout the UK for around £200 to £300.

Private health insurance isn't usually intended to replace NHS treatment but to complement it. Most health insurance policies fall into one of two main categories: those providing immediate private specialist or hospital treatment (e.g. BUPA, PPP and WPA) and so-called 'budget' or 'waiting-list' policies, where you're treated as a private patient only when waiting lists exceed a certain period. Under waiting-list policies, if you cannot obtain an appointment with an NHS specialist or an NHS hospital admission within a certain period (e.g. six weeks), you can do so as a private patient.

The cost of private health insurance depends on your age and the state of your health. There are maximum age limits for taking out health insurance with some insurers, e.g. 65 for BUPA, although age limits may be higher if you're willing to accept some restrictions. Some companies have special policies for those aged over 50 or 55. There are generally no restrictions on continuing membership, irrespective of age. Treatment of any medical condition for which you've already received medical attention or were aware existed up to five years before the start date of the policy may not be covered. However, existing health problems (often referred to as 'pre-existing' conditions) are usually covered after two years' membership, provided that no further medical attention has been necessary during this period. Some group policies do, however, include cover for existing or previous health problems. Other exclusions are listed in the policy rules.

Standard policies may offer three scales (usually designated A, B and C) of hospital treatment, which may include London NHS teaching hospitals (A, high scale), provincial NHS teaching hospitals (B, medium scale) and provincial non-teaching hospitals (C, low scale). Accommodation is usually in a private room, but in some hospitals it may be in a twin or four-bedded ward. Premiums range from a few pounds a week for a budget plan offering limited benefits (e.g. HSA) up to hundreds of pounds a month for a comprehensive policy with a major insurance company. Comprehensive, top-of-the-range cover costs from £40 a month for a single person and from around £100 for a family (some companies offer lower premiums but have a compulsory annual excess of £500 or £1,000).

When deciding on the type and extent of health insurance, make sure that it covers **all** your family's present and future health requirements in the UK **before** you receive a large bill. A health insurance policy should cover you for essential health care required as a result of an accident and injuries (e.g. a sporting injury), whether they occur in your home, at your place of work or when travelling. Don't take anything for granted, but check in advance that you're covered. Long-stay visitors should have travel or long-stay health insurance or an international health policy. If your stay in London is limited, you may be covered by a reciprocal agreement between your home country and the UK (see **National Health Service** on page 250).

If you need private treatment in the UK, you may be required to pay in advance and reclaim the cost from your insurance company later, although some foreign insurers will pay bills directly (in which case your choice of hospital may be limited). If you must pay up front, you will need to ensure that you have sufficient funds available to pay for medical care while you're in the UK and that you understand how to make claims.

PRIVATE HEALTH TREATMENT

If you aren't entitled to treatment under the NHS, you will be treated as a private patient by a doctor or hospital (except in an emergency) and the cost will be borne by you or your health insurance company. Private hospital care in the UK is provided in private clinics and hospitals, which are completely independent of the NHS, and in private wings or wards of large NHS hospitals. Private patients can choose to pay for treatment in most NHS hospitals and NHS consultants also treat private patients.

In addition to specialist appointments and hospital treatment, people commonly use private health treatment to obtain second opinions, and for private health checks and screening, complementary medicine and cosmetic surgery. Over 6 million people have private health insurance of some kind in the UK and around a quarter of all operations are performed privately. If you need to see a GP or specialist privately, you (or your insurance company) must pay the full fee, which is usually left to the doctor's discretion. You should expect to pay at least £30 for a routine visit to a GP.

London's Harley Street is the most famous address for private medicine in the UK (and possibly the world), where leading practitioners are skilled in virtually every medical discipline, from cardiac surgery to liposuction. It has the greatest concentration of medical expertise anywhere in the world, with over 1,400 specialist medical and dental consultants and practitioners in 'residence'. If money's no object and you're seeking the best treatment available, your first stop should be the website of The Harley Street Bureau (☎ 0171 580 9966 ⌨ www.harleystreet medical.com/bureau), which is a non-profit organisation that provides a free service to patients seeking specialist private medical services. Simply fill in the online questionnaire and the bureau will provide details regarding the availability of treatment in the area.

Always make sure that a 'doctor' or medical practitioner is qualified to provide the treatment you require, as (surprisingly) anyone can call himself a doctor in the UK. When selecting a private specialist or clinic, you should be extremely cautious and only choose someone who has been recommended by a doctor or organisation that you can trust. It's sometimes advisable to obtain a second opinion, particularly if you're diagnosed as having a serious illness or requiring a major operation (but don't expect your doctor or specialist to approve). According to some reports, unnecessary operations are becoming increasingly common in the UK. Private patients don't have the same protection as NHS patients, although complaints about treatment paid for by a private health insurance policy may be taken up by your insurance company. As a last resort, you can complain to the General Medical Council, provided a medical practitioner is a qualified doctor.

Note that the quality of private treatment isn't necessarily superior to that provided by the NHS and you shouldn't assume that because a doctor (or any other medical practitioner) is in private practice he is more competent than his NHS counterpart. In fact, often you will see the same specialist or be treated by the same surgeon on the NHS and privately. If you see a private doctor, his offices will be plush and welcoming, you will be greeted courteously by his receptionist, he will have more time to spend on you (NHS GPs can be abrupt and even downright rude!) and his bedside manner will be impeccable. However, he won't necessarily be a better doctor than the one in the high street community clinic.

Drop-In Medicentres

An innovation in recent years has been the introduction of private drop-in 'medicentres' (☎ 0870-600 0870, ⌨ www.medicentre.co.uk) where doctors and nurses are on hand for consultations and to perform tests, screening, health checks, vaccinations and minor treatment. A medicentre offers a walk-in service – there's no need to be registered and you don't require an appointment. Medicentres are located in the high street, e.g. in branches of Boots the chemist, and in shopping centres. Patients pay around £60 for a consultation and package deals are available from insurers such as Norwich Union (☎01603 622200, 💻 www.norwichunion.com). Medical Express, 117a Harley Street, W1 (☎ 020 7499 1991, Mondays to Fridays 9am to 6pm, Saturdays 9.30am to 2.30pm) operates a walk-in casualty clinic and health screening service in central London.

COMPLEMENTARY MEDICINE

Growing fears about the side-effects of medicines and general disillusionment with the NHS have led to a huge growth in complementary (or alternative) medicine in the last decade, although the UK is still way behind many other EU countries, particularly France and Germany. Complementary medicine is is chosen by some 5 million British patients a year, although with the exception of certain fields such as acupuncture, chiropractic, homeopathy and osteopathy it isn't usually covered by the NHS or private health insurance in the UK. To find a homeopath or homeopathic chemist in your area, contact the British Homeopathic Association, Hahnemann House, 29 Park Street West, Luton LU1 (☎0870 444 3950). London is also the base for Europe's largest provider of complementary medicine, the Royal London Homeopathic Hospital NHS Trust, which is the only independent public sector hospital in Europe dedicated to complementary medicine. If you're seeking a chiropractor, contact the British Chiropractic Association, 59 Castle Street, Reading, RG1 7SN (☎ 0118-950 5950, 💻 www.chiropractic-uk.co.uk). To find a doctor practising acupuncture, contact the British Acupuncture Council, 63 Jeddo Road, London, W12 9HQ (☎ 020-8735 0400, 💻 www.acupuncture.org.uk) and for a holistic practitioner contact the British Holistic Medical Association, PO Box 371, Bridgwater, Somerset, TA6 9BG (☎ 01278 722000, 💻 www.bhma.org.uk). If you're interested in Reflexology, the specialist foot massage therapy, contact the Association of Reflexologists, 5 Fore Street, Taunton, Somerset, TA1 1HX (☎ 0870-567 3320, 💻 www.aor.org.uk) to find a therapist in your area. A list of professional bodies governing alternative medical practitioners is contained in the *Time Out Guide to Shopping & Services in London*.

DOCTORS

There are excellent family doctors, generally referred to as General Practitioners (GPs), in all areas of Britain. The best way to find a doctor, whether as a NHS or a private patient, is to ask your colleagues, friends or neighbours if they can recommend someone. Alternatively you can consult a list of GPs for your Strategic Health Authority in your Community Health Council (CHC) office or contact your local Family Health Services Authority (FHSA). FHSAs publish lists of doctors, dentists, chemists and opticians in their areas. These are available at libraries, post offices, tourist information offices, police stations and Citizens' Advice Bureaux. You can also look up doctors in the Medical Directory, available in public reference libraries. If you're a student, some colleges have a student health centre, where you should register. GPs or family doctors are listed under Doctors (Medical Practitioners) in yellow pages.

Surgery hours vary but are typically from 8.30am to 6pm or 7pm, Mondays to Fridays, with early closing one day a week, e.g. 5pm or 5.30pm on Fridays (evening surgeries may also be held on one or two evenings a week). Emergency surgeries may be held on Saturday mornings, e.g. from 8.30 to 11.30am or noon. Most doctors' surgeries have answering machines outside surgery hours, when a recorded message informs you of the name of the doctor on call (or deputising service) and his telephone number.

GP fundholding, under which individual GP practices had control of their own healthcare budgets, was scrapped in favour of a system of Primary Care Trusts by New Labour in 1999. The old system, introduced by the Conservative government in 1991, allowed GPs to manage their own budgets, enabling them to shop around and buy services for their patients direct from hospitals and other health service providers. However, fundholding created a two-tier health system, patients of non-fundholders being disadvantaged by longer waits for hospital beds and a more limited range of services because their GPs couldn't shop around. Under the new system of GP commissioning and Primary Care Trusts, committees of around 50 GPs decide together, and in collaboration with other health and social services professionals chosen by the government, how NHS budgets should be spent in their area.

NHS Doctors

NHS doctors are contracted by their local FHSA to look after a number of patients (average around 2,000) who make up their list. Doctors are paid by the NHS according to the number of NHS-registered patients on their list and an NHS doctor can refuse to register you as a patient if he has no vacancies. If you're looking for an NHS doctor, you must live within a doctor's catchment area. If you have trouble getting onto an NHS doctor's list, contact your local FHSA, which has a duty to find you a doctor. If you're living in a district for less than three months or have no permanent home, you can apply to any doctor in the district as a temporary resident. After three months, you must register with the doctor as a permanent patient or you may register with another doctor. An NHS doctor must give 'immediate necessary treatment' for up to 14 days to anyone without a doctor in his area, until the patient has been accepted by a doctor as a permanent or temporary resident.

Group Practices

Around 80 per cent of GPs work in a partnership or group practice, around 25 per cent of those in health centres, which provide a range of medical and nursing services. Health centres may have facilities for immunisation, cervical smears, health education (known as a 'well person clinic'), family planning, speech therapy, chiropody, hearing tests, physiotherapy and remedial exercises. Many also include dental, ophthalmic, hospital outpatient and social work support. Most health centres and group practices have district nurses, health visitors, midwives and clinical psychologists in attendance at fixed times.

If your doctor is part of a partnership or group practice, when he's absent you will automatically be treated by a partner or another doctor (unless you wish to wait until your doctor returns). All NHS GPs must produce practice guides for patients, containing the names of the doctors, times of surgeries and any special services provided, such as ante-natal, family planning, 'well woman' or diabetic clinics.

It's often advisable to meet a prospective doctor before deciding whether to register with him. When you've found a suitable NHS doctor who'll accept you (a doctor can refuse to accept a patient or remove anyone from his list without giving a reason), you must register with him by completing part A of your medical card and giving it to his receptionist. If you don't have an NHS medical card, you must complete a form provided by the GP, which he will send to the local FHSA (which will send you a medical card within a few weeks of registration).

Appointments & House Calls

Most doctors operate an appointment system, where you must make an appointment in advance. You cannot just turn up during surgery hours and expect to be seen. If you're an urgent case (but not an emergency), your doctor will usually see you immediately, but you should still phone in advance. Surgeries are often very busy and you may have to wait well past your appointment time to see a doctor. NHS doctors make free house calls and emergency visits outside surgery hours (at their discretion) in cases where patients are bedridden or unable to visit their surgery. In the UK, a doctor is responsible for his patients 24 hours a day and, when he's unavailable, must make alternative arrangements, either through his partners in a group practice, a voluntary rota between individual doctors or a commercial deputising service. When you call your GP outside normal hours, he's unlikely to attend you personally at home. Most GPs use an outside medical service, which exists to provide house calls and an 'after hours' service.

Changing Doctors

Under recent NHS reforms, it's easy to change doctors: you don't need to inform your old doctor and can simply visit a new doctor's surgery and ask to be registered. If, out of courtesy, you inform your existing doctor that you intend to change, be careful what reason you give, as doctors tend to be wary of accepting a patient who has had a 'disagreement' with a colleague. One 'legitimate' reason for changing doctors is that you wish to be treated by a doctor of the opposite sex to your present one (it's hard luck if all doctors in your area are of the same sex).

Your doctor is able to give advice or provide information on any aspect of health or medical after-care, including preventive medicine, blood donations, home medical equipment and special counselling. If you're an NHS patient, he should also be able to advise you about the range of medical benefits provided under the NHS, including maternity care, contraceptive help and psychiatric treatment. NHS patients must always be referred by a GP to a specialist, e.g. an eye specialist, gynaecologist or orthopaedic surgeon.

If you'd like a second opinion on any health matter, you may ask to see a specialist, although, unless it's a serious matter, your doctor will probably refuse to refer you. If your doctor refuses, you won't be able to obtain a second opinion from another NHS doctor unless you change doctors. The only other possibility is to consult another doctor or specialist as a private patient. Patients who have a foreign (i.e. not British) private health insurance policy may be free to make appointments directly with specialists. **In many cases where a second opinion is sought, the second doctor doesn't confirm the first doctor's diagnosis.** GPs often drop patients who ask questions and almost 100,000 are removed from GP lists each year. Most GPs don't like answering medical questions or patients who question or refuse treatment or ask for a second opinion - you're simply supposed to do as you're told!

Complaints

If you have a complaint against your NHS GP, you should first contact your local FHSA, usually within eight weeks of the event. If you need help to make a complaint, you can ask your Community Health Council or a Citizens' Advice Bureau. In the event of serious professional misconduct, your complaint will be passed to the General Medical Council. Information booklets are published by the British Medical Association (BMA) and are available from doctors' surgeries, clinics and chemists or direct from the BMA.

CHEMISTS & MEDICINES

Medicines ('drugs' in British English normally refers to illegal drugs or narcotics) are obtained from a chemist (pharmacy) in the UK, most of which provide free advice regarding minor ailments and suggest appropriate medicines. There are three categories of medicine in the UK: those that can be prescribed only by a doctor (via an official form called a prescription) and purchased from a chemist; medicines that can be sold only with the approval of a chemist; and general-sale medicines (such as aspirin and paracetamol) that can be sold in outlets such as petrol stations and supermarkets.

Some medicines requiring a doctor's prescription in the UK are sold freely in other countries, although other medicines that are controlled elsewhere are freely available in the UK. Increasing numbers of previously restricted medicines are now available over the counter. Some medicines aren't recognised by the NHS, in which case your doctor will usually inform you and may offer to prescribe an alternative. If you insist on having an unrecognised medicine, you must usually pay for it yourself. Requests for repeat prescriptions may be accepted by your doctor by post or telephone. If you have regular repeat prescriptions, you can have a chemist pick up your prescription from your doctor. Many chemists use a computer to keep information about the health problems and medicines of regular customers.

If you need medicines after normal hours, there are a number of chemists that regularly open late in central London including Bliss (5/6 Marble Arch, W1H 7AP, ☎ 020-7723 6116), which is open from 9am until midnight daily, and Boots (75 Queensway, W2 4QH, ☎ 020-7229 9266, 🖥 www.wellbeing.com), open from 9am to 10pm Mondays to Saturdays and from 2pm to 10pm on Sundays. If you require medicine urgently when all chemists' are closed, you should contact your GP or local police station.

To obtain medicines prescribed by a doctor, simply take your prescription form to any chemist. Your prescription may be filled immediately if it's available off the shelf or you may be asked to wait or come back later. NHS prescriptions for medicines are charged at a fixed rate of £6.75 per item, although certain categories of person qualify for free medicines (see below). Prepayment certificates cost £33.90 for four months (you save money if you have more than four prescriptions) and £93.20 for a year (you save if you have more than 12 prescriptions). You can order by telephone (☎ 0845-850 0030) or online (🖥 www.ppa.org.uk).

Many people qualify for free prescriptions, including hospital outpatients and day patients, children under 16, students under 19 in full-time education, pensioners (men over 65, women over 60), expectant mothers and those who have had a baby in the last year, those with certain medical conditions (e.g. diabetes or epilepsy) or a permanent disability which prevents them getting around without help, and people on low incomes receiving state benefits. With the exception of children under 16 and pensioners, all those entitled to free prescriptions must apply for an exemption certificate or a refund.

When you're exempt, you must complete and sign the declaration on the back of the prescription form. Claim form AGI is available from local social security offices, hospitals, dentists and opticians. Those with comprehensive private (e.g. foreign) health insurance may be able to reclaim the cost of prescriptions from their insurance company.

Leaflet HC12, *NHS Prescriptions*, contains information about NHS charges, and Leaflet HC11 will tell you who is exempt from payment. Both leaflets are available from your local social security office or can be downloaded from the Department of Health website (⌨ www.doh.gov.uk).

Some medicines prescribed by a doctor (e.g. certain painkillers) can be replaced by substitute medicines that can be purchased over the counter for less than the prescription charge. The Consumers' Association (⌨ www.which. net) publishes a booklet entitled *Cheaper than a Prescription*, listing medicines that you can buy over the counter and prescription-only medicines costing less than a prescription (which your GP may prescribe privately). Boots, the UK's largest chain of chemists with over 1,300 stores, and supermarkets are often the cheapest place to buy non-prescription medicines (many sell 'own brand' products).

Most chemists also sell toiletries, cosmetics, health foods and cleaning supplies. Some chemists, such as Boots, may have departments selling anything from records and books to electrical and photographic equipment and kitchen appliances (in addition to those items mentioned above). Boots also sells a range of healthcare equipment. A health food shop sells health foods, diet foods, homeopathic medicines and eternal-life-virility-youth pills and elixirs, which are quite popular in the UK (even though their claims are usually in the realms of fantasy).

Always use, store and dispose of unwanted medicines and poisons safely, e.g. by returning them to a chemist or doctor, and never leave them where children can get their hands on them.

HOSPITALS & CLINICS

All London boroughs have one or more NHS hospitals or clinics, indicated by the international hospital sign of a red 'H' on a white background. There are many kinds of hospital in London, including community hospitals, district hospitals, teaching hospitals and cottage hospitals. Major hospitals are called general hospitals and provide treatment and diagnosis for in-patients, day patients and outpatients. Most have a maternity department, infectious diseases unit, psychiatric and geriatric facilities, rehabilitation and convalescence units, and cater for all forms of specialised treatment.

Some general hospitals are designated teaching hospitals, which combine treatment with medical training and research work. In addition to general hospitals, there are specialist hospitals for children, the mentally ill and disabled, the elderly and infirm, and for the treatment of specific complaints or illnesses. There are also dental hospitals. Only major hospitals have an Accident & Emergency (A&E) department. Many NHS hospitals have sports injury clinics, although you must usually be referred by your GP, and some have minor injuries units. In many areas there are NHS 'Well Woman' Clinics, where women can obtain medical check-ups and cervical smear tests, and NHS Family Planning. Clinics. You can be referred to these clinics by your GP or can refer yourself.

You can also refer yourself to an NHS Sexually Transmitted Diseases (STD) Clinic for an examination.

Since mid-2003 hospitals have been 'star graded' and the 'best' hospitals given Foundation status, which means that they receive extra funding and enjoy greater autonomy from the NHS – a move that has been criticised as being a step towards the privatisation of the health service.

Choosing A Hospital

Except for emergencies, you may be admitted or referred to an NHS hospital or clinic for treatment only after consultation with a GP or a consultant (or from an NHS clinic such as a family planning or well woman clinic). Patients with private health insurance may be treated at the hospital of their choice, depending on their insurance cover. NHS patients can ask to be treated at a particular hospital or to be referred to a particular consultant, but have no right to have their request met. In an emergency you will be treated at the nearest hospital.

Accommodation

NHS hospital accommodation is in wards of various sizes, e.g. 12 beds, some of which are mixed. Many NHS hospitals have private rooms (known as 'pay beds') and they're permitted to charge for extras such as a single room with a telephone, a TV or a wider choice of meals. In most NHS hospitals, you choose the meals you'd like the day before and provision is made for vegetarian and other diets. Some wards have dining rooms for those sufficiently mobile and most have day rooms for mobile patients. The service, facilities and standards of NHS hospitals vary considerably with the area, and the best of them compare favourably with private hospitals (apart from a possible lack of modern conveniences). On the other hand, some NHS hospitals are dingy and depressing and are perhaps the last place on earth you'd wish to be when you're ill. However, there's some consolation to being in an NHS general ward – just think how lonely and bored those poor private patients must be, ensconced in their luxury rooms with nobody to talk to all day!

Note that in early 2004, the NHS was given the go-ahead to introduce US-style 'treatment' methods, which would mean a reduction by up to two-thirds in the average length of hospital stay.

Private Hospitals & Clinics

In addition to NHS hospitals, there are around 50 private hospitals and clinics in London, many of which are owned by provident associations such as BUPA and PPP and other health insurers. The most striking difference between NHS and private hospitals is in the standard of accommodation. Instead of being housed in a public ward with other patients, you will have a private room equipped with all the comforts of home, including a radio, TV, telephone, en-suite bathroom and room service (a visitor can usually enjoy a meal with a patient in the privacy of his room). The corridors will be carpeted, the food will be edible and there will be frills and extras galore – which may even include interpreters and special diets for overseas patients – and the nurses and other staff will wait on you hand and foot.

If you don't have health insurance or are a visitor to the UK, you may be asked to pay a (large) deposit in advance, particularly if there's any doubt that you will survive the ordeal (private hospitals usually accept credit cards). Many private hospitals provide fixed-price surgery, subject to an examination by a consultant surgeon. Some hospitals offer interest-free loans to pay hospital bills (e.g. a 10 per cent deposit with the rest payable over 12 months). This is one solution for those who cannot afford health insurance and don't want to wait for an operation. However, make sure that you aren't being overcharged, as you can often have an operation cheaper elsewhere in the UK or even abroad (e.g. in France) and possibly save thousands of pounds.

According to Action for Victims of Medical Accidents (AVMA), there are higher health risks in private hospitals than in NHS hospitals, and there may be less emergency equipment and fewer experienced staff. **You have almost no protection under the law when you're treated at a private clinic or hospital compared with your rights as an NHS hospital patient, and when things go wrong (as they occasionally do) you're usually better off in an NHS hospital.** Many experts believe that the best solution is a private ward in an NHS teaching hospital, where, if anything goes wrong and your life is on the line, you're far better off than you are in a small private clinic. Private hospitals and clinics in London include the following:

- **The Clementine Churchill Hospital**, Sudbury Hill, Harrow HA1 3RX (☎ 020-7872 3872, 🖳 www.bmihealth.co.uk, Harrow-on-the Hill tube or rail), which provides sophisticated diagnostic services, including a new imaging centre and comprehensive health screening;

- **The Cromwell Hospital**, Cromwell Road, SW5 0TU (☎ 020-7460 2000, 🖳 www.cromwell-hospital.co.uk, Earls Court/Gloucester Road/High St Kensington tube), which is one of the major private hospitals in the capital. Its specialities include cancer treatment, liver disease and transplants, pancreas and kidney transplants, neurosurgery, spinal surgery, heart surgery, gamma knife surgery (radiosurgery) and IVF.

- **The Devonshire Hospital**, 29–31 Devonshire Street, W1G 6PU (☎ 020-7486 7131, Baker Street tube), which specialises in the rehabilitation of those suffering from neurological conditions such as head and spinal cord injuries and strokes;

- **The Harley Street Clinic**, 35 Weymouth Street, W1G 8BJ (☎ 020-7935 7700, 🖳 www.theharleystreetclinic.com, Regent's Park tube), which is an acute care hospital specialising in cardiology and cancer treatment;

- **The Lister Hospital**, Chelsea Bridge Road, SW1W 8RH (☎ 020-7730 5932, 🖳 www.thelisterhospital.com, Sloane Square/Victoria tube), which has a wide range of specialities, including assisted conception and skin lasers;

- **The London Bridge Hospital**, 27 Tooley Street, SE1 2PR (☎ 020-7407 3100, 🖳 www.londonbridgehospital.com, London Bridge tube), which specialises in breast care, physiotherapy, cardiology and sports medicine;

- **The London Clinic**, 20 Devonshire Place, W1G 6BW (☎ 020-7935 4444, 🖳 www.thelondonclinic.co.uk, Regent's Park tube), which caters particularly to overseas patients, particularly (rich) Arabs and Greeks. It provides a wide range of diagnostic services and treatment options.

- **The Portland Hospital for Women and Children**, 205–209 Great Portland Street, W1W 5AH (☎ 020-7580 4400, 🖳 www.theportlandhospital.com, Great Portland St/Regent's Park tube), which is the only private London hospital entirely dedicated to caring for women and children. It specialises in obstetrics, gynaecology and paediatrics.

- **The Princess Grace Hospital**, 42–52 Nottingham Place, W1U 5NY (☎ 020-7486 1234, 🖳 www.theprincessgracehospital.com, Baker St/Regent's Park tube) is another acute unit specialising in many disciplines. It also has a sleep apnoea (excessive snoring) clinic and is a major centre for the diagnosis and treatment of all forms of hepatitis.

- **The Wellington Hospital**, Wellington Place, St Johns Wood Road, NW8 9LE (☎ 020-7586 5959, 🖳 www.thewellingtonhospital.com, St John's Wood tube), which is one of the largest, purpose-built private hospitals in the UK offering all the resources of a first-class general hospital. It also has a major sport injuries clinic.

- **The Wellman Clinic**, 32 Weymouth Street, W1G 7BU (☎ 020-7637 2018, 🖳 www.wellmanclinic.org, Regent's Park/Gt Portland Street tube), which is a preventative healthcare centre designed exclusively for men. Treatments offered include prostate cancer treatment, impotence treatment and testosterone replacement therapy, as well as treatment for sport injuries and general health screening.

COSMETIC SURGERY

A glance through the advertisements in any women's, and increasingly men's magazines will give you some indication of just how big (and lucrative) a business cosmetic surgery has become in London. If your nose, ears or derrière are too big, or you'd love to fill a full C cup, just pop down to your local plastic surgeon, who will remove those unwanted bits (or make others more prominent) as fast as you can say £2,000. If you're contemplating cosmetic surgery, you'd be well advised to contact one of the professional associations listed below for advice before parting with any money. They also provide informative websites with search facilities for surgeons in a particular speciality, and the BAPS site also contains a handy glossary of esoteric medical terms.

The most respected professional associations include the British Association of Plastic Surgeons (BAPS), c/o The Royal College of Surgeons of England, 35–43 Lincoln's Inn Fields, London WC2A 3PE (☎ 020-7831-5161/2, 🖳 www. baps.co.uk); the British Association of Aesthetic Plastic Surgeons (BAAPS), c/o The Royal College of Surgeons of England, 35–43 Lincoln's Inn Fields, London WC2A 3PE (☎ 020-7405-2234, 🖳 www.baaps.org.uk); and the Breast Implant Information Society (BIIS), PO Box 1084, Mitcham, Surrey CR4 4ZU (☎ 070-4147 1225).

A few of the best-known clinics specialising in plastic surgery in and around London are the Pountney Clinic (☎0800-028 2114, 🖳 www.pountneyclinic. co.uk) near Heathrow Airport, which performs the whole range of cosmetic surgery for face and body; the Cosmetic Surgery Clinic, 100 Harley Street, W1 (☎ 020-7486 5111, 🖳 www.100harleystreet.com), which specialises in breast enhancement; and Guy's Nuffield House (☎020-7188 7188), which is attached to Guy's Hospital and emphasises extensive consultation and counselling before surgery.

CHILDBIRTH

Childbirth in the UK usually takes place in a hospital, where a stay of a few days is usual. If you wish to have a child at home, you must find a doctor or midwife (see below) who's willing to attend you, although it's generally impossible for the birth of a first child. Some doctors are opposed to home births, particularly in cases where there could be complications and when specialists and special facilities (e.g. incubators) may be required. You can also choose to hire a private midwife (a nurse specialising in delivering babies), who'll attend you at home throughout and after your pregnancy.

For hospital births, you can usually decide (with the help of your GP or midwife) the hospital where you wish to have your baby. You aren't required to use the hospital suggested by your GP but should book a hospital bed as early as possible. Your GP will also refer you to an obstetrician. Find out as much as possible about local hospital methods and policies on childbirth, either directly or from friends or neighbours, before booking a bed.

The policy regarding a father's attendance at a birth varies depending on the hospital. A husband doesn't have the right to be present with his wife during labour or childbirth (which is at the consultant's discretion), although some doctors expect fathers to attend. If the presence of your husband is important to you, you should check that it's permitted at the hospital where you plan to have your baby and any other rules that may be in force.

In the UK, midwives are responsible for educating and supporting women and their families during the childbearing period. Midwives can advise women before they become pregnant, in addition to providing moral, physical and emotional support throughout a pregnancy and after the birth. Your midwife may also advise on parent education and antenatal classes for mothers. After giving birth, mothers are attended at home by their midwife for the first ten days or so, after which they see a health visitor and their GP to monitor their child's health and development.

DENTISTS

Britons' annual consumption of over 750,000 tonnes of sweets (over 13kg per person) ensures that dentists (and sweet manufacturers) remain financially healthy. Despite the efforts of dentists to promote preventive dentistry, millions of Britons never go near a dentist (mostly out of fear) unless they're dying from toothache. Fortunately, when you need help there are excellent dentists in all areas, although the number of dentists offering treatment on the NHS has dwindled to a mere handful (see below).

The best way to find a good dentist, whether as an NHS or a private patient, is to ask your colleagues, friends or neighbours (particularly those with perfect teeth) if they can recommend someone. Dentists are listed under Dental Surgeons in the yellow pages and are permitted to advertise any special services they provide, such as emergency or 24-hour answering service, dental hygienist, and evening or weekend surgeries. The British Dental Association (64 Wimpole Street, London W1G 8YS, ☎ 020-7935 0875, ⌨ www.bda.org) can also provide a list of dentists in your area.

In some areas, community dental clinics or health centres provide a dental service for children, expectant and nursing mothers, and disabled adults. Some hospitals provide a free emergency service, e.g. on Sundays and public holidays. Dental hospitals in London provide a free emergency service on most days. Around 50 per cent of dentists hold an evening surgery one day a week or open on Saturday mornings. There are mobile dentists in some regions.

Many family dentists in the UK are qualified to perform special treatment, e.g. periodontal work, although you must usually see a specialist. In the UK, false teeth (dentures) are made by a dental technician and prescribed and fitted by dentists. Most dental technicians carry out emergency repairs on dentures (see yellow pages).

Fees vary considerably according to the area and the dentist. The cost of dental treatment has risen considerably in recent years and you can pay at least £35 for a check-up, which are recommended every six months in the UK. However, dental care isn't particularly expensive in the UK compared with many other western countries.

NHS Treatment

In theory, dental care is covered by the NHS, although it's only completely free to those under the age of 18 (19 if in full-time education), pregnant women, mothers with a baby under one year of age and those who are receiving state benefits (Income Support, Jobseeker's Allowance, Family Credit or Disability Working Allowance). Other patients must pay a proportion of their treatment costs, which is currently around £5 for a check-up, plus the cost of any work carried out.

In practice, however, dentists are over-stretched in London (as elsewhere in the UK) and many are unwilling to accept new NHS patients onto their lists if their quotas are already full, although a dentist may offer to treat you as a private patient. If applicable, and to avoid misunderstandings, you should ensure that the dentist knows you expect NHS treatment when you register and that you remain entitled to NHS-subsidised treatment by attending regular check-ups – otherwise you may find yourself dropped from the dentist's NHS list. You should take your NHS medical card to the dentist when you have your initial examination. Each time you visit a dentist, whether the same dentist or another one, you must re-confirm that you will be treated as an NHS patient. NHS dental patients aren't required to live within a certain catchment area and can change dentists whenever they like. Once you're registered as an NHS patient, a dentist cannot refuse to treat you and essential work is always completed under the NHS when clinically necessary.

Patients who aren't exempt (see the list below) pay 80 per cent of the set NHS fees (up to a maximum of £372 per treatment) for 'normal' dental treatment (e.g. fillings, extractions and hygiene work), and standard bridges and dentures, according to a fixed scale of fees. There's a standard NHS charge of around £15.50 for a dental check-up. There's no extra charge for stopping bleeding, denture repairs, home visits or opening a surgery in an emergency (although you must pay for treatment as usual).

Exemptions include children and young people in full-time education, the over-60s, expectant mothers and those who have had a baby in the last year, and those on low incomes receiving state benefits. NHS patients who aren't under 18 or receiving unemployment or supplementary benefits must usually pay a proportion of their dental treatment and for the whole cost of cosmetic treatment, e.g. bridges and crowns. A list of dental charges and exemptions is published by the NHS and is available from them or your FHSA.

Private dentistry usually involves less waiting, and treatment may be of a better quality (e.g. you can decide the quality of fillings, etc.), but it's much more expensive. Dentists may ask for payment in advance and NHS dentists must receive prior permission from the Dental Estimates Board (DEB) before certain expensive work can be undertaken. If you miss a dental appointment without giving 24 hours' notice, your dentist may charge you a standard fee. If a dentist sees you as an emergency NHS patient outside normal surgery hours, he isn't permitted to make an extra charge. In some areas an emergency dental service is operated by the local health authority.

Note that a dentist isn't obliged to treat someone who isn't a patient, even in an emergency. Many dentists operate an emergency service and in some areas an emergency dental service is operated by the local health authority. If you're suffering from agonising toothache and you can't find a dentist who will see you, you can try the Emergency Dental Care Service (☎ 07 07 44 55 999, 24hr care), which will refer you to a dental surgery. Alternatively, Guy's Hospital Dental School, Guy's Tower, St Thomas Street, SE1 (☎ 020-7955 4317, London Bridge tube) provides a free emergency dental service from 9.30am to 4pm Mondays to Fridays, as does the Eastman Dental Hospital, 256 Gray's Inn Road, WC1X 8LD (☎ 020-7915 1038, 🖥 www. eastman.ucl.ac.uk, Chancery Lane/King's Cross tube) from 8.30am until 5.30pm weekdays.

Complaints

If you have a complaint about dental treatment completed under the NHS, you should write to your local FHSA within six months of the end of the course of treatment. For complaints about private treatment, you must contact the General Dental Council, 37 Wimpole Street, London W1M 8DQ (☎ 020-7887 3800, 🖥 www.gdc-uk.org). The British Dental Association doesn't handle complaints.

OPTICIANS

Opticians are listed under 'Opticians-dispensing' or 'Opticians-ophthalmic (optometrists)' in the yellow pages and may advertise their services, such as contact lenses or an emergency repair service. Opticians (like spectacles) come in many shapes and sizes. Your sight can be tested only by a registered ophthalmic optician (or optometrist) or an ophthalmic medical practitioner, who tests eyesight, prescribes glasses and diagnoses eye diseases. Most 'high street' opticians are both ophthalmic opticians and dispensing opticians, who make up spectacles. An eye specialist may be an ophthalmic medical practitioner (a doctor who treats eye diseases and also tests eyesight and prescribes lenses), an ophthalmologist (a senior specialist or eye surgeon) or an orthoptist (an ophthalmologist who treats children's eye problems).

If you need to see an eye specialist, you must usually be referred by your GP. The Eye Care Trust (☎ 0845-129 5001, 💻 www.eye-care.org.uk) can provide advice and direct you to an appropriate eye specialist. The optometrist business is competitive in the UK and, unless someone is highly recommended, you should shop around for the best deal. Recent years have seen a flood of 'chain store' opticians such as Vision Express, Specsavers, Dollond and Aitchinson (and those in Boots stores) opening in high streets and shopping centres.

Prices for both spectacles and contact lenses vary considerably, so it's wise to compare costs (although make sure you're comparing like with like) before committing yourself to a large bill, particularly for contact lenses. The prices charged for most services (spectacle frames, lenses, hard and soft contact lenses) are often loser in the UK than elsewhere in Europe, although higher than North America.

Sight Tests

Certain people receive free sight tests under the NHS including children under 16, full-time students under 19, the registered blind or partially sighted, diagnosed diabetic or glaucoma sufferers, and people on low incomes receiving state benefits. NHS leaflet G11, *NHS Sight Tests and Vouchers For Glasses*, explains who's entitled to free sight tests and NHS vouchers for glasses, and is available from social security offices, NHS family doctors and opticians.

If you aren't entitled to a free sight test under the NHS, you must have the test as a private patient, which usually costs between £15 and £20. Some opticians offer a special low price (or even free tests) for pensioners. Sight tests are valid for two years, although you should be aware that your eyesight could change considerably during this time. You don't need to buy your spectacles (lenses or frames) or contact lenses from the optician who tests your sight, irrespective of whether you're an NHS or private patient, and you have the right to a copy of any prescription resulting from an NHS or private sight test.

Laser Surgery

In the last few years, laser surgery to correct short sight has become increasingly popular in the UK. It's heavily promoted by laser surgery clinics, which are unregulated and don't need any particular qualifications or registration, and costs between around £500 and £1,000 per eye. There are conflicting reports about its effectiveness, particularly for those with severe short sight, who are generally considered poor candidates. Some eye specialists warn against having it done, as it can cause permanent eye damage in certain cases, although it also achieves some remarkable results. However, the long-term effects are unknown and it should be treated with caution.

Complaints

If you have a complaint regarding your optician, which you're unable to resolve, you should write to the Association of Optometrists, Consumer Complaints Service, 61 Southwark Street, London SE1 0HL (☎ 020-7261 9661, ⌨ www. assoc-optometrists.org) or, for dispensing opticians, the Association of British Dispensing Opticians, 199 Gloucester Terrace, London W2 6LD (☎ 020-7298 5100, ⌨ www.abdo.org.uk). Help the Aged, Pentonville Road, London N1 9UZ, (☎ 020-7278 1114, ⌨ www.helptheaged.org.uk) collects unwanted spectacles, which they distribute to the elderly in Africa and Asia.

FAMILY PLANNING SERVICES

Family planning services such as the provision of contraceptives (including the morning-after pill), advice on how to use them and, if necessary, abortions, are free to foreign nationals living and working in the UK. For information visit your doctor or a family planning clinic. To find the nearest clinic to your home contact the Family Planning Association (FPA), 50 Featherstone Street, EC1Y 8QU (☎ 020-7608 5240 or their low-cost national helpline number 0845-310 1334 available Monday to Friday 9am to 6pm, ⌨ www.fpa.org.uk, Angel tube). The International Planned Parenthood Federation, 4 Newhams Row, SE1 3UZ (☎ 020-7939 8200, ⌨ www. ippf.org) provides general information on contraception, condoms and abortion, while the National Childbirth Trust (Enquiry Line: ☎ 0870-444 8707 9am to 5pm Mondays to Thursdays, 9am to 4pm Fridays; Breastfeeding Line: ☎ 0870-444 8708 8am to 10pm daily, ⌨ www.nct.org.uk) provides information and support to women during pregnancy, childbirth and early parenthood. Information about contraception, pregnancy and abortion is available from a number of organisations, including the British Pregnancy Advisory Service (☎ 0845-7304 030, ⌨ www.bpas.org.uk, Victoria tube), the Brook Advisory Centre, 421 Highgate Studios, 53--79 Highgate Road, NW5 1TL (☎ 020-7284 6040, Helpline 0800-0185 023, ⌨ www.brook.org.uk, Highgate tube) and Marie Stopes International, 153–160 Cleveland Street, W1T 6QW (☎ 0845 300 8090, ⌨ www.mariestopes.org.uk).

If you want an abortion, you must satisfy two UK doctors that the operation is justified under British law. If you're pregnant and don't want to consider an abortion, contact LIFE (☎ 01926 421 587, ⌨ www.lifeuk.org) for practical help and support, counselling and advice.

SEXUALLY TRANSMITTED DISEASES

Like most western countries, the UK has its share of sexually transmitted diseases, including the deadly Acquired Immune Deficiency Syndrome (AIDS). The furore over AIDS has died down in the past few years, which many fear may cause those most at risk to be lulled into a false sense of security. **AIDS is always fatal (over 10,000 people have died from it in the UK) and to date there's no cure.**

The spread of AIDS is accelerated by the sharing of syringes by drug addicts, among whom AIDS is rampant (many of the UK's heroin addicts are infected with the HIV virus). In an effort to reduce syringe sharing among HIV positive drug addicts, syringe exchange centres have been set up throughout England (☎ 0800-567123, 24 hours), and free syringe vending machines have been provided. The spread of AIDS is also accelerated by prostitutes, many of whom are also drug addicts, which is an increasing international problem. Prostitution is illegal in the UK, so it's impossible to effect any control over the spread of sexually transmitted diseases by prostitutes.

Condoms are on sale at chemists, some supermarkets, men's hairdressers, and vending machines in public toilets in pubs and other places. They're also available free from family planning clinics.

Many hospitals have clinics for sexually transmitted diseases such as HIV/AIDS, syphilis or gonorrhoea, or you can go to a Sexually Transmitted Diseases (STD) or VD clinic. Both provide free tests, treatment and advice. You can also obtain free confidential advice, diagnosis and treatment at the Centre for Sexual Health, Genito-Urinary Clinic, Jefferiss Wing, St Mary's Hospital, Praed Street, W2 (☎ 020-7886 6666), which will also help with non-sexually transmitted diseases such as cystitis and thrush.

Gonorrhoea is on the increase (there are over 20,000 cases per year) and the anti-biotic ciprofloxacin is losing its effectiveness. Cases of chlamydia, which is thought to affect one in ten sexually active British women but also affects men, cases rose by 14 per cent last year to over 80,000.

If you'd like to talk to someone in confidence about AIDS, there are many organisations and self-help groups providing information, advice and help in all areas. These include the National AIDS Helpline (☎ 0800-012 322, ▭ www.aidshelpline.org.uk). Those who have been diagnosed with AIDS can obtain help and advice from the Terrence Higgins Trust (☎ 020-7812 1600, ▭ www.tht.org.uk) or Body Positive (☎ 020-7287 8010, ▭ www.bodypositive.org.uk). All cases of AIDS and HIV-positive blood tests in the UK must be reported to the local health authorities (patients' names remain anonymous).

INFORMATION & HELP

There are many health helplines in London covering a broad range of medical and related problems, many operated by volunteers. Some helplines provide a 24-hour service, although most have limited 'business' hours, so if you don't receive a reply the first time, try again later. Some of the most useful helplines are listed below.

- **Alcoholics Anonymous** (☎ 0845-769 7555, 24 hours a day) is the number to ring if you want help with an alcohol-related problem. AA organises meetings where alcoholics support each other in their efforts to kick the habit and will even send someone to go with you and offer support when you attend your first meeting.

- **Childline** (Freepost 111, London N1 0BR, ☎ 0800-1111 or 020-7239 1000) is a free, confidential, 24-hour national helpline for children and young people in danger or trouble.

- **Healthline** (☎ 0345-678 444, 10am to 5pm Mondays to Fridays) provides pre-recorded advice and information on some 400 health problems.

- The **Rape & Sexual Abuse Centre** (☎ 020-8683 3300, noon to 2.30pm and 7 to 9.30pm Mondays to Fridays and 2.30 to 5pm weekends and bank holidays) helps with counselling and advice if you've been raped or sexually abused. The Rape Crisis Federation (☎ 0115-900 3560 9.30am to 4.30pm Mondays to Fridays) can put you in touch with your nearest Rape Crisis Centre and itself offers advice and information for anyone who has been raped or sexually abused, their families, friends and partners.

- The **Medical Advisory Service** (☎ 020-8995 8503, 5pm to 10pm Mondays to Fridays) can offer you help on almost any health-related problem.

- **Narcotics Anonymous** (☎ 020-7251 4007, 10am to 10pm daily) provides the same sort of services for drug addicts as Alcoholics Anonymous does for those with an alcohol problem.

- **NHS Direct** (☎ 0845-4647) is a 24-hour nurse advice and health information service staffed by NHS nurses, who can advise on what to do if you or a relative are feeling ill, particular health conditions, local healthcare services, such as doctors, dentists or late night opening chemists' and self-help and support organisations.

- The **Samaritans** (☎ 0845-790 9090, 24 hours) will help anyone talk through emotional problems and isn't, as many believe, purely for those contemplating suicide.

Useful websites on UK health issues include:

- **Your NHS** (💻 www.nhs.uk) – the official NHS site;

- **BBC Health News** (💻 www.bbc.co.uk/health) – part of the encyclopaedic BBC Online site;

- **Surgery Door Health Magazine** (💻 www.surgerydoor.co.uk) – has information on a wide range of family health topics, from pregnancy to immunisation;

- **NHS Direct** (💻 www.nhsdirect.nhs.uk) provides information on particular health conditions, local healthcare services, such as doctors, dentists or late night opening chemists' and self-help and support organisations.

- **Handbag Health & Beauty** (💻 www.handbag.com/healthfit) – contains health resources and up-to-date news stories;

- **Wired For Health** (💻 www.wiredforhealth.gov.uk) – contains health information for young people;

- **Healthworks** (💻 www.healthworks.co.uk).

Note that information obtained from recorded telephone helplines, websites and books, although usually recorded, written or approved by medical experts, must be used with caution and shouldn't be used as a substitute for consulting your family doctor.

The College of Health publishes a *Consumers' Guide to Health*, and the Health Development Agency (270 Kilburn High Road, London NW6 2BY, ☎ 020-7624 2484) publishes information on a wide range of health topics (a catalogue is available), much of which is available free from chemists, clinics and doctors' surgeries.

BIRTHS & DEATHS

Births and deaths in the UK must be reported to your local Registrar of Births, Deaths and Marriages (look in your local telephone directory or on the website of your London borough – see **Chapter 1**).

Births

In recent years the British birth rate has fallen to its lowest level for 150 years (1.8 children per family in 2003), despite the fact that the UK has the highest rate of teenage pregnancies in Europe. Either parent can register a birth by simply going to the registrar within six weeks of a birth and giving the child's details (no proof of birth is necessary). Both parents must report to the registrar if they aren't married and they both want their details to be included on the birth certificate; otherwise the mother registers the birth and only her details are listed. A birth is usually registered in the area where the baby was born but can be registered with another office. Births and deaths of foreigners in the UK may need to be reported to a consulate or embassy, for example to obtain a national birth certificate and passport for a child or to register a death in the deceased's country of birth.

Deaths

When someone dies in the UK, a medical certificate must be completed by a doctor and taken to the registrar (see above) within five days. If someone dies suddenly, accidentally, during an operation or in unusual circumstances, or if the cause of death is unknown, the doctor will notify the police and/or a coroner, who will decide whether a post-mortem is necessary to determine the cause of death. The registrar will need to know the personal details of the deceased, including his date and place of birth and death, details of a marriage (if applicable), and whether he was receiving a state pension or any welfare benefits. The registrar then issues a death certificate and the 'notification of disposal', which authorises the funeral to take place. The death certificate must be given to a funeral director (or undertaker) to arrange the burial or cremation or to arrange for the body to be shipped to another country for burial. If you wish to remove a body from London, permission must be obtained from a coroner at least four days before shipment.

You may wish to announce a death in a local or national newspaper, giving the date, time and place of the funeral, and your wishes regarding flowers or contributions to a charity or research. In the UK, the traditional dress for a Christian funeral is black or dark dress.

Cost

Funerals are expensive in the UK (many think they're a rip-off), partly as a result of many family and small funeral businesses being gobbled up by large national and international companies, which have grabbed a large slice of the market (the increase in the cost of dying in the last few decades has exceeded the increase in the cost of living). In the last ten years, the cost of the average London funeral has doubled to around £2,600. You can save money by having a body cremated rather than buried, although the cost is still high at around £1,250.

You can pay in advance for your funeral through a variety of pay-now-die-later schemes, with price and service guaranteed, although there are no legal safeguards and the prepaid funeral trade is ripe for fraud, mismanagement and over-selling (a number of companies offering funeral plans have gone bust in recent years). Pre-paid funeral schemes cost between £1,000 and £2,000 and have been taken out by some 250,000 people (this is expected to increase tenfold in the next few years).

Information

The Pension Service (💻 www.thepensionservice.gov.uk), which is a government agency, gives advice about procedures to be followed in the event of a death. The Inland Revenue has a telephone helpline for inheritance information (☎ 0845-3020 900) and publishes a leaflet *What Happens When Someone Dies* (IR45). Help the Aged (💻 www.helptheaged.org.uk) publishes a free booklet entitled *Bereavement*. Other useful books include *What to Do When Someone Dies* by Paul Harris (Which? Books) and *Through Grief* by Elizabeth Collick (Darton, Longman and Todd). Cruse Bereavement Care (126 Sheen Road, Richmond upon Thames, London TW9 1UR, ☎ 0870-167 1677, 💻 www.crusebereavementcare.org.uk) can also provide comprehensive help and advice.

8

9

TIME OFF

Whether your idea of a good time is a quiet stroll round an art gallery or a night out at one of the capital's hottest night-spots, London is one of the best places in the world to enjoy yourself. It doesn't matter whether you're 19 or 90, a drinker or a thinker, gay or straight, single or a mother of four, there's something here for you. The variety of leisure opportunities in London is enormous and it provides more cultural activities than any other city in the world, including over 1,500 events per week and some 60,000 seats at cultural events each night. Whatever your favourite leisure pursuits, you will find them in abundance in London, including art galleries, museums, cinemas, theatres, dance, music, gambling, pubs and restaurants, gardens, stately homes, zoos, theme parks, children's entertainment and much more.

This chapter provides just a taste of what London has to offer and doesn't include details of famous sights such as 'Big Ben', the Tower of London and the recent London Eye (a giant wheel opposite the Houses of Parliament offering superb views of the city). Information about these and details of other attractions is available from a multitude of tourist guides, newspapers (many of which publish free weekly entertainment guides) and magazines, including London's weekly *Time Out* and *What's On* leisure guides. *Time Out* also publishes a number of excellent annual guides for visitors and residents alike, including the essential *London Visitors' Guide*. The latest tourist information is available from Visit London, (☎ 020-7932 2000, 🖳 www.visitlondon.com). You can make general enquiries about the city by contacting ✉ enquiries@visitlondon.com. There are many other excellent websites including 🖳 www.londontown.com, 🖳 www.thisislondon.co.uk (*Evening Standard*), 🖳 www.timeout.com (*Time Out*), 🖳 www.londonnet.co.uk, 🖳 www.sorted.org/london, 🖳 www.bbc.co.uk/london and 🖳 www.virgin.net. There are numerous organisations in London working for the disabled, many of which help the disabled gain access to the arts and entertainment in London such as Artsline (☎ 020-7388 2227) – a number of others are listed on the *Time Out* website (🖳 www.timeout.com/ london/esinf/ disabled_london. html).

9

ART GALLERIES & MUSEUMS

London has an international reputation for its art galleries and boasts some of the world's finest collections of art and antiquities. Many galleries don't charge for admission and you can wander in and out as you please, making it worthwhile browsing even if you've only an hour or two to spare. However, opening hours vary, so you should check before making a special journey.

London's flagship art gallery is the National Gallery (☎ 020-7747 2885, 🖳 www.nationalgallery.org.uk) in Trafalgar Square (Leicester Square/Charing Cross tube) where you can see over 2,000 priceless paintings dating from the 13th to 20th centuries, including masterpieces such as Constable's *The Hay Wain* and Van Gogh's *Sunflowers*. Admission is free, an audio guide can be rented at the entrance and you can even lounge on leather sofas when you get tired or are all cultured out. Don't miss a visit to the Micro Gallery, where you can display any of the gallery's paintings on a screen and print a reproduction.

The National Portrait Gallery (☎ 020-7306 0055, 💻 www.npg.org.uk) is close to the National Gallery in St Martin's Place (Leicester Square/Charing Cross tube) and, as the name suggests, it specialises in portraits of famous people through the ages. Here you can look into the eyes of William Shakespeare or Diana, Princess of Wales, plus a host of kings, queens and political figures from the past. Admission is free and the gallery also stages regular themed exhibitions. The Tate Britain (☎ 020-7887 8000, 💻 www.tate.org. uk) at Millbank (Pimlico tube) takes over where the National Gallery ends. It houses an impressive collection of British Art from the 16th century to the present day, including Hogarth, Constable, Reynolds and Turner masterpieces as well as showcasing contemporary artists such as Lucian Freud and David Hockney. Admission is free. A Tate to Tate boat service links Tate Britain to its highly successful younger sister, the Tate Modern and runs every 20 minutes, stopping at the London Eye on the way. Tickets are available from desks at both museums, on board the boat, or by calling ☎ 020 7887 8888 or online at 💻 www.tate.org.uk.

Housed in the old Bankside Power Station, the cavernous interior of the Tate Modern, Bankside, SE1 9TJ (☎ 020-7887 8000, 💻 www.tate.org.uk), Blackfriars tube) is as awe-inspiring as the displays. The Courtauld Institute (☎ 020-7848 2777, 💻 www.courtauld.ac.uk) at Somerset House in the Strand (Covent Garden tube) usually charges £5 (£4 concessions) for admission, although it provides free admission from 10am to 2pm on Mondays. Recently restored, the building houses some wonderful paintings by impressionists and post-impressionist artists such as Degas, Cezanne, Monet, Renoir, Gauguin and Toulouse-Lautrec, as well as works by Botticelli, Breughel and Rubens. The Hayward Gallery (☎ 020-7960 5226, 💻 www.hayward.org.uk) is part of the South Bank Centre by the river (Embankment/Waterloo tube) which also houses the National Theatre and Royal Festival Hall complex. It has no permanent collection of its own, but is one of the best venues in London to see temporary exhibitions, although admission charges can be high depending in the particular exhibition. The Royal Academy of Arts (☎ 020-7300 8000, 💻 www.royalacademy.org.uk) in Piccadilly (Piccadilly Circus/Green Park tube) is famous for its annual Summer Exhibition, as well as for a range of themed arts events. The Institute of Contemporary Arts (☎ 020-7930 3647, 💻 www.ica.org.uk) in the Mall (Piccadilly Circus/Charing Cross tube) is celebrated for its exhibitions of challenging avant-garde work.

Two notable smaller galleries outside the central area include the Dulwich Picture Gallery (☎ 020-8299 8709, 💻 www.dulwichpicturegallery.org.uk, North Dulwich/West Dulwich rail), which houses a magnificent collection of old masters by Rembrandt, Poussin, Watteau, Rubens, Canaletto, Gainsborough and many more. The critically acclaimed loan exhibitions and its setting in the beautiful 18th

9

century village of Dulwich make the Gallery a must for all art lovers. The Gallery has recently undergone extensive refurbishment and now has impressive new facilities, including a Picture Gallery Café. The Queen's Gallery (☎ 020-7766 7301, 💻 www.royal.gov.uk) at Buckingham Palace (St James's Park/Victoria tube) re-opened in 2002 as one of the key events of the Golden Jubilee provides a year-round showcase for displays from the Royal Collection.

Museums

London has some 300 museums, many containing world-renowned collections and covering a wide range of subjects. Although some national museums introduced entrance fees in the last 15 years due to a new government policy, most have now returned to being free. Other private London museums and art galleries charge an admission fee, although students, the unemployed, the disabled, carers and pensioners often receive a reduction (or 'concession') on production of an identity card, and are sometimes admitted free. A London Pass (☎ 01664 485 020, 💻 www.londonpass.com) could save you money if you want to visit a number of more expensive sights such as the Tower of London in a single day. The pass gives you pre-paid access to more than 50 sights and attractions and costs from £34 daily per adult. Some museums also offer annual family season tickets. Many museums allow free entrance for the last hour or two of the day, and most have special access for the disabled or provide wheelchairs.

The Victorian method of displaying artefacts in dusty wooden cabinets within silent, cavernous halls has largely been consigned to history's dustbin. Nowadays, many of London's museums have replaced static displays with bright new interactive models and themed multimedia exhibitions that appeal to everyone – not just scholars and enthusiasts.

Probably the best place to start is the British Museum (☎ 020-7323 8000, 💻 www.thebritishmuseum.ac.uk) in Bloomsbury (Holborn/Russell Square/ Tottenham Court Road tube). The museum is one of the wonders of the capital and its number one tourist attraction, attracting six million visitors a year. It's also free! It takes days to see the whole museum and many treasures are tucked away, but venture if you can into the eerie Clocks Room and don't miss the unrivalled collection of Egyptology, the Anglo-Saxon Sutton Hoo Ship Burial artefacts and the famous Elgin Marbles (still the subject of a vociferous ownership wrangle between the UK and Greece).

You will find the greatest concentration of museums in South Kensington. Here you can spend several days exploring the delights of the Natural History Museum (☎ 020-7942 5000, 💻 www.nhm.ac.uk) in Cromwell Road (South Kensington tube). The museum has changed out of all recognition in the past decade, although the famous dinosaur skeletons remain (and have been joined recently by a robotic T Rex), and it's worth visiting for the extraordinary Victorian architecture alone. The fusty displays have given way to the interactive

'Life Galleries' featuring a wonderful section of 'creepy crawlies', including a giant animatronic scorpion and the 'Earth Galleries', which replaced the old Geological Museum. This is as much fun as any theme park and educational to boot. Here you can ride a vast escalator through the centre of a rotating globe, experience an earthquake and marvel at real moon rocks.

The Science Museum (☎ 0870 870 4868, 💻 www.sciencemuseum.org. uk) in Exhibition Road (South Kensington tube) contains a wealth of historical technological wonders from Stephenson's Rocket to the command module of Apollo 10. In the Flight Lab you can take the controls inside a full-size aeroplane cockpit and kids can experiment with a range of interactive machines at the Launch Pad. There's even a special hands-on area for 3 to 6-year-olds in the basement, called 'The Garden' and another for 7 to 11-year-olds called simply 'Things'. There is also the new, ultra-modern 'Wellcome Wing', heralded as the 'world's leading centre for the presentation of contemporary science and technology.'

The Victoria & Albert (V&A) Museum (☎ 020-7942 2000, 💻 www. vam. ac.uk) in Cromwell Road (South Kensington tube) houses unrivalled collections of sculptures, historical costumes and examples of the applied and decorative arts, from Korean ceramics and Lalique glassware to famous Raphael cartoons, an unparalleled jewellery collection, historical musical instruments and a whole gallery devoted to Frank Lloyd Wright (one of the UK's foremost architects). In recent years the museum has tried to attract a trendier market, housing retrospectives on such fashion luminaries as Gianni Versace, Giorgio Armani and Coco Chanel.

The Imperial War Museum (☎ 020-7416 5320, 💻 www.iwm.org.uk) is situated south of the river in the Lambeth Road (Lambeth North/Waterloo tube). Nearly 200 years ago the building housed the infamous 'Bedlam' lunatic asylum, but it's now a grim reminder of the horror and heroism of warfare. In addition to static exhibits of the machinery of war, including a Spitfire and V2 rocket, it also features multimedia 'experiences' which bring to life the First World War trenches and London's Blitz in World War II.

The National Maritime Museum (☎ 020-8858 4422, 💻 www.nmm.ac.uk) is located at Greenwich (Greenwich/Maze Hill rail or Islands Gardens DLR). This is where you can appreciate the UK's historic role as a great sea-going power. There's an interactive gallery called 'All Hands' where you can send a signal in Morse Code or with flags, or, more poignantly, view the uniform in which Admiral Nelson died at the Battle of Trafalgar.

The Horniman Museum (☎ 020-8699 1872, 💻 www.horniman.ac.uk) is an odd little place in the south London suburbs (Forest Hill rail), but well worth the trip from the centre. Founded by 19th century tea merchant Frederick Horniman, it boasts a marvellous gallery of African art and culture, an underwater aquarium (Living Waters), and the eco-friendly 'Centre for Understanding the Environment'. A £13 million refurbishment in 2002 has further boosted the museum with a spanking new café, music room and intriguing 'environment' room. A great day out for families, it even boasts a small menagerie of farmyard animals.

Madame Tussauds (☎ 0870 999 0046, ☐ www.madame-tussauds.co.uk) is a traditional waxworks museum that continues to draw the crowds. It has become more interactive in recent years, visitors can now sing to a waxwork of pop idol judge Simon Cowell – and receive a torrent of abuse for their troubles! You can also see disturbingly life-like models of historical and modern-day figures, from kings and queens to Hollywood stars – there's even an infamous Chamber of Horrors with its roster of serial killers and criminals. You can buy a joint ticket for Tussauds and the adjacent London Planetarium (☎ 0870-400 3000), where you sit in comfort and view the night sky projected onto the domed roof and enjoy a 30-minute show about the cosmos enhanced by modern computer graphics.

If you enjoyed the Chamber of Horrors, you might like to pay a visit to the even grislier London Dungeon (☎ 020-7403 7221, ☐ www.thedungeons.com) in Tooley Street (London Bridge tube). Not one for young children (or squeamish parents) who might be terrified by the graphic scenes of torture and death or by the costumed actors who 'enliven' the experience. The Museum of London, (☎ 0870 444 3852, ☐ www.museumoflondon.org.uk) on London Wall near the Barbican Centre (Barbican/Moorgate or St Paul's tube) presents the capital's history from prehistoric times to the present day. Don't miss the Roman London gallery which uses thousands of original Roman objects, including recent archaeological discoveries, to recreate the life of Londinium's Roman culture.

CINEMAS & THEATRES

London's cinemas are divided into mainstream commercial cinema, usually catered for by large central London cinemas mostly in and around Leicester Square, and by suburban multiplexes with several screens showing different current movies. There are also arthouse cinemas showing fringe movies and foreign films, usually with subtitles. Films on general release are classified by the British Board of Film Censors according to their suitability for a given audience, as shown below:

Classification	Age Restrictions
U	A 'U' film should be suitable for children aged four years and over;
Uc	Particularly suitable for pre-school age children;
PG	Parental guidance advised (not mandatory);
12A	No one under 12 may see a 12A film in the cinema unless accompanied by an adult;
12	No one under 12 may rent or buy a 12 rated video;
15	No one under age 15 admitted;
18	No one under age 18 admitted.

In practice, most 'U' and 'PG' films are family movies or summer blockbusters, while 12, 15 and 18 rated movies have increasingly more adult content – either 'bad' language or scenes of a violent or sexual nature.

The best places to see the new blockbusters and summer hits are the Odeon Leicester Square and the Empire which face each other across Leicester Square. Both these huge cinemas stage star-studded premières, are the first to get the new releases, and have huge screens and excellent sound systems. Most suburban high streets have a local cinema or two, many owned by the ABC, Odeon, Virgin or Warner chains. These chains offer passes for participating cinemas that are good value for film buffs. Notable independent art house cinemas in London include the National Film Theatre (☎ 020-7928 3232, ▣ www.bfi.org.uk/nft) on the South Bank (Embankment/Waterloo tube/rail), the Lux Cinema (☎ 020-7684 0201) in Hoxton Square (Old Street tube) and the Everyman Cinema in Hollybush Vale, NW3 6TX (☎ 0870-0664 777, ▣ www. everymancinema.com, Hampstead tube). You can see German films at the Goethe Institut (☎ 020-7596 4000, ▣ www.goethe.de/ins/gb/lon) in Princes Gate (South Kensington tube) and French films at the Ciné Lumière (☎ 020-7073 1350, ▣ www.institut.ambafrance.org.uk) at the Institut Français in Queensberry Place (South Kensington tube).

You can find reviews and details about films old and new, plus details of where they're currently showing, in *Time Out* magazine (who also publish an annual *Film Guide*), *What's On in London* magazine, the *Evening Standard* and other local newspapers.

Theatres

London is renowned for the quality, quantity and variety of its theatre, which is the most vibrant in the world. There are over 150 commercial and subsidised theatres in London (50 in the West End) producing up to 25 new productions every week. Theatre entertainment includes modern drama; classical plays; comedy; modern and traditional musicals; revue and variety; children's shows and pantomime; opera and operetta; and ballet and dance. The theatre is widely patronised throughout the country and is one of the delights of living in London. Fringe theatre is both lively and extensive, and provides an excellent training ground for new playwrights and companies. Many London and provincial theatres support youth theatres (e.g. 14 to 21) and people of all ages who see themselves as budding Lawrence Oliviers or Katherine Hepburns can audition for local amateur dramatic societies.

The cost of tickets for most London musicals and plays range from under £10 to over £50. When buying tickets for any event, whether theatre, cinema, opera or a concert, it's advisable to purchase them direct from the venue. If you're in central London and wish to buy tickets for a West End show, it's usually convenient to buy tickets in person from a theatre box office, most of which

9

are open from around 10am daily on performance days. Tickets can also be purchased from most box offices by post, simply by writing and requesting tickets for a particular performance (give alternatives if possible). However, it's advisable to telephone in advance and make a reservation. Tickets must either be collected in person or payment sent, usually within three days. Telephone credit card bookings can also be made, usually by telephoning a special number.

Tickets can also be purchased from ticket agencies, who charge a booking fee anywhere from 15 to 25 per cent of the face value of the ticket (similar to ticket touts). Before buying tickets from any source other than from a theatre, you should check the official box office price first (printed on the ticket) so that you know exactly how much commission you're being asked to pay. Most ticket agencies don't actually have any tickets but simply ring the box office, which you can do yourself. If you desperately want to see a show and cannot wait, you may be able to buy tickets from ticket touts, although you may be asked two or three times a ticket's face value.

Theatre listings are provided in newspapers and magazines, including London's weekly *Time Out* and *What's On* guides, and information is also available (and booking can also be made) via the internet (⌨ www.official londontheatre.co.uk and ⌨ www.whatsonstage.com).

MUSIC

London is one of the world's great music centres and you can hear every type of music imaginable somewhere in the capital.

Classical

As far as classical music goes, London is one of the great music capitals of the world. It has five major orchestras: the London Symphony Orchestra or LSO (⌨ www.lso.co.uk), the London Philharmonic, the Royal Philharmonic (⌨ www.rpo.co.uk), the Philharmonia and the BBC Symphony Orchestra, plus many excellent smaller ensembles such as the English Chamber Orchestra and the Academy of St Martin-in-the-Fields.

London also has a wealth of excellent music venues. The major classical venues include:

- **The Barbican Centre** (☎ 020-7638 4141, ⌨ www. barbican.org.uk) in the City's Silk Street (Barbican/Moorgate tube) which is an enormous, confusing concrete jungle on several levels containing theatres, libraries and galleries as well as a concert hall.

- The **South Bank Centre** (☎ 020-79604242, 🖥 www.southbankcentre.co.uk) at Waterloo (Waterloo tube) incorporates the Royal Festival Hall, the smaller Queen Elizabeth Hall and the intimate chamber music venue, the Purcell Room.

Other chamber music venues include:

- **St John's** (☎ 020-7222 1061, 🖥 www.sjss.org.uk), a deconsecrated church in Smith Square (Westminster tube).

- The **Wigmore Hall** (☎ 020-7258 8200, 🖥 www.wigmore-hall.org.uk) in Wigmore Street (Bond Street tube).

- **Blackheath Concert Hall** (☎ 020-8318 9758, 🖥 www.blackheathhalls.com) in Lee Road, SE3 (Blackheath rail).

As well as secular venues, many central London churches provide live music, particularly free lunchtime recitals which are popular with workers. Drop in at St Bride's (☎ 020-7427 0133 in Fleet Street (Blackfriars tube), St James's (☎ 020-7734 4511, 🖥 www.st-james-picadilly.org) in Piccadilly (Piccadilly Circus tube) or best of all, St Martin-in-the-Fields (☎ 020-7839 8362, 🖥 www.stmartin-in-the-fields.org) in Trafalgar Square (Charing Cross tube), which also stages 'ticketed' concerts in the evenings featuring its own top-class classical ensemble. You can also catch free lunchtime concerts by the students at the Royal Academy of Music (☎ 020-7873 7373, 🖥 www.ram.ac.uk) in Marylebone Road (Regent's Park/Baker Street tube) or the Royal College of Music (☎ 020-7589 3643, 🖥 www.rcm.ac.uk) in Prince Consort Road, Kensington (South Kensington tube).

One of the great joys of London is its summer music festivals. One of the most famous classical music seasons anywhere in the world is the Proms (promenade concerts), or to give them their full name, the BBC Sir Henry Wood Promenade Concerts. They're performed between July and September at the Royal Albert Hall (☎ 020-7589 3203, 🖥 www.royalalberthall.com) in Kensington (South Kensington tube). This budget-price season – if you're prepared to queue for promenade (standing) tickets costing just £4 – combines musical favourites with cutting-edge works and culminates in the celebrated 'Last Night of the Proms' concert for which tickets are allocated by ballot. Maybe it's jingoistic, but it's also huge, good-natured fun as the audience, many knowledgeable music students, wave flags and outsize mascots as they sing Rule Britannia and Land of Hope and Glory at the concert's climax. Details are available from the annual *Proms* guide, published in May, or on the internet (🖥 www.bbc.co.uk/proms).

Other festivals include the City of London Festival (🖥 www.colf.org) that's held at the Barbican Centre and other city venues during June and July; Meltdown at the South Bank Arts Centre in June/July featuring avant-garde music; and the Kenwood Lakeside Concerts, which are outdoor events featuring classical favourites (and often firework displays) held on Saturday evenings from June to September outside Kenwood House (☎ 020-8233 7435, 🖳 www. picnicconcerts.com) in Hampstead (East Finchley/Golders Green tube then courtesy shuttle bus on concert nights).

Pop

The main venues for big rock and pop concerts are divided between the mega-stadiums and the smaller concert halls and clubs. Stadium gigs can be spectacular, but what you gain on the lasers and inflatables you often lose on the human scale – the performers are likely to be dots in the distance or blown-up images on a huge screen above the stage. Unless you're down the front, you're often better off buying the tour video. Nevertheless, you can see the big bands on tour at the soulless Earl's Court exhibition hall (☎ 020-7385 1200, 🖳 www. eco.co.uk, Earl's Court tube), the huge London Arena in the Isle of Dogs (DLR) (☎ 020-7538 1212, 🖳 www.londonarena.co.uk) the indoor Wembley Arena (☎ 0870-739 0739, 🖳 www.wembleyticket.com, Wembley Park/ Wembley Central tube). Better places to see live bands are the concert hall venues, most of which are seated venues where you can buy drinks only before the show or in the interval, theatre-style. Usually there's a support band whose thankless task is to warm up the audience before the main attraction, although in practice, most people forego the experience for an extra half-hour in the bar. Carling Apollo Hammersmith (☎ 020-748 8660, 🖳 www. cclive.co.uk) in Queen Caroline Street (Hammersmith tube), the former Hammersmith Odeon, is the largest of these. The Carling Brixton Academy (☎ 020-7771 3000, 🖳 www.brixton-academy.co.uk) in Stockwell Road (Brixton tube) is a converted Victorian hall that welcomes medium-league bands rather than the really big names. The Forum (☎ 020-7284 1001, 🖳 www. meanfiddler. com) in Highgate Road (Kentish Town tube) was once called the Town and Country Club and is possibly the best place to see live bands in London. Finally, there's the Astoria (☎ 020-7434 9592, 🖳 www. meanfiddler.com) in Charing Cross Road (Tottenham Court Road tube), another converted theatre that welcomes bands during the week and hosts club nights at weekends, and the grand old London Palladium (☎ 020-7494 5020) in Argyll Street (Oxford Circus tube), which stages all kinds of music and theatre, occasionally featuring something of interest to rock or pop fans.

Bottom of the pecking order are the clubs – the places where all live bands begin their apprenticeships, desperately angling for a following while their début single languishes in the shops or their demo tapes do the rounds of record companies. Like dance clubs, these come and go, but some of the best and most established are The Borderline (☎ 020-7534 6970, www.borderline.co.uk) in Orange Yard, W1 (Tottenham Court Road tube) which sometimes features 'secret' gigs by mega-bands playing under pseudonyms, the Mean Fiddler (☎ 020-8961 5490, 💻 www.meanfiddler.com) in Harlesden High Street (Willesden Junction tube) and pub venues such as the Dublin Castle (☎ 020-7485 1773, 💻 www.dublincastle.co.uk) in Parkway (Camden Town tube) and the Half Moon (☎ 020-8780 9383, 💻 www. halfmoon.co.uk) in Lower Richmond Road (Putney Bridge tube). More obscure bands, some playing their first live gig, can be seen at talent scout haunts such as the Rock Garden (☎ 020-7836 4052) in Covent Garden's piazza (Covent Garden tube), the Bull & Gate (☎ 020-7093 4820) in Kentish Town Road (Kentish Town tube) and the Hope & Anchor (☎ 020-7354 1312) in Upper Street (Angel/Highbury & Islington tube).

Jazz

The most famous jazz club in London is the poky and smoky Ronnie Scott's (☎ 020-7439 0747, 💻 www.ronniescotts.co.uk) in Frith Street (Leicester Square tube) where you can book a table or stand at the back. Big jazz names play here. The 100 Club (☎ 020-7636 0933, 💻 www.the100club.co.uk) in Oxford Street (Tottenham Court Road tube) used to be a punk club in the late '70s, but has now reverted to its original purpose as a jazz venue. Other worthwhile central places to hear good jazz are Chelsea's 606 Club in Lots Road off the King's Road (☎ 020-7352 5953, 💻 www.606club.co.uk, Earl's Court or Fulham Broadway tube) and the Jazz Cafe in Parkway (☎ 020-7916 6060, 💻 www.jazzcafe. co.uk, Camden Town tube), which has a broad definition of what passes for 'jazz'. If you don't mind heading out of town a bit, visit the excellent Vortex in Stoke Newington Church Street (☎ 020-7254 6516, 💻 www.vortexjazz.co.uk, Stoke Newington rail) or the Bull's Head on Barnes Bridge (☎ 020-8876 5241, 💻 www.thebullshead.com, Hammersmith tube) then the No. 9 bus or Barnes rail) which attracts some big national names.

NIGHTLIFE

When the sun goes down in London, the city really comes alive and the sheer diversity of entertainment on offer can bewilder even the most dedicated night owls. During the last decade or so, the accent has shifted from pubs and discos to a well-established club culture – no other European city offers such a variety and choice of constantly changing venues. The secret of the club scene's success is its mutability; it's in a constant state of flux, reacting swiftly to the latest developments in style and underground dance music.

Most clubs open between 10pm and midnight and don't close until after dawn. The majority of clubs are open every night, others at weekends only, while some are strictly 'one-nighters' hosted by an umbrella venue that features a different attraction each night of the week. It would be impossible to list every club on offer and such information would, in any case, swiftly become out-of-date, but listed below are some of the more established club venues.

Before making plans, phone or check their websites, or obtain up-to-date information from a weekly listings magazine such as *Time Out* (💻 www. timeout. com). If you want the latest information on music, opening times and door policy, ask around, as the 'bouncers' (doormen) won't let you in if your face or outfit doesn't fit. Find out the best times to arrive and the appropriate clothes to wear if you want to avoid disappointment, and remember that virtually no place will let you in wearing jeans and trainers or a business suit. As for music venues – you will find clubs playing techno, hard house, hardcore, deep house, garage, drum 'n' bass, jungle and speed garage, as well as the older hybrids acid-jazz and swing/hip-hop.

The Ministry of Sound, 103 Gaunt Street, SE1 (☎ 020-7378 6528, 💻 www. ministryofsound.co.uk, Elephant & Castle tube) is London's most famous dance club and still one of the trendiest, despite its downmarket setting in one of the poorest parts of town. It has an exceptional sound system and attracts some of the biggest name DJs from the US as well as home-grown talent. The Fridge Brixton, 1 Town Hall Parade, Brixton Hill, SW2 1RJ (☎ 020-7326 5100, 💻 www. fridge.co.uk, Brixton tube/rail) is south London's biggest night out. It hosts occasional club nights like Saturday's gay Love Muscle and Friday's trance/psychedelic night Escape from Samsara, but musical policy runs the gamut from funk to techno and garage. In the City, Turnmills, 63B Clerkenwell Road, EC1M 5PT (☎ 0871 075 1740, 💻 www.turnmills.com, Farringdon tube.rail) is host to three popular one-nighters – The Gallery house party on Fridays, Heavenly Jukebox on Saturdays, which morphs into gay marathon Trade (💻 www.dircon. co.uk/trade) from 4am until Sunday afternoon.

Heaven (☎ 0871 332 3352, 💻 www.heaven-london.com) in Villiers Street, WC2 (Embankment/ Charing Cross tube) is probably the most famous gay club in the capital. Packed to the rafters on a Saturday night, it entertains gay revellers with an uplifting set of commercial house. Since a recent refit, you can get to new underground techno club The Soundshaft (☎ 020-7930 2020) from Heaven on Saturdays and Sundays, and the original venue still has three floors playing different music. The End, 18 West Central Street, WC1A 1JJ (☎ 020-7419 9199) is owned by Mr. C of The Shamen, who you will have heard of if you're up on dance music history. It's spacious, minimalist chrome and plays a wide range of music. Hanover Grand, Hanover Street, W1 (☎ 020-7499 7977, Tottenham Court Road tube) is a super-cool club catering to the top-notch glitterati. It has a balconied dance floor upstairs, an incredible light show and some serious 'style-police' on the door at weekends. Midweek, it's home to Fresh 'n' Funky playing R&B and hip-hop.

The Cross (☎ 020-7837 0828, 💻 www.the-cross.co.uk) under the arches in Goods Way Depot, off York Street, N1 (King's Cross tube/rail) has a marvellous garden as well as a rave reputation for garage and hard-house music. Subterania (☎ 020-8960 4590) under the Westway at 12 Acklam Road, W10 (Ladbroke Grove tube)

▲ Cheyne Walk, Chelsea

▲ Columbia Road flower market

◄ The City

▼ Houses of Parliament & Big Ben

▼ Richmond

▲ Fortnum & Mason

The Dorchester Hotel

▲ Kew

◀ Chinatown, Soho

▼ Canary Wharf, Docklands

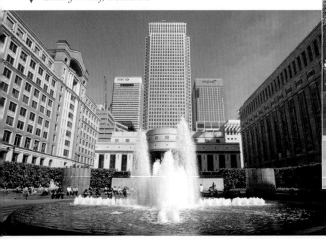

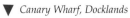

▲ Coffee Shop

▲ Covent Garden

► A Pearly King

Richmond Park

▼ Hampstead

▲ The Thames by night

▲ Hyde Park

▲ Prospect of Whitby pub, E1

▲ St. Paul's Cathedral &
the Millennium Bridge

▼ Camden Lock

◄ Changing of the Guard

attracts a trendy west London crowd and is hugely popular for Friday's Rotation and Saturday's Soulsonic, which is a very dressy event. Islington's The Complex (☎ 020-7288 1986) in Parkfield Street, N1 (Angel tube) is a fashionable club as far as music goes and plays a wide variety of radical sounds. It has four floors, including the Love Lounge where you can chill out and get friendly in a restful rosy glow. Catch its Camouflage night on Saturdays for excellent funk, swing and US garage.

The latest development in club culture is a new club/pub hybrid called, unsurprisingly, the Club Bar. These are bars that stay open later than standard pub closing time of 11pm (although they charge for admission after a certain time) and have in-house DJs playing club-style music. Although drinks tend to be expensive, food is usually on offer and you can sit around and hold conversations more easily than in a club, while still enjoying the music. Now becoming popular with the in-crowd, club bars fill the void between traditional London pubs and full-scale night-spots, and can be great places for a late night out. Here are some good examples from around the capital.

Dogstar (☎ 020-7733 7515, 💻 www.thedogstar.com) is at 389 Coldharbour Lane, Brixton (Brixton tube). A converted pub, it's almost a club in its own right at weekends playing techno, house and disco, but also staging comedy improvisation from the Top Dog Players on Thursdays. The Embassy Bar (☎ 020-7226 7901) at 119 Essex Road, Islington (Angel tube) is a retro-styled, suave joint with a sweeping chrome bar and a fashionable and diverse music policy. Jerusalem (☎ 0871 332 5652) at 33-34 Rathbone Place, W1 (Tottenham Court Road tube) is stratospherically trendy, with velvet drapes and chandeliers, giving it an air of *fin de siècle* decadence; it plays all kinds of music.

Alphabet (☎ 020-7439 2190, 💻 www.alphabetbar.com) in the heart of the West End at 61-63 Beak Street, W1 (Oxford Circus tube) serves gorgeous food – try the upstairs lounge with its luxurious leather sofas. Village Soho (☎ 020-7434 2124) at 81 Wardour Street, W1 is a gay club bar with two separate entrances leading to its cafe and very busy bar. A.K.A. (☎ 020-7836 0110, 💻 www.akalondon.com) in West Central Street, WC1 (Tottenham Court Road tube) is a chrome-infested minimalist bar next door to The End and shares its design philosophy.

If all this is a little cutting-edge for you and all you want is a good old-fashioned night-club or disco, there's still plenty of choice. Many places cater for the more mature, conservative crowd, so don't feel you have to stay in with your pipe and slippers if you're over 40. Here are some alternatives to the fashionable club scene, ranging from smart and exclusive night-clubs to mass-market discos and haunts for tired businessmen.

The Equinox (☎ 020-7437 1446) in Leicester Square (Leicester Square tube) is a typical cavernous West End disco with lots of lights and lasers where you can dance to mainstream 'commercial' music. The Hippodrome (☎ 020-7437 4311) round the corner in Charing Cross Road, WC2 (Leicester Square tube) is another monster disco that attracts tourists, albeit of the smarter variety, by the coach load. It's clad in retro chrome, but watch out for the trapeze artists who swing dangerously back and forth over your head. Stringfellows is run by and named after the ageing 'king of clubs', Peter Stringfellow, and attracts a clientèle of besuited businessmen and trendies in pursuit of pleasure. It features table-dancing from Mondays to Thursdays, filling the gap between a disco and strip joint. At weekends it fills up with a more straight-ahead disco crowd. There's a restaurant if you're hungry.

If you're after something smarter and want to try a bit of celeb-spotting, try Browns at 4 Great Queen Street, WC2 (Holborn tube). Lots of celebrity parties are held in this two-floor, very chic night-spot. Alternatively, you could pop along to The Emporium at 62 Kingly Street, W1 (Oxford Circus tube) which is a busy club popular with the rich and famous. Another chic night-spot is the recently refurbished Café de Paris (☎ 020-7395 5806, 🖥 www.cafedeparis.com) at 3 Coventry Street, W1 (Leicester Square/Piccadilly Circus tube); a classic '20s ballroom beautifully restored to its original elegance with a balcony from where you can watch the dancing, and an excellent restaurant.

London, particularly Soho, positively pulsates with seedier places to spend your leisure time, from strip bars and lap-dancing joints to so-called 'gentlemen's clubs'. If this is your thing, information is readily available on the internet and there's a forthright and amusing book, *The Good Striptease Guide to London,* which you can order direct from the publishers (Tredegar Press, Dept IN/CO, PO Box 4830, London SW11 4XQ, 🖥 www.stripguide.co.uk).

PARKS

If a visit to a museum isn't for you, why not try a relaxing stroll through one of London's many parks – few cities in the world are better endowed with public parks and open spaces and almost 30 per cent of London is comprised of green space. Although surrounded on all sides by some of the busiest roads in the world, it's surprising how peaceful these oases of calm are, even when packed with sandwich-toting office workers, boisterous schoolchildren and tourists.

Hyde Park, Kensington Gardens, Green Park and St James's Park are all part of a huge green area in central London, although bisected by the hurly-burly of Hyde Park Corner and the grandeur of Buckingham Palace, the main London residence of the British Royal Family. You could almost say St James's Park is the Queen's front garden, but you can rest assured that she has ample private grounds to the rear of her palace! Further north is Regent's Park (and London Zoo) and the kite-flyers' Mecca, Primrose Hill, not forgetting the dog-walker's 900-acre paradise of Hampstead Heath. These parks have for centuries been the scene of many urban children's first outings with mummy or nanny, an almost infinite number of lover's trysts and numerous peaceful afternoon naps. There's plenty to see, too: palaces, villas, gardens, statuary and water features fill the parks, and are there to be enjoyed by all, mostly free of charge.

In Hyde Park you can see Rotten Row, where the fashionable members of society used to parade on horseback. Near Long Water in Kensington Gardens keep an eye out for two beautiful Edwardian statues; George Frampton's 'Peter Pan' by the Long Water and George Frederick Watt's bronze statue of 'Physical Energy' before marvelling at that Victorian monument to 'bad taste', the Albert Memorial, which stands opposite the Royal Albert Hall. Alternatively, you can make a 'pilgrimage' to Kensington Palace, another royal residence and the home of the late Diana, Princess of Wales. In Hyde Park you can swim at the Serpentine's open-air Lido (☎ 020-7706 3422, 🖳 www.serpentinelido.com) during the summer months.

Regent's Park has a boating lake fed by an underground river, a bandstand, a ravishing rose garden and a magical open-air theatre where Shakespearean productions are performed in summer in an enchanting evening atmosphere – provided it doesn't rain! Non-Muslims are also sometimes allowed to visit the London Central Mosque at the park's western edge. Further from the centre, you might consider a visit to Victoria Park in the east, Finsbury Park in the north, Battersea Park to the south, and Richmond Park, and Kew Gardens (London's celebrated botanical gardens) to the west.

PUBS & BARS

Leaving aside the new 'club bar' hybrids described above, most London pubs (short for public houses) – and there are literally hundreds – are an institution. Many began life as coaching inns in the days long before motor travel and served as the focal point for local communities in much the same way as a church or village hall. The best traditional pubs serve good, unpretentious food, as well as a range of traditional 'real ales' and have a buzzy, convivial atmosphere. The worst pubs cut corners, serving poor food, fizzy lager and flat, warm beer to tourists in depressing surroundings. The only way to find a really good one which suits you is to try as many as you can: it's a tough job, but someone's got to do it.

A few London pubs still cling to the old division between 'public' and 'saloon' (or lounge) bars. The former is a 'rough-and-ready' room for men in working clothes to unwind after their labours, while the latter is a more comfortable place for the well-dressed where young men can take their girlfriends for a quiet drink. You will tend to find the snooker and pool tables, dartboards, jukeboxes and gambling machines in the public bar, and the nice upholstery and buffet in the saloon.

Nowadays, however, many pubs have undergone a transformation and shed their old class-consciousness and have just one huge 'lounge' bar. Many welcome anyone and everyone to all areas and some even have special areas for families with children or gardens where the young ones can play. Children aren't supposed to sit in a bar until they're 14 years old and cannot drink alcohol until they're 18, but are allowed entry to a restaurant area, family room or outdoor area. Don't expect many non-smoking pubs, however, as breweries and landlords have rather dug their heels in when it comes to smoking. If you want fresh air, if such a thing exists anywhere in London, sit outside or find a non-smoking table in a restaurant.

Although the UK is supposed to have gone metric, you will be hard-pressed to find a pub that sells beer by the litre – you can have a pint or half-pint. If you have the option you should try a 'real ale', which is brewed from fresh barley, hops and oats – it's superior to most other beers and a truly traditional British drink. Avoid anything that comes out of an electric pump if you want real ale, which is pumped by hand from a barrel; it's also perishable (unlike modern pasteurised brews), so go somewhere with a high turnover. If you don't know what to look for, ask the bar staff or seek out London pubs owned by Fullers or Youngs.

If you visit a 'free house', i.e. a pub that isn't tied to a specific brewery for its supplies, you will be able to sample a range of real ales from around the UK from companies such as Greene King, Flower's or smaller independents. Another option is draught Guinness, the rich black Irish 'stout' that's pumped electrically but is far superior to pasteurised beers. It now has UK competitors such as Beamish and Murphy's (also from Ireland) to keep it on its toes, although any Irishman will tell you the stuff they sell in Dublin is entirely different and much better! There's also a wide range of bottled beers available from good brewers throughout the UK and farther afield, many of which are excellent. If you want to learn more about good British ale, buy a copy of the CAMRA (Campaign for Real Ale) *Good Beer Guide* edited by Jeff Evans. *The Good Pub Guide* (Ebury Press) edited by Alisdair Aird is also worth a read.

Spirits such as whisky, vodka, gin and rum are sold in measures of 24ml, (although you can order a 'double', also called a 'large', or even a 'triple' measure if you are 'thirsty' or have had a hard day at the office!). Mixers and soft drinks are where publicans make most of their money, so don't expect a non-alcoholic option to be cheaper than the hard stuff (which is a sore point among teetotallers). Wine is simply sold by the glass (size unspecified), which gives publicans a lot of leeway! Most wine sold in traditional pubs is of poor quality and you may get a choice of 'red' or 'white' only (it saves having to remember all those fancy names). Go to a wine bar if you want some decent stuff, although dedicated wine bars were rather an '80s fashion and aren't as common now as they were.

Many pubs feature entertainment such as live music or stand-up comedy, while others have karaoke or single-sex nights featuring male or female strippers. Some are gay or lesbian haunts and some attract ethnic minorities of one kind or another, for example Irish pubs in predominantly Irish areas such as Kilburn. London's licensing laws allow pubs to open from 11am until 11pm, Mondays to Saturdays, and from noon until 10.30pm on Sundays. On public holidays such as Christmas Day, Boxing Day and New Year's Eve, pubs are usually allowed to stay open until midnight or even 1am. Drink-driving laws are sensibly strict in the UK and strictly enforced by London's police, but the densely-populated city is a great place for a pub crawl on foot or by tube or taxi. Just make sure you don't get too drunk to find your way home!

Hotel bars are another option if you have someone to meet and fancy a quiet drink before a show or a night-club. All the larger, ritzier hotels (mostly in the Mayfair area) open their bars to non-residents, although drinks (particularly those extravagant cocktails) are **very** expensive and the dress code is usually a jacket and tie for men. Outside normal pub opening hours they may insist you buy food before serving you with alcohol. Some hotel bars are also unofficial pickup joints where high-class prostitutes hang out – many hotels turn a blind eye to the practice and don't wish to be reminded. Pick of the hotel bars has to be Claridge's (☎ 020-7629 8860, 💻 www.claridges.co.uk) in Brook Street, W1 (Bond Street tube), which serves marvellous cocktails at stratospheric prices, is furnished in Art Deco style and staffed by waiters who have stepped straight from a P.G. Wodehouse (Jeeves) novel.

In Park Lane (Hyde Park Corner tube) you will find the Dorchester (☎ 020-7629 8888, 💻 www.dorchesterhotel.com), owned by the Sultan of Brunei and recently refurbished in fantastic style to his specifications. The Langham Hilton (☎ 020-7636 1000, 💻 www.hilton.com) in Portland Place (Oxford Circus tube) is frequented by BBC staff from Broadcasting House over the road and serves a ridiculous number of different vodkas in its Tsar Bar. Don't confuse it with the London Hilton (☎ 020-7493 8000) in Park Lane (Hyde Park Corner tube), where Trader Vic's bar resembles a tacky film set complete with costumed waitresses. Le Meridien Waldorf (☎ 020-7836 2400) in Aldwych (Covent Garden tube) has a wonderfully relaxed Palm Court bar where you don't need to wear a tie and a pianist entertains during the evenings.

Note that in February 2004, London's Mayor, Ken Livingstone, was considering a range of measures to curb public drunkenness, including limits on happy hours and crowding regulations. One in 25 Londoners has a drink problem and over 230,000 consume harmful quantities of alcohol.

For more information consult the *Evening Standard London Pub and Bar Guide* by Edward Sullivan (Simon & Schuster) or the *Time Out Eating and Drinking Guide*.

RESTAURANTS & CAFÉS

Most foreigners are familiar with the infamous (and previously well-deserved) image of a London full of 'greasy spoon' establishments specialising in fried food, burnt meat and overcooked vegetables. However, those who think that a period spent in London means bringing your own food supply or facing starvation or death by food poisoning are in for a pleasant surprise. There has been a revolution in London restaurants in the last few decades and it now provides a wealth of excellent eateries offering a quality and variety of culinary delights rivalling those of Paris (the only city in the world with more Michelin-starred restaurants). You need only open the pages of the latest restaurant guide to realise that British food doesn't always live up (or down) to its dreadful reputation, and London is now at the cutting edge of food fashion. On the negative side, prices for good food are often astronomical (wine is also **very** expensive) and even modest food can be costly.

It's a cliché that the UK has no recognisable cuisine of its own, although with the renaissance of traditional English cooking in recent years, this is no longer true. However, you're unlikely to come across much English cuisine in London's ubiquitous foreign restaurants. In fact the UK's national dish is now officially curry! London has a huge variety of ethnic restaurants (representing some 70 countries) and some of the best Chinese and Indian restaurants outside Asia (it's said that the British founded an Empire so they could get some decent food!), and numerous establishments serving admirable French, Italian and international cuisine. The best bet for those wishing to eat well and cheaply are ethnic restaurants, where the standard of food is invariably high and a filling meal can be had for around £10 to £15 a head (without wine).

Always phone ahead to check opening hours and ask whether you need to book a table. Most restaurants stop serving early, e.g. between 10.30 and 11.30pm, so it's usually best to eat before going to a show, pub or club. There are, however, a number of notable exceptions, mainly in the traditionally nocturnal Soho area. Indian restaurant Soho Spice (see below) takes last orders at 2.30am, Chinese restaurant Mr Kong (☎ 020-7437 7341/9679, Leicester Square/Piccadilly Circus tube) at 3am and if you're gay you might like to drop in at the 24-hour Old Compton Cafe in Old Compton Street. Most restaurants accept all major credit cards and are licensed to serve alcohol. Tipping is discretionary, but check whether a service charge is added to your bill before leaving a tip, as there's no need to pay twice. If you're American, be warned; British appetites aren't as large as on the other side of the pond and you may be disappointed by the portion size until your stomach acclimatises!

Many of London's best restaurants are concentrated near the centre around Soho, where they outnumber the ubiquitous peep shows and sex shops, and include some of the best eateries in London, such as the many Chinese restaurants in the 'Chinatown' district south of Shaftesbury Avenue. For Cantonese cuisine try Chuen Cheng Fu (☎ 020-7437 1398) at 17 Wardour Street (Leicester Square). It's an enormous and wholly authentic Hong Kong-style restaurant serving real dim sum as well as a huge range of dishes from the menu. If sushi's more to your taste, avoid the trendier media spots and go to Kulu Kulu (☎ 020-7734 7316) at 76 Brewer Street (Piccadilly Circus tube), which is a friendly and compact restaurant with the accent on excellent food rather than expensive decor. For European food try Andrew Edmunds (☎ 020-7437

5708) at 46 Lexington Street (Oxford Circus/Piccadilly Circus tube), which is a tiny but very popular bistro.

Covent Garden is another hotspot for restaurants, although there are some terrible tourist traps serving overpriced burgers and other 'fast' foods. For superb French food at an affordable price look no further than Mon Plaisir (☎ 020-7836 7243) at 21 Monmouth Street (Covent Garden/Leicester Square tube). If you're starving, Café Pacifico (☎ 020-7379 7728) serves enormous portions of superior Mexican food at 5 Langley Street (Covent Garden tube) or Stephen Bull (☎ 020-7379 7811) at 12 Upper St Martin's Lane (Leicester Square tube) is one of those new wave of restaurants serving 'modern British food'; its fish and puddings are highly recommended and good value.

Bloomsbury and Fitzrovia traditionally make up London's intellectual quarter, although based on the number of good restaurants, one could be forgiven for thinking its inhabitants are keener on feeding their stomachs than their minds. The Diwana Bhel Poori House (☎ 020-7387 5556) in the oriental quarter of Drummond Street (Euston tube) serves vegetarian southern Indian food and is a great place for a weekday lunch. Interlude is an unpretentious French restaurant in Charlotte Street (Goodge St/Tottenham Court Road tube), and at 67a Tottenham Court Road (Goodge Street tube) you will find Ikkyu (☎ 020-7636 9280), which serves authentic Japanese cuisine.

St James's and Mayfair are home to the 'poshest' of haute cuisine restaurants with strictly formal dress codes (e.g. jacket and tie for men). Try the elegant but not too expensive Mirabelle in Curzon Street (☎ 020-7499 4636, Green Park tube). Terence Conran's Quaglino's (☎ 020-7930 6767) at 16 Bury Street (Green Park tube) was one of the most fashionable places in London a couple of years ago, but now the beautiful people have largely moved on to be replaced by tourists who gawp at its splendid converted ballroom ambience. If you must be informal, try the ultra-hip Momo (☎ 0871 223 8015) in Heddon Street (Piccadilly Circus tube), where the Moroccan food is so good you need to book three weeks in advance. Nobu (☎ 020-7447 4747, 💻 www.nobu restaurants.com, Hyde Park Corner tube) is another celebrity favourite and features the famous black cod with miso. Gordon Ramsay at Claridge's (020-7499 0099, 💻 www.gordonramsay.com, Bond Street tube) is one of London's top restaurants – with prices to match!

Stylish European restaurants abound in Kensington and Chelsea. Try ultra-smart Polish restaurant Wodka (☎ 0871 332 7307) at 12 St Albans Grove, W8 (Gloucester Road/High St Kensington tube), named after its extensive range of flavoured iced vodkas, or the noisy and popular Portuguese eaterie O Fado (☎ 020-7589 3002) in Beauchamp Place (Knightsbridge tube). For well-cooked Italian fare try Zafferano (☎ 020-7235 5800) at 15 Lowndes Street (Knightsbridge tube), which gets booked out very early, or head over to Boisdale (☎ 020-7730 6923) at 15 Ecclestone Street (Victoria tube), owned by a latter-day clan chief, for gamey Scottish haute cuisine.

The business and financial quarter of the City isn't exactly packed with fine restaurants but you could do worse than Singapura (☎ 020-7329 1133) in Limeburner Lane off Ludgate Hill (St Paul's/Blackfriars tube) which serves a strange hybrid of Chinese and Malay food from Singapore. Rampant carnivores might like to brave the portals of St John (☎ 020-7251 0848) near Smithfield meat market at 26 St John Street (Farringdon tube), a vegetarian's nightmare specialising in offal dishes including unusual dishes made from brains and bones. The East End boasts some fine Asian restaurants such as Cafe Spice Namaste (☎ 020-7488 9242) at 16 Prescott Street (Tower Hill tube) serving Kashmiri and Goan delicacies, or the cheap but authentic Pakistani restaurant Lahore Kebab House (☎ 020-7488 2551) which has stewed sheep's feet on the menu along with more mainstream fare. There's also a splendid Vietnamese restaurant beyond the reach of the tube in Shoreditch called the Viet Hoa (☎ 020-7729 8293) at 70-72 Kingland Street, E2. Catch a No. 67, 242 or 149 bus to get there or push the boat out and get a taxi.

Further out in arty, middle-class Hampstead and Camden, go for cheerful African eaterie Wazobia (☎ 020-7284 1059) at 257 Royal College Street (Camden Town tube) which serves Nigerian and West African dishes. If you fancy Russian cuisine, head for Primrose Hill and book a table at Trojka (☎ 020-7483 3765) in Regent's Park Road (Chalk Farm tube). Solly's (☎ 020-848 8088) is a popular kosher restaurant in Golders Green Road (Golders Green tube) and excellent Greek food can be found at the popular Lemonia (☎ 020-7586 7454) in Regent's Park Road (Chalk Farm tube). In the Marylebone/Bayswater/Notting Hill area, try the classy Sudanese restaurant, The Mandola (☎ 020-7229 4734), at 139 Westbourne Grove – the spiced coffee comes highly recommended – while nearby at 21–23 Westbourne Grove is The Standard, serving some of the most delicious (and best value) Indian food in London. Brazilian restaurant Rodrizio Rico (☎ 020-7792 4035) in Westbourne Grove (Notting Hill Gate/ Queensway tube) specialises in grilled meats; and if you want good English fish and chips there are few better places than Sea-Shell (☎ 020-7224 9000) in Lisson Grove (Marylebone tube).

South of the river, try Brixton's 'global' eaterie Helter Skelter (☎ 020-7274 8600) at 50 Atlantic Road (Brixton tube), the welcoming Gujerati restaurant and takeaway Hot Stuff (☎ 020-7720 1480) at 19 Wilcox Road (Vauxhall tube) or Fina Estampa (☎ 020-7403 1342) at 150 Tooley Street, London's only Peruvian restaurant with lots of yummy seafood.

If you want to check out these or any other restaurants further before paying them a visit, get yourself a copy of a good restaurant guide such as the *Time Out Eating and Drinking Guide*, listing over 1,300 restaurants, cafés and bars, the *Evening Standard London Restaurant Guide* by Nick Foulkes (Simon & Schuster) or *London Restaurants: The Rough Guide* by Charles Campion (Rough Guides). If you love eating out but cannot afford the wine, obtain a copy of *Capital BYOs: A Guide to London's Bring Your Own Wine Restaurants* by

Victoria Alers (Hankey VBAH). If you prefer internet reviews, try the excellent *Restaurant & Food Guide* (💻 www.thisislondon.com), which contains reviews of over 800 restaurants, or *Eat London* (💻 www.londontown.com).

Internet Cafés

Internet (or Cyber) cafés have proliferated in London in recent years in order to meet the demand for internet access from those who aren't on-line at home and don't have access at their workplace or college. Most London cyber-cafés also serve drinks and food, and a few even offer free websurfing, although most charge around £2 to £5 an hour.

The bright orange frontage of the Easyinternetcafes makes them easy to spot and there are 17 branches dotted across London, including outlets at Baker Street, Camden, Kensington High Street and Trafalgar Square. (💻 www.easyeverything.com). Room Service @ the Vibe Bar (☎ 020-7247 3479, 💻 www. vibe-bar.co.uk) in the Truman Brewery, Brick Lane doesn't charge for net access but only has four terminals (Aldgate East tube). Café Internet (☎ 020-7233 5786) at Victoria tube/rail has 22 terminals and charges £2 an hour or £1 after 8pm. The Global Cafe (☎ 020-7287 2242, 💻 http://gold.globalcafe.co.uk) in Golden Square (Oxford Circus/Piccadilly Circus tube) serves great food and the Buzz Bar (☎ 020-7460 4906, 💻 www.portobellogold.com) in Portobello Road (Notting Hill Gate/Ladbroke Grove tube) also charges £2 an hour and is one of the friendliest places to surf the web in London.

RIVER TRIPS & EXCURSIONS

For an alternative view of the capital, you can take one of several river trips, which include the following:

- **Greenwich To Gravesend/Tilbury** – Wednesdays and Saturdays during the summer. Operated by the Lower Thames & Medway Passenger Boat Company (☎ 01732–353448);

- **MV Balmoral & Paddle Steamer Waverley From Tower Pier** – Trips to Tilbury and Southend and up the River Medway aboard these historic vessels during June, July, September and October. Operated by Waveley Excursions (☎ 0141-243 2224);

- **From Embankment Pier** – Trips including lunch or dinner with entertainment passing Westminster and the Tower of London daily. Operated by Bateaux London (☎ 020-7925 2215, 💻 www.bateaux london.com);

- **From Festival Pier** – Circular trip passing Westminster, the Tower of London and the Globe Theatre after a ride on the London Eye daily from mid-April until the end of October and at weekends the rest of the year (☎ 0870-443 9185, 🖳 www.ba-londoneye.com);

- **From Greenwich Pier** – Circular trip passing the Tower of London and Westminster on Sundays from early May until the end of September. Operated by the London Borough of Greenwich (☎ 020-8312 5576);

- **From Waterloo Pier** – Multi-lingual circular trip passing many famous landmarks daily from mid-April until the end of October. Operated by Catamaran Cruisers (☎ 020-7987 1185, 🖳 www.catamrancruisers.co.uk);

- **From Westminster Pier** – Trips including dinner and entertainment passing Westminster and the Tower of London daily. Operated by City Cruises (☎ 020-7740 0400, 🖳 www.citycruises.com).

There are also trips to various places of interest from the piers listed below. Further information is available from London River Services/LRS (☎ 020-7941 4500, 🖳 www.tfl.gov.uk/river).

- **Bankside** – Clink Museum, Globe Theatre, Tate Modern and Vinopolis City of Wine;

- **Blackfriars** – City of London and St Paul's Cathedral;

- **Canary Wharf** – Canary Wharf Tower, Isle of Dogs and London Arena;

- **Embankment** – Cleopatra's Needle, Covent Garden, London Transport Museum and Trafalgar Square;

- **Festival** (in front of the South Bank complex) – Imax Cinema, and Royal Festival Hall and South Bank complex;

- **Greenwich** – Cutty Sark, Greenwich Market, Greenwich Park, National Maritime Museum, Royal Naval College and Royal Observatory;

- **Hampton Court** – Hampton Court Palace;

- **Kew** – Kew Bridge Steam Museum and Kew Gardens;

- **London Bridge** – Britain at War Museum, City Hall, Clink Museum, Hay's Galleria, HMS Belfast, London Dungeon, Old Operating Theatre Museum and Southwark Cathedral;

- **Millbank** – Tate Modern Museum;

- **Richmond** – Richmond Town and Richmond Park;

- **St Katharine's** – St Katharine's Dock and Tower Bridge;

- **Tower** – St Katharine's Dock, Tower Bridge and Tower of London;
- **Waterloo** – FA Premier League Hall of Fame, Imax Cinema, London Aquarium, London Eye, Royal Festival Hall and South Bank complex;
- **Westminster** – Houses of Parliament and Westminster Abbey.

Excursions

If you want a change from the big city, there are many interesting places and attractions to visit within a few hours of London. Many historic cities and towns are within easy reach of the capital by train or road, including the world-renowned university cities of Oxford and Cambridge plus many fine cathedrals, castles and stately homes.

The ancient university city of Cambridge is just 50 minutes from King's Cross or you can drive there on the M11 (exit at junction 11 or 12). The oldest college buildings (at Peterhouse in Trumpington Street) date from the 13th century and Corpus Christi in the same street was built in the 14th century. Most famous of all, though, is the Gothic King's College Chapel, home to the world-famous boys' choir that sings at evensong each afternoon during term time. Check out the university's main website (💻 www.cam.ac.uk), which has links to the colleges and their attractions. You can picnic on the grassy area called the Backs behind the main parade of colleges or hire a punt on the river Cam and lie back lazily as you drift along, propelled by one of the professional boatmen (or by a friend if you choose to do-it-yourself). While you're in the city don't miss the marvellous Fitzwilliam Museum in Trumpington Street which has a collection as grand as many London museums and galleries. There are also excellent second-hand bookshops and a bustling open-air market in the central square. The Tourist Information Centre (☎ Tourist Information line 0906-586 2526, calls charged at 60p per minute, or enquiries on 0122-345 7577) is in Wheeler Street.

Oxford, the UK's other world-famous university city, is an hour from London by train from Paddington or by road via the M40 (junction 8) and the A40. Its oldest college buildings are at University College (13th century), but the finest architecture is to be seen at Christ Church with its wonderful chapel and Magdalen with its unparalleled grounds. Information is available on the university website (💻 www.ox.ac.uk). You can punt on both the Isis, a tributary of the River Thames, and the Cherwell. Oxford also has an excellent Museum of Modern Art (☎ 01865-722733, 💻 www.moma.org.uk) in Pembroke Street and the Pitt Rivers Museum of Archaeology and Anthropology (☎ 01865-270949, 💻 www.prm.ox.ac.uk), which has an amazing collection of ethnic art. There's a covered market dating from 1774 and a huge range of antique shops in Park End Street. The Tourist Information Centre (☎ 01865-726871, 💻 www.visit oxford. org) is at 15-16 Broad Street, Oxford OX1 3AS.

9

Windsor Castle (☎ 020-7766 7304, 💻 www.royal.gov.uk), standing on a steep chalk bluff overlooking the River Thames, is the world's largest inhabited castle. It's one of the UK's premier tourist attractions and has been a home to British royalty (from which the family took its name) continuously for over 900 years, having been originally built by William the Conquerer in 1070. The castle is open to the public from 10am to 5.30pm from 13th March to October 31st and closes an hour earlier during the rest of the year. Highlights include the State Apartments (badly damaged in a horrendous fire in 1992, but now restored to their former glory), St George's Chapel and Queen Mary's Dolls' House. If you have any energy left afterwards you may wish to take a stroll in Windsor Great Park, from where there are marvellous views of the castle. Nearby Eton College (☎ 01753-671000, 💻 www.etoncollege.com), which is open to the public from 2 to 4.30pm during term time and from 10.30am to 4.30pm during Easter and summer holidays) dates from the 15th century (founded in 1440) and is the UK's most exclusive public school (where the royal princes William and Harry were educated). Windsor is just 20m (32km) from central London taking 50 minutes by train from Waterloo (direct) to Windsor & Eaton Riverside station or 35 minutes from Paddington to Windsor & Eton Central station (change at Slough), or around the same time by car (via the M4).

Brighton, 50 minutes from London (Victoria) by train, is in many ways an outpost of London by the sea. It's bright, breezy, and incorrigibly trendy with a liberal, slightly eccentric atmosphere, due in part to its large student population and thriving gay community. It also has much that has survived from the forgotten age of British seaside towns and has now acquired its own delightfully camp charm. Don't fail to visit the gaudy Brighton Pier – where fish and chip shops and candy-floss vendors rub shoulders with slot machines and a summer funfair. The outrageous Royal Pavilion (☎ 0127-329 2820, 💻 www. royalpavilion.org.uk) bears an uncanny resemblance to the Kremlin and was built by Nash in 1823 for the Prince Regent. Children love the Sea Life Centre (☎ 01273-604234, 💻 www.sealife.co.uk) with its huge glass tanks housing enormous aquatic life-forms and you can spend your life savings shopping for antiques and nick-nacks in The Lanes, with its maze of specialist shops, pubs and cafés. As for nightlife, it's worth staying late to sample places such as the Zap Club (☎ 01273-821147) and Honey (☎ 01273-202807). There's also a fine art house cinema in the Duke of York's (☎ 01273-626261) in Preston Circus. Brighton's tourist information centre is at 10 Bartholomew Square (☎ 07906-711 2255, 💻 www.visitbrighton.com)

Stratford-upon-Avon is, of course, Shakespeare's birthplace, and not surprisingly one of the UK's most visited towns. It's a relatively long haul from London, taking 2 hours 10 minutes from Paddington by train or you can drive via the M40 (junction 15) and the A46. The literary tourist trail takes in Shakespeare's birthplace (☎ 01789-204016), his wife Anne Hathaway's cottage (☎ 01789-292100) and his mother Mary Arden's childhood home (☎ 01789-293455). Round off your 'day' with a trip to the Royal Shakespeare Theatre

(☎ box office 0870-609110 or for tours 01789-403405, 💻 www.rsc.org.uk – be sure to book well in advance), home of the world-famous Royal Shakespeare Company (RSC). When you've had your fill of Shakespeare, you can admire the brightly-painted narrowboats on the River Avon and Stratford Canal.

LONDON FOR CHILDREN

London can sometimes seem an unfriendly place to bring up a family, mainly due to the lingering English attitude that children should be seen and not heard. Kids aren't made welcome in many restaurants and pubs, unless they're the kind that serve plastic burgers, chips and chicken nuggets and have a multicoloured squashy play centre in the corner. Still, there are the parks (see above), the largely child-friendly museums (see page 274) and a wealth of shows, special events and workshops, particularly during the school holidays.

London also provides plenty of attractions for days out with the children. London Zoo (☎ 020-7722 3333, 💻 www.londonzoo.co.uk) is situated in the north-eastern corner of Regent's Park (Camden Town or Baker Street tube). It's great fun for kids (there's even a petting zoo where they can touch and handle the animals), although older animal-lovers may find it vaguely depressing. The zoo does its level best to make the enclosures humane and, along with its out-of-town partner at Whipsnade in Bedfordshire, carries out valuable work in saving endangered species. Don't miss the '30s spiral penguin pool or the Lord Snowdon-designed aviary resembling a huge aluminium tent.

Children also adore the London Aquarium (☎ 020-7967 8000 or for tours 020-7967 8007, 💻 www.londonaquarium.co.uk) in County Hall, Westminster Bridge Road (Westminster/Waterloo tube/rail). It's a wonderful display of aquatic life on three levels, with scary sharks and friendly rays which you can even touch. Battersea Park (☎ 020-8871 7540) in Albert Bridge Road, SW11 (Battersea Park rail/Queenstown tube) has a small children's zoo plus an adventure playground. The playground is free and you can also visit the Buddhist Peace Pagoda in the park. In August the park hosts a huge Teddy Bear's Picnic.

London is also home to many 'city farms' where children can get a feel for rural life without leaving the city. One of the best is Mudchute City Farm (☎ 020-7515 5901) in Pier Street, Isle of Dogs, E14 3HP (Crossharbour/Mudchute/Island Gardens DLR) which, at 35 acres, is London's largest city farm. As well as farmyard animals, it has llamas, a pet's corner, a riding school, Young Farmers' club and a study centre. College Farm (☎ 020-8349 0690) in Fitzalan Road, Finchley (Finchley Central tube) is a former dairy farm where you can see horses, donkeys, pigs, highland cattle and rabbits. To the south of the city, Crystal Palace Farm (☎ 020-8778 4487) is also well worth a visit (Crystal Palace rail), boasting some rare farm animals and birds. Finally, right in the centre of town in Guildford Street, WC1 (Russell Square tube) lie Coram's Fields (☎ 020-7837 6138) on the site of the old Foundling Hospital where illegitimate and abandoned children were once cared for. The grounds are closed to adults

9

unless accompanied by a child and there's a large free playground plus farmyard animals and birds. There are huge sandpits, a basketball court and football pitches.

If the weather is bad (as it so often is, even in summer), then London has a wide variety of indoor play centres for children of all ages. Try the Discovery Zone (☎ 020-7223 1717) at Clapham's Junction shopping centre which has many activities for 2 to 12-year-olds. At Ladbroke Grove there's Bramley's Big Adventure (☎ 020-8960 1515) in Bramley Road (Ladbroke Grove/Latimer Road tube) with a wide range of activities for all ages and an adult crèche where kids can park their parents to read in peace!

If your children aren't the active type, many local London cinemas hold Saturday morning or afternoon shows especially for kids. One of the best events in the centre is the Barbican Children's Cinema Club (☎ 020-7382 7000, 🖥 www.barbican.org.uk) on a Saturday afternoon at the city's cavernous Barbican Centre (Barbican/Moorgate tube). For a £4 annual membership, children can bring up to three guests with them. Alternatively, the National Film Theatre (☎ 020-7928 3232, 🖥 www.bfi. org.uk/nft) on the south bank (Waterloo tube) holds regular Junior NFT matinees on Saturday and Sunday afternoons (adults £4.75, children £3.35).

London boasts several dedicated children's theatres. In Autumn 2003, building work began on a brand new venue for The Unicorn Theatre for children (☎ 08700 534 534, 🖥 www.unicorntheatre.com, Holloway Road tube) The oldest professional children's theatre in London stages plays, mimes and puppet shows at weekends and during school holidays. The Unicorn hopes to be able to move into its new premises, which will boast a 350-seat auditorium, 120-seat studio theatre, rehearsal studio and cafe, by 2005. Islington's Little Angel Theatre (☎ 020-7226 1787, 🖥 www.littleangeltheatre.com) in Dagmar Passage, N1 (Angel/ Highbury & Islington tube) is a permanent puppet theatre and has shows for three to six-year-olds on weekend mornings and for older children in the afternoons. The Bull Theatre (☎ 020-8449 0048) in High Street Barnet (High Barnet tube) to the north of the city has also gained a reputation for good shows in recent years. Many of London's smaller, independent theatres cater for children with special shows at weekends including the Lyric Theatre (☎ 020-8741 2311) in Hammersmith (Hammersmith tube) and the impressive, glass-fronted Tricycle Theatre (☎ 020-7328 1000) in Kilburn High Road (Kilburn tube), which also runs courses and workshops for budding junior actors.

There are a number of books dedicated to entertaining children in London including *Children's London* (Nicholson) and *Evening Standard Children's London* by Linda Conway (Prentice Hall). See also **Excursions** on page 292.

Theme Parks

If you've children to amuse, you might prefer a trip to an out-of-town theme park. The most accessible from London is Chessington World of Adventures

(☎ 0870-444 7777, 💻 www.chessington.com) in Surrey, just 30 minutes by train from Waterloo to Chessington South or by car via the M25 (junction 9). It's expensive and perhaps a little tacky, but kids love the terrifying white-knuckle rides – don't miss Rameses' Revenge and the Samurai ride. There's also a zoo, so arrive early! Thorpe Park (☎ 0870-444 4466, 💻 www.thorpepark.co.uk) is a larger, more modern theme park 45 minutes from Victoria by train (change at Clapham Junction for Staines, then catch a shuttle bus), or by car via the M25 (junction 11 or 13). It's a 500-acre park with all the usual Disneyland-style rides and shows as well as a real working farm.

Legoland (☎ 0870-504 0404, 💻 www.legoland.co.uk) situated just outside Windsor (train as above for Windsor or by car via the M25, junction 13). As its name suggests, it promotes the perennial building toy and includes not only incredibly complex miniature copies of cities from around the world, but inventive and original theme park rides for all ages, including some gentle ones for tiny tots and grannies, and a chance to pan for gold (children get a medal when they've found enough) in the Wild Woods. The accent is on originality and good design rather than thrills and nausea, but food and drink is expensive and the park is so popular that the time spent queuing for the main attractions can eat into your fun-time to an alarming degree.

If your kids prefer animals to rides, take a trip to Whipsnade Wild Animal Park in Dunstable (☎ 01582-872171, 💻 www.londonzoo.co.uk/whipsnade), set in 600 acres of parkland. It's around 30 minutes from King's Cross to Luton followed by a bus ride or by car via the M1 (junction 9), A5 and B4540. As well as doing valuable work in the conservation of endangered species – you will see elephants, hippos, wallabies and Chinese water deer – it features a children's farm, miniature railway and a great play area. Not far from Whipsnade is Woburn Abbey (☎ 01525-290666, 💻 www.woburnabbey.co.uk), which is 30 minutes from Euston to Bletchley by train or by car via the M1 (junction 13) and the A4012. Woburn Abbey is an 18th century stately home built on the foundations of a 12th century monastery. Children love it, not least because of the Safari Park (💻 www.woburnsafari.co.uk) in the grounds where you can see lions, tigers and bears. There are also five adventure playgrounds, including one for under-fives.If you're looking for historic sites, the National Trust (NT) should be your first point of reference. Membership gives you free access to all NT properties and you receive a free *Family Handbook* packed with ideas for family day trips. Contact the National Trust, Membership Department, Freepost MB1438, Bromley, Kent BR1 3XL (☎ 0870-458 4000, 💻 www. nationaltrust.org.uk) or you can join at any NT property. You can also join English Heritage which provides free admission to over 350 properties and special events. For information contact English Heritage (Membership Department, Freepost WD214, PO Box 570, Swindon SN2 2UR, ☎ 0870-333 1182, 💻 www.english-heritage.org). If you're keen on gardens, you may wish to join the Royal Horticultural Society (Membership Department, 80 Vincent Square, London SW1P 2PE, ☎ 0845-130 4646, Mondays to Fridays 9am to 5.30pm), in return for which you receive free entry to beautiful gardens throughout the country.

10

SPORT & FITNESS

Sports facilities are generally excellent throughout the UK, whether you're a novice or an experienced competitor. Among the most popular sports are football (soccer), rugby (union and league rules), cricket, athletics, fishing, snooker, horse racing, golf, walking, cycling, squash, badminton, tennis, swimming and skiing, an inordinate number of which were British inventions. A good general website for further information about several of these activities in the UK is 🖳 www.24hoursport.co.uk.

The sport industry in the UK is big business and new sports facilities and complexes, including golf clubs, indoor tennis clubs, dry slope ski centres and health and fitness clubs are opening all the time. They're all part of a huge growth market which is expected to gain even greater momentum as more people retire early and have more time for leisure and sport, even if the number of those who cannot even afford to retire at 65 is also growing remorselessly. Many sports owe their popularity (and fortunes) to TV and the increased TV coverage (and competition for TV rights) generated by the proliferation of cable and satellite TV stations. Both professional and amateur sports have also benefited hugely in recent years from the increase in the commercial sponsorship of individual events, teams, and league competitions.

In contrast to the extensive and often excellent sports facilities for competitors in the UK, facilities for spectators often leave a lot to be desired. Most football stadia have now left a primitive past behind in which most spectators were expected to stand on the 'terraces', with no protection from the cold and rain. Following a number of tragedies, football clubs were obliged (for safety reasons) to convert to these to all-seat stadia, many of which are among Europe's best. London's flagship stadium at Wembley is near completion after a being demolished in 2002 to build a new 90,000 capacity venue at a cost of approx £795 million, originally intended to re-open in 2006 but now delays mean a target of opening in time for the 2007 FA cup. You can watch the stadium take shape for yourself on the webcam at (🖳 www.wembleystadium.com) Other major stadia in London are the Wembley Arena and Conference Centre – Engineers Way, Wembley, HA9 0DH (☎ 020-8782 5500, 🖳 www.wembley.co.uk) Wembley Park tube, Wembley Stadium rail and the Crystal Palace National Sports Centre, Ledrington Road, Crystal Palace, SE19 2BB (☎ 020-8778 0131, 🖳 www. crystalpalace.co.uk, Crystal Palace rail.) which hosts the Grand Prix athletics every summer and activities and competitions year round.

Despite the excellent sports facilities in the UK and the estimate that over 25 million people over the age of 13 regularly participate in sport and exercise, around half the population takes part in none at all (apart from strolling to the local pub and staggering back).

Sports results are given on the television, numerous internet sites such as 🖳 www.skysports.co.uk, teletext information service and published widely in daily newspapers. The Sunday broadsheet newspapers provide comprehensive cover and a nationwide results service (particularly for football and rugby). Numerous magazines are published for all sports, from angling to yachting, most of which are available (or can be ordered) from any newsagent. For information about sports facilities in the UK, contact Sports England, Third Floor, Victoria House, Bloomsbury Square, London WC1B 4SE (☎ 08458 508 508, 🖳 www. sportengland.org). The Central Council of Physical Recreation (CCPR), Francis House, Francis Street, London SW1P 1DE (☎ 020-7854 8500, 🖳 www.ccpr. org.uk) is the national association of governing bodies of sport and recreation in the UK. The names and addresses of sports associations and federations can be obtained from either Sports England or the CCPR.

BUNGEE JUMPING

If you fancy a thrill, try a bungee jump from Adrenalin Village (☎ 070-0028 6433) in Queenstown Road, SW8 (Sloane Square tube). It'll cost you in the region of £50 to jump from the 300ft (92m) Chelsea Bridge tower, which has a cage ride to the top so your friends can see you off!

CRICKET

If cricket's more your thing, the season runs from April to September. Although the English invented cricket, they're regularly beaten nowadays by their ex-colonies, including Australia, India, New Zealand, Pakistan, South Africa and the West Indies. The big events of the London season are the two five-day test matches, played at Lord's, St John's Wood Road, St John's Wood, NW8 8QN. (Tickets £10–£50, ☎ 020-7432 1000, 🖳 www.lords.org, St John's Wood tube) and The Oval, Kennington Oval, Kennington, SE11 5SS (Tickets £5–£50 ☎ 08712 461 100, 🖳 www.surreycricket.com, Oval tube). Touring sides also play at least two, one-day international games in London at the aforementioned grounds. You can also see top county cricket played at the Oval (Surrey) and Lord's (Middlesex).

CYCLING

Cycling isn't as popular in the UK as on the continent and not much more than 2.3 per cent of journeys are made by bicycle in the UK compared to an average of 18 per cent in Denmark and 27 per cent in Holland. However, around 1.5 million cycles are sold each year (over a third bought to replace stolen machines!), which adds up to an awful lot of cyclists. Cycle use has increased some 12 per cent since its nadir in 1998 with an increase of 4 per cent last year. In fact it is estimated that in 2002 4.4 billion kilometres were cycled in the UK. Most people in the UK buy cycles for shopping or getting around towns, rather than cycling purely for pleasure, exercise or sport (e.g. touring or racing). If you aren't exhausted from trying to commute across town using pedal power, you can let off steam at the Lee Valley Cycle Circuit (☎ 01992 702 200) at Temple Mills Lane, E15 (Leyton tube).

You can also hire a bike here and take part in BMX, time-trialling, road racing and cyclo-cross. Alternatively, try the oldest cycle circuit in the world at the Herne Hill Velodrome, Burbage Road, Herne Hill, SE24 9HE (☎ 020-7737 4647, 🖥 www.hernehillvelodrome.org.uk) Herne Hill rail. It costs £8 with bike hire or £5.50 if you have your own. An interesting book for Londoners is *On Your Bike*, published by the London Cycling Campaign, 2 Newhams Row, London, SE1 3UZ (☎ 020-7234 9319, 🖥 www.lcc.org.uk). Other useful books include *Richard's New Bicycle Book* by Richard Ballantine (Pan), which is a guide to choosing and using a bicycle and the *Complete Bike Book* by Chris Sidwells (Penguin). Around 15 magazines are published for cyclists in the UK including *Cycling Plus*, *Cycling Weekly*, *Cycle Sport* and *Mountain Biking* .The Bicycling Bookshop at 🖥 www. pennyfarthing.dabsol.co.uk/bicycle-books.htm has a vast array of books on the subject, both new and old.

FOOTBALL

Football is the UK's national spectator and participation sport. The league season in England officially runs from August to May (although professional football seems to be expanding continually in one way or another, with competitions such as the international UEFA Cup in the summer). There's no mid-season winter break, as in many other European countries, although many clubs would like one. Most matches are played on Saturdays, although some clubs play regularly on Friday evenings and there are Tuesday, Wednesday, Sunday afternoon and Monday evening Barclaycard Premiership and Nationwide Football League matches most weeks which are televised live on Sky TV. It isn't necessary to buy a ticket in advance for most matches, although Premiership games, local derbies (matches between neighbouring clubs) and cup matches are usually 'all-ticket', meaning tickets must be purchased in advance. The thriving market for tickets which are acquired and sold on at a fat profit is testimony to demand far exceeding supply.

The Football Association (FA) runs the world's oldest league competition, the FA Cup (instituted in 1888). England's top 20 clubs play in the Premiership, which was formed in the 1992/93 season. There are three lower divisions with 24 teams in each. The three worst-performing Premiership clubs face relegation to the First Division each season, and three First Division teams are promoted in their place. The Premiership has created a huge gulf between its top clubs and those in the lower leagues. Relegation from the Premiership can cost a club over £20 million in lost revenue from TV, sponsorship, advertising and ticket sales (and precipitate the loss of a club's best players).

The cost of tickets in England has risen at well over double the rate of inflation in recent years to fund expensive new all-seat stadia and they now average around £45 for Premiership games. Season tickets are even more expensive and English football fans can pay up to four times more than their continental counterparts. One of most exorbitant London clubs is Chelsea, which charges from £495 to £805. The high price of tickets does not deter supporters: many premier league clubs sell out every home game. However, it is beyond argument that the top clubs are pricing many traditional working class fans out of the game. Tickets for big matches are difficult to obtain; try the club ticket office first and if they cannot help, seats are sometimes available from the main London ticket agencies. The FA Cup Final is currently being played at the Millennium Stadium, Cardiff (☎ Information 0870-013 8600, ticket hotline ☎ 08705-582 582, 🖳 www. millenniumstadium.com) while the new Wembley stadium is being built.

Thanks to the millions pumped into football by sponsors and TV companies in recent years, top British clubs now compete with the richest Italian and Spanish clubs for the best foreign players. British football has been revitalised over the past decade by this, although it has had a detrimental affect on the development of up and coming home-grown stars (some Premiership teams regularly field only one or two English players). It's often cheaper to buy top-class players abroad than in the UK and many clubs have resorted to doing this as prices in the UK have skyrocketed. Transfer fees of £5 million or £10 million are commonplace and top players command far more, notably Rio Ferdinand who was bought by Manchester United for £30 million. This has also put severe pressure on clubs' wage bills: salaries have gone through the roof since the Bosman ruling removed transfer fees for players who have reached the end of their contracts. Many clubs (often without huge resources) spend tens of millions of pounds on wages in an attempt to remain in the Premiership. Premiership salaries are typically £20,000 a week but many better players receive over double this and world class players far more in some cases. (By contrast many players in lower divisions earn around £500 a week).

Not surprisingly, as the capital of a football-mad nation, football clubs ranging from world-class sides to lowly conference teams can be found in all corners of the capital. London's premiership clubs are Arsenal (Arsenal Stadium, Avenell Road, Highbury, N5 1BU ☎ 020-7704 4040, 🖳 www. arsenal.com, Arsenal tube, tickets £32–£70), Charlton Athletic (The Valley, Floyd Road, Charlton, SE7 8BL, ☎ 020-8333 4010, 🖳 www.cafc.co.uk, Charlton rail, tickets £25–£35), Chelsea (Stamford Bridge, Fulham Road, Chelsea, SW6 1HS, ☎ 020-7386 7799, 🖳 www.chelseafc.co.uk, Fulham Broadway tube, tickets £35–£65), Fulham, Rangers Stadium (temporary ground-share with Queens Park Rangers, South Africa Road, Shepherd's Bush, W12 7PA, ☎ 0870-442 1234, 🖳 www.fulhamfc.co.uk, White City tube, tickets £30–£55), Tottenham Hotspur (White Hart Lane Stadium, 748 High Road, Tottenham, N17 0AP, ☎ 0870-420 5000, White Hart Lane rail, tickets £25–£70). You can obtain more information about these clubs and their fixtures from the premiership's official website (🖳 www.fa-premier.com).

London's Division One clubs are Crystal Palace (Selhurst Park, Whitehorse Lane, Selhurst, SE25 6PU, ☎ 020-8771 8841, 🖥 www.cpfc.co.uk, Selhurst rail, tickets £25–£45), Millwall (The Den, Zampa Road, Bermondsey, SE16 3LN, ☎ 020-7231 1199, 🖥 www.millwallfc.co.uk, South Bermondsey rail, tickets £16–£26) and West Ham United (Boleyn Ground, Green Street, West Ham, E13 9AZ, ☎ 0870-112 2700, 🖥 www.whufc.com, Upton Park tube/Stratford rail, tickets £26–£46).

London's current Division Two clubs are West London neighbours, Brentford (Griffin Park, Braemar Road, Brentford, TW8 0NT, ☎ 020-8847 2511, 🖥 www.brentfordfc.co.uk, South Ealing tube, Brentford rail, tickets £14 standing, £18 seated) and Queens Park Rangers (Rangers Stadium, South Africa Road, Shepherd's Bush, W12 7PA, ☎ 020-8740 2575, 🖥 www.qpr.co.uk, White City tube, tickets £14–£24).

Other London clubs include Division Three side Leyton Orient (Matchroom Stadium, Brisbane Road, E10, 🖥 www.leytonorient.com, Leyton tube, tickets £12–£16) and Conference club Barnet (Underhill Stadium, Westcombe Drive, Barnet, EN5 2BE, 🖥 www.barnetfc.com).

British football fans have a terrible reputation for drunkenness and violence abroad, although it's generally safe for women and children to attend a major premier league match. Nearly every London stadium is now all-seat and much of the old violence and hooliganism has disappeared along with the terraces, although the experience certainly isn't what you could call 'refined'. **Don't go if you have a sensitive nature and are shocked by bad language!**

GOLF

Yes, you can play golf in the big city! If it's tuition you want, contact the English Golf Union (☎ 01526-354500) for details. You may like to start with Regent's Park Golf School (☎ 020-7724 0643), Outer Circle, Regent's Park (Baker Street tube). If you just fancy a quick round, there are 18-hole public courses throughout the suburbs as well as more exclusive clubs, although none are on the tube network. It isn't necessary to purchase a set of clubs, as they can be hired for around £7 for 18 holes. Second-hand beginner's sets of clubs can be snapped up for as little as £50, while new sets start at around £230. Green fees (the cost of a round) are reasonable at most public golf clubs, averaging around £5 to £10 per round (18 holes), although fees at top private courses are from between £30 and £50 a day. Fees are usually increased by around 20 to 25 per cent at weekends and on public holidays.

Green fees are reduced for 9-hole courses and many municipal courses allow juniors (under 18s) to play at a cheap rate. Fees may be reduced in winter. Try one of the two courses at Richmond Park (☎ 020-8876 3205) or Chingford Golf Course at Bury Road, E4 (☎ 020-8529 5708). Another option is Dulwich and Sydenham Hill, Grange Lane, College Road, Dulwich, Se21 7LH (020-8693

8491, 💻 www.dulwichgolf.co.uk) West Dulwich rail. Green fee £30 Mondays to Fridays. You can find a complete list of courses at 💻 www.thelondongolfer. com.

Numerous golf books are published, including *Britain's 100 Extraordinary Golf Holes* by Geoff Harvey and Vanessa Strowger (Aesculus Press) and *The Thinking Man's Guide to Golf* by Colin Montgomerie (Orion). Excellent websites also exist including 💻 www.golfuk.co.uk, 💻 www.golfingguides.net, and 💻 www.uklinks.org/sport/golf.

GREYHOUND RACING

For an authentic East End experience and the chance to win some 'bread and honey' (money), try Walthamstow Stadium, Chingford Road, Walthamstow, E4 8SJ (☎ 020-8498 3300, 💻 www.wsgreyhound.co.uk) Walthamstow Central tube/rail then 97, 215 bus. Races 2pm Mondays, 11.30am Fridays and 7.30pm Tuesdays, Thursdays and Saturdays. Admission costs between £1–£6 and is free at lunchtimes from Monday to Friday. A south London alternative is Wimbledon Stadium, Plough Lane, Wimbledon, SW17 0BL (☎ 020-8946 8000) Tooting Broadway tube/Wimbledon tube/rail Haydons Road rail. Races are at 7.30pm on Tuesdays, Fridays and Saturdays and admission costs £5.50.

GYMNASIA & HEALTH CLUBS

There are gymnasia and health and fitness clubs in most towns in the UK. Working out is popular and many companies provide their own health and leisure centres or pay for corporate membership for staff. In addition to many private clubs, most public sports and leisure centres have tonnes of expensive bone-jarring, muscle-wrenching apparatus, designed either to get you into shape or kill you in the attempt. Middle-aged 'fatties' shouldn't attempt to get fit in five minutes (after all it took years of dedicated sloth and over-eating to put on all that weight), as overexertion can result in serious sports injuries. A good gymnasium or health club will ensure this doesn't happen and will carry out a physical assessment, including a blood pressure test, fat distribution measurements and heart rate checks. In your pursuit of the body beautiful it pays to take the long route and give the intensive care unit (or mortuary) a wide berth. London has a huge range of gyms and fitness clubs to suit every budget. Here are a selection of the most popular chains to be found in the capital:

- **Cannons Health Fitness Club** (☎ 0208 336 2288fit, 💻 www.cannons.co.uk). Branches in Battersea, Bloomsbury, Brondesbury Park, City, Covent Garden, Fulham, Norbury, Paddington, Richmond, Twickenham, Wandsworth, West End, Wimbledon.Membership rates vary from Club to Club. You will need to pay an initial joining fee followed by a monthly subscription. Most Cannon clubs are well equipped, with top notch fitness rooms and at least one aerobics studio. Many clubs also have ladies-only areas plus pools and health and beauty suites with a spa, steam room and sauna.

- **David Lloyd Leisure** (☎ 0158-2844 899, ⌨ www.davidlloydleisure.co.uk) Branches in Ealing, Enfield, Finchley, Fulham, Hounslow-Heston, Kensington, Kingston, Raynes Park. David Lloyd Leisure Clubs have hi-tech gymnasiums and aerobic and dance studios, top notch indoor and outdoor tennis courts, squash courts and non-slip badminton courts plus the usual sauna, spa, steam-room and relaxation areas. Prices vary from club to club.

- **Esporta Health Fitness Club** (☎ 0118-912 3500, ⌨ www.esporta.com) Clubs in Chigwell, Chislehurst, Chiswick, Croydon, Enfield, Friern Barnet, Ilford, Islington, Kingston, Northwood, Romford, Swiss Cottage, Wandsworth, Wimbledon. Firmly at the top (and priciest) end of the market, Esporta clubs have spanking new machines, swimming pools, squash and tennis facilities in all clubs. Some of the sites have physiotherapy and sports injury treatment available plus the ubiquitous health suites with saunas, steam rooms, spa, whirlpools and solarium.

- **Fitness First** (☎ 01202-845000, ⌨ www.fitnessfirst.com.) Branches in Acton, Alperton, Balham, Bow Wharf, Brixton, Camden, Clapham, Croydon, North Finchley, Hammersmith, Harrow, Holloway, Islington, Kilburn, Kingsbury, Lewisham, Leyton Mills, Central London - America Square, Berkeley Square, Bloomsbury, Chancery Lane, Covent Garden, Embankment, Fetter Lane, Gracehurst Street, Great Marlborough Street, High Holborn, Kingly Street, Liverpool Street, London Bridge, Old Street, Palace Street, Regent's Park, Victoria, Pinner, Shepherd's Bush, South Kensington, Teddington, Uxbridge, Walworth Road, Woolwich. Currently the largest health club operators in Europe, Fitness First clubs have large gym and fitness rooms. As well as the gym, clubs have aerobics studios with a wide range of classes. Most clubs also have health suites. A one-off joining fee is payable along a monthly membership fee that depends on the club and type of membership you have.

- **Holmes Place** Clubs in Barbican, Bromley, Brook Green, Canary Riverside, Chelsea, Chigwell, Clapham, Crouch End, Croydon, Ealing, Fulham Pools, Hendon, Holloway Road, Kensington, Kingston, Marylebone, Moorgate, Notting Hill, Oxford Street, Putney, Regent's Park, South Wimbledon, Strand and Streatham. (☎ 0845 130 4747, ⌨ www.virginactive.co.uk). Holmes Place now part of Virgin Active also caters for the premium end of the market, offering luxurious health and fitness facilities which include a swimming pool, sauna, steam room, gym and studios. There is a range of memberships available depending on the club, the location and the type of membership you want. The most expensive are in the centre of London and once you have paid the joining fee you will have monthly fees to pay. Contact the club directly for current fees.

- **LA Fitness Gym** (☎ 020-7366 8020, 💻 www.lafitness.co.uk). Clubs in Aldgate, Bayswater, Croydon, New Barnet, Bromley, Edgware, Finchley, Golders Green, Hallam Street, Highgate, Holborn, Isleworth, Leadenhall, London Wall, Marylebone, New Barnet, Piccadilly, South Kensington, Southgate, St Pauls, Sydenham, Victoria, Waldorf, West India Quay. Some clubs have a 'ladies only' workout area. The clubs all have spas, saunas and steam rooms. The joining fee depends on level of membership required and the location.

HORSE RIDING

Once again, the parks turn up trumps. Hyde Park Stables (☎ 020-7723 2813, 💻 www.hydeparkstables.com) in Bathurst Mews, W2 (Lancaster Gate tube) is one of the nicest places to ride in London. A group riding session for an hour costs £40, the same price as a group lesson. Hourly private tuition fees are £50 per hour during the week and £60 at weekends. Further out, try Belmont Riding Centre (☎ 020-8906 1255) in The Ridgeway, NW7 (Mill Hill East tube), which has a full-scale indoor school, a cross-country course on 160 acres, and provides tuition for all ages and levels from beginner to advanced. Wimbledon Village Stables (☎ 020-8946 8579, 💻 www.wvstables.co.uk) in High Street, SW19 (Wimbledon tube) is a smaller operation, offering a range of classes and riding in Richmond Park or on Wimbledon Common (but watch out for the Wombles!).

ICE SKATING

If you're looking for something central, try Leisurebox (☎ 020-7229 0172, 💻 www.queensbowling.com) in Queensway, W2 (Bayswater/Queensway tube) which offers general and family sessions and trains young skaters after school. Friday and Saturday night are disco nights! In the City area you will find an outdoor ice rink. Broadgate Ice Rink (☎ 020-7505 4068, 💻 www. broadgateice.co.uk) at Broadgate Circus, EC2 (Liverpool Street tube) is a friendly and fun place to visit and is famous for a bizarre game called 'broomball', played on Monday to Wednesday evenings. Out in the suburbs you can visit Streatham Ice Arena (☎ 020-8769 7771, 💻 www.streatham icearena.co.uk) in Streatham High Road, SW16 (Streatham rail) or Lee Valley Ice Centre (☎ 020-8533 3154, 💻 www.leevalleypark.org.uk) in Lea Bridge Road, E10 (Blackhorse Road tube).

10

LEISURE CENTRES

Most towns have a community sports or leisure centre (also called recreation centres), usually run and financed by London Borough Councils. A huge range of sports and activities are catered for, including badminton, basketball, netball, swimming and diving, squash, indoor football (five-a-side), roller-skating, BMX bikes, gymnastics, yoga, weight training, table tennis, tennis, racquetball, aerobics, cricket, climbing, canoeing (in the swimming pool), archery, bowls, hockey, martial arts and snooker. Councils publish a wealth of information about local sports and leisure centres on their websites. London has facilities to suit every pocket. There are far too many to list here, but you can obtain details from your London Business phone book or call Sportsline (☎ 020-7222 8000) for information. Remember to book ahead if you're after a squash court or wish to join a class. Some of the most popular central facilities include the following:

- The **Jubilee Hall Leisure Centre** (☎ 020-7836 4835) in the Covent Garden piazza (Covent Garden tube) is enormous, well-equipped, and provides a vast selection of free weights in its cavernous gym, plus aerobics, step and martial arts classes.

- The **Seymour Leisure Centre** in Seymour Place, W1 (Edgware Road/ Marble Arch tube) is another centrally located fitness centre with a sports hall and cardiovascuiar suite as well as the usual steam room, sauna and Jacuzzi. It also offers classes in aerobics, step and body conditioning. (☎ 020-7723 8019).

- The **Michael Sobell Leisure Centre** (☎ 020-7609 2166) at Hornsey Road, N7 (Finsbury Park/Holloway Road tube) is another enormous centre boasting a climbing wall, trampolining and a gym.

- The **Queen Mother Sports Centre** (☎ 020-7630 5522) in Vauxhall Bridge Road, SW1 (Victoria tube) has not only a gym, but two dance studios, a sauna and steam room, martial arts, aerobics and a swimming pool.

- The **Arches Leisure Centre**, Trafalgar Road, Greenwich, SE10 9UX (☎ 020-8317 5000), Maze Hill rail, Greenwich DLR is in the heart of historic Greenwich in the original 1930s "Greenwich Baths" building. The Arches Leisure Centre gained national recognition by winning the Fitness Industry Association "Flame" award for "Best Leisure Centre" in 2000.

Slightly farther out of town options include:

10

- The **Kentish Town Sports Centre,** Prince of Wales Road, London NW5 3LE (☎ 020-7267 9341), which has two swimming pools, a teaching pool, exercise studios, gymnasium and belly dancing, body conditioning and Tai Chi Yoga classes.

- The **Archway Leisure Centre** MacDonald Road, N19 5DD (☎ 020-7281 4105, 💻 www.acquaterra.org/Islington/archway). The centre has a leisure pool with a river run, spa pools, water slide, water jets, waves, lane swimming and lessons. The centre also provides children's parties, a hi-tech gym with computerised machines and satellite television, magic boat soft play area and water aerobics.

- The **Putney Leisure Centre**, Dryburgh Road, London SW15 1BL (☎ 020-8785 0388), with its 395m^2 air-conditioned gym, a precision cycling studio, new air conditioned dance studio, cafeteria and a purpose built creche.

- **The Sanctuary** (☎ 0870-770 3350, 💻 www.thesanctuary.co.uk) **for women only** in Floral Street, WC2 (Covent Garden tube). It's ruinously expensive at £65 for a day ticket (Mondays to Thursdays), £75 Fridays to Sundays and £40 for an evening, but it's worth it just to luxuriate in the tropical plant-filled interior or swim naked in the wonderful pool. Your admission fee also includes unlimited use of the sauna, Jacuzzi and steam room, and there's a range of beauty treatments on sale if you have any money left.

MOTORSPORTS

Motor racing has a huge following in the UK and embraces everything from Formula One grand prix to stock car racing. Among the many classifications of motor racing in the UK are Formulas One, Two and Three; Formula 3000; sports car and Formula Ford racing; rallying; hill-climbing; historic sports car racing; competitions among special one-make series (such as TVR, Renault 5, Maxda MX-5 and Honda CRX, to name but a few); autocross; go-karting and bantam racing for kids. The most famous motor racing venues in the UK are Brands Hatch and Silverstone, host to the British Grand Prix, which is part of the F1 World Motor Racing Championship. This is one of the UK's most expensive sporting events, with tickets for the 2004 race costing from up to £300. Motorcycle racing is almost as popular and includes grand prix racing at 125cc, 250cc, 350cc, 500cc levels and superbikes over 1,000cc. There are a number of magazines dedicated to motor sports in the UK and lots of websites including 💻 www.fia.com, 💻 www.motorsport.org.uk, 💻 www.motorsport.co.uk and 💻 www.f1-racing.org.

10

RACKET SPORTS

There are excellent facilities in the UK for most racket sports, particularly badminton, squash, racketball and tennis. If you're an advanced player, you may find the level of competition is higher at private clubs than at community leisure centres. Racket sport leagues and competitions are also organised by many companies and schools, and some of the latter have their own courts.

Court costs for all racket sports are usually cheaper before 5pm and after 5pm at weekends, although lunch-time periods may be charged at peak rates for some sports, e.g. squash. Courts in public sports and leisure centres can be booked up to two weeks in advance, while private clubs may allow bookings to be made further in advance. You must usually cancel a booked court 24 or 48 hours in advance, otherwise you must pay for it if it isn't re-booked. Rackets, shoes and towels can usually be hired (or purchased) from both public sports centres and private clubs. Most centres and clubs organise internal leagues, ladders and knockout competitions, and also participate in local and national league and cup competitions.

To find the rackets clubs in your local area look in the yellow pages, enquire at your local library or contact the appropriate national association.

Badminton

Badminton in the UK, with an estimated 2.5 million players, is more popular than tennis. The cost of hiring a badminton court in a sports centre is around £5 to £8 an hour or around £4 an hour at off-peak times.

Squash

Squash (or more correctly squash rackets) has been declining in popularity since its heyday in the '80s but is still widely played and there's an abundance of courts in sports centres and private squash clubs in all areas. England has a larger number of players and courts than any other country in the world and boasts the current world number one player, Peter Nicol. Private clubs usually cater exclusively for squash, and clubs combining squash and tennis (or some other sport) are rare. Many private squash clubs have a resident coach, providing both individual and group lessons.

The cost of hiring a court in a sports centre is from around £5 to £7 for a 40 or 45 minute session or £6 to £10 for an hour. Off-peak (before 5pm) fees may be around £3 or £4 for 45 minutes (students and the unemployed are entitled to use council facilities for half price during off-peak hours in some areas). Annual membership of a private squash club varies from around £50 to £120 a year; off-peak, family and junior membership may also be available.

Court fees are usually around the same or a little lower than for municipal courts, although there may be an extra charge for guests.

Squash is an energetic sport and you should think twice about taking it up in middle age, particularly if you're unfit, have high blood pressure or a heart or respiratory problem. Players of any age should get fit to play squash and shouldn't play squash to become fit. Doctors recommend that players don't take a sauna after a squash game, which can be dangerous as it increases the heart rate and body temperature. Tennis or badminton are better choices for the middle-aged, as they aren't as frenetic as squash and encourage oxygen to enter the body (although singles badminton can be a hard slog). Further information can be found on 💻 www.squashplayer.co.uk and 💻 www.squash.uk.com.

Racketball

Racketball is an 'easy' version of squash and is played in the UK on a squash court; rackets and balls can be hired at most squash clubs.

Table Tennis

Table tennis is popular in the UK and is played both as a serious competitive sport and as a pastime in social and youth clubs. Most sports centres have a number of table tennis tables for hire for as little as £4 an hour and bats can be hired for a small fee. If you want to play seriously there are clubs in most areas. Costs vary, but it's an inexpensive sport with little equipment necessary.

Tennis

Despite the popularity of tennis as a spectator sport in the UK (particularly Wimbledon), actually playing tennis only seems popular for a few weeks of the year when the prestigious tournament inspires couch potatoes to venture on to a court. Tennis isn't much fun in the cold and rain and indoor tennis courts are relatively scarce and prohibitively expensive. Everyone's heard of Wimbledon and Queens, but you don't need to join a fancy club to play in London – in any case, the most prestigious clubs have long waiting lists that reflect their lofty status. Many of London's parks provide tennis courts, most for little or no fee, but you must make a reservation. Courts are available at Hyde Park (☎ 020-7298 2100), Regent's Park (☎ 020-7486 7905), Victoria Park (☎ 020-8533 2057), Hampstead Heath (☎ 020-7485 3873) and Battersea Park (☎ 020-8871 7530). Alternatively, there's the fashionable (and more expensive) Islington Tennis Centre (☎ 020-7700 1370) in Market Road, N7 (Caledonian Road tube) which has three floodlit outdoor and three indoor courts and also provides coaching.

10

For further information write to the Lawn Tennis Association Trust (Queen's Club, West Kensington, London W14 9EG, ☎ 020-7381 7000) for a copy of their leaflet, *Where to Play Tennis in London*. Some centres have outdoor courts with artificial surfaces which can be used in all weathers and some parks and most sports centres have floodlit outdoor courts. There may be a nominal membership fee of around £5 to use some municipal courts. If you're a serious tennis player you may be interested in joining a private club. Costs vary but can be high, e.g. a £150 enrolment fee plus a £300 annual subscription (or a monthly fee of around £25) for single membership of an exclusive tennis club, with both indoor and outdoor courts. Many private clubs also have gymnasia and swimming pools that can be used by members for an increased payment. Special rates are usually available for couples and families. Sports centres and private clubs usually have coaches available for both private and group lessons. The official website of the Lawn Tennis Association is 🖥 www.lta.org.uk. If you're a tennis fan, chances are you will be keen to attend Wimbledon where the Grand Slam championship is played in the last week of June and the first week of July on the hallowed lawns of the All England Lawn Tennis and Croquet Club, Church Road, Wimbledon (☎ 020-8946 2244, 🖥 www.wimbledon.org, Southfields/Wimbledon Park tube). If you want a ticket for centre or number one court and aren't connected with a club member or corporate sponsor, you must first obtain an application form. You need to apply by post between 1st September and 31st December of the previous year, enclosing a stamped addressed envelope. You will then go into a ballot and will be informed later whether you've been successful, although there's nothing to stop you queuing for hours each day during the championships for a ticket to the outside courts. You need to arrive before 9am for a realistic chance of getting in when play starts at noon. If you wish to have a chance at the tiny number of centre and number one court tickets sold on match days then you'll need to be prepared to spend a night under the stars with the other die-hard fans!

You can also see top-class men's tennis at the Queen's Club tournament (☎ 020-7385 3421) in Palliser Road, W14 (Baron's Court tube) which is the main curtain-raiser to Wimbledon. Once again, application forms must be obtained the previous year and returned by 30th September in order to go into the ballot for tickets, although returns are for sale on match days.

10

RUGBY

There are two kinds of rugby football played in the UK: 15-a-side rugby union, the code most common in London, and 13-a-side rugby league, which is played mainly in the north of the country. London has two major local rugby union teams: the Harlequins, based at Stoop Memorial Ground (☎ 020-8410 6000, 🖥 www.quins.co.uk) in Twickenham (Twickenham rail) and the Wasps who are based at Twyford Avenue Sports Ground, Twyford Avenue, W3 9QA

(💻 www.wasps.co.uk) Ealing Common tube. However, there are a number of other teams, including London Scottish, London Irish and the London Broncos. The headquarters of rugby union is Twickenham Stadium, Whitton Road (Twickenham rail) which stages international matches and the highlight of the club season, the Pilkington Cup Final in April.

SKIING

Skiing is a popular sport with the British, who have made up for their lack of snow (and mountains) with dry-slope skiing. As well as being an excellent training ground for the 'real thing', dry-slope skiing has become a popular sport in its own right. Most centres have a ski racing team and dry-slope competitions are held regularly throughout the year. Learning to ski on a dry-slope can save you both time and money when you arrive in a winter resort, and also helps experienced skiers find their ski-legs before arriving. A dry-slope consists of around 2,000m² of ski-matting, usually with separate areas for beginners and advanced skiers. The maximum descent of 'pistes' is around 500m, although most are 200m to 300m. Poma or button ski tows (or even a chair lift) are usually provided and floodlights light up evening skiing in winter. You should use your own ski boots (they can also be hired) and wear old clothes, as the matting can damage expensive ski suits. Gloves are usually compulsory. **Don't use good skis as they don't take kindly to the artificial surface and make sure that the bindings of hired skis are adjusted to your weight and ability.** Equipment hire is usually included in the hourly rate, which varies considerably. Many centres offer weekly and season tickets which are usually good value for money. It's best to ski at quiet times, as centres can get extremely crowded at weekends, particularly towards Christmas when everyone is keen to get in a bit of practice before heading off to the Alps. Tuition is provided at all levels for both adults and children, although off-piste skiing is frowned upon! A three-hour course costs from around £45 to £65, depending on the centre.

Skiing can also be practised indoors in the UK on a new type of artificial snow, which genuinely feels like the real thing. The only centre currently offering this within reasonable proximity to London is the Snowzone in Milton Keynes, Buckinghamshire. The Snowzone gets really cold – the temperature is never more than -3°C and with the wind-chill factor when skiing it can feel like -15°C – so wrap up accordingly. If you're looking for a book about learning or improving your skiing, the *Sunday Times* book *We Learned to Ski* (Collins) is an excellent choice for all standards. A number of ski magazines are published in the UK. The *Daily Mail* International Ski Show is held at Earls Court in November, where all the latest equipment and clothing can be seen. Dry ski slopes are handy when it comes to learning the basics and brushing up on your ski skills before a holiday.

The main dry ski slope in London, Hillingdon Ski Centre in Uxbridge is currently closed until further notice due to a fire on the slope. Another slope at Beckton in East London has also been shut and is due to reopen as a 'snowdome' in 2007. Two other possibilities a little further out of town are:

- **Bromley Ski Centre**, Sandy Lane, St Paul's Cray, Orpington, Kent, BR5 3HY (☎ 01689-876812, 🖥 www.c-v-s.co.uk/bromleyski), which boasts a 120 metre main slope served by two lifts, a mogul run for accomplished skiers plus a nursery slope for beginners. The Centre is open 12 months of the year and there is even a fully licensed bar so you can enjoy an après-ski shandy or two after your endeavours.

- **Warley Ski Centre**, Holdens Wood Warley Gap Brentwood, Essex, CM13 3DP (☎ 01277-211994), has an outdoor dry slope and offers ski tuition, snowboard tuition.

SWIMMING POOLS

London has a fine selection of lidos (swimming pools) for those all too infrequent hot summer days, including Brockwell Lido, Dulwich Road, London SE24 0PA (☎ 020-7274 3088, 🖥 www.thelido.co.uk). With its 1930s Art Deco cafe, this south London pool is something of a local landmark. Charlton Lido, Charlton Park Lane, Charlton, SE7 (☎ 020-8856 7180), Charlton rail, is open only throughout the school summer holidays. Facilities include a 50m pool and toddlers splash pool. Finchley Lido, Great North Leisure Park, High Road, Finchley, N12 0AE (☎ 020-8343 9830), East Finchley or Finchley Central tube, is a good option for north Londoners. Parliament Hill Lido, Parliament Hill Fields, Gordon House Road, London NW5 2LT (☎ 020-7485 3873, 🖥 www. cityoflondon.gov.uk/openspaces), Gospel Oak rail/C11 bus, has a 60m (200ft) long open-air unheated swimming pool and the early morning swimming session is free. Serpentine Lido, Hyde Park, W2 2UH (☎ 020-7706 3422, 🖥 www.serpentinelido.com), Knightsbridge or South Kensington tube, is open to the public in the summer and is the perfect place to cool off if you work in central London. Tooting Bec Lido, Tooting Bec Common, London, SW16 1RU (☎ 020-8871 7198), Tooting Bec tube/Streatham rail, is open to the public from late May until the end of September. The Lido has a 90m (300ft) pool and children's paddling pool. Facilities for those with disabilities include showers, toilets and changing areas.

Two of the best indoor pools are the Ironmonger Row Baths in Finsbury (☎ 020-7253 4011, 🖥 www.aquaterra.org), near Old Street tube, and, more centrally, the Oasis Sports Centre in Convent Garden (☎ 020-7831 1804), Holborn tube. For details of other indoor pools, visit individual London Borough Council websites.

10

WATERSPORTS

This is where London's River Thames comes into its own. The Docklands boast three separate clubs. If it's sailing that you're after, try the Docklands Sailing and Watersports Club at Millwall Dock E14 which provides a variety of courses. At King George V Dock (Gallions Reach DLR/North Woolwich rail) you can learn to jet-ski at the Docklands Watersports Club (☎ 020-7511 7000) or water-ski at the Royal Docks Waterski Club (☎ 020-7511 2000) inside London City Airport. If you'd rather learn to row, try the Capital Rowing Centre (☎ 020-8395 2190) in Ibis Lane, W4 (Chiswick rail) which has beginner's courses starting at £4 for an hour and a half. If you'd rather go it alone, you can rent a rowing boat in Hyde Park, Regent's Park or Battersea Park.

MISCELLANEOUS SPORTS

The following are a selection of other popular sports in the UK. For addresses and telephone numbers of national sports associations contact Sport England or the Central Council of Physical Recreation.

Archery

Still a popular sport in the UK, many years after the British army was issued with more modern weapons. The UK is still searching for a modern Robin Hood who can win an elusive Olympic gold medal. Crossbow shooting is also practised in some clubs.

Basketball

Basketball is becoming increasingly popular in the UK (there are over 1,000 clubs). Basketball doesn't have a strong following as a professional sport in the UK, although the top teams participate in the European Clubs Championship.

Boxing

Legalised punch-ups for violent types. Popular throughout the country, particularly as a spectator 'sport' (many people enjoy watching a good fight, as long as they're out of harm's way). Most towns have a boxing club and gymnasia for budding professionals are common in the main cities. the UK has produced a stream of world champions over the years.

Darts

Not actually a sport, but an excuse to get drunk. Around 5 million people play darts regularly in the UK (which dominates the world championship), usually in pubs, most of which have teams playing in local leagues.

Fencing

A sport which has lost a lot of its popularity since the invention of the gun, although a hard core of enthusiast swordsmen are holding out in a small number of clubs.

Foreign Sports

Many foreign sports and pastimes have a group of expatriate fanatics in the UK including American football, baseball, *boccia*, *boules* (and *pétanque*), Gaelic sports (hurling, Gaelic football), handball and softball. For information enquire at council offices, libraries, tourist offices, expatriate social clubs, embassies and consulates.

Frisbee

Believe it or not, throwing plastic discs around has actually developed into a competitive 'sport', with national and local league and cup competitions.

Hockey

Hockey is a very old sport in the UK and has gained wider appeal since the UK won the Olympic gold medal in Seoul in 1988, although it still faces an uphill battle to woo youngsters away from football, rugby and cricket. Equally popular among both sexes.

Horse Racing

Horse racing is popular in the UK, although not because the British are a nation of equestrians or horse lovers, but rather inveterate gamblers. Horse racing is known as the sport of kings and you certainly need a king's ransom to buy and keep a horse in training. An extensive programme of events is organised throughout the year consisting of national hunt racing (steeplechasing and hurdles races) from August to April and flat racing from March to October.

Horse Riding

Equestrianism is popular in the UK and needn't be expensive unless you wish to own your own horse. The UK has a proud tradition of breeding and horsemanship and is one of the world's leading show jumping nations.

Martial Arts

For those brought up on a diet of Bruce Lee, unarmed combat such as Aikido,

Judo, Karate, Kung Fu, Kushido, Taekwon-Do and T'ai Chi Ch'uan, are taught and practised in many leisure centres and clubs. Judo is the most popular martial art in the UK and a sport in which the UK has had considerable international success.

Rollerskating & Rollerblading

Rollerskating rinks are widely available and are sometimes located in leisure centres. Skates can be hired, coaches are to hand, and roller-discos for teenagers are often organised. Rollerblading - using skates on which the wheels are set in a line - was a craze for a while. It's now less popular and its practice has been curbed on public paths due to the risks to cyclists and pedestrians (some of whom have been killed in collisions). Keen rollerskaters and rollerbladers often play roller hockey.

Rounders

The forerunner to baseball, which is popular in schools and is usually played in the UK by females, and with a little less razzmatazz.

Skateboarding & BMX

Rinks and specially designed circuits are provided in many towns for skateboarding and BMX cycles (acrobatics on a bicycle). Children can start at around seven but participants of all ages should be protected against falls with crash helmets and elbow and knee pads. It's difficult to hire equipment as it's too easily stolen, although BMX bikes can usually be hired. The cost of using purpose-built facilities is around £2 to £5 (including the hire of a bike) or nearer £1 if you provide your own bike.

Tenpin Bowling

After a decline in the 1970s, the sport made a comeback at the end of the 20th century. Two options to try are Rowans Bowl in Finsbury Park (☎020-8800 1950, 🖥 www.rowans.co.uk) which has 24 lanes and charges £2.50–£3.70 per game or the 36 lane Acton MegaBowl (☎ 0871 550 1010, 🖥 www.mega bowl. co.uk) which has 28 lanes and charges £6.25 per game for adults.

Wrestling

This refers to the real sport of wrestling (as practised in the Olympics) rather than the cabaret stuff shown on TV. However, when it comes to mass popularity, showbiz wrestling is streets ahead.

11

SPEND, SPEND, SPEND

London is one of the world's great shopping cities, catering for all tastes and pockets. It has an abundance of smart department stores and designer shops, the equal of any European or American city, although the prices aren't always as keen. However, whilst it's true that London's most exclusive shops are ruinously expensive, there's also much to offer the budget shopper, including a wealth of discount stores, street markets and out-of-the-way shops.

Opening hours for shops in central London are usually from between 9 and 10am until 5.30 or 6pm, Mondays to Saturdays. Shops don't shut for lunch and some stay open until between 7 and 8pm, especially on 'late night shopping day' (usually Wednesday or Thursday) and in the run-up to Christmas. Shops are permitted to open on Sundays between the hours of 10am and 6pm and many major stores open from noon until 6pm, although you should check in advance if you're planning to visit a particular store.

In most shops you have a choice of payment methods; cash, cheques (with a guarantee card), debit cards and major credit cards are almost universally accepted, although some shops won't accept them for purchases under £5 or £10. Most of the larger department stores and chains also issue their own store cards. However, travellers' cheques and foreign currency are rarely accepted. It's worth noting that if you're a foreign national living outside the European Union you can apply for reimbursement of British value added tax (17.5 per cent) on purchases. Shops will give you a form to complete, which you must have stamped by customs when you leave the country with the goods.

British law allows you to return goods that prove to be faulty for a full refund or a replacement, but make sure you keep your receipt as proof of purchase. If you simply change your mind about something you've bought or discover it doesn't fit, a shop isn't obliged to change it for another item or refund your money. However, many chain stores (such as Marks & Spencer) will make cash refunds for any reason and most will give you a credit note if a purchase is returned in mint condition.

Most London shops hold at least two sales a year – in January and July – when you can buy branded goods at greatly reduced prices. Old stock and ends of lines are sometimes marked down by 50 per cent or more, so it's worthwhile earmarking some money from your Christmas and holiday budgets to spend in the sales (the 'January' sales often start on 26th December!). Other 'minor' sales may be held throughout the year. Many stores will post or deliver goods to you if you order by phone and pay by credit or debit card.

Many large stores make free home deliveries within a certain radius and many also despatch items by post to anywhere in the country (and abroad). Shopping from home has recently taken a giant leap forward with the advent of the internet (see page 334), although Londoners tend not to be dedicated internet shoppers, as they have virtually everything they need on their doorstep. However, most major supermarket chains now offer home shopping via the internet if you live within a certain distance of a participating store.

Although little more than a pilot scheme a year ago, this service has now spread throughout London – if you're interested try Sainsbury's (🖥 www. sainsburystoyou.com), Tesco (🖥 www.tesco.com) or Waitrose (🖥 www.ocado. com). Those with Sky digital television (see page 365) can use the recently launched interactive shopping service, Open, to order goods from a growing number of stores, including groceries from Somerfield, CDs from Woolworths and books from WH Smith (but check to see whether your area qualifies for home delivery).

Although central London's crowded streets can present difficult terrain for wheelchair users, some shops and malls operate 'shop mobility' schemes. Access to London's shops for disabled people is detailed on a useful website (🖥 www. visitlondon.com/plan_a_visit/disabled) and in a book entitled *Access in London* by Gordon Couch, William Forrester and Justin Irwin (Quiller Press).

The UK officially converted to metrication on 1st October 1995 and all retailers must now price goods in kilograms, litres and metres, despite the fact that many Britons haven't got a clue whether a pound (454 grams) weighs more or less than a kilogram (1,000 grams). However, British measures such as pounds, pints and feet can be used alongside metrication and many stores display conversion tables. For those who aren't used to buying goods with British measures and sizes, a list of comparative weights and measures is provided in **Appendix D**.

It's often said that London isn't so much a city as a collection of villages (from which it grew) – and nowhere is this more evident than when shopping. The cheap tourist 'trinkets' on sale in the eastern half of Oxford Street have little in common with the exotic fare of Soho or the exclusive goods to be found in Old Bond Street, yet these areas are little more than a mile apart.

On the other hand, in every suburb of the metropolis you will find branches of supermarkets and chain stores that have spread throughout the UK, which makes one city shopping street seem much like any other. These include the mid-range fashion stores Accessorize, French Connection, Gap, Laura Ashley, Monsoon, Next, Oasis and Warehouse; cheap-and-cheerful budget fashion stores BHS, H&M, Miss Selfridge, New Look and Top Shop/Top Man; toiletries giants The Body Shop, Boots and Superdrug; record stores HMV, Our Price and Virgin; book chains Books Etc, Dillons, Waterstones and WH Smith; and supermarkets Co-op, Safeway, Sainsbury's, Tesco and Waitrose – not to mention stalwarts such as Marks & Spencer and the budget-conscious Woolworths..

To make the most of shopping in London you need to know where the really interesting independent shops are: where you can buy a chic pair of shoes or an organic sausage, and how to find industrial work-wear or a left-hand potato peeler. Below is a region by region 'tour' of some of the best and most fascinating stores London has to offer. For further information, obtain a copy of the annual *Time Out Guide to Shopping & Services in London*, listing over 2,000 shops, *The Serious Shoppers' Guide to London* by Beth Reiber, *Frommer's Born to Shop*

London by Suzy Gershman (both John Wiley & Sons) or *The Markets of London* by Alec Forshaw & Theo Bergström (Penguin). If you're looking for second-hand bargains, try the periodicals *Exchange & Mart* or *Loot* or any local newspaper.

WEST END

Let's start our shopping tour where everyone begins: in the central area of the capital known as the West End (it isn't really in west London but is merely to the west of the City).

Oxford Street

Oxford Street represents the heart of London's West End shopping and is the UK's busiest street (although it's increasingly under threat from vast out-of-town shopping centres). At peak shopping times the pavements are almost gridlocked and it isn't uncommon for workers to be late back to their offices after a lunchtime shopping dash, having got stuck in a 'people-jam' of purchase-laden pedestrians. In addition, around 9 million foreign tourists trudge up and down the street each year, accounting for some 20 per cent of its income.

Until the '60s, Oxford Street was a smart place to shop with Edwardian department stores Selfridges, Debenham & Freebody and Waring & Gillow dominating its length. Only Selfridges (see below) remains now in anything like its original form, and much of Oxford Street, particularly the eastern half, is dominated by tatty tourist souvenir shops, jeans emporia, record stores, snack bars and employment agencies. However, its Christmas lights still draw the crowds, and the police and the Oxford Street Association (a trader's organisation) between them do their best to control shoplifting and pickpockets through all-seeing CCTV cameras. Don't pick your nose or scratch your backside here – you're on candid camera!

Despite the crowds, the crime and the tatty souvenirs, the pick of Oxford Street is well worth visiting. In the part of the street west of the central crossroads known as Oxford Circus, the mighty department store Selfridges (☎ 0870-837 7377, 🖳 www.selfridges.co.uk) at 400 Oxford Street (Bond Street/Marble Arch tube) has recently undergone a major refit to drag it kicking and screaming into the 21st century. It's still a delightfully eccentric and sprawling place to go browsing, with the largest cosmetics department in Europe and a wide range of fashion clothing, although some departments are strangely disappointing.

Close to Selfridges at 458 Oxford Street (Bond Street/Marble Arch tube) is the flagship branch of national chain Marks & Spencer (☎ 020-7935 7954, 🖳 www.marksandspencer.com). A long-term British institution, 'M&S' (also referred to as 'Marks & Sparks' and simply 'Marks') has been having problems in recent years, which have been blamed on its unexciting fashion ranges, thier focus now is to turn this around with a more up-to-date feel.

The stores specialise in sensible, classic clothes for both sexes – and are the chief purveyors of comfortable and reasonably-priced underwear to the nation. This enormous store has the best choice of any branch in London, although you can find them in any high street, and there's a second branch at 173 Oxford Street, near Oxford Circus.

Further east, towards Oxford Circus at 278–306 Oxford Street (Oxford Circus tube) is the John Lewis department store (☎ 020-7629 7711, 🖥 www.johnlewis.com), which is also part of a national chain. Once again, this is their flagship store and it tends to concentrate on goods that the other stores don't stock. The furniture and haberdashery departments are excellent and in recent years has imported all kinds of exotica from India and other Asian countries.

Another department store, House of Fraser (☎0870 160 7258, 🖥 www.houseoffraser.co.uk), can be found at 318 Oxford Street (Oxford Circus tube) at the more downmarket, eastern end of the street. Like Debenhams (☎ 0844 561 6161, 🖥 www.debenhams.com) at 334–338 Oxford Street (Oxford Circus/Tottenham Court Road tube) it handles the mid-range goods available in almost any urban shopping centre.

Like all London shopping streets, Oxford Street is also dotted with branches of run-of-the-mill chain stores. Of these, probably the best examples are the flagship branches of Top Shop and H&M at Oxford Circus, and Miss Selfridge at 40 Duke Street, just round the corner from its parent Selfridges store. HMV has stores selling CDs, videos, computer games and entertainment-linked merchandise at 150 and 363 Oxford Street and its main rival, the enormous Virgin Megastore, is at 14 and 527 Oxford Street.

Oxford Street also features two noteworthy shopping malls: The Plaza at 120 Oxford Street (☎ 020-7637 8811) is a recent development at the eastern end (Tottenham Court Road tube), while the smarter West One shopping centre within the Bond Street underground station complex is at the western half of the street.

Regent Street

Running at right angles to Oxford Street is the crescent-shaped thoroughfare Regent Street, once a gloriously upmarket area now looking more down-at-heel with the influx of a plethora of travel agencies and chain stores. One of the best shops here is Liberty (☎ 020-7734 1234) at 210–220 Regent Street (Oxford Circus tube). Home of the original Liberty print fabrics, this rambling mock-Tudor department store has a decidedly late 19th century feel to it and stocks some wonderful women's fashion and jewellery.

A stone's throw from Liberty is Dickins & Jones (☎ 020-7734 7070) at 224–244 Regent Street (Oxford Circus tube), part of the House of Fraser group and devoted to fashion and beauty items, with a particularly strong line in accessories. Classic English outdoor fashion for weekends in the country can be found at Burberry (☎ 020-7806 1328) at 165 Regent Street (Piccadilly Circus tube), while a classic of a different cut can be found at the Levi's store at 174–176 Regent Street (☎ 020-7409 2692, Oxford Circus tube).

If you have children or grandchildren, don't miss Hamleys (☎ 0800 2802 444) at 188–196 Regent Street (Oxford Circus tube). Although it isn't cheap, it has a greater range of toys than you're liable to see anywhere outside an out-of-town branch of Toys 'R' Us. There are five floors and the largest selection of board games anywhere in London. At Christmas time it's a war zone!

Tottenham Court Road

Running north to south at the extreme eastern end of Oxford Street is Tottenham Court Road, best known for its 'electronics' shops, selling hi-fi, computers and cameras, and for its furnishing and interior design stores. Gultronics (☎ 020-7323 2838) at 52 Tottenham Court Road (Tottenham Court Road/Goodge Street tube) stocks a wide range of computer hardware but specialises in laptops. You can pick up second-hand equipment at Computer Exchange (☎ 020-7419 2590) at No.70 (Goodge Street tube). For hi-fi, head for Hi-Fi Care (☎ 020-7637 8911) at No.231 (Tottenham Court Road tube) or the oddly named Cornflake Shop (☎ 020-7323 4554) round the corner at 37 Windmill Street (Goodge Street tube). Jessops (☎ 020-7240 6077), another national chain, has one of the world's largest camera shops nearby at 63–69 New Oxford Street.

Competition in Tottenham Court Road is fierce and most shops will match or beat any advertised price, so this is the place to buy the latest electronic gizmos. If you're looking for some new furniture, scout around stylish Heal's (☎ 020-7636 1666) at No.196 (Goodge Street tube), the adjacent branch of Habitat (☎ 020-7631 3880) or Purves & Purves (☎ 020-7580 8223) at No.220–224 (Goodge St/Warren Street tube).

Carnaby Street

For many years the pedestrianised Carnaby Street and its satellites survived on the myth of a glorious past in the swinging '60s, but lately the shabby souvenir shops and jeans chains have begun to give way to more interesting fare once again. Carnaby Street itself is still dominated by tatty fashion boutiques and Soccer Scene (☎ 020-7439 0778), 'Europe's leading football store', on the corner with Great Marlborough Street (Oxford Circus tube), but in Newburgh Street there's the designer menswear shop Fletcher, while at 22a Conduit Street (Oxford Circus tube) there's Rigby & Peller (☎ 0845 076 5545), corsetieres to the Queen. If you're tired of making do with badly-fitting off-the-peg underwear, splash out here, where your 'protruding bits' can be expertly corralled into shape by friendly, understanding assistants.

11

Old & New Bond Street

Old Bond Street and New Bond Street and their tributaries make up much of the Mayfair district. This is the province of the seriously rich and almost every major designer name has a foothold here. If your credit cards will take it, visit Gucci (☎ 020-7629 2716) at 32/33 Old Bond Street, Nicole Farhi (☎ 020-7499 8368) at 158 New Bond Street, Donna Karan (☎ 020-7493 3100) at 19 New Bond Street (its sister store DKNY – ☎ 020-7499 6238 – selling younger and slightly cheaper clothes, is at 27 Old Bond Street, both Bond Street/Green Park tube), Comme des Garçons (☎ 020-7493 1258) at 59 Brook Street (Bond Street tube), Joseph (☎ 020-7629 3713) at 23 Old Bond Street or Vivienne Westwood (☎ 020-7629 3757) at 6 Davies Street (Bond Street tube).

Fenwick's (☎ 020-7629 9161) at 63 New Bond Street and Browns (☎ 020-7514 0000) at 23–27 South Molton Street (both Bond Street tube) stock a range of designer names, and Watches of Switzerland (☎ 020-7493 5916) at 16 New Bond Street (Green Park tube) is worth a visit if you're after an elegant and expensive timepiece. If you're after fine jewellery or silverware, try Asprey & Garrard (☎ 020-7493 6767), the royal jewellers, who have their base at 167 New Bond Street (Green Park tube), or you can choose Tiffany & Co (☎ 020-7499 4577) at 25 Old Bond Street (Green Park/Piccadilly Circus tube) or Cartier (☎ 020-7290 5150) at 40-41 Old Bond Street.

Slightly less stratospherically-priced jewellery can be found at the Electrum Gallery (☎ 020-7629 6325) at 21 South Molton Street (Bond Street tube), where over 100 designers sell their wares. Mulberry (☎ 020-7491 3900) at 41-42 New Bond Street (Bond Street tube) is the place to go for expensive leather bags and accessories, or try the hand-made leather goods at Osprey in St Christopher's Place (Bond Street tube). Sotheby's (☎ 020-7293 5000), the auction house, can also be found here at 34 New Bond Street (Green Park tube).

Piccadilly

Piccadilly (a street, not a district) could be said to be part of Mayfair, although it's at the rather less salubrious end. The gaudy neon signs of Piccadilly Circus (no longer a 'circus' since the statue of Eros was moved from its centre a few years ago) have, surprisingly, been around since Edwardian times – the drug addicts and rent-boys who cluster round the statue not quite so long. Piccadilly itself is home to several notable stores. The ground floor of Fortnum & Mason is London's food store *par excellence*, a cornucopia of yummy goodies from around the world, from truffles to pickled walnuts. Their food hampers are internationally famous and are despatched around the globe. Fashion clothes can be found upstairs.

Hatchards at 187 Piccadilly has been a bookshop since 1797 but has now become the flagship branch of the Dillons chain, while at number 203–206 the former Simpsons store has become Waterstone's new flagship outlet and the biggest bookshop in Europe.

Near Piccadilly Circus at 24–36 Lower Regent Street, Lillywhites (☎ 0870-333 9600) has six floors of sportswear and equipment; whatever you're into, it's here. There's also the quirky Burlington Arcade, a Grade II listed arcade built in 1819 with a glass canopy and shops with Regency styled mahogany fronts. Patrolled by 'beadles' in period costume, it's famous for quality leather goods, bespoke shoes, antique and contemporary jewellery, cashmere and perfumes.

Trocadero

The Trocadero is about as far from the period charm of the Burlington Arcade as it's possible to get. It's a horribly tacky place – a kind of hi-tech amusement arcade with overpriced rides including those at Segaworld, where there are also six floors of video games to play (heaven for kids!). Elsewhere in the mall you will find more branches of those same old chain stores. Another shrine to modern consumerism is Tower Records (☎ 020-7439 2500) at 1 Piccadilly Circus, which has possibly the best all-round selection of modern music in the capital, including exhaustive rock and indie sections.

St James's

Venture south of Piccadilly and you enter the time warp area known as St James's. It's a world of gentlemen's clubs, bespoke tailoring shops and strange little places dedicated to traditional male 'grooming'. If this is your thing, you can order a made-to-measure suit for a modest £2,000 from a tailor such as Gieves & Hawkes (☎ 020-7434 2001) at 1 Savile Row (Piccadilly Circus tube). Bespoke shirts are available from Turnbull & Asser (☎ 020-7808 3000) at 71 Jermyn Street (Green Park tube) and you can complete your outfit with a hat from James Lock (☎ 020-7930 8874) at 6 St James's Street and luxurious, made-to-measure shoes from John Lobb (☎ 020-7930 3664/5) at No.9 (Green Park tube). While you're there, you may wish to have an old-fashioned shave, with a cut-throat razor, and a high-class haircut at G F Trumper (☎ 020-7499 1850) at 9 Curzon Street (Green Park tube) or buy gentleman's cologne (and perhaps a floral scent for a special lady) at Floris (☎ 0845 702 3239) at 89 Jermyn Street (Green Park/Piccadilly Circus tube).

Soho

Nearby but worlds away from the elegant retro of St James's and smart and expensive Mayfair is Soho, which with its neighbouring district of Covent Garden houses many of the more interesting shops to be found in central London, including grocers and delicatessens to delight any gourmet's taste buds.

Soho is the area cornered by the four tube stations: Tottenham Court Road, Leicester Square, Piccadilly Circus, and Oxford Circus.

Soho and Covent Garden are divided by Charing Cross Road, which is the focus for the London book trade; numerous book shops can be found here selling both new and second-hand/antiquarian titles (the latter also buy books from the public). Their future is less certain since the scrapping of the Net Book Agreement in 1995, as major booksellers can now discount books and there are fears that they will price the smaller independent shops out of the market. Take a break from the superstores and try Blackwell's (☎ 020-7292 5100) at 100 Charing Cross Road (Tottenham Court Road tube) or the endearingly chaotic Foyles (☎ 020-7437 5660) at 119 Charing Cross Road (Tottenham Court Road tube), staffed by eccentric assistants who arrange books by publisher rather than author or subject and make you queue twice to buy a book.

If it's second-hand books you're after, try the excellent Henry Pordes (☎ 020-7836 9031) at 58–60 Charing Cross Road and Quinto (☎ 020-7379 7669) at No.48a (Leicester Square tube). Specialist bookshops in this quarter include Grant & Cutler (☎ 020-7734 2012) at 55–57 Great Marlborough Street (Oxford Circus tube), the best bookshop in London for foreign-language books, Murder One (☎ 020-7539 8820) at 76–78 Charing Cross Road (Leicester Square tube), which specialises in genre books (not just whodunits but science-fiction, fantasy, horror and romance as well), Forbidden Planet (☎ 020-7836 4179) at 179 Shaftesbury Avenue (Leicester Square tube), which carries a vast range of adult comic books and magazines, and Stanford's (☎ 020-7836 1321), the map and travel book specialists at 12–14 Long Acre (Covent Garden/Leicester Square tube).

Soho proper – or rather improper – is known first and foremost as the capital of London's sex industry, with public call boxes littered with prostitutes' business cards and walk-up flats advertising the attractions of 'new young models'. There are also sex shows, hostess bars, triple-X cinemas and sex shops aplenty, mostly around the area west of Wardour Street, home of London's movie and advertising industries. There's also a thriving gay scene here, based around the pubs and bars of Old Compton Street which has some fine, long-established specialist shops.

Stop off at the Algerian Coffee Store (☎ 020-7437 2480) at 52 Old Compton Street (Leicester Square/Piccadilly Circus tube) and sample a choice of over 40 different coffees from one of London's oldest wholesale merchants, or if you're after something stronger, try The Vintage House off-licence which stocks literally hundreds of malt whiskies. Italian salami, pasta and oils are on sale at I. Camisa & Son (☎ 020-7437 7610) at 6 Old Compton Street (Leicester Square/Piccadilly Circus tube). There's also plenty of interesting fashion on offer – try American Retro (☎ 020-7734 3477) at 35 Old Compton Street for themed fashion and quirky bits and pieces, or Paradiso (☎ 020-7287 2487) at No.41 for fetish-wear in PVC, rubber and leather! Prowler Soho (☎ 020-7734 4031,

⌨ www.prowler direct.co.uk) at 5–7 Brewer Street is a 'gay lifestyle' shop selling everything from clothes to books and videos. It even has its own travel agency!

Interesting little shops abound in Brewer Street, such as Anything Left-Handed (☎ 020-8770 3722), which sells everything from scissors and knives to pens and potato peelers in left-handed versions. Tinks at 53 Brewer Street is one of Soho's best delicatessens, specialising in additive-free foods including unpasteurised cheeses and ham on the bone. The Vintage Magazine Shop (☎ 020-7439 8525) at 39–43 Brewer Street sells magazines, collectables and memorabilia relating to the movies and theatre.

Chinatown is the area around Gerrard Street, where you can find some of the best Chinese food shops and restaurants in London. Two of the best food stores in which to buy your exotic ingredients are Loon Fung (☎ 020-7437 7332) at No.42–44 and New Loon Moon (☎ 020-7734 3887) at No.9 (both Piccadilly Circus tube).

Recording studios, music stores and rehearsal spaces are concentrated in Denmark Street, where the biggest and most important shop is World of Music (☎ 020-7836 4656) at 28 Denmark Street (Tottenham Court Road tube). Here you can buy almost anything connected with music – pianos, guitars, drums, amps, recording equipment and sheet music. If you're a guitarist, you cannot afford not to know about Andy's Guitar Centre and Workshop (☎ 020-7916 5080) at 27 Denmark Street (Tottenham Court Road tube), which specialises in electric and acoustic guitars and also does repairs. Round the corner at 144 Shaftesbury Avenue (Leicester Square/Tottenham Court Road tube) is Bill Lewington (☎ 020-7240 0584), sellers of brass instruments, while Turnkey (☎ 020-7419 9999) at 114–116 Charing Cross Road (Tottenham Court Road tube) stocks studio gear and computer-based musical equipment.

Soho also has a vast concentration of independent record stores, so if you're tired of the stranglehold exerted by the mainstream giants, HMV, Our Price and Virgin, head over here. There are far too many to list them all, but some of the best are Daddy Kool (☎ 020-7437 3535) at 12 Berwick Street (Piccadilly Circus tube) for ska and reggae, Ray's Jazz at Foyles (inside the bookshop, ☎ 020-7440 3205), Black Market (☎ 020-7437 0478) at 25 D'Arblay Street (Tottenham Court Road tube) for hip-hop and rap, Sister Ray (☎ 020-7287 8385) at 94 Berwick Street for indie, and Rough Trade (☎ 020-7240 0105) at 16 Neal's Yard round the corner in Covent Garden (Covent Garden tube).

Soho has its own fruit and vegetable market in Berwick Street (Leicester Square/Tottenham Court Road tube) offering some of the lowest prices in central London. You can also get good fish, cheeses, herbs and spices here, where Simply Sausages (☎ 020-7329 3227) at 341 Central Markets are purveyors of superior bangers to go with your mash.

11

Covent Garden

On the other side of the Charing Cross Road, Covent Garden, and to some extent Soho as well, has become the home of London's small, idiosyncratic shops, although the mainstream is beginning to make itself felt here as everywhere else. The Piazza, the pedestrianised site of the old fruit and vegetable market near the Opera House, is the place to go if you're looking for upmarket souvenirs, superior toiletries or designer nick-knacks. You can also browse through the interesting Apple Market in the disused market halls for crafts and clothes, or the Jubilee Market containing cheaper goods aimed mainly at tourists. Both markets change on Mondays, when the stalls are given over to antiques and collectables.

Also pedestrianised, the Neal Street area is the place for anything 'alternative' such as whole-food shops, arts and crafts, esoterica and so on. The midnight blue-fronted Astrology Shop (☎ 020-7813 3051) at No.78 has plenty for the fans of esoterica, as does Mysteries (☎ 020-7240 3688), one of the best new age shops in the capital, at 9-11 Monmouth Street. Clubbers can pick up new clobber at Red Or Dead at 43 Neal Street (Covent Garden tube). Kids will love Benjamin Pollock's Toy Shop (☎ 020-7379 7866), which is full of traditional toys, at 44 The Market. Kaleido at 11 Long Acre (☎ 020-7836 3444) sells mostly silver jewellery with other items in gold and platinum and is well worth a look (Covent Garden tube). If you're into conservation, head for the Natural Shoe Store (☎ 020-7836 5254) at 21 Neal Street, where everything has been produced without cruelty to animals or environmental damage, or Birkenstock (☎ 020-7240 2783) at No.37.

Long Acre offers minimalist Japanese store Muji (☎ 020-7379 0820) at No.135, but is otherwise packed with chain stores and other uninteresting stuff (apart from Stanford's – see above).

For some reason, Southampton Street leading to the Strand has several camping and outdoor shops, while Floral Street is full of interesting fashion retailers selling the kind of clothes you'd wear to enjoy the local nightlife – try Robot (☎ 020-7836 6156) at No.37 and Agnes B (☎ 020-7379 1992) at No.35/36 (Covent Garden tube for all the above)

Fine foods and natural remedies are also available in Covent Garden. Carluccio's at 28a Neal Street has a stunning selection of Italian groceries and Neal's Yard Dairy (☎ 020-7240 5700) at 17 Shorts Gardens sells mature farmhouse cheeses, chutneys and breads. If you need some extra pots and pans to cook all your goodies, look no further than the Elizabeth David Cookshop at 3a North Row. Neal's Yard Remedies (☎ 020-7379 7222) at 15 King St. Neal's Yard stocks medicinal herbs, oils and potions, and Lush (☎ 020-7240 4570) on the Piazza has environmentally friendly cosmetics and soaps (Covent Garden tube for all the above).

11

WEST LONDON

The West End or central area ends at Marble Arch, where Hyde Park begins. South of here you enter an area between the park and the river that includes the fashionable shopping centres of Knightsbridge, Kensington and Chelsea, known as West London.

Knightsbridge

Like Mayfair, Knightsbridge is an upper-crust (i.e. expensive) area servicing the rich of Belgravia to the immediate west of the capital's centre. It's here that you will find the 'world's most famous department store', Harrods (☎ 020-7730 1234, 🖳 www.harrods.com) at 87 Brompton Road (Knightsbridge tube). Harrods started life as a humble family grocer's in the 19th century; 150 years later (having lost its apostrophe) it's rated the third most popular tourist attraction in London. It has been owned for some years by Mohammed Al Fayed, whose son perished in the same car crash as the Princess of Wales and who reputedly rules the store with a rod of iron, turning away customers whose costume is deemed too revealing (don't wear shorts or crop-tops!). Harrods has a reputation as the 'top people's store' (an interesting *double entendre*), where you can buy all the world's best brand names under one roof, and it claims to be able to obtain virtually anything.

Almost as interesting as Harrods is Harvey Nichols (☎ 020-7235 5000) at 109–125 Knightsbridge (Knightsbridge tube). This is another decidedly upmarket department store, concentrating on designer fashion and food, although the fifth floor bar is known to be something of a pick-up joint.

Like Mayfair, Knightsbridge also boasts some of London's smartest fashion boutiques. At its western end, towards Kensington, you will find all the designer names that you didn't find in Bond Street – in Sloane Street, Beauchamp Place and Brompton Road. Check out Jean-Paul Gaultier (☎ 020-7584 4648) at 171 Draycott Avenue, Issey Miyake (☎ 020-7581 3760) at 270 Brompton Road (South Kensington tube), MaxMara (☎ 020-7235 7941) at 32 Sloane Street (Knightsbridge tube) and Betty Jackson (☎ 020-7589 7884) at 311 Brompton Road (South Kensington tube). For beautiful Chinese and Indian designs, visit Egg (☎ 020-7235 9315) at 36/37 Kinnerton Street (Knightsbridge tube). If you're after exotic underwear that flatters rather than flattens a good figure, you need Janet Reger (☎ 020-7584 9360) at 2 Beauchamp Place or Agent Provocateur (☎ 020-7235 0229) at 16 Pont Street (both Knightsbridge tube). If you're a well-built chap – either unusually tall or 'well rounded' – you can find clothes to fit at High & Mighty (☎ 0800-298 8083) at 81–83 Knightsbridge (Knightsbridge tube).

11

Kensington

In Kensington there's plenty for shopaholics of all persuasions. Kensington High Street features a parade of designer shops, including Kookai (☎ 020-7938 1427) at No.125 and the Urban Outfitters (☎ 020-7761 1011) at No.36–38 (High Street Kensington tube). The Edwardian department store Barkers of Kensington is also worth a visit. Next door, the old Derry & Toms (later Biba) department store is now closed but you can still gain access (from Derry St) to its spectacular roof garden and gaze out over the city. The original Kensington Market has also closed but there's a new market on Kensington Church Street. A short stroll away at 1–22 Church Street (High Street Kensington tube) is Amazon – no, not a real-world outpost of the famous internet bookstore but a 'designer' clothes outlet selling at cut-to-the-bone prices. There's no phone, so you have to pay a visit if you want to know what's on offer.

Chelsea

The King's Road, like Carnaby Street, owes much of its cachet to the '60s and '70s. However, unlike the pedestrianised West End streets, it's still a living part of London and fashion victims still prance and preen here on Saturdays. When the swingers and hippies departed, the peacock punks moved in and, like a long-surviving pop star, the street has succeeded in repeatedly reinventing itself to move with the times. The King's Road stretches from the upmarket Sloane Square at one end to the World's End pub at the other before becoming the New King's Road and continuing to Putney Bridge.

At the posh end visit the department store Peter Jones or, if you have fashion-conscious children, call in at Trotters (☎ 020-7259 9620) at 34 King's Road, which even has a children's library. At No.121 try the CM Store (☎ 020-7351 9361) for trendy club-wear or Steinberg & Tolkien (☎ 020-7376 3660) at No.193 for quality second-hand designer wear. If it's antiques you're after, there's plenty of choice, such as Antiquarius at No.131–141. Further down you can visit World's End at No.430, once the notorious punk emporium 'Sex', where Vivienne Westwood's outrageous gear sold by the truckload in the mid-'70s. Despite her recent elevation to *haute couture*, she still sells some of her designer clobber from this address. At 49–51 Old Church Street (Sloane Square tube, then take a cab or catch an 11, 19 or 22 bus) you will find the most marvellous shoes in the world at Manolo Blahnik (☎ 020-7352 3863).

Even further into west London, at 42 Westbourne Grove (Bayswater/Queensway tube), you can find Planet Organic (☎ 020-7727 2227), one of London's best organic supermarkets with a butcher's, fresh fish counter, juice bar, and 'miles' of fresh produce and groceries, all produced without the aid of nasty chemicals.

11

Notting Hill is famous for its Portobello Road Market (⌨ www.portobello road. co.uk) which has expanded and flourished in recent years and now caters for both the affluent 'trustafarians' of the area (rich kids living off their trust funds) and the genuinely impecunious. Portobello is really several markets rolled into one: at the top end it sells antiques, bygones and collectibles, including quality antiques at prices which are almost modest compared with the fancy antique emporiums in other parts of London; further down, there's a fruit and veg market; and at the bottom end (which disappears under the Westway) you will find clothes, jewellery, books and music. The market starts slowly at around 5.30 each morning, when professional antique dealers trade among themselves. Most traders arrive between 6.30 and 8.30am and by 10am the street is bustling. Some traders disappear after lunch but many stay until late afternoon. If you're after some cutting-edge fashion, try The Dispensary (☎ 020-7221 9290) at 25 Pembridge Road (Notting Hill Gate tube).

EAST LONDON

City of London shopping tends to be geared to the bright, moneyed yuppies heading for burnout on the trading floors and in the merchant banks of the financial quarter. Here there's an abundance of fancy shops selling silk ties, flashy accessories, classy smokes and luxury chocolates. However, there's also more down-to-earth shopping to be found and the redeveloped Liverpool Street Station, with its quality chain stores and food outlets (including an amazing cheese shop), is a good place to start while you're waiting for your train home. If you're choosier, spend your lunch hour at Spitalfields Market in Brushfield Street (Liverpool Street tube), where organic foods are on sale alongside jewellery and clothes. There's also a fashion market every Thursday at which young designers exhibit their wares.

On Sundays (9am to 2pm), Petticoat Lane Market in Middlesex Street (Aldgate/Aldgate East tube) is more of a tourist attraction but still worth a look, while if you're after good household goods go on a weekday pilgrimage to Leather Lane Market (Chancery Lane tube). If you're looking for unusual jewellery, try Beau Gems (☎ 020-7623 7634) at 33 Leadenhall Market, EC3V (Bank tube), which sells antique pieces.

Further into the wilds of the East End, try Brick Lane Market (Aldgate East/Shoreditch tube), which sells fruit and veg as well as cheap clothes and household goods (8am to 1pm). The further east you go from Brick Lane into Cheshire Street, the tattier the market becomes – although if it's East End authenticity you're seeking, you will certainly find it here. Another East End market worthy of mention is Walthamstow Market (Walthamstow Central tube), Europe's longest daily street market (Mondays to Saturdays 8am to 6pm) with some 300 shops and 450 stalls.

11

NORTH LONDON

North London has an atmosphere quite unlike the sophistication and glitz of much of the West End. Bloomsbury stands at the border between central and northern London and has a tradition of being a centre for academic and specialist shops, perhaps because of the presence of the British Museum and much of London University. However, it becomes increasingly rundown and ugly as it stretches northwards into the rough, red-light area of King's Cross, where prostitutes and drug dealers have traditionally plied their trades after dark, although the area is currently being regenerated as part of the Channel Tunnel Link scheme (see page 110), due for completion in 2005. Nevertheless, Bloomsbury contains many fascinating little specialist book shops, including Bookmarks (☎ 020-7637 1848) at 1 Bloomsbury Street (Tottenham Court Road tube), which specialises in left-wing literature, Gay's The Word (☎ 020-7278 7654) at 66 Marchmont Street (Russell Square tube), and Unsworths (☎ 020-7436 9836) at 12 Bloomsbury Street (Tottenham Court Road tube), which is good on arts subjects.

Towards Euston, army surplus and militaria can be found at the chaotic Lawrence Corner (☎ 020-7387 6134) at 62 Hampstead Road (Warren Street tube), while devotees of African music are sure to find what they're looking for at Stern's African Record Centre (☎ 020-7387 5550) at 293 Euston Road (Warren Street tube).

Camden Town

Further north, Camden Town is a bustling bohemian area full of aspiring actors, musicians, artists and misfits. Camden Market stretches from Camden High Street to Chalk Farm Road (Camden Town tube). The covered section (Thursdays to Sundays only) is where you will find rare records and interesting clothes; the fruit and veg market in Inverness Street is open daily except Sundays. At Camden Lock there are arts and crafts, jewellery and clothes, although not all shops and stalls are open or even there during the early part of the week – go between Wednesdays and Sundays for the best choice. In The Stables is the flea market with the cheapest stalls of all, where the Electric Ballroom opens its doors to a jewellery and alternative clothing market on Sundays. Feeling stressed? Learn to keep all those balls in the air at Oddballs Juggling, Kites & Skates (☎ 020-7284 4488) at Camden Lock (Camden tube).

Hampstead

Hampstead is a sophisticated, well-heeled quarter just north of Camden, where the natives are largely middle-class intelligentsia. When you aren't walking

11

on the still-charming heath, browse along the High Street with its arty little eateries– try the Louis Patisserie at No.32 for its fabulously sticky cakes – and fashion boutiques. In neighbouring Highgate, stock up on intellectual property at Fisher & Sperr, a great second-hand bookshop specialising in books about London.

Islington

Along with Hampstead, Islington is one of the habitats of the 'chattering classes': middle-class, well-educated and possessed of too much money. Consequently, many of the shops in the area cater to refined or specialist tastes. If you're fed up with the kind of plastic 'junk' that you find at high street toy shops, Donay Traditional Games and Pastimes (☎ 020-7359 1880) at 3 Camden Passage (Angel tube) stocks antique and early 20th century toys and games, although the prices will probably mean your children don't get to play with them. If your sartorial tastes veer some way from the mainstream, Regulation (☎ 020-7226 0665) at 17a St Albans Place (Angel tube) is reputedly one of the capital's foremost suppliers of fetish-wear and industrial clothing. Or, if you're into taxidermy, try Get Stuffed (☎ 020-7226 1364) at 105 Essex Road (Angel tube), where stuffed wildlife of every description can be found.

SOUTH LONDON

South London is often portrayed as a cultural and shopping desert but, although its outer suburbs are dull and ordinary, there are some treasures to be found among the suburban dross. Immediately south of the river, the South Bank area has much to recommend it shopping-wise. The Oxo Tower in Barge House Street is a complex of retail studios selling 'the best in UK contemporary design' from Tuesdays to Sundays (Blackfriars/Waterloo tube). It has an expensive restaurant (☎ 020-7803 3888) on the top floor with wonderful views across the Thames. Gabriel's Wharf is also good for designer crafts; check out Ganesha (☎ 020-7928 3444) at No.3, which sells vibrant, hand-crafted, Indian textiles and crafts, including tiger rugs and hand-stitched wall-hangings.

In the wilds of Waterloo, at 87 Lower Marsh, you can find Radio Days (☎ 020-7928 0800) with its stock of '50s memorabilia, collectables, books, magazines and posters. At the rear of the store is Masquerade, a store within a store selling second-hand retro clothing. If you happen to be in the area on a Friday or Saturday, don't miss Borough market (London Bridge tube), one of the best – and most popular – farmers' markets in London, where you can stock up on everything from organic cider to French cheeses. In the One World Shop (☎ 020-7401 8909) at St John's Church, Waterloo Road, you can buy goods from the developing world, including Tanzanian honey, Central American coffee,Lombok pottery tableware and Indonesian silver jewellery, plus craft toys,T-shirts and Christmas cards.

11

Greenwich has much more than museums and the Observatory and there's a tangle of markets to tempt the shopper, including a good antiques market on Thursdays in Greenwich High Road, a central covered market selling hand-made crafts (Fridays to Sundays), and a Sunday flea market on Thames Street (Greenwich rail).

Further south, Brixton Market in Electric Avenue (Brixton tube) is loved by outsiders, but many local residents reckon it's overrated. A large West Indian community is based here and the goods on offer, such as plantain, breadfruit, strange varieties of fish, exotic herbs and incense, reflect this. There are some second-hand clothes and bric-a-brac stalls to explore at the east of the market proper and some interesting shops – check out Alltone Records for dancehall, dub and reggae. If you like fun retro gifts and clothes, take a look at Joy (☎ 020-7787 9616) on Coldharbour Lane, where you will find lava lamps, glitter balls, movie star cufflinks and a host of other items of dubious taste (Brixton tube).

INTERNET SHOPPING

Shopping via the internet has finally begun to take off following the premature predictions of an explosion in this area before the collapse of the dot-com bubble a few years ago. It is also expected that Britons will spend on average in excess of £1,000 each in 2007 and such increases are expected to continue.

There are numerous shopping site portals, including 💻 www.shopguide.co.uk, 💻 www.virgin.net, which provides a good directory of British sites, and 💻 www.shopping.net. One of the best bargain websites is 💻 www.buy.com, which offers over 10,000 electronic items at discount prices and has forced UK high street retailers to cut theirs. Other useful sites include 💻 www.shopper.uk.net and 💻 www.onlineclothesshops.co.uk. Price comparison sites are numerous and include 💻 www.computerprices.co.uk, 💻 www.priceguide.uk.com, 💻 www.pricechecker.co.uk, 💻 www.bookbrain.co.uk (for books), 💻 www.camera tag.co.uk (for cameras) and 💻 www.price-tracker.co.uk (for video-games).

With internet shopping, the world is very much your oyster and savings can be made on a wide range of goods, including CDs, clothes, sports equipment, electronic gadgets, jewellery, books, wine, computer software, and services such as insurance, pensions and mortgages. Huge savings can also be made on holidays and travel. Small high-price, high-tech items (e.g. cameras, watches and portable computers) can usually be bought more cheaply somewhere else in Europe or (more likely) in the US, with delivery by courier within as little as three days.

However, while shopping on the internet is sometimes claimed to be very secure, research has shown that your credit card details are more likely to be discovered by thieves when shopping via the internet than when doing so by phone or mail order. The limitations of assurances given by over-confident experts were underlined in February 2003, when a computer hacker gained access to over 5 million Visa and MasterCard credit accounts in the US.

Buying Overseas

When buying goods overseas, ensure that you're dealing with a bona fide company and that the goods will work in the UK. If possible, pay by credit card when buying over the internet (or by mail-order) because, for bills between £100 and £30,000, the credit card issuer is usually jointly liable with the supplier under the Consumer Credit Act 1974. (Although many card companies claim that the law doesn't cover overseas purchases, some will consider claims up to the value of the goods purchased). **When you buy expensive goods abroad, always have them insured for their full value.**

VAT & Duty

When buying overseas, take into account shipping costs, duty and VAT. There's no duty or tax on goods purchased within the European Union or on goods from most other countries worth £18 or less (or £36, if a gift). Don't buy alcohol or cigarettes abroad, as the duty is usually too high to make it pay. When VAT or duty is payable on a parcel, the payment is usually collected by the post office or courier company on delivery.

12

MISCELLANEOUS MATTERS

This chapter contains miscellaneous information of interest to anyone planning to live or work in London. Subjects covered include climate, crime, government, monarchy, police, pets, postal services, telephone, television and radio, and time difference. For further details of topics covered in this book, refer to *Living and Working in Britain* by David Hampshire (Survival Books).

CLIMATE

London has a generally mild and temperate climate and is often damp, although the weather can change rapidly within relatively narrow 'extremes'. The least hospitable months are November to February, when it's often very cold and the days are short; March and October are slightly better but can still be quite cold. Although temperatures drop below freezing in winter, particularly at night, it's rarely below freezing during the day, although the average temperature is a chilly 4°C (39°F). The most unpleasant features of British winters are fog and ice, which make driving hazardous. However, the 'pea-soup' fog that was usually the result of pollution, and which many foreigners still associate with London, is thankfully a thing of the past.

April to September are the best months, with July and August the warmest. Spring is generally the most pleasant time of year, although early spring is often very wet. Summer temperatures are often around 26°C (75°F) and occasionally rise above 30°C (86°F), although the average temperature is 15° to 18°C (60° to 65°F). Average high and low temperatures are: January 6/2°C (43/36°F), April 13/6°C (55/43°F), July 22/14°C (72/57°F) and October 14/8°C (57/46°F).

Rain is fairly evenly distributed throughout the year (many Londoners carry an umbrella at all times), although the wettest month is usually November. Average rainfall is January 54mm, April 37mm, July 59mm and October 57mm. The worst aspect of British weather is the frequent drizzle (light rain) and grey skies, particularly in winter. This has given rise to a condition known as 'seasonal affective disorder' (SAD), which is brought on by the dark, dull days of winter and causes lethargy, fatigue and low spirits. However, there's some good news – British winters are becoming milder and in recent years have been nothing like as severe as in earlier decades, although whether this is a permanent change is unclear. In fact, British weather is becoming warmer all round, recent years experiencing some of the driest summers since records began in 1659, and 2003 recording the highest temperatures on record, even exceeding 40°C (104°F) in London and a few other places in the south.

To add a little spice to the usual diet of cold and rain, in recent years the UK has been afflicted with gales and torrential rain (including the infamous storms of 1987 and 1990), which have caused severe damage and flooding in many areas. Tornadoes also occur in the UK, but are extremely rare. There's considerable debate among weather experts and scientists as to whether the climatic changes (not just in the UK, but worldwide) are a result of global warming or just a temporary change. If present trends continue, some scientists predict that temperatures will increase considerably in the next century and the south of England could become frost-free. 2007 has seen the warmest January recorded since 1916.

Weather forecasts are available via TV teletext services, in daily newspapers, via premium rate telephone services, on the internet, and on TV and radio (usually after the news). Warnings of dangerous weather conditions affecting motoring, e.g. fog and ice, are broadcast regularly on all BBC national and local radio stations. The most detailed weather forecasts are broadcast on BBC Radio 2 and BBC Radio 4, the latter also providing weather forecasts for shipping. During the early summer, when pollens are released in large quantities, the pollen count is given on radio and TV weather forecasts and in daily newspapers. In summer, the maximum exposure time for the fair-skinned is also included in TV weather forecasts on hot days.

CRIME

Overall, the number of reported crimes (apart from violent crimes) has fallen in the last decade, although some sceptics believe it's because people are simply reporting crime less often because they consider it a waste of time (in some areas 95 per cent of crimes are unsolved). The number of violent crimes has increased in the last decade, although they're still relatively low compared with many other countries – the risk of being a victim of crime is around the European average. There are around 800 murders a year in the UK, which is less than in most other European countries, and you're more likely to choke to death on your food than you are to meet a violent death.

The level of street crime (where men under 30 are most at risk) is higher than official figures suggest and the actual number of crimes is reckoned to be around four times the number recorded by the police. However, muggings and crimes of violence are still rare in most areas of London, where you can safely walk in most places day or night, although the police warn people (particularly young women) against walking alone in dark and deserted areas late at night. Many crimes are drug-related and due to the huge quantity of drugs flooding into the UK in recent years. The use of hard drugs (particularly cocaine) is a major problem in London, where gangs increasingly use guns to settle their differences. Nearly half of London street crime is committed by cocaine addicts, and some 40 per cent of UK gun crime is committed in London (around 20 people are shot dead in London each year in drug-related incidents).

Crime is a major concern for residents of some London suburbs, where elderly people are often afraid to leave the relative safety of their homes at any time of day or night. The increase in crime is attributed by psychologists to poverty, the breakdown of traditional family life, the loss of community and social values in society, and a growing lack of parental responsibility and skills. The failure to deal with juvenile crime is one of the biggest threats facing the UK, and particularly London, and many children are totally out of control by the age of ten or even younger.

Crimes against property are escalating, particularly burglary, car theft and theft from vehicles. In London, where around 20 per cent of all crime takes place, professional thieves even steal antique paving stones, railings and antique doors and door casings. Fraud or so-called 'white-collar' crime (which includes credit card fraud, income tax evasion and VAT fraud), costs billions of pounds a year and accounts for larger sums than the total of all other robberies, burglaries and thefts added together.

Although the foregoing catalogue of crime may paint a depressing picture, London is a generally safe place to live. In comparison with many other countries, including most European countries, the UK's crime rate isn't high and the incidence of violent crime is low. If you take care of your property and take precautions against crime, your chances of becoming a victim are small. Note, however, that the crime rate varies considerably from area to area, and anyone planning on living in London should avoid high crime areas if at all possible.

The Metropolitan Police publishes annual crime statistics for each borough, indicating the number of crimes of various types committed each month. These can be found on ⌨ www.met.police.uk/crimestatistics/statbody.htm. The table below shows numbers of crimes per 1,000 population in 2003 in five categories of crime: violence (including murder, bodily harm, assault and possession of weapons), burglary of private dwellings, theft of motor vehicles and theft from motor vehicles. There are no comparable statistics for the City of London, which has its own police force (see **Police** on page 358).

Borough	Crimes Per 1,000 Population (2006)			
	Violence	Burglary	Stolen Cars	Theft From Cars
Average	29	11	12	13
Barking & Dagenham	26	8	11	11
Barnet	18	8	6	10
Bexley	18	5	7	8
Brent	26	11	8	14
Bromley	16	10	7	10
Camden	31	15	10	34
Croydon	23	7	7	8
Ealing	24	10	8	19

Enfield	18	10	8	12
Greenwich	31	9	11	14
Hackney	34	16	11	23
Hammersmith & Fulham	26	14	7	21
Haringey	27	14	11	17
Harrow	15	9	4	10
Havering	17	4	8	11
Hillingdon	20	9	7	16
Hounslow	33	10	7	16
Islington	36	15	13	33
Kensington & Chelsea	21	13	7	17
Kingston	22	4	4	7
Lambeth	36	14	8	14
Lewisham	27	11	8	9
Merton	19	6	4	7
Newham	32	9	13	21
Redbridge	17	9	8	14
Richmond	14	7	3	8
Southwark	33	13	11	17
Sutton	18	4	5	8
Tower Hamlets	38	10	11	24
Waltham Forest	26	10	9	16
Wandsworth	21	9	6	12
Westminster*	56	14	9	26

* Figures in Westminster are distorted by non-resident visitors, e.g. temporary workers and tourists.

12

GOVERNMENT

The UK is a constitutional monarchy, under which the country is governed by ministers of the crown in the name of the sovereign (Queen Elizabeth II), who's head of both the state and the government. Nowadays the monarchy has no real power and its duties are restricted to a ceremonial and advisory role only, although there are certain acts of government that require the participation of the sovereign, such as the opening and dissolving of parliament and the approval of parliamentary bills. Parliament is the ultimate law-making authority in the UK (although the Channel Islands and the Isle of Man make their own laws on island affairs) and consists of two houses or chambers, the House of Commons and the House of Lords, which together make up the Houses of Parliament.

Parliament sits in the Palace of Westminster in the eponymous borough, which was built in the 19th century after the previous building was destroyed by fire, and whose clock, Big Ben (actually the name of the large bell), is London's most famous landmark. The roots of the UK's democratic traditions date from 1265 (when King Henry III was forced to acknowledge the first parliament). Westminster, which is often referred to as the mother of parliaments, is the model for many democracies around the world.

The House of Commons is the assembly chamber for the 646 Members of Parliament (MPs) who are commoners (i.e. not Lords or titled people), elected by the people of the UK in a general election, which must be held every five years if parliament isn't dissolved earlier. Each MP represents an area called a constituency, of which there are 529 in England, 59 in Scotland, 40 in Wales and 18 in Northern Ireland.

All British and Commonwealth citizens and citizens of the Republic of Ireland over the age of 18 and resident in the UK can vote in parliamentary elections, provided they're registered voters. To be eligible to vote, your name must appear in a register of electors maintained and updated annually in autumn by councils. If you fail to register, you're liable to a fine of up to £1,000. Voting isn't compulsory and there's no penalty for not voting (but don't complain about the government if you don't vote). Anyone who's a registered voter and who's away from his constituency during parliamentary, European or local government elections, can vote by post or appoint a proxy to vote on his behalf.

The government of the day is formed by the political party that wins the largest number of seats at a general election. If no party has a clear majority, i.e. 326 seats, a coalition government may be formed between a number of parties. This is extremely rare in the UK as, unlike other countries in Western Europe, it doesn't have a system of proportional representation. The candidate in each constituency who polls the most votes is declared the winner ('first past the post'). All votes cast for other candidates are disregarded, which means that a party such as the Liberal Democrats (the third force in UK politics) often receives millions of votes and ends up with just a few seats. Many people believe this system is outdated and undemocratic (particularly the Liberal Democrats), although it's difficult to see the major parties changing the system voluntarily (Labour went through the motions of investigating electoral reform on entering government but then quietly forgot all about it). MPs hold weekly or fortnightly 'surgeries' (like doctors!) in their constituencies, when constituents can visit them and discuss their problems. Constituents can also write to their MP and telephone or visit him at the House of Commons.

The head of the government is the Prime Minister, who's the leader of the party with the majority of seats (or the leader of the principal party in a coalition) and who chooses an inner cabinet of around 20 ministers. In addition to the cabinet, the government appoints at least 80 junior ministers, of which there may be two to five in each ministry. The Leader of the Opposition, who's the head of the largest defeated party (and not part of a government coalition), appoints a 'shadow' cabinet, whose job is to respond to government ministers in Parliament on behalf of the party. MPs who are members of the cabinet or shadow cabinet sit on the front benches (on opposite sides) in the House of Commons. All other MPs are known as back-benchers.

The highlight of the week in the House of Commons is question time, during which MPs can question Ministers (and which often becomes heated when the PM and the leader of the opposition trade insults). The proceedings of both houses are public (except for rare occasions involving national security) and both houses have a public gallery. Television was introduced into Parliament in 1989, although strict rules apply, which are designed to hide the fact that the chambers are often sparsely attended.

There are three main national parties in the UK: the Conservatives or Tories, Labour (or New Labour as it prefers to be called) and the Liberal Democrats. There are a few other smaller parties, most of which contest seats in particular regions or constituencies only. These include the Scottish Nationalist Party (SNP); the Ulster Unionist Party, the Democratic Unionist Party, the Social and Democratic Labour Party (SDLP) and Sinn Fein, all of Northern Ireland; Plaid Cymru (Welsh nationalists); the Green Party and the Communist Party of Great Britain (as distinct from the Communist Party, which is now defunct).

The UK was long plagued by its predominantly two-party system, with its extremes of left (Labour) and right (Conservatives) and very little between. Now, however, the difference often seems more a battle for personal power than ideology. The Conservatives remain – more or less – the party of big business, from which they receive the vast majority of their finances (although this connection has been muted during the current predominance of New Labour, with which business has sought to maintain reasonable relations, and which anyway often seems quite right-wing). The The Labour party was traditionally the party of the workers and still receives most of its funds from the trade unions, although this connection has been thrown in doubt and it now appears more to represent the interests of public sector professionals, of which there are many.

12

It seems an age since it believed in the public ownership of industry (nationalisation). After almost a decade in government, it still dominates the political scene.

The House of Lords is referred to as the 'Other Place' in the House of Commons and is the geriatric ward of the constitution, where retired MPs and a declining number of blue-blooded landowners spend their days in retirement. The Lords consists of the Lords Spiritual (archbishops and bishops) and Temporal, which includes a fixed number of 90 hereditary peers and peeresses, all life peers and peeresses, and the Law Lords, with the precise total depending on the number of life peers the Prime Minister chooses to create. Until the beginning of the 20th century, the House of Lords had extensive powers and could veto any bill submitted to it by the House of Commons. It still retains powers to block government legislation temporarily, which sometimes can have the same result in practice. It remains the highest court of appeal in the UK, with the exception of criminal cases in Scotland, but proposals to replace it with a Supreme Court are under consideration. Members of the House of Lords are unpaid, although they receive travelling and other expenses when on parliamentary business within the UK.

The House of Lords is presided over by the Lord Chancellor, who's the ex-officio Speaker of the House. Proposals are under discussion to abolish this ancient office which combines a number of functions in a way which is considered no longer desirable.

The House of Lords has long been considered an anachronism in the UK and has been partially reformed – until a few years ago all hereditary peers belonged to it – but currently nobody knows quite what more to do about it. It could be replaced by an elected second house (similar to the US Senate) or a completely appointed house, but the likelihood is that it will continue in some form similar to its present one for the time being. The general government intention is to get rid of the remaining hereditary peers, but it's easy to imagine circumstances in which this doesn't happen.

Local Government

The administration of local affairs in the UK is performed by local government or local authorities. In most areas of England and Wales, services are divided between two authorities, a district council and a county council. In large cities, services are usually provided by a single authority, e.g. a borough council in London. Borough councils provide the main local government services that require planning and administration over wide areas, or that require substantial resources. These include the police, fire service, libraries and museums, traffic regulation, magistrates courts, the probation service, waste disposal, highways and road safety, trading standards and personal social services. Other essential services include area health authorities funded by central government.

London borough councils hold elections every four years. All local government councils are organised along party political lines, although some councillors are independent. All councils elect a chairman, who in boroughs or cities has the ceremonial title of mayor (or Lord Mayor in the City of London and other large cities). The turnout in local government elections is usually much lower than for parliamentary elections (around 30 per cent). Voting qualifications are broadly the same as for parliamentary elections, but additionally EU citizens can participate. Councillors are unpaid, although they can claim an allowance for attending council meetings and travel and subsistence allowances. Local authority finances come from a variety of sources, including around 25 per cent from council tax (see page 205), a further 25 per cent from the uniform business rate and the remainder from central government.

MONARCHY

The British royal family is the longest reigning monarchy in the world and certainly the most famous. Apart from the period from 1649 to 1660, it has reigned continuously for a thousand years. The head of the royal family is the monarch or sovereign, Her Majesty (HM) Queen Elizabeth II, who's married to His Royal Highness (HRH) the Duke of Edinburgh, Prince Philip (who's the son of Princess Andrew of Greece). The monarch is head of state and head of the British Commonwealth, although these are ceremonial titles involving no real power. The UK is governed by HM Government in the name of the Queen (see above).

The Queen and Prince Philip have four children: Prince Charles (the Prince of Wales), who's the heir to the throne (and remarried to the Duchess of Cornwall after being divorced from the late Diana, Princess of Wales); Princess Anne (the Princess Royal), also divorced; Prince Andrew (the Duke of York, divorced from Sarah Ferguson, the Duchess of York); and Prince Edward (who married Sophie Rhys-Jones in 1999). The most popular member of the Royal Family by far was the late Queen Elizabeth the Queen Mother, who died aged 101 in 2002. The Queen's sister, Princess Margaret (who was married to the Earl of Snowdon – formerly Anthony Armstrong-Jones), died in the same year. The Royal Family includes other major and minor royals, many of whom are descended from King George V's other children, Henry (the 1st Duke of Gloucester), George (the 1st Duke of Kent) and Mary.

The most important functions of the Queen are ceremonial and include the state opening of Parliament; giving Royal Assent to bills; the reception of diplomats; entertaining foreign dignitaries; conferring peerages, knighthoods and other honours; the appointment of important office-holders; chairing meetings of the Privy Council; and sorting out family squabbles. She also attends numerous artistic, industrial, scientific and charitable events of both national and local interest (the Queen and other members of the royal family are patrons or honorary heads of many leading charities and organisations in the UK). The sovereign's official birthday is celebrated in June with the Trooping of the Colour ceremony on Horse Guards' Parade. Each year the Queen and other members of the royal family visit many areas of the UK and undertake state visits and royal tours of foreign and Commonwealth countries.

Around 85 per cent of the cost of the royal family's official duties is met by public departments, including the upkeep of royal palaces and the Queen's various modes of private transport. The Queen's public expenditure on staff and the expenses incurred in carrying out her official duties are financed from the Civil List, which is approved by Parliament. Annual allowances are made in the Civil List to other members of the royal family, with the exception of the Prince of Wales, who as the Duke of Cornwall receives the net revenue of the estate of the Duchy of Cornwall. The Queen is estimated to be the richest person in the UK, although a lot of the property attributed to her actually belongs to the state.

The antics of the British royal family are the longest-running soap opera in the world and hundreds of column inches of newsprint are devoted to their affairs, both in the UK by the popular press, who delight in printing sensational stories about royalty and anyone famous, and abroad. Nonetheless, as the overwhelming public enthusiasm for the Queen's Golden Jubilee celebrations in 2002 showed, despite the vicissitudes of life which she has endured, she is still a focus for abiding affection and real respect.

PETS

Britain is generally regarded abroad as a country of animal lovers and has over 14 million pet owners (including some 7 million dog owners). This is attested to by the number of bequests received by the Royal Society for the Prevention of Cruelty to Animals (RSPCA), which far exceeds the amount left to the Royal Society for the Prevention of Cruelty to Children (RSPCC). It's even possible (and not uncommon) in the UK for people to leave their entire estate to their pets! The British are almost uniquely sentimental about animals, even those reared for food. Protests about various forms of commercial cruelty to animals make headline news at regular intervals. Britons are also prominent in international animal protection organisations that attempt to ban cruel sports and practices in which animals are mistreated (such as bullfighting).

Dogs

After a series of vicious attacks on children, the British government introduced a controversial ban on the ownership of certain breeds of dog bred for fighting. These include pit bull terriers, Japanese tosas, dogo argentinos and fila brazilieros, all of which can no longer be imported or bred in the UK (males must be neutered), and must be registered and muzzled in public. If the law is broken, a dog can be destroyed and if it attacks anyone you will be liable to a fine (and your dog may also be destroyed). You can be fined up to £400 (in addition to compensation) if your dog kills or injures livestock and a farmer can legally shoot a dog that molests farm animals. There isn't a dog registration or licence scheme in England, Wales or Scotland.

Quarantine

The UK has the toughest quarantine regulations in the world in order to guard against the importation of rabies and other animal diseases, and has been virtually free of rabies for over 60 years. Apart from those participating in the Pet Passports scheme (see below), all mammals, other than specific breeds of horses and livestock, must normally spend a period of six months in quarantine in an approved kennel to ensure they're free of rabies and Newcastle disease. Rabies is a serious hazard throughout the world, including many parts of Europe. You can catch this disease if you're bitten, scratched or even licked by an infected animal. Quarantine regulations also apply to guide dogs for the blind and hearing dogs.

If you're coming to the UK for a short period, it may not be worth the trouble and expense of bringing your pet and you may prefer to leave it with friends or relatives during your stay. Before deciding to import an animal, check the website of the Department for Environment, Food and Rural Affairs (DEFRA – see below) or contact them at Hook Rise South, Tolworth, Surbiton, Surrey KT6 7NK (☎ 020-7238 6951) for the latest regulations, application forms, and a list of approved quarantine kennels and catteries. (The ministry also publishes a number of free brochures about rabies).

Applications for the importation of dogs, cats and other mammals should be made at least eight weeks before the proposed date of importation. To obtain a licence to import your pet, you must have a confirmed booking at an approved kennel and have enlisted the services of an authorised carrying agent (who will transport your pet from the port to the quarantine kennels). Your pet must arrive at an approved port or airport, must be transported in an approved container, available from air transport companies and pet shops, and must be shipped within six months of the date specified by the licence.

The cost of quarantine is from £250 to £320 per month for a dog, depending on its size (and what it eats) and around £200 per month for a cat. You must also pay for any vaccinations and veterinary costs incurred during your pet's quarantine period. You're permitted – in fact encouraged – to visit your pet in quarantine but won't be able to take it out for exercise. There are different regulations for some creatures. Birds, for example, serve a shorter quarantine period than animals, until it's established that there's no danger of psittacosis. Pet rabbits must be inoculated against rabies and cannot be imported from the US.

12

There's no quarantine for cold-blooded animals such as fish and reptiles. Around 5,000 dogs and 3,000 cats are quarantined each year in the UK.

The Pet Passport Scheme

The Pet Passport Scheme (PETS) was introduced recently and enables you to bring your dog, cat, rabbit, mouse, rat, guinea pig or ferret into the UK and avoid quarantine, **but only under stringently controlled conditions.** Animals must be microchipped, have a 'passport' listing their vaccinations and other necessary veterinary treatments, have had an officially approved blood test no less than six months previously, have an official PETS certificate from a government-authorised vet, come from certain countries only and only on certain routes from those countries, and on certain specified flights, ferries or railways. Their owners must also sign a declaration that the pet has not been outside of any of the countries participating in the scheme (most of which are listed here) during the past six months.

The specified countries include Australia, Austria, Bahrain, Belgium, Canada, Cyprus, Denmark, Finland, France, Germany, Greece, the Netherlands, Iceland, Italy, Jamaica, Japan, Luxembourg, Malta, New Zealand, Norway, Portugal, Singapore, Spain, Sweden, Switzerland, mainland US, the Vatican and a variety of dependent territories of European powers.

The list is growing and it's **essential** in any event to check the DEFRA website (🖳 www.defra.gov.uk/animals/quarantine/index.htm) to ensure that your country is still covered by the scheme and to elicit the latest details connected with it. There are additional demands made on people travelling from certain countries, which vary according to the country in question. Other regulations of a general nature pertaining to animal welfare while travelling also apply and are given in detail on the website.

For some domestic animals, e.g. horses, of which only certain breeds are kept in quarantine, an import licence and a veterinary examination is required. Dangerous animals (e.g. poisonous snakes) require a special import licence. You require a licence from your local council to keep a poisonous snake or other dangerous animal, which must be properly caged with an adequate exercise area, and must pose no risk to public health and safety. It's a criminal offence to attempt to smuggle an animal into the UK and it's almost always discovered. **Illegally imported animals are either exported immediately or destroyed and the owners are always prosecuted.** Owners face (and invariably receive) a heavy fine of up to £1,000 or an unlimited fine and up to a year's imprisonment for deliberate offences.

There's no VAT or duty on animals brought into the UK as part of your 'personal belongings', although, if you import an animal after your arrival, VAT and duty may need to be paid on its value.

Kennels & Catteries

If you don't have a friend or relative who will look after your dog or cat while you're on holiday, you must board it in a kennel or cattery. If you leave a pet with a friend, always provide full instructions regarding diet, exercise and vets. Ask your friends, neighbours or colleagues if they can recommend somewhere (if they cannot help you, ask your vet). It's important not to take pot luck, as standards vary from excellent to poor. If a kennel or cattery isn't highly recommended, check it personally before boarding your pet and ask what services are charged as extras, such as grooming and medicine. Any veterinary fees incurred while boarding are charged to the owner. If you plan to leave your pet at a kennel or cattery, book well in advance, particularly for school holiday periods. Dogs left at kennels may need to be vaccinated against certain diseases, although the requirements vary with the kennel.

Vets

You can take your dog or cat to a veterinary surgeon (vet) for a course of vaccinations, boosters or neutering, the cost of which varies greatly with the region and the vet. It isn't mandatory to have your dog (or any pet) vaccinated against any disease in the UK, although most dog owners have dogs vaccinated against a number of them, including distemper, hepatitis, and leptospirosis. After the initial primary vaccinations (fee around £20 to £30), annual boosters are necessary. You will receive a 'record of primary and booster vaccination' from your vet.

Shop around, compare fees and always agree one in advance. Unfortunately, London is among the most expensive places in the UK. A list of local vets can be obtained from the Royal College of Veterinary Surgeons, Belgravia House, 62–64 Horseferry Road, London SW1P 2AF (☎ 020-7222 2001) or the British Veterinary Association (BVA), 7 Mansfield Street, London W1G 9NQ (☎ 020-7636 6541), which publishes a series of booklets on pet care. If you cannot afford a vet's fees, the People's Dispensary for Sick Animals, Whitechapel Way, Priorslee, Telford, Shropshire TF2 9PQ (☎ 01952-290999) may provide free treatment. It's one of a network of centres throughout the country; for further information call the information line free (☎ 0800-917 2509).

Animal Welfare

The Royal Society for the Prevention of Cruelty to Animals (RSPCA, Wilberforce Way, Southwater, Horsham, West Sussex RH12 9RS, ☎ 0870-335 5999) is the main organisation for animal protection and welfare in the UK and operates a number of animal clinics and welfare centres. The work of the RSPCA is

12

complemented by the National Canine Defence League (NCDL, Dogs Trust, 17 Wakely Street, London EC1V 7RQ, ☎ 020-7837 0006), a national charity devoted to the welfare of dogs, which takes in lost, abandoned and abused dogs, and turns them into healthy, well-adjusted pets. No healthy dog is ever destroyed by the NCDL. The most famous animal shelter in London is The Dogs' Home (Battersea), but there are many others, including those run by the Cats' Protection League. Many Britons are also concerned about the survival of wild animals and there's even a British Hedgehog Protection Society (BHPS), although they have yet to teach the creatures how to cross roads safely.

POLICE

Britain doesn't have a national police force but 52 regional police forces (43 in England and Wales, eight in Scotland and one in Northern Ireland), each responsible for a county (or a region in Scotland) or a metropolitan area. In the case of London, there are two police forces: the City of London Police, which was formally established in 1839 and covers only the City of London, and the Metropolitan Police, which covers the rest of London. Further information can be found on 💻 www.cityoflondon.police.uk and 💻 www.met.police.uk respectively. There are no special uniformed traffic or tourist police in the UK, all routine duties being performed by standard policemen and policewomen.

Police forces in England, Scotland and Wales are among the few in the world that don't carry guns (their only weapon is a truncheon), although in recent years an increasing number of policemen have been armed for special services such as the prevention of terrorism and when dealing with armed suspects. This is a controversial issue, as a number of innocent people have been shot dead by police marksmen over the past decade. Some police forces have also been issued with telescopic truncheons that can cause severe injuries and pepper sprays that can cause blindness. After the deaths of a number of police officers on duty in recent years, there has been an intense debate among the police concerning the carrying of arms. However, the great majority of police officers are against routinely carrying them and many would leave the force rather than do so.

The uniform worn by police forces is generally the same throughout the UK and male 'bobbies' (police constables or PCs) on the beat in England and Wales wear the famous British police helmet. Other police officers (e.g. in cars) wear a flat cap with a chequered black and white band.

In addition to full-time police officers, each force has a part-time attachment of unpaid volunteer special constables. Traffic wardens are responsible for traffic and parking and come under the control of the local police force. There's also an auxiliary force of security wardens in some urban areas with fewer powers than police officers.

British policemen used to be the most respected in the world, not least by the British people. However, in recent years they've had a bad press in England and Wales and their reputation has been badly tarnished. According to a number of surveys, many people have lost faith in the integrity and efficiency of their police force. Many are unhappy about police responses when they ring 999 or their local police station, and over half the victims of crime are dissatisfied with the police response. There has been an increase in complaints against the police, many concerning prejudice, harassment, and even brutal and violent treatment. Even more worrying, a public inquiry into the handling of the murder investigation of a black teenager (Steven Lawrence) found that racism was rife in the Metropolitan Police force. There are very few black and Asian officers in the UK (and they're often subject to racial abuse and prejudice from their white colleagues).

The police in England and Wales have consistently refused to allow independent investigations of complaints, which means that successful complaints against the police are extremely rare. Most people don't even bother to complain, as they consider it a waste of time. The Police Complaints Authority (PCA) claims to be independent, yet investigations into complaints against police are carried out by police officers. If you're seeking compensation against the police in England or Wales, you must usually seek redress in a county court, as the PCA cannot ensure that you receive compensation. The level of compensation paid by the police to the victims of illegal arrest and police brutality is increasing, often as a result of civil actions for damages. To make a complaint against a police officer, you can write to the Chief Constable of the force involved, go to any police station or write directly to the Police Complaints Authority (PCA), 5th Floor, 90 High Holborn, London WC1V 6BH (☎ 08453 002 002).

If the foregoing catalogue of complaints has given the impression of an incompetent, prejudiced and dishonest police force, it would be quite wrong. The UK still has one of the best police forces in the world and the vast majority of people rate the police performance as good or very good. What is evident is that the actions of a small minority of officers are increasingly bringing the whole force into disrepute. Unlike some countries, the British public expects its police to be above reproach and, although it may seem old-fashioned in the 21st century, are unwilling to accept anything less than absolute honesty, impartiality and efficiency from their police officers.

POSTAL SERVICES

There's a post office in most London districts and suburbs, providing over 100 different services, which (in addition to the usual post office services provided in most countries) include a number of unique services. The term 'post office' is used in the UK as a general term for three separate businesses: the Royal Mail, Post Office (formerly Post Office Counters) and Parcelforce Worldwide (formerly

Royal Mail Parcels). Girobank plc, the former post office banking division, still operates from post offices, but is now owned by Alliance & Leicester.

Of some 14,000 post offices in the UK, only around 500 are operated directly by the post office. The remainder are franchise offices or sub-post offices, which don't offer all the services provided by a main post office and are operated on an agency basis by sub-postmasters. There are plans to partly privatise the post office – the government has already been accused of back-door privatisation with the transfer of many post offices from the high street to supermarkets, stationery stores, newsagents and other shops. There are angry reactions to recent announcements in January 2007 that between 2,500 and 3,000 post offices, mostly in rural areas, face phased closure to save money.

In addition to offering postal services, the post office acts as an agent for a number of government departments and local authorities (councils), for example, the sale of TV licences (exclusive to post offices), national insurance stamps and road tax. You can also pay many bills at a post office, including electricity, gas, water, telephone, cable, store cards, mail-order bills, council tax, rent payments and housing association rents. The post office is also the largest chain of outlets for the National Lottery and a distribution centre for social security leaflets. It provides bureaux de change facilities in main branches (although you may need to order foreign currency) and provides an (expensive) international money transfer service in conjunction with Western Union International.

The post office (founded in 1635) is the last bastion of the old state sector and like all nationalised companies it's over-staffed and inefficient in some areas. Despite this, it provides one of the best postal services in the world. Services have improved considerably in recent years and it's now one of the world's most modern and automated post offices, offering a vast range of services compared with most foreign post offices. However, overseas rivals are muscling in on Royal Mail services and a number of overseas groups also handle post in the UK.

Post office business hours in the UK are usually from 9am to 5.30pm, Mondays to Fridays, and from 9am to 12.30pm on Saturdays. Sub-post offices usually close for an hour at lunchtime, e.g. 1 to 2pm, Mondays to Fridays, and may also close one afternoon a week, usually Wednesdays. Main post offices don't close at lunchtime. Some post offices at airports are open on Sundays and public holidays. Details of individual post offices, including their opening hours, are available from Post Office Counters (☎ 0845-722 3344).

If you want to receive post in London and don't have a permanent address, you can use the *poste restante* service and have post sent to any London post office. Post is kept for a month and an identity card or passport is required to collect it.

Letter Post

The post office provides a choice of first and second class domestic post delivery (further evidence of the British preoccupation with class). Domestic post refers to all post to addresses in Great Britain, Northern Ireland, the Channel Islands and the Isle of Man. The target for the delivery of first class post is the next working day after collection and for second class post, the third working day after collection. Some 95 per cent of first class post is delivered the next day, although some letters fail to arrive until weeks after posting (probably those that are delivered by rail). It's unnecessary to mark post as first or second class, as any item that's posted with less than first class postage is automatically sent second class.

To ensure delivery within the UK the next day, first class post should be posted by 5pm for the local area (e.g. a letter posted in London to another London address) or by 1pm for other parts of the UK, excluding northern Scotland.

Airmail letters take an average of two to three days to Denmark, Norway and Switzerland and up to seven days to Italy and some other European countries (which provides a good indication of the relative efficiency or otherwise of European postal services). Airmail to other destinations usually takes four to seven days. Surface post takes up to two weeks to Europe and up to 12 weeks outside Europe. Underpaid airmail items may be sent by surface post or will incur a surcharge. Leaflets are published in September, listing the latest post international posting dates for Christmas.

Second class domestic letter post mustn't exceed 750g, although there's no limit for first class post. This means that packages weighing between 750g and 1kg must be sent by first class post. International letters, small packets and printed papers (both airmail and surface) are limited to a maximum of 2kg (books and pamphlets 5kg).

Domestic letters weighing up to 60g now cost 23p second class and 32p first class. The cost of sending a letter weighing up to 20g by airmail is 44p to Europe or 72p to the rest of the world. Postcards cost 50p. It's possible to send a letter by surface mail to destinations outside Europe, costing 42p, but delivery can take weeks (see above).

Private couriers are able to handle only urgent and valuable post, subject to a minimum fee of £1. The courier industry, particularly in London and other major cities, is growing by some 20 per cent a year and the UK is a major centre for international air courier traffic. Major companies include Federal Express, DHL, UPS and TNT, plus the post office's own Parcelforce service.

The post office produces a wealth of brochures about postal rates and special services, including a *Mini Mailguide* containing information about all Royal Mail products and services. It also has a telephone helpline (☎ 0845-774 0740 or 01752-387112) and a website (🖳 www.royalmail.co.uk).

TELEPHONE

Nearly all homes in London have a fixed-line telephone and mobile phone use is among the highest in the world. You can make calls to anywhere in the UK and to most countries in the world without contacting the operator and, because telephone exchanges now operate digitally, a wide range of additional services such as call diversion and call waiting can be also accessed (see below).

The cost of making telephone calls has gone down sharply in the last decade. Long-distance and international call charges have particularly fallen because of competition among the many indirect access providers, who buy time from British Telecom (BT) or other companies to re-sell it to their own customers.

The general emergency telephone number throughout the UK is 999.

Telephone Companies

The telephone system in the UK is dominated by British Telecom (BT), created and given a 25-year licence in 1984 when the state-owned monopoly was privatised. When the telecommunications market was opened to national and international competition in 1991, the UK stood at the forefront of technology in this sector, but other European countries, having subsequently liberalised their own telecoms industries, have now largely caught up. Well over 100 companies are licensed to operate telecoms services, and competition, although less intense than a few years ago, is still keen, so shopping around to compare rates could save you money.

Users can choose between BT, cable companies, a large number of indirect operators and one or two small radio-based organisations (operating in remote areas only). Cable companies now offer convenient connections to over 50 per cent of homes, the major providers of services to consumers being Telewest and NTL, whose areas of coverage don't overlap. To find out if either operates in your district, check their websites (💻 www.telewest.co.uk and 💻 www.ntl home. com/ntl_telephone) or look in your local telephone directory.

The major companies which provide telephones and infrastructure as well as the opportunity to make calls are BT, Telewest, Kingston, and NTL. The most prominent indirect service provider is Talk Talk. Kingston offers attractive overall rates but is active only in certain parts of the country, while Telco is among the cheapest of the indirect companies, closely followed by Talk Talk, British Gas and Tiscali. However, the increasing number and complexity of different schemes on offer, even from the same company, means that the cheapest option for you depends ever more on how high your monthly bill is, when you make most calls, what sort of calls you make (e.g. local, national or international), and how frequently you call mobiles. Consult the internet site 💻 www.uswitch.com, which provides tariff calculations for numerous permutations of these variables, in order to establish which company will offer you the best deal.

Connection costs are free in the case of indirect operators – who don't, of course, have to install a telephone line – while the major infrastructure providers normally charge unless a special offer happens to be current. Installation costs £60 from Kingston if an engineer needs to visit your home and £23.50 if you're taking over a line. Telewest's standard rate is £75 but the frequency of special offers means you're likely to pay less – sometimes as little as £10. NTL also charges £75 but this is for a broadband connection.

Most households still rent their phone line from BT but many additionally use indirect services for specific purposes, such as making international calls. Occasionally it's cheaper to switch companies entirely if your pattern of telephone usage changes markedly. Where BT scores heavily is in reliability and being able to put right anything which goes wrong quickly. A significant consideration when choosing a telecoms company is whether it looks likely to stay in business for the foreseeable future! **Smaller companies have come and gone with regularity in recent years, some going bankrupt and causing difficulties for their customers.**

It should be noted that BT charges more for a local call than some other providers charge for a call to the US or Australia (as little as 2p per minute). If you make a lot of international calls, you should investigate the companies mentioned under **International Calls** on page 358.

For information about providers contact your local telecoms advisory service (see your local telephone directory) or the Telecommunications Users' Association, Woodgate Studios, 2–8 Games Row, Barnet, Herts EN4 9HN (☎ 020-8449 8844).

Installation & Registration

Before moving into a new home, check whether there's a telephone line and that the number of lines or telephone points is adequate (most new homes already have phone lines and points in a number of rooms). If a property has a cable connection, you could decide not to have a BT phone line installed. If you move into an old house or apartment, a telephone line will probably already be installed, although there won't be a phone. If you're moving into accommodation without a phone line, e.g. a new property, you must ask BT or one of the other infrastructure providers (see above) to install one.

BT's target for residential line installation is three working days, depending on the area. The installation of a line where there wasn't one previously costs £75 but to take over an existing line is free. If, unusually, a property still has an old-style phone point (which cannot be unplugged), it should be replaced with a new-style 'linebox' or master socket. **This can be done by BT only and it's illegal to do it yourself or get anyone other than a BT engineer to do it.** Once you have a BT linebox or master socket, you can install as many additional sockets as you like but you shouldn't connect more than four telephones to one telephone line. You can install additional sockets yourself by buying DIY kits from BT or a DIY shop, or BT can install them for you (although their labour charges are astronomical). BT sells a wide range of extension kits, sockets and cords.

12

New residential subscribers, particularly tenants in rented property, may need to pay a deposit (in rare instances when BT doubts their capacity to meet bills). BT will retain the deposit for a maximum of a year (provided bills are paid on time) and pay interest on it. You can appeal against this demand to your local district general manager. However, it's far more likely that new customers will be asked to agree to a maximum bill level with BT, which eliminates this requirement. If this level is exceeded before the end of the quarter, BT will contact you to agree a course of action.

If you're moving to a new address in the same code area, it's usually possible to retain your existing number. The number to ring for information is ☎ 0800-800880.

Using The Telephone

Using the telephone in the UK is much the same as in any other country – with a few British eccentricities thrown in for good measure.

London telephone numbers were changed (unnecessarily) in 1995 and again in 1999 (to rectify the mistake) – a national scandal that cost residents and businesses millions of pounds but somehow escaped the notice of both the media and consumer organisations. All London numbers now have the code 020, followed by eight digits, the first of which is 7 for numbers in 'inner' London – an area which, needless to say, doesn't correspond with the geographical concept of 'inner' London (see page 20) – and 8 for 'outer' London. It's widely believed, even by Londoners, that the code for inner London is 0207 and for outer London 0208, but that isn't the case and it's possible to dial a number within the same area without using the 020 code but not if the 7 or 8 is omitted.

Free numbers, sometimes called 'freefone numbers' by BT, have the prefix 0800. They're usually provided by businesses that are trying to sell you something or, having sold you something, provide a free telephone support service. Numbers with the prefix 0845 are charged at the local rate, irrespective of where you're calling from. Numbers with the prefix 0870 are charged at the national rate even when you're calling locally. Note also that charges (which are around 4p and 8p per minute respectively) are the same whichever call provider you use. Premium rate (information and entertainment numbers) begin 09 and can cost as much as 60p per minute. **If you use these numbers frequently, you can go bankrupt!**

When dialling a British number from overseas, you must dial the international access code used in the country from which you're calling (e.g. 011 from the US or 00 from most other countries), followed by the UK's international code (44), the area code **without** the first 0 (e.g. 20 for London) and the subscriber's number. For the London number 7123 4567, you would dial the access code followed by 44-20-7123 4567.

Telephone numbers are usually dictated one digit at a time on the phone, except for repeated numbers, e.g. 11 or 222, which are given as double one or treble two. Zero is usually read as the letter 'O' (oh).

If you get a bad line, e.g. you're unable to hear the caller or the caller is unable to hear you, or a crossed line where you can hear voices in the background, the connection may improve if you redial the number.

Extra Services

BT's variety of additional services includes alarm call, call barring, caller display, 'choose to refuse' (which allows you to block certain incoming calls), call diversion, call minder (an answerphone service), message alert, call return, call waiting, reminder call, reverse charge call, ring back, and 'ring me free'. Some of these are free; others are quite expensive.

BT Chargecard

Direct-dialled calls and calls via an international operator can be made using a BT Chargecard to over 130 countries and to the UK from over 100 countries using the BT Direct service. BT Chargecards can be used to dial direct from any tone phone, which includes all BT payphones and most private phones, although they cannot be used from mobile phones. For domestic calls, there's a basic charge of 20p for the first minute, after which the price is calculated per second. If you call via the operator, there's an additional handling charge of £1.75 for all calls (even local ones). Calls from payphones are charged at BT public payphone rates (see below).

BT Call Charges

BT remains by far the largest telephone company in the UK and therefore its call rates are listed here for comparison purposes. **This isn't meant as an endorsement of the company, which charges some of the country's highest rates.** BT levies a quarterly line rental fee of £31.50 (including VAT) for a residential line (there's a £1 per month reduction when your is bill paid by direct debit). For a large percentage of BT's customers, the line rental fee accounts for over half their bill. The VAT rate of 17.5 per cent is applicable to line rental and call charges and is included in all rates shown unless otherwise noted.

BT has three charge rates for self-dialled, domestic calls from ordinary lines (not payphones or mobile phones), depending on the time and day. Daytime Rate is in operation from 8am to 6pm, Mondays to Fridays; Evening and Night time Rate is from 6pm to 8am, Mondays to Fridays; and Weekend Rate from midnight Friday until midnight Sunday. However, BT charges a minimum of 5p for all calls, so your cheap weekend local call must be at least five minutes in length to take advantage of the 1p per minute rate. Some companies offer national calls for 4p per minute at all times and are therefore cheaper during the day.

12

BT Tariff/Cost Per Minute			
Type Of Call	Daytime	Evening/Night	Weekend
Local*	3.95p	1p	1p
National	7.91p	3.95p	1.50p

* To clarify what constitutes a local call, consult your telephone directory.

BT Bills

You're billed by BT for your line rental, phone rental (if applicable) and calls every quarter (three months). If applicable, the telephone connection fee is included in your first bill. BT provides all customers with itemised bills, which state the date and time, duration and cost of each call. Customers can choose to have only certain calls itemised.

BT phone bills can be paid by budget account (to spread bills evenly over 12 months), quarterly direct debit, or by cheque using the envelope provided or at your bank (using the form provided) or at a post office. The best way for most people to pay their phone bill is monthly via a budget account or quarterly from an interest-bearing bank or building society account. With quarterly direct debit, your account is debited 14 days after you receive the bill. BT sells £1 telephone stamps (available from BT shops and post offices) to help spendthrifts save for their phone bills. However, these pay no interest and, if you lose them, you've lost your money.

If you don't pay your phone bill within around 14 days of receipt, you will receive a red Reminder of Payment, after which you will have another 14 days in which to pay it. If you don't pay your bill within this period, your phone will be disconnected, usually without any further notification.

If you have a query about your account, dial ☎ 150. If you cannot obtain satisfaction from your local BT area manager (the phone number is on your bill) or district general manager, you should contact the secretary of your national Advisory Committee (the address is listed in your telephone directory under Code of Practice for Consumers). Complaints about the telephone service are dealt with by the Office of Communications (Ofcom), 50 Ludgate Hill, London EC4M 7JJ (☎ 020-7634 8700). Ofcom has taken over from the Office of Telecommunications (Oftel) as regulator of broadcasting media as well as telephone services. As a last resort you can go to legally-binding arbitration if your dispute is for less than £5,000.

12

International Calls

All private telephones in the UK are on International Direct Dialling (IDD), allowing calls to be dialled direct to over 190 countries and reverse charge (collect) calls to be made to some 140 countries. To make an international call, dial 00, the country code, the area code without the first zero (with a few exceptions, such as Italy) and the subscriber's number. Dial 155 for the international operator to make non-IDD calls, credit card calls, person-to-person and reverse charge calls (which aren't accepted by all countries). Dial ☎ 118505 for international directory enquiries. The codes for the major cities of many countries are listed in telephone directories in Section 3: International Information, including the time difference. (One sure way to upset most people is to wake them at 3am!)

BT charges for dialled international calls from ordinary lines are based on charge bands (1 to 16), which are shown in telephone directories with international dialling information. In 2003 BT's standard weekend rates were around 24p per minute to Australia, 23p to France and Germany, 18p to Ireland, 54p to Japan, 67p to South Africa and 21p to the US. International charges are listed on the BT website (🖳 www.bt.com). **Rates are much higher during the day from Mondays to Fridays. Using an alternative company to BT, e.g. an indirect access company (see below), can result in huge savings, even when comparing their standard charges with BT's lowest.**

Indirect Access Companies

The cheapest companies for international calls are indirect access companies. You must usually dial a code before dialling a number, although it may be possible to route all calls automatically via the company. It's even possible to buy a box that you connect between your phone and wall socket which automatically routes long-distance and international calls via the cheapest carrier. Companies may offer low rates for all calls or just national and international calls. Some charge a subscription fee. Calls are charged at a flat rate 24 hours a day, seven days a week. Some companies allow you to make calls from any tone phone (even abroad), while others restrict you to a single (e.g. home or office) number. Calls may be paid for with a credit or debit card, either in advance, when you must buy a number of units, or by direct debit each month. Alternatively, you may be billed monthly in arrears.

Low-cost companies have devastated BT's erstwhile share of the international market, particularly with regard to transatlantic calls, which isn't surprising when you consider the savings that can be made. For example, Talk Talk (☎ 0845-308 1878) charges a flat rate of 3p per minute to the US and Germany, 4p to Australia, Canada, France, and Ireland and New Zealand, 7p to Japan and 14p to South Africa (these rates aren't applicable to mobile phones or payphones). Compare these rates with BT's above! Most other indirect access companies,

12

such as Telco (☎ 0800-594 1004, 🖳 www.cheap-telephone-calls.com), Alpha Telecom (☎ 0800-279 0000/3205, 🖳 www.alphatelecom.com), Callmate (☎ 0113-244 9955, 🖳 www.callmate.com), Swiftcall (🖳 www.swift call.co.uk).

Country Direct

Many European countries, including the UK, subscribe to a Country Direct service that allows you to call a special number giving you direct access to an operator in the country you're calling. The number varies according to the country from which you're making the call and you must establish this before you travel. The operator will connect you to the number required and will also accept credit card payment and reverse charge calls. The number to dial is shown in telephone directories in the International Code section. **You should be extremely wary of making international reverse charge calls to the UK using BT's UK Direct scheme, as you will pay at least double the cost of using a local payphone.** For example, a call from the US to the UK would cost £6.07 for the operator's assistance and £1.68 per minute for the call. For information about countries served by the Country Direct service call BT International Directory Enquiries on ☎ 118505 or the international operator on ☎ 115 (the latter is free).

International Calling Cards

You can obtain an international telephone calling card from telephone companies in many countries. It allows you to make calls from abroad and charge them to your telephone bill in your home country. American long-distance telephone companies (e.g. AT&T, MCI and Sprint) compete vigorously for overseas customers and all offer calling cards allowing foreign customers to bill international calls to a credit card. AT&T's service, for example, allows you to make calls from almost any phone in over 100 countries (call ☎ 0800-220679 or visit 🖳 www.att.com for information).

Information

To find out more about international direct dialling, country codes, BT international services and related topics you can visit 🖳 www.bt.com or ring the international operator on ☎ 155.

Public Telephones

Most public telephones (officially called 'payphones') permit international direct dialling (IDD) as well as domestic calls and calls made via the operator. Older ones are sterile grey 'vandal-proof' steel and glass booths containing push-button payphones, ancient and stylish red boxes surviving only in some locations of historic interest (and, curiously, in Malta!). The latest payphones also also offer internet, email and SMS texting facilities while video email phones were trialled in London in 2003. Some humbler payphones aren't enclosed and offer little protection from the elements and surrounding noise (although if they remain in working order, most people are happy). A limited number offer more convenience for people with disabilities and better wheelchair access. There are also private 'call shops' in London, where you can usually make calls in more comfort. A large number of London's licensed taxis, called 'taxifone cabs', are fitted with metered passenger payphones accepting all leading credit cards (taxifone cabs can be booked in advance).

Payphones in the UK are operated by BT and now chiefly accept credit cards – Visa, Visa Delta, MasterCard, Eurocard, American Express, Diners Club International and JCB – rather than coins as formerly. A BT Chargecard can be used to make calls from payphones, but there's a high charge. Note that pre-paid phonecards are no longer in use. This eliminates theft because, of course, there is nothing in the phonebox to steal, and consequently it's easier than in the past to find payphones that work. Public payphones are to be found throughout London: in public streets, inside and outside post offices and railway stations, and in hotels, pubs, restaurants, shops and other private and public buildings. If you're driving, finding a payphone is more difficult than in the past but nowhere near as difficult as finding somewhere to park.

Some payphones at airports, ferry ports and main railway stations are reserved for international calls. This is indicated by a sign. Others may display a '999 calls only' (emergency calls) sign, which means you will be unable to make an ordinary call but may be able to contact the operator and make a reverse charge or BT Chargecard call. Emergency calls are free from any payphone. Not all payphones accept incoming calls, so check for a sign before asking someone to call you back. If you need additional information dial ☎ 100 for the inland or ☎ 155 for the international operator. Calling from payphones, the BT Domestic Directory Enquiry number is ☎ 118141 (calls cost 60p per minute) and the International Enquiry number ☎ 118505 (£1.50 per minute).

The minimum charge for a call from a payphone is 20p, four times the minimum for a local call made from a private phone. For your 20p, you can make a local call lasting 67 seconds, a national call lasting 47 seconds or a call to a mobile phone lasting just 8.9 seconds. There's a 75p minimum charge when using a credit card, in which case all inland calls are charged at 20p per minute. Credit card international calls involve an additional £1 'set-up' fee. Operator-connected calls from payphones cost far more than dialled calls and should be avoided if possible. **Payphones should be avoided at all costs when making international calls, as the rates are exorbitant.**

Be wary of using private payphones, e.g. those located in pubs, restaurants, hotels, shopping centres and petrol stations. The charge rate for these phones is set by the owners, many of whom levy extortionate rates. The call charge should be displayed on all private payphones. You should also avoid using hotel room phones, where fees can be astronomical. Some hotels even charge a fee to connect guests to free (e.g. 0800) numbers used to make chargecard calls!

12

Mobile Phones

Few countries in the world have as many mobile phone (mobile) users as the UK. Practically anyone who wants one now owns one. Whereas they were once status symbols among yuppies and the young they have now become just another everyday 'necessity'. Mobiles are so widespread that many businesses (e.g. restaurants, cinemas, theatres, concert halls, etc.) ban them and some even use mobile phone jammers, which can detect and jam every handset within 100m.

In recent years there has been widespread publicity regarding a possible health risk to users from the microwave radiation emitted by mobile phones. Nothing has been reliably established yet, but you can visit the Department of Health's official website on the subject to discover the facts (🖳 www. doh.gov.uk/mobilephones).

Mobile phone network providers in the UK include Vodaphone, T-mobile, Orange, O2, and 3G. There are also a number of 'virtual' providers such as Virgin, One.Tel and Sainsbury's, who buy time from the major operators and operate their own services. BT, having abandoned the mobile phone business a couple of years ago, is now returning with a new technology which uses its own landline network and wireless connections in order to provide what is claimed will be a cheaper and more reliable service.

Coverage is most limited in the case of the newcomer G3, but there's little discernible difference between the two major companies, O2 and Vodafone, although you should check the reception in your area. Details about areas of coverage are available on websites such as 🖳 www.mobileshop.org. Some companies have been criticised for the quality of reception offered in many parts of the country (and even worse customer service).

Subscribers can buy a GSM phone, which can be used in many countries worldwide, including much of western Europe, Australia, Hong Kong, South Africa and parts of the Middle East. You must have a contract with a 'roaming' agreement if you wish to use your mobile phone abroad and should check the countries your service provider has contracts with.

Phones are sold by retail outlets such as BT shops, specialist dealers (e.g. Carphone Warehouse, The Link, and Phone City), department and chain stores (e.g. Dixons) and supermarkets, all of whom have arrangements with service providers or networks to sell airtime contracts along with phones. **Don't rely on always getting good or impartial advice from retail staff, some of whom know little or nothing about phones and networks.** Always deal with an independent company that sells a wide range of phones and can connect you to any network.

Retailers advertise almost daily in magazines and newspapers, where a wide range of special offers is common and prices vary considerably. Phones are even available free if you're willing to sign a contract which ensures that retailers and network providers can make a profit through line rental and call charges

Before buying a phone, compare battery life, memory capacity, weight, size and features, which may include automatic call back, unanswered call store, mailbox, call timer, minute minder, lock facility and call barring.

The most important point is where you're going to use your phone, followed by when and how often and whether you will make mostly local or long distance and international calls. **Don't be tempted by a cheap phone if there are high call and line rental charges.**

Before buying a mobile phone (or pager), check the reviews and comparison tests in surveys conducted by *Which?, What Cellphone?* and *W@MOB* magazines.

TELEVISION & RADIO

Most British homes have at least one TV, over 60 per cent have more than one (25 per cent have three or more) and over 80 per cent have a video recorder – not simply to watch video tapes, but also to record their favourite TV soaps such as *Coronation Street, Eastenders, Neighbours, The Bill, and Home and Away*, which are easily the most popular programmes in the UK (now joined by the National Lottery draw). DVD is becoming increasingly popular and is now coming close to superceding the video. The British are avid radio listeners and over 90 per cent of the population listen to the radio for 20 hours or more each week. There's a wide variety of stations, including a plethora of independent broadcasters.

Television

Although it produces a surfeit of nonsense (e.g. inane quiz shows and soaps, otherwise known as 'tabloid' TV) to cater for those who have nothing better to do with their lives, British TV (i.e. British-produced TV programming) is generally recognised as the best – or least bad – in the world. British TV companies produce many excellent programmes, including documentaries, wildlife and nature programmes, serialised adaptations of novels, TV films, situation comedies, and variety shows, which are sold throughout the world. Other excellent programmes include current affairs, music programmes, chat shows and sports coverage. Some three-quarters of Britons get their main information about the world from TV news, although the presentation is becoming more showbiz (newscasters are stars in their own right). Explicit sex and extreme violence are becoming commonplace and the Broadcasting Standards Council is trying to ban gratuitous sex scenes.

Standards

The standards for TV reception in the UK aren't the same as in many other countries. TVs and video recorders manufactured for use in the US (NTSC standard) and continental Europe, won't function in the UK because of different transmission standards. Most European countries use the PAL B/G standard, except for France, which has its own standard called SECAM. The British standard is a modified PAL-I system, where the audio signal is shifted to avoid the buzz plaguing the conventional PAL system when, for example, transmitting subtitles or other white areas.

If you bring a TV to the UK from the US or the continent, you will get either a picture or sound, **but not both.** A TV can be converted to work in the UK, but it's usually not worth the trouble and expense. If you want a TV and video recorder (VCR) that will work in the UK and other European countries (including France) and/or the US, you must buy a multi-standard model. Some multi-standard TVs also handle the North American NTSC standard and have an NTSC jack plug connection, allowing you to play American videos.

VCRs manufactured for non-British markets are unusable in the UK, and recordings made for the North American market are unplayable on British video recorders. Video recordings made on a PAL VCR can usually be played back on any other PAL VCR with both sound and vision. Most modern VCRs have a feature called 'Video Plus', which allows you to record programmes simply by entering a 'Video Pluscode' (shown in most programme listings).

Stations

BBC television (🖳 www.bbc.co.uk) has been broadcasting regularly since 1936 and introduced a second station (BBC2) in 1964. There are now six BBC channels, the other four – BBC3 (🖳 www.bbc.co.uk/bbcthree), offering comedy, drama, films and news, BBC4 (🖳 www.bbc.co.uk/bbcfour), for arts, science, history and business programmes, BBC News 24 (🖳 www.bbc. co.uk/bbcnews24) for news, BBC Parliament for political programmes and two children's channels – being available only digitally or via satellite or cable (see below). The first regular commercial programmes began in London in 1955 – originally called Independent Television (ITV, 🖳 www.itv.com), renamed Channel 3 in 1990 but now called ITV1. ITV1 broadcasts regional programmes (there are 15 regions) as well as national programmes, such as news and soaps. ITV2 (🖳 www.itv2. co.uk), a 'younger entertainment' channel, was launched in 1998 but is available only digitally or via satellite or cable (see below). Two more terrestrial national commercial TV stations, Channel 4 (🖳 www.channel4.com) and Channel 5 (🖳 www.channel5.co.uk), were launched in 1982 and 1997 respectively.

In most London and suburban areas, all five terrestrial stations can be received, although reception for Channel 5 is sometimes poor. The BBC channels carry no advertising and are publicly funded through an annual TV licence (see below), sales of *Radio Times*, and the trading activities of BBC Enterprises. The other stations have regular 'commercial breaks' (approximately every 20 to 30 minutes). All terrestrial TV stations broadcast for 24 hours a day, as do many satellite and cable stations. Programmes on BBC begin at odd times (e.g. 6.20, 8.05), depending on the length of programmes, as they aren't subject to commercial breaks. Other broadcasters' programmes usually start on the hour or half hour.

TV Licence

An annual TV licence (£131.50 for colour, £44 for the three people who still have black and white sets) is required by all TV owners in the UK. Registered blind people are generously offered a reduction of 50 per cent on production of the local authority's certificate for the blind. The fee is linked to the cost of living and is subject to a three-year agreement under the BBC's charter.

A licence is required by anyone who has a TV or video (or has one installed) that can receive or record BBC, Channel 3, Channel 4, Channel 5, satellite or cable TV programmes. If a TV is used for video playback, as a computer monitor or to receive satellite TV only, the licence fee isn't payable. However, your TV must be incapable of receiving BBC and ITV channels, which can be done only by permanently disconnecting your TV aerial and tuner circuitry.

The licence fee covers any number of TVs owned by the licence holder, members of his family and domestic staff, at his main home. The licence fee also covers a TV at a second home in the UK, provided that both TVs aren't used simultaneously. If you've paid for a licence for a TV in a second home, you're entitled to a full refund.

TV licences must be renewed annually and can be purchased from post offices or from TV Licensing, Freepost (BS6689), Bristol BS98 1TL (☎ 0870-850 1202, 🖳 www.tvlicensing.co.uk). A Television Licence Application form must be completed. The licence fee can also be paid by direct debit from a bank or building society account in one payment or in quarterly or monthly payments (which include a small premium). The post office operates a TV licence saving scheme, through the purchase of £1 TV licence stamps. If you're leaving the UK, you can obtain a refund on any unexpired three-month period of a TV licence by applying in writing to Customer Services at the address above.

Digital TV

Digital TV was launched on 1st October 1998 by BSkyB in the UK. The benefits include a superior picture, better (CD quality) sound, widescreen cinema format and access to many more stations. Digital TV also allows interactive services.

To watch digital TV, you require an integrated digital TV or a set-top Digibox and a (digital) Minidish, which cost around £80. Customers must sign up for a 12-month subscription and agree to have the connection via a phone line (to allow for future interactive services). **This occasionally causes problems with your telephone, resulting in massive phone bills – for which BSkyB naturally denies any responsibility.**

In addition to the five terrestrial channels, digital TV offers ITV2 and four more BBC channels (see above), all of which are available free, plus many other channels (a total of 200, with up to 500 possible). For information about free digital TV channels, ☎ 0870-880 9980 or 🖥 www.freeview.co.uk.

Satellite TV

There are hundreds of channels, in addition to the five terrestrial channels, ITV2 and the four additional BBC channels, available in London via satellite, which is the only choice for those who want to watch foreign-language TV. Many satellite stations provide teletext information, which includes programme schedules.

The UK's biggest satellite TV provider is Sky (☎ 0870-240 4080 or 🖥 www. sky.com). Installation of a satellite dish and decoder costs around £120, although this cost is reduced if you take one of a number of subscription packages.

Satellite programmes are also listed in most national daily newspapers, general TV magazines and satellite TV magazines such as *What Satellite*, *Satellite Times* and *Satellite TV*, available from newsagents or on subscription. The annual *World Radio and TV Handbook* by David G. Bobbett (Watson-Guptil Publications) contains information and frequencies about all radio and TV stations worldwide.

Cable TV

Cable television in the UK was originally confined to areas of poor reception (e.g. due to geographical features or high-rise buildings) or where external aerials weren't permitted. However, there has been an explosion in cable TV in the last decade and it's the fastest-growing sector of the UK TV industry. Over 16 million homes can now receive cable TV and there are around 3 million subscribers (although the UK still has a long way to go to match European countries such as Belgium, the Netherlands and Switzerland, where 90 per cent of the populations have access to cable TV).

The latest broadband cable systems can carry up to 30 channels, including terrestrial broadcasts, satellite and digital TV programmes (see above) and local services. Cable TV is offered by a number of companies on a regional basis. Two of the main providers are Ntl and Telewest. A useful website offering comparisons between the services offered by the main cable companies is 🖥 www.uswitch.com.

Most cable TV companies provide all the stations offered by satellite TV plus a few others (possibly including local cable TV companies, such as Channel One in London). There's an initial connection fee of around £25 for cable TV, and a subscription of around £15 per month for the basic package or up to £35 per month for a package including all the most popular channels. One of the main advantages of taking out a cable subscription is that most cable companies offer inexpensive telephone services, possibly including free local off-peak calls, and therefore internet access, which can save you enough on your phone bill to pay for your cable TV. (One of the disadvantages is that cables are run underground

12

involving the digging of trenches across your carefully tended lawn and flower-beds.) Cable TV is controlled by the Independent Television Commission. For information about cable TV, contact the Cable Communications Association, 5th Floor, Artillery House, Artillery Row, London SW1P 1RT (☎ 0800-300750).

Video & DVD

There are numerous video and DVD hire shops in the UK, which reached (or exceeded) saturation point in the early 1990s. The British video market is the second-largest in the world after that of the US, and the UK has the highest ownership of VCRs in Europe (around three-quarters of households). Many video shops are open until 8pm or even 10pm, seven days a week.

To hire a video or DVD, you must usually be a member, for which shops require proof of your address and verification of your signature. If you're under 18, a parent is required to stand as a guarantor. Some video shops have a children's membership scheme with special deals for kids and cheap rental rates for children's films. Daily hire charges range from around £1.50 to £4 according to popularity (new top ten films are the most expensive). There's usually no extra charge for weekend hire (e.g. Saturday to Monday) when a shop doesn't open on a Sunday.

Members are issued with a membership card, which must be shown when hiring videos or DVDs. Usually you can take out up to three or four films at any time, which must usually be returned by 7pm the following day. If you're late returning a film, you're charged an extra day's rental for each day overdue. If you lose or damage a film, you must usually pay for a replacement at retail price. Insurance against loss or damage is sometimes available for a one-time payment, e.g. £5.

Videos can also be hired from public libraries, where the cost is usually 50p or £1 per night.

Recently released videos usually cost about £16 and DVDs around £25. HMV, Virgin and Woolworths stores have a wide selection of the latest videos and DVDs for sale and major supermarkets also stock a good range. Both videos and DVDs can be bought, often at discount, by mail order from Mr Benson (💻 www.bensons-world.co.uk) and Amazon (💻 www.amazon.co.uk). Most video and DVD shops also sell second-hand films at reduced prices.

Radio

Radio reception in London is excellent, including stereo reception (although FM reception isn't always good in cars). The radio audience in the UK is almost equally split between the British Broadcasting Corporation (BBC) and commercial radio stations (although the BBC has been losing listeners to commercial stations at an alarming rate in recent years). Community and ethnic radio is also popular in many areas and a number of universities and colleges operate their own radio stations. In addition to the FM or VHF stereo wave band, medium wave (MW or

12

AM) and long wave (LW) bands are in wide use throughout the UK. Shortwave (SW) band is useful for receiving foreign radio stations.

BBC

The BBC operates five network radio stations with easy to remember (if unimaginative) names: BBC Radio 1 (FM 97.6-99.8) for contemporary music, BBC Radio 2, (FM 88-90.2) for light entertainment and music, BBC Radio 3 (FM 90.2-92.4) for classical music, jazz and occasionally drama and poetry, BBC Radio 4 (FM 92.4-94.6, LW 198) for conversation, comedy, drama, documentaries, magazine programmes and news, and BBC Radio 5 Live (MW 693, 909) for news, current affairs and sport. There are also around 40 BBC local radio stations with some 10 million listeners. There's no advertising on BBC radio stations, although it's the main source of income for commercial radio stations. BBC radio is financed by the government and the revenue from TV licence fees, as no radio licence is necessary in the UK.

BBC radio programmes are publicised in national newspapers and Radios 1, 3 and 4 are broadcast both in stereo on FM and in mono on AM. BBC radio programmes are also listed on the BBC TV teletext information service. If you have difficulty locating the BBC's stations, send an SAE to the BBC, Listener Correspondence, PO Box 1922, Glasgow G2 3WT (☎ 08700-100 222).

Commercial Radio

Commercial radio is hugely popular in the UK, where it's the fastest-growing entertainment medium. However, there are still only some 200 commercial radio stations in the whole of Britain, compared with around 1,000 in France and Italy, and over 9,000 in the US. It's possible to receive more than ten commercial stations in London. National Commercial radio is reported to have some 36 million listeners or almost 80 per cent of adults.

Stations vary from large national stations with vast budgets and millions of listeners to tiny local stations run by volunteers with just a few thousand listeners. Stations provide a comprehensive service of local news and information, music and other entertainment, education, consumer advice, traffic information and local events, and provide listeners with the chance to air their views, often through phone-in programmes. Advertising on commercial radio is limited to nine minutes an hour but is usually less. Britain has three national commercial radio stations: Classic FM (🖳 www.classicfm.com, FM 100-101.9), which broadcasts classical music, Virgin Radio (🖳 www.virginradio.co.uk, FM 105.8, MW 1197, 1215) for popular music, and Talk Radio UK (🖳 www.talk-radio.co.uk, MW 1053, 1089), Britain's first 24-hour, national, speech-only commercial station. The UK's most popular commercial radio station is London's Capital Radio (🖳 www. capitalradiogroup.com), which includes Capital FM (🖳 www.capitalfm.com), Capital Gold (🖳 www.capitalgold.com) and other regional radio stations, and is the world's largest metropolitan radio station with over 3 million listeners.

12

Digital Radio

Digital radio offers better sound quality, less interference and no frequency changing. It's available in around 90 per cent of the UK, including all of London, although you need a digital radio to receive it (it can also be received on a PC with a digital card). All national BBC radio stations are broadcast digitally and new BBC digital radio programmes include BBC Radio 5 Live Sports Plus, BBC Parliament and BBC Xtra. Commercial radio has also gone digital with seven new national stations available only on digital. Digital One was awarded the franchise to launch a range of commercial radio channels and Classic FM, Virgin Radio and Talk Radio (see above) all broadcast digitally.

Satellite Radio

If you have satellite TV, you can also receive radio stations via your satellite link. For example, BBC Radio 1, 2, 3, 4 and 5, BBC World Service, Sky Radio, Virgin 1215 and many foreign (i.e. non-English) stations are broadcast via the Astra satellites. Satellite radio stations are listed in British satellite TV magazines such as *Satellite Times*. If you're interested in receiving radio stations from further afield, you should obtain a copy of the *World Radio TV Handbook* by David G. Bobbett (Watson-Guptil Publications).

TIME DIFFERENCE

London, like the rest of the UK, is on British Summer Time (BST) in summer and Greenwich Mean Time (GMT) in winter. The changes are made at 2am on the last Sunday in October (when the clocks go back an hour) and at the same time on the last Sunday in March, when they go forward. In case you forget, time changes are announced in local newspapers and on radio and TV and are usually indicated on diaries and calendars. The exact time is given by the telephone 'speaking clock' (☎ 123) and on televisions with teletext services (most remote controls have a 'time' button). When making international telephone calls or travelling long distances by air, check the local time difference, which is shown in the International Dialling section of telephone directories. The time in some foreign cities when it's noon GMT in London is shown below.

LONDON	CAPE TOWN	BOMBAY	TOKYO	LOS ANGELES	NEW YORK
Noon	2pm	5.30pm	9pm	4am	7am

12

APPENDICES

APPENDIX A: USEFUL ADDRESSES

Embassies & Consulates

A selection of foreign embassies and high commissions (Commonwealth countries) in London are listed below. Many countries also have consulates in other cities, e.g. Belfast, Birmingham, Cardiff, Edinburgh, Glasgow and Manchester, which are listed in phone books. All London embassies are listed in The London Diplomatic List (The Stationery Office).

Antigua: 2nd Floor, 45, Crawford Place, London W1H 4LP (☎020-7258 0070).

Argentina: 65, Brook St, Westminster, London W1U 3JT (☎ 020-7318 1300).

Australia: Australia House, Strand, London WC2B 4LA (☎ 020-7379 4334).

Austria: 18 Belgrave Mews West, London SW1X 8HU (☎ 020-7235 3731).

Bahamas: 10 Chesterfield Street, London W1J 5JL (☎ 020-7408 4488).

Bangladesh: 28 Queen's Gate, London SW7 5JA (☎ 020-7584 0081).

Barbados: 1 Great Russell Street, WC1B 3ND (☎ 020-7631 4975).

Belgium: 17, Grosvenor Crescent, London SW1 7EE (☎ 020-7470 3700).

Belize: 45, Crawford Place, London SW1H 4LP (☎ 020-7723 3603).

Bolivia: 106 Eaton Square, London SW1W 9AD (☎ 020-7235 4248/2257).

Bosnia & Herzegovina: 5-7, Lexham Gardens, London W8 5JJ (☎ 020-7373 0867).

Brazil: 32 Green Street, Mayfair, London W1Y 7AT (☎ 020-7499 0877).

Brunei: 19/20 Belgrave Square, London SW1X 8PG (☎ 020-7581 0521).

Bulgaria: 186–88 Queen's Gate, London SW7 5HL (☎ 020-7584 9400).

Cameroon: 84 Holland Park, London W11 3SB (☎ 020-7727 0771).

Canada: MacDonald House, 1 Grosvenor Square, London W1K 4AB (☎ 020-7258 6600).

Chile: 12 Devonshire Street, London W1G 7DS (☎ 020-7580 1023).

China: 49–1 Portland Place, London W1N 4JL (☎ 020-7299 4049).

Colombia: Flat 3a, 3 Hans Crescent, London SW1X 0LN (☎ 020-7589 9177).

Croatia: 21 Conway Street, London W1T 6BN (☎ 020-7387 2022).

Cuba: 167 High Holborn, London WC1 6PA (☎ 020-7240 2488).

Cyprus: 93 Park Street, London W1K 7ET (☎ 020-7499 8272).

Czech Republic: 26, Kensington Palace Gardens, London W8 4QY (☎ 020-7243-1115).

Denmark: 55 Sloane Street, London SW1X 9SR (☎ 020-7333 0200).

Dominica: 1 Collingham Gardens, South Kensington, London SW5 0HW (☎ 020-7370 5194).

Ecuador: Flat 3b, 3 Hans Crescent, Knightsbridge, London SW1X 0LS (☎ 020-7584 2648).

Egypt: 26, South St, Westminster, London SW1X (☎ 020-7499 2401).

El Salvador: 8 Dorset Sq. London NW1 6PU (☎ 020-7224 9800).

Fiji: 34 Hyde Park Gate, London SW7 5DN (☎ 020-7584 3661).

Finland: 38 Chesham Place, London SW1X 8HW (☎ 020-7838 6200).

France: 58 Knightsbridge, London SW1X 7JT (☎ 020-7073 1000).

The Gambia: 57 Kensington Court, Kensington, London W8 5DG (☎ 020-7937 6316).

Germany: 23 Belgrave Square, 1 Chesham Place, London SW1X 8PZ (☎ 020-7824 1300).

Ghana: 13 Belgrave Square, London SW1X 8PN (☎ 020-7201 5900).

Greece: 1A Holland Park, London W11 3TP (☎ 020-7229 3850).

Grenada: The Chapel, Archel Road, West Kensington, London W14 (☎ 020-7385 4277).

Guatemala: 13 Fawcett Street, London SW10 9HN (☎ 020-7351 3042).

Guyana: 3 Palace Court, Bayswater Road, London W2 4LP (☎ 020-7229 7684).

Holy See: Apostolic Nunciature, 54 Parkside, London SW19 5NF (☎ 020-8944 7189).

Honduras: 115 Gloucester Place, London W1U 6JT (☎ 020-7486 4880).

Hungary: 35 Eaton Place, London SW1X 8BY (☎ 020-7201 3440).

Iceland: 2a Hans Street, London SW1X (☎ 020-7259 3999).

India: India House, Aldwych, London WC2B 4NA (☎ 020-7836 8484).

Indonesia: 38 Grosvenor Square, London W1K 2HW (☎ 020-7499 7661).

Iran: 16 Prince's Gate, London SW7 1PT (☎ 020-7225 3000).

Ireland: 17 Grosvenor Place, London SW1X 7HR (☎ 020-7235 2171).

Israel: 2 Palace Green, Kensington, London W8 4QB (☎ 020-7957 9500).

Italy: 14 Three Kings Yard, Davies Street, London W1K 4EH (☎ 020-7312 2200).

Jamaica: 1–2 Prince Consort Road, London SW7 2BZ (☎ 020-7823 9911).

Japan: 101–104 Piccadilly, London W1J 7JT (☎ 020-7465 6500).

Jordan: 6 Upper Phillimore Gardens, Kensington, London W8 7HB (☎ 020-7937 3685).

Kenya: 45 Portland Place, London W1B 1AS (☎ 020-7636 2371).

Korea (South): 60 Buckingham Gate, London SW1E 6AJ (☎ 020-7227 5500).

Kuwait: 2 Albert Gate, London SW1X 7JU (☎ 020-7590 3400).

Lebanon: 15–21 Palace Gardens Mews, London W8 8QM (☎ 020-7229 7265).

Lesotho: 7 Chesham Place, Belgravia, London SW1X 8HN (☎ 020-7235 5686).

Luxembourg: 27 Wilton Crescent, London SW1X 8SD (☎ 020-7235 6961).

Malawi: 33 Grosvenor Street, London W1K 4QT (☎ 020-7491 4172).

Malaysia: 45 Belgrave Square, London SW1X 8QT (☎ 020-7235 8033).

Malta: Malta House, 36–38 Piccadilly, London W1J 0LE (☎ 020-7292 4800).

Mauritius: 32/33 Elvaston Place, London SW7 5NW (☎ 020-7581 0294).

Mexico: 42 Hertford Street, Mayfair, London W1Y 7JR (☎ 020-7499 8586).

Morocco: 49 Queen's Gate Gardens, London SW7 5NE (☎ 020-7581 5001).

Mozambique: 21 Fitzroy Square, London W1T 6EL (☎ 020-7383 3800).

Namibia: 6 Chandos Street, London W1G 9LU (☎ 020-7636 6244).

Nepal: 12a Kensington Palace Gardens, London W8 4QU (☎ 020-7229 6231).

Netherlands: 38 Hyde Park Gate, London SW7 5DP (☎ 020-7590 3200).

New Zealand: New Zealand House, Haymarket, London SW1Y 4TQ (☎ 020-7930 8422).

Nigeria: Nigeria House, 9 Northumberland Avenue, London WC2N 5BX (☎ 020-7839 1244).

Norway: 25 Belgrave Square, London SW1X 8QD (☎ 020-7591 5500).

Oman: 167 Queen's Gate, London SW7 5HE (☎ 020-7225 0001).

Pakistan: 35/36 Lowndes Square, London SW1X 9JN (☎ 020-7664 9200).

Papua New Guinea: Ground Floor, 14 Waterloo Place, London SW1Y 4AR (☎ 020-7930 0922).

Paraguay: 344, High St., Kensington, London W14 8NS (☎ 020-7610 4180).

Peru: 52 Sloane Street, London SW1X 9SP (☎ 020-7235 1917).

Philippines: 9a Palace Green, London W8 4QE (☎ 020-7937 1600).

Poland: 47 Portland Place, London W1B 1JH (☎ 020-7580 4324).

Portugal: 11 Belgrave Square, London SW1X 8PP (☎ 020-7235 5331).

Qatar: 1 South Audley Street, London W1K 1NB (☎ 020-7493 2200).

Romania: Arundel House, 4 Palace Green, London W8 4QD (☎ 020-7937 9666).

Russia: 6-7 Kensington Palace Gardens, London W8 4QP (☎ 020-7229 2666).

Saudi Arabia: 30 Charles Street, Mayfair, London W1X 7PM (☎ 020-7917 3000).

Serbia Republic: 28, Belgrave Square, London, SW1 X (☎ 020-7235 9049).

Sierra Leone: 41, Eagle St., Holborn, London WC14TL (☎ 020-7404 0140).

Singapore: 9 Wilton Crescent, London SW1X 8RW (☎ 020-7235 8315).

Slovak Republic: 25 Kensington Palace Gardens, London W8 4QY (☎ 020-7243 0803).

Slovenia: 10 Little College Street, London SW1P (☎ 020-7222 5400).

South Africa: South Africa House, Trafalgar Square, London WC2N 5DP (☎ 020-7451 7299).

Spain: 39 Chesham Place, London SW1X 8SB (☎ 020-7235 5555).

Sri Lanka: 13 Hyde Park Gardens, London W2 2LU (☎ 020-7262 1841).

Swaziland: 20 Buckingham Gate, London SW1E 6LB (☎ 020-7630 6611).

Sweden: 11 Montagu Place, London W1H 2AL (☎ 020-7917 6400).

Switzerland: 16–18 Montagu Place, London W1H 2BQ (☎ 020-7616 6000).

Syria: 8 Belgrave Square, London SW1X 8PH (☎ 020-7245 9012).

Tanzania: 43 Hertford Street, London W1Y 8DB (☎ 020-7499 8951).

Thailand: 29/30 Queen's Gate, London SW7 5JB (☎ 020-7589 2944).

Tonga: 36 Molyneux Street, London W1H 6AB (☎ 020-7724 5828).

Trinidad & Tobago: 42 Belgrave Square, London SW1X 8NT (☎ 020-7245 9351).

Turkey: 43 Belgrave Square, London SW1X 8PA (☎ 020-7393 0202).

Uganda: Uganda House, 58/59 Trafalgar Square, London WC2N 5DX

(☎ 020-7839 5783).

Ukraine: 60 Holland Park, London W11 3SJ (☎ 020-7727 6312).

United Arab Emirates: 30 Prince's Gate, London SW7 1PT (☎ 020-7581 1281).

United States Of America: 24 Grosvenor Square, London W1A 1AE (☎ 020-7499 9000).

Uruguay: 2nd Floor, 140 Brompton Road, London SW3 1HY (☎ 020-7589 8735).

Venezuela: 1 Cromwell Road, London SW7 2HW (☎ 020-7584 4206).

Zaire: 26 Chesham Place, London SW1X 8HH (☎ 020-7235 6137).

Zambia: 2 Palace Gate, Kensington, London W8 5NG (☎ 020-7589 6655).

Zimbabwe: Zimbabwe House, 429 Strand, London WC2R 0SA (☎ 020-7836 7755).

Government Departments

Department for Culture, Media & Sport, 2–4 Cockspur Street, London SW1Y 5DH (☎ 020-7211 6200, ⌨ www.culture.gov.uk).

Department for Education and Skills, Sanctuary Buildings, Great Smith Street, London SW1P 3BT and other addresses listed on website (☎ 0870-000 2288, ⌨ www.dfes.gov.uk).

Department for Environment, Food & Rural Affairs, Eland House, Bressenden Place, London SW1E 5DU (☎ 020-7890 3333, ⌨ www. defra. gov.uk).

Department for Health, Richmond House, 79 Whitehall, London SW1A 2NS (☎ 020-7210 3000, ⌨ www.doh.gov.uk).

Department for International Development, 94 Victoria Street, London SW1E 5JL (☎ 020-7917 7000, ⌨ www.dfid.gov.uk).

Department of Social Security, Richmond House, 79 Whitehall, London SW1A 2NS (☎ 020-7238 0800, ⌨ www.dss.gov.uk).

Department of Trade & Industry, DTI Enquiry Unit, 1 Victoria Street, London SW1H 0ET (☎ 020-7215 5000, 💻 www.dti.gov.uk).

Department for Work & Pensions, Correspondence Unit, Room 540, The Adelphi, 1–11 John Adam Street, London WC2N 6HT (☎ 020-7712 2171, 💻 www.dwp.gov.uk)

Foreign & Commonwealth Office, King Charles Street, London SW1A 2AH (☎ 020-7270 1500, 💻 www.fco.gov.uk).

Home Office, 50 Queen Anne's Gate, London SW1H 9AT (☎ 020-7273 4000, 💻 www.homeoffice.gov.uk).

Ministry of Defence, Main Building, Whitehall, London SW1A 2HB (☎ 020-7218 9000, 💻 www.mod.uk).

Tourist Information

British Tourist Authority, (BTA), Thames Tower, Black's Road, Hammersmith, London W6 9EL (☎ 020-8846 9000, 💻 www.visit britain.com).

Britain Visitor Centre, 1 Regent Street, London, SW1Y 4XT, (☎ 020- 7808 3838, 💻   www.visitbritain.com).

English Tourist Board, Thames Tower, Black's Road, Hammersmith, London W6 9EL (☎ 020-8846 9000, 💻 www.enjoyengland.com).

Irish Tourist Board, 150 New Bond Street, London W1Y 0AQ (☎ 020-7493 3201, 💻 www.tourismireland.com).

London Tourist Board, 1 Warwick Row, London SW1E 5ER (recorded information service, (☎ 0906-866 3344, 💻 www.visitlondon.com).

Scottish Tourist Board, 23 Revelstone Terrace, Edinburgh EH4 3EU (☎ 0131-557 1700, 💻 www.visitscotland.com).

Welsh Tourist Board, Brunel House, 2 Fitzalan Road, Cardiff CF2 1UY (☎ 01222-227 281, 💻 www.visitwales.co.uk).

Transport & Travel

Association of British Travel Agents, 68-71 Newman Street, London W1T 3AH (☎ 020-7637 2444, 💻 www.abta.co.uk).

Automobile Association (AA), Fanum House, PO Box 50, Basingstoke, Hampshire RG21 2EA (☎ 01256-20123, 🖳 www.theaa.com).

British Airports Authority, Corporate Office, Gatwick Airport, West Sussex RH6 0HZ (☎ 01293-517755, 🖳 www.baa.co.uk).

British Airways, Head Office, Belgrave House, London, SW1W 9TQ (☎ 020-7834 9449, 🖳 www. british-airways.com).

British Midland, Donington Hall, Castle Donington, Derby DE7 2SB (☎ 01332 854 000, 🖳 www.flybmi.com).

National Express, Ensign Court, 4 Vicarage Road, Edgbston, Birmingham, B15 3ES (☎ 08705 808080, 🖳 www.nationalexpress.com).
P&O, Channel House, Channel View Road, Dover, CT17 9TJ (☎ 08705 980 333, 🖳 www.poferries.com).

Transport For London, 55 Broadway, London SW1H 0BD (☎ 0845 330 9880, 🖳 www.tfl.gov.uk).

Miscellaneous

British Council, 10 Spring Gardens, London SW1A 2BN (☎ 020-7930 8466, 🖳 www.britishcouncil.org).

British Broadcasting Corporation (BBC), Broadcasting House, Portland Place, London W1A 1AA (☎ 020-7580 4468, 🖳 www. bbc.co.uk).

BBC Television Centre, Wood Lane, London W12 7RJ (☎ 020-7743 8000, 🖳 www.bbc.co.uk).

British Telecom, 81 Newgate Street, London EC1A 7AJ (☎ 020-7356 6666, 🖳 www.bt.com).

Central Office of Information, Hercules Road, London SE1 7DU (☎ 020-7928 5037, 🖳 www.coi.gov.uk).
Confederation of British Industry (CBI), Centre Point, 103 New Oxford Street, London WC1A 1DU (☎ 020-7379 7400, 🖳 www. cbi.org.uk).

Consumers' Association, Castlemead, Gascoyne Way, Hertford SG14 1LH (☎ 01992-828557, 🖳 www.which.co.uk).

Driver & Vehicle Licensing Agency (DVLA), Swansea SA99 1AR (☎ 0870 240 0009, 🖳 www.dvla.gov.uk).

Good Housekeeping Institute, National Magazine House, 72 Broadwick Street, London W1V 2BP (☎ 020-7439 5000, 💻 www.good housekeeping. co.uk).

HM Customs and Excise, New King's Beam House, 22 Upper Ground, London SE1 9PJ (☎ 020-7620 1313, 💻 www.hmce.gov.uk).

Immigration & Nationality Directorate, Lunar House, 40 Wellesley Road, Croydon, CR9 2BY (☎   0870 606 7766, 💻 www.ind.home office.gov.uk)

Inland Revenue, Somerset House, Strand, London WC2R 1LB (☎ 020-7438 6622, 💻 www.inlandrevenue.gov.uk).

National Association of Citizens' Advice Bureau, Myddelton House, 115-123 Pentonville Road, London N1 9LZ (☎ 020-7833 2181, 💻 www.nacab.org.uk).

National Consumer Council, 20 Grosvenor Gardens, London SW1 0DH (☎ 020-7730 3469, 💻 www.ncc.org.uk).

National Federation of Women's Institutes, 39 Eccleston Street, London SW1W 9NT (☎ 020-7730 7212, 💻 www.womens-institute.co.uk).

Office of Fair Trading, Fleetbank House, 2-6 Salisbury Square, London, EC4Y 8JX (☎ 020-7211 8000, 💻 www.oft.gov.uk).

Office for National Statistics, 1 Drummond Gate, London SW1V 2QQ (☎ 0845 601 3034, 💻 www.statistics.gov.uk).

Public Record Office, Ruskin Avenue, Kew, Richmond, Surrey TW9 4OU (☎ 020-8876 3444, 💻 www.pro.gov.uk).

Royal Automobile Club (RAC), RAC House, Lansdowne Road, East Croydon, Surrey CR9 2JA (☎ 020-8686 2525, 💻 www.rac.co.uk).

The Stationery Office, National Publishing, 51 Nine Elms Lane, Vauxhall, London SW8 5DR (☎ 071-873 0011, 💻 www.the-stationery-office.co.uk).

UK Council for International Education (UKCOSA), 9 St Alban's Place, London N1 0NX (☎ 020-7354 5210, 💻 www.ukcosa.org.uk).

APPENDIX B: FURTHER READING

There are many useful reference books for those seeking general information about London, the UK and the British. Published annually since 1868, Whitaker's Almanack (The Stationery Office) contains a wealth of information about the British government, finances, population, commerce and general statistics of the nations of the world. Another comprehensive publication is Enquire Within Upon Everything by Moyra Bremner (Helicon), first published in 1856 and containing information on a multitude of subjects from social behaviour to organisations. Newcomers to the UK may also be interested in Britain (The Stationery Office), an annual reference book describing many features of life in the UK, including the workings of the government and other major institutions.

Books

In the lists below, the publication title is followed by author's name and the publisher (in brackets). All books prefixed with an asterisk are recommended by the author.

Tourist Guides

*Access London, Richard Saul Wurman & Lucy Koserski (Access)

American Walks in London, Richard Tames (Interlink Publishing)

*Baedeker Guide: London (AA Publishing)

The Best of London, Andre Gayot (Gault Millau)

Blue Guide: London, Ylva French (A&C Black)

** Buying, Selling & Letting Property, David Hampshire (Survival Books)

Cadogan London, Andrew Gumbel (Cadogan)

Companion Guide to London, David Piper (Companion Guides)

*David Gentleman's London, David Gentleman (Phoenix)

Essential London, Paul Murphy (AA Publishing)

Everybody's Historic London, Jonathan Kiek (Quiller Press)

Everyman Guide to London (Everyman)

Explorer London, Christopher Catling (AA Publishing)

*Eyewitness Travel Guides: London, Michael Leapman (DK Publishing)

The Faber Book of London, A.N. Wilson (Faber & Faber)

*Fodor's London Companion, Louise Nicholson (Fodor)

Fodor's Up Close London (Fodor)

Frommer's London from $70 a Day (Macmillan Reference)

In and Around London (Pitkin Unichrome)

*Let's Go London (St Martin's Press)

*London, England – A Daytripper's Travelogue from the Coolest City in the World, Derek Hammond (Mainstream)

London for Free, Peter & Richard Harden (Harden's Guides)

London for Free, Brian Butler (Mustang)

*London: The Rough Guide, Rob Humphreys (Rough Guides)

London Step by Step, Christopher Turner (Independent Traveller)

*Lonely Planet: London, Pat Yale (Lonely Planet)

*Michelin Green Tourist Guide: London (Michelin)

*The National Geographic Traveller: London (National Geographic)

Rick Steves' London, Rick Steves & Gene Openshaw (John Muir)

Secret London, Andrew Duncan (New Holland)

*Time Out London Guide (Penguin)

Living & Working

Buying or Renting a Home in London, David Hampshire & Sue Harris (Survival Books)

Guide to Good Living in London (Francis Chichester)

**Living and Working in Britain, David Hampshire (Survival Books)

*Living in London, Karen Howes (Editions Flammarion)

London Living, Lisa Lovatt-Smith & Paul Duncan (Weidenfeld)

London Living (Ramboro Books)

*The New London Property Guide, Carrie Seagrave (Mitchell Beazley)

Summer Jobs in Britain (Vacation Work)

*Where to Live in London, Sarah McConnell (Simon & Schuster)

Miscellaneous

*Access in London, Gordon Couch (Quiller Press)

*The Art & Architecture of London, Anne Saunders (Phaidon)

*A–Z Big Street Atlas of London (Geographers A-Z Map Co.)

The Bookshops of London, Matt Jackson (Mainstream)

*Capital BYOs: A Guide to London's Bring Your Own Wine Restaurants, Victoria Alers (Hankey VBAH)

*Cheap Eats in London, Sandra A. Gustafson (Chronicle)

*The English, Jeremy Paxman (Michael Joseph)

*Enquire Within Upon Everything, Moyra Bremner (Helicon)

*Evening Standard Children's London, Linda Conway (Prentice Hall)

*Evening Standard London Pub and Bar Guide, Edward Sullivan (Simon & Schuster)

*Evening Standard London Restaurant Guide, Nick Foulkes (Simon & Schuster)

Focus on London (Office for National Statistics); can be downloaded or viewed online at : www.statistics.gov.uk/london/ or purchased as hard copy.

*Frommer's Born to Shop London, Suzy Gershman (IDG Books)

Gay London, Will McLoughlin (Ellipsis)

*Geographers' London Atlas (Geographers A-Z Map Co.)

*Guide to Ethnic London, Ian McAuley (Immel Publishing)

The Heinz Guide to Days Out with Kids: South East, Janet Bonthron (Bon Bon)

Holistic London, Kate Brady (Brainwave)

*How to be a Brit, George Mikes (Andre Deutsch)

*In and Around London Pathfinder Guide (Jarrold/Ordnance Survey)

*London Restaurants: The Rough Guide, Charles Campion (Rough Guides)

London Schools Guide (Mitchell Beazley)

*Notes From a Small Island, Bill Bryson (Doubleday)

*On Your Bike, Guide to Cycling in London (London Cycling Campaign)

*The Penguin London Mapguide, Michael Middleditch (Penguin)

*Residence in Britain: Notes for People from Overseas (Central Office of Information)

*The Serious Shoppers' Guide to London, Beth Reiber (Prentice Hall Press)

*The State We're In, Will Hutton (Vintage)

*Top Towns (Guiness Publishing)

Which London School, Derek Bingham (John Catt)

*Whitaker's Almanack (The Stationery Office)
Zagat Survey 1999: London Restaurants (Zagat)

Magazines

The Big Issue, 1–5 Wandsworth Rd, London SW8 2LN (☎ 020-7526 3200 ☐ www.bigissue.com). Weekly 'street' magazine.
Evening Standard, Associated Newspapers Ltd., Northcliffe House, London W8 5EE (☎ 020-7938 6000 ☐ www.thisislondon.co.uk). London's evening newspaper.

Girl About Town, Midweek, Ms London and **Nine to Five,** Independent Magazines (UK), 7–9 Independent House, 191 Marsh Wall, London E14 9RS (☎ 020-7636 6651, ☐ www.londoncareers.net). Free weekly
careers and recruitment magazines.

The London Magazine, 32 Addison Grove, London W4 1ER (☎ 020-8400 5882, ☐ www.thelondonmagazine.net). Bi-monthly literature and arts magazine.

Loot, Wembley Point 1, Harrow Rd, Wembley, Middlesex HA9 6DE (☎ 020-8900 4500, ☐ www.loot.com). Daily newspaper for buying/selling properties (and just about everything else) privately and property rentals in an around London.

Metro London, Harmsworth Quays Printing, Surrey Quays Road, Rotherhithe, London SE16 7ND (☎ 020-7651 5200, ☐ www.london metro.co.uk). Free daily newspaper (Mondays to Fridays).

Southern Cross Magazine, 14/15 Child's Place, Earls Court, London SW5 9RX (☎ 020-7373 3377, ☐ www.sxmagazine.com). Weekly magazine for Australians and New Zealanders living in London.

Time Out, Universal House, 251 Tottenham Court Road, London W1P 0AB (☎ 020-7813 3000, ☐ www.timeout.com). Weekly (Tuesdays) entertainment guide.

TNT Magazine, 14/15 Child's Place, Earls Court, London SW5 9RX (☎ 020-7373 3377, ☐ www.tntmag.com). Weekly magazine for expatriate Australians and New Zealanders living in London.

Which? Magazine, Business Research Centre, 2 Marylebone Road, London NW1 4DF (☎ 020-7770 7000, ☐ www.which.co.uk). Monthly consumer magazine, available on subscription only.

APPENDIX C: USEFUL WEBSITES

The following lists of internet sites are by no means definitive but include many sites that will be of help and interest to those planning to live or work in London.

London Sites

Accommodation London (⌨ www.accommodationlondon.net) – Help finding a place to live, with text available in English, French, Spanish, Italian and Swedish.

BBC London Weather (⌨ www.bbc.co.uk/london/weather) – Check whether to take an umbrella or a sunhat.

BT Directory Enquiries (⌨ www.bt.com/118500) – Free directory enquiries, no longer available over the phone.

Cockney Rhyming Slang (⌨ www.cockneyrhymingslang.co.uk) – The biggest list of East End vernacular; helpful in case someone asks if you "saw the wooden pews [news] last night."

Greater London Authority (⌨ www.london.gov.uk) – The Mayor of London's website, with information on campaigns, London issues and forthcoming events.

In London (⌨ www.inlondon.com) – Information on jobs, accommodation, entertainment and travel, focused on Australians, New Zealanders and South Africans.

Itchy London (⌨ www.itchylondon.co.uk) – Online version of the city guidebook, with reviews of bars, clubs and pubs and suggestions for places to go out.

London (⌨ www.londonby.com or www.londonnet.co.uk) – Two of the most comprehensive London websites for residents and visitors.

London Town (⌨ www.londontown.com) – Comprehensive site featuring articles and reviews of restaurants, films and theatre shows, hotel and travel bookings and general information.
Multimap (⌨ www.multimap.co.uk) – Invaluable resource for find-

ing your way around if you haven't got an 'A–Z'.

National Rail (💻 www.nationalrail.co.uk) – For when you want to get out of London. Timetables, special offers and a journey planner for all the UK's railway services.

Greater London Authority (💻 www.london.gov.uk) – GLA official site, with links to other London authority sites.
Streetmap (: www.streetmap.co.uk) – Another invaluable resource for finding your way around.

This Is London (💻 www.thisislondon.com) – General information site published by the Evening Standard newspaper.

Toptable (💻 www.toptable.co.uk) – Online restaurant booking service, offering deals such as two-for-one offers and tables at hard-to-book London restaurants.

Transport For London (💻 www.tfl.gov.uk) – Everything you need to know about London's public transport systems.

Virtual London (💻 www.a-london-guide.co.uk) – Tourism and travel guide, including webcams and travel and theatre bookings.

Work Gateways (💻 www.workgateways.com) – Organises work for visitors on temporary working visas.

Professional Associations

Building Societies' Association (💻 www.bsa.org.uk) – Central representative body for building societies.

Council For Licensed Conveyancers (💻 www.theclc.gov.uk).

Council Of Mortgage Lenders (💻 www.cml.org.uk) – Trade association for mortgage lenders.

Federation Of Master Builders (💻 www.fmb.org.uk) – Includes a directory of members.

Land Registry (💻 www.landreg.gov.uk) – Practical information about registering land and land registry archives.

The Law Society (💻 www.lawsoc.org.uk) – Professional body for solicitors in England and Wales.

National Association Of Estate Agents/NAEA (💻 www. naea. co.uk) – The main organisation for Estate Agents.

Ombudsman For Estate Agents (💻 www.oea.co.uk) – Independent arbitration for property buyers with complaints about registered estate agents.

Mortgages & Finance

Charcol Online (💻 www.charcolonline.co.uk) – Online mortgage brokers.

Council Of Mortgage Lenders (💻 www.cml.org.uk) – The trade association for mortgage lenders.

Finance For Professionals (💻 www.f4p.com) – Finance for members of certain professions, e.g. architects, engineers and teachers.

Home Buyer & Mortgage Advisor Magazine (💻 www.homebuyer mag.co.uk) – The UK's most popular mortgage magazine. Good general information about buying and selling property.

Market Place (💻 www.marketplace.co.uk) – Search for the best mortgage deals.

Money Extra (💻 www.moneyextra.co.uk) – Financial services, including the best mortgage deals.

Money Net (💻 www.moneynet.co.uk) – Financial services, including the best mortgage deals.

Money Quest (💻 www.moneyquest.co.uk) – Mortgage brokers.

Money Supermarket (💻 www.moneysupermarket.com) – General finance including mortgages.

Mortgage Next (💻 www.mortgage-next.com) – Financial advisers.

This Is Money (💻 www.thisismoney.co.uk) – Data and statistics on money matters as well as useful money guides.

Virgin Money (⌨ http://uk.virginmoney.com) – The Virgin Group's financial services online.

What Mortgage Magazine (⌨ www.whatmortgageonline.co.uk) – Mortgage information and comprehensive advice on buying a property.

Your Mortgage Magazine (⌨ www.yourmortgage.co.uk) – Provides a wealth of information about mortgages and all aspects of buying and selling property.

Neighbourhood Information

Environment Agency (⌨ www.environment-agency.gov.uk) – Check the occurrence of flooding and other natural hazards in an area.

Enviro Search (⌨ www.home-envirosearch.com) – Check whether a property is adversely affected by environmental factors.

Get A Map (⌨ www.getamap.co.uk) – Free downloadable Ordnance Survey neighbourhood maps.

Home Check (⌨ www.homecheck.co.uk) – Local information about the risks of flooding, landslip, pollution, radon gas, landfill, waste sites, etc. Also provides general information about neighbourhoods.

Hometrack (⌨ www.hometrack.co.uk) – Online property reports.

Knowhere (⌨ www.knowhere.co.uk) – An alternative look at over 2,000 UK towns.

My Village (⌨ www.myvillage.com) – Community sites for London and 20 other cities.

Neighbourhood Statistics (⌨ http://neighbourhood.statistics.gov.uk) – Contains a wide range of statistics for neighbourhoods in England and Wales.

Proviser (⌨ www.proviser.com) – Local property prices and street maps for England and Wales.

UK Online (⌨ www.ukonline.gov.uk) – Comprehensive information about local services and neighbourhoods, including local schools, health, housing and crime statistics.

Up My Street (⌨ www.upmystreet.co.uk) – Information about neighbourhoods, including property prices, local services, schools, local government, etc..

Estate Agents

Asserta Home (⌨ www.assertahome.com) – Large database of properties for sale around the country.

Find A Property (⌨ www.findaproperty.com) – Property for sale in London and surrounding counties.

Fish 4 Homes (⌨ www.fish4homes.co.uk) – Selection of properties and directory of estate agents around the UK.

Foxtons (⌨ www.foxtons.co.uk) – London's largest chain of estate and letting agents.

Home Sale (⌨ www.home-sale.co.uk) – National network of over 700 estate agents.

Hot Property (⌨ www.hot-property.com) – The Hot Property magazine website featuring property in London and the south-east.

House Web (⌨ www.houseweb.co.uk) – Independent property website that contains comprehensive advice and tips for the home-buyer.

London Property Guide (⌨ www.londonpropertyguide.co.uk) – Buy, sell or rent in London.

My Property (⌨ www.mypropertyforsale.co.uk) – Internet estate agent.

New-Homes (⌨ www.new-homes.co.uk) – Comprehensive database of new home developments throughout the UK.

Number One For Property (⌨ www.numberone4property.co.uk) – Property website.

Property Finder (⌨ www.propertyfinder.co.uk) – Internet estate agent.
Property Live (⌨ www.propertylive.co.uk) – The National Association of Estate Agents' property website.

Prime Location (🖳 www.primelocation.com) – Consortium of estate agents advertising properties.

Right Move (🖳 www.rightmove.co.uk) – Buying, selling and letting.

Smart Estates (🖳 www.smartestates.com) – Independent property website selling new and resale property.

Smart New Homes (🖳 www.smartnewhomes.co.uk) – Search for new homes.

Ugly Properties (🖳 www.uglyproperties.com) – Specialists in selling vandalised and empty properties, 'brownfield' development land and just plain ugly homes.

Vebra (🖳 www.vebra.com) – One of the UK's most visited property sites run by a consortium of estate agents.

Winkworth (🖳 www.winkworth.co.uk) – Property database for London and ... Yorkshire.

Private Sales

The following websites are online property agents who advertise property for sale, usually for a modest one-time fee (many also contain comprehensive general information).

4 Sale By Owner (🖳 www.4salebyowner.co.uk).

Estate Agent (🖳 www.estateagent.co.uk) – Advertise free of charge.

Home Pages (🖳 www.homepages.co.uk).

Home Sale Network (🖳 www.home-sale.co.uk).

House Web (🖳 www.houseweb.co.uk).

Internet Homes (🖳 www.internethomes.co.uk).

My Property For Sale (🖳 www.mypropertyforsale.co.uk).

Private House for Sale (⌨ www.privatehousesforsale.co.uk).

Property Broker (⌨ www.propertybroker.co.uk).

Property Finder (⌨ www.propertyfinder.co.uk).

Smart Estates (⌨ www.smartestates.com).

Use The Mouse (⌨ www.use-the-mouse.com).

Moving Resources

British Association Of Removers (⌨ www.bar.co.uk) – Association of removal companies offering a professional service with a conciliation and arbitration service.

I Am Moving (⌨ www.iammoving.com) – Will inform companies on your behalf that you're moving.

The Move Channel (⌨ www.themovechannel.com) – General property website containing everything you need to know about moving house.

Really Moving (⌨ www.reallymoving.com) – Comprehensive information about property, including home-moving services and a property finder.

Websites For Women

Career Women (⌨ www.womenconnect.com) – Contains career opportunities for women abroad plus a wealth of other useful information.

Expatriate Mothers (⌨ http://expatmoms.tripod.com) – Help and advice on how to survive as a mother on relocation.

Spouse Abroad (⌨ www.expatspouse.com) – Information about careers and working abroad. You need to register and subscribe.

Third Culture Kids (⌨ www.tckworld.com) – Designed for expatriate children.

Women Abroad (⌨ www.womanabroad.com) – Advice on careers, expatriate skills and the family abroad. Opportunity to subscribe to a monthly magazine of the same name.

Worldwise Directory (⌨ www.suzylamplugh.org/worldwise) – Run by the Suzy Lamplugh charity for personal safety, the site provides practical information about a number of countries with special emphasis on safety, particularly for women.

General Information

Able to Go (⌨ www.abletogo.com) – Excellent website that lists hotels, motels, guest houses, self-catering, caravans and holiday centres for those with mobility difficulties.

Advice Guide (⌨ www.adviceguide.org.uk) – Established by the Citizens' Advice Bureau (CAB) and full of down-to-earth advice, including information about civil rights, benefits and the legal system.

At UK (⌨ www.atuk.co.uk) – The foremost UK travel search engine and directory.

Au Pair Forum (⌨ www.aupair-forum.com) – Experiences of au pairs and tips for those thinking of becoming one.

Australia Shop (⌨ www.australia.shop.com) – Expatriate shopping for homesick Australians.

BBC (⌨ www.bbc.co.uk) – Excellent, comprehensive website from one of the UK's great institutions.

BBC Homes (⌨ www.bbc.co.uk/homes) – Lifestyle homes from the BBC.

Black Britain (⌨ www.blackbritain.co.uk) – Jobs and career pages along with helpful feature pages on ethnic issues.

Business Link (⌨ www.businesslink.org) – Includes hot topics and the latest news, plus e-commerce and e-business pages with masses of links to other useful sites.

Charity Choice (⌨ www.charitychoice.co.uk) – Excellent portal to all areas of charity work from hospices to family welfare organisations.

Childcare Link (🖳 www.childcarelink.gov.uk) – Allows you to find childcare facilities in your area.

Consumers' Association (🖳 www.which.net) – The UK's consumer watchdog, which publishes the monthly Which? consumer magazine.

Crime Reduction (🖳 www.crimereduction.gov.uk) – A government site providing crime statistics and advice on avoiding and preventing crime.

Direct Moving (🖳 www.directmoving.com) – General expatriate information, tips and advice, and numerous links.

Education UK (🖳 www.educationuk.org) – Everything foreign students need to know about education in the UK, from the British Council.

Escape Artist (🖳 www.escapeartist.com) – One of the most comprehensive expatriate sites, including resources, links and directories covering most expatriate destinations. You can also subscribe to the free monthly online expatriate magazine, Escape from America.

Ethnic Pages (🖳 www.ethnic-pages.co.uk) – A useful insight into multicultural Britain and all it has to offer in terms of topical issues such as books, music, arts and crafts, dance and disabilities.

ExpatAccess (🖳 www.expataccess.com) – Aimed at those planning to move abroad, with free moving guides.

ExpatBoards (🖳 www.expatboards.com) – A comprehensive site for expatriates, with popular discussion boards and special areas for Britons and Americans.

Expat Exchange (🖳 www.expatexchange.com) – Reportedly the largest online 'community' for English-speaking expatriates, including articles on relocation and a question and answer facility.

Expat Forum (🖳 www.expatforum.com) – Provides cost of living comparisons as well as over 20 country-specific forums.

Expat Mums (🖳 www.expat-moms.com) – Information for expatriate mothers.

Expat Network (🖳 www.expatnetwork.com) – The UK's leading expatriate website, which is essentially an employment network for expatriates, although it also includes numerous support services and a monthly online magazine, Nexus.

Expat Shopping (🖥 www.expatshopping.com) – Order your favourite foods from home.

Expat World (🖥 www.expatworld.net) – Information for American and British expatriates, including a subscription newsletter.

Expatriate Experts (🖥 www.expatexpert.com) – Run by expatriate expert Robin Pascoe, providing advice and support.

Global People (🖥 www.peoplegoingglobal.com) – Includes country-specific information with an emphasis on social and political issues.

Government (🖥 www.ukonline.gov.uk and www.gateway.gov.uk) – Easy access to over 1,000 government websites. Government Gateway is a centralised registration service that enables you to sign up for online government services.

Homes Online (🖥 www.homes-on-line.com) – Useful information about buying, selling, home improvements and financing a property.

Home Pages (🖥 www.homepages.co.uk) – Comprehensive property database and information about buying and selling.

Jobcentre (🖥 www.jobcentreplus.gov.uk) – The government website for job seekers, with advice on job hunting, training, recruitment and benefits.

Knowhere Guide (🖥 www.knowhere.co.uk) – An unofficial look at over 2,000 places in the UK.

Living Abroad (🖥 www.livingabroad.com) – Includes an extensive list of country profiles, which are available only on payment.

Loot (🖥 www.loot.com) – Log on to buy and sell virtually anything under one roof.

Medical Care (🖥 www.med4u.co.uk) – The leading UK online medical service. Obtain health advice and a second opinion with ease.

The Move Channel (🖥 www.themovechannel.com) – Comprehensive information on all aspects of buying and selling property.

National Health Service (⌨ www.nhsdirect.nhs.uk) – Your gateway to government health information, services and assistance.

Nomis (⌨ www.nomisweb.co.uk) – Labour market statistics provided by the University of Durham on behalf of the Office for National Statistics.

Outpost Information Centre (⌨ www.outpostexpat.nl) – Contains extensive country-specific information and links operated by the Shell Petroleum Company for its expatriate workers, but available to everyone.

Parental Help (⌨ www.parentcentre.gov.uk) – A centre for parents and carers with a 'search for a school' facility.

Public Transport Information (⌨ www.pti.org.uk) – Covers all travel by rail, air, coach, bus, ferry, metro and tram within the UK (including the Channel Islands, Isle of Man and Northern Ireland) and between the UK and Ireland.

Rail (⌨ www.rail.co.uk) – The best independent rail information, including timetables.

Real Post Reports (⌨ www.realpostreports.com) – Includes relocation services, recommended reading lists and 'real-life' stories written by expatriates in cities throughout the world.

Reception Bell (⌨ www.receptionbell.com) – A comprehensive guide to UK travel accommodation.

Refugee Council (⌨ www.refugeecouncil.org.uk) – The largest organisation in the UK working with asylum seekers and refugees. A good way of keeping up to date on topical issues and FAQs.
Save Britain's Heritage (⌨ www.savebritainsheritage.org) – Conservation of historic buildings.

Save Wealth Travel (⌨ www.savewealth.com/travel/warnings) – Travel information and warnings.

Scoot (⌨ www.scoot.co.uk) – Find essential services for homeowners.

Shelternet (⌨ www.shelternet.co.uk) – The website of Shelter, a charity for the homeless and the leading provider of independent housing advice in the UK.

Shopping Net (⌨ www.shopping.net) – The UK's most comprehensive shopping website, which allows you to search thousands of websites for products and services at the best prices.

Sport Link (⌨ www.sportlink.co.uk) – Lists sports and leisure facilities throughout the UK.

Student Accommodation (⌨ www.accommodationforstudents.com) – A search engine for students seeking accommodation in and around the UK's major cities.

The Foot Rule (⌨ www.omnis.demon.co.uk). - Conversions and calculations.

Tourism (⌨ www.visitbritain.com) – The official website of the UK tourist authority.

Trade Partners (⌨ www.tradepartners.gov.uk) – A UK government-sponsored site providing trade and investment (and general) information about most countries.

The Travel Doctor (⌨ www.tmvc.com.au/info10.html) – Includes a country-by-country vaccination guide.

Travelfinder (⌨ www.travelfinder.com/twarn/travel_warnings.html) – Travel information with warnings about danger areas.

Unit-Conversion (⌨ www.unit-conversion.info).

UK Government Guide (⌨ www.ukgovernmentguide.co.uk) – A hassle-free way to access local UK government websites.

UK Visas (⌨ www.ukvisas.gov.uk) – All you need to know about UK visas.

Visit England (⌨ www.visitengland.com) – The website of the English Tourist Board.

Volunteering (⌨ www.volunteering.org.uk) – A useful site for those looking for volunteering work, with helpful 'I want a volunteer' pages to help you to find a job in the UK.

World Health Organization (⌨ www.who.int) – Health information.

The World Press (🖥 www.theworldpress.com) – Links to media sites in practically every country.

World Travel Guide (🖥 www.wtgonline.com) – A general website for world travellers and expatriates.

Yankee Doodle (🖥 www.yankeedoodleiow.com) – Import American products.

Your New Home Magazine (🖥 www.yournewhome.co.uk) – The magazine for new homebuyers.

APPENDIX D: WEIGHTS & MEASURES

Officially, the UK converted to the international metric system of measurement in 1995 and the use of imperial measures was due to finish at the end of 1999, but it has been given a reprieve until the end of 2009. Therefore, you can expect to find goods marked in both metric and imperial measures. The conversion tables on the following pages may prove useful. Some comparisons shown are approximate but close enough for most everyday uses.

The following websites allow you to make instant conversions between different measurement systems: 💻 www.omnis.demon.co.uk and 💻 www.unit-conversion.info.

Women's Clothes

Continental	34	36	38	40	42	44	46	48	50	52
UK	8	10	12	14	16	18	20	22	24	26
US	6	8	10	12	14	16	18	20	22	24

Pullovers

	Women's						Men's					
Continental	40	42	44	46	48	50	44	46	48	50	52	54
UK	34	36	38	40	42	44	34	36	30	40	42	44
US	34	36	38	40	42	44	sm	med		lar		xl

Men's Shirts

Continental	36	37	38	39	40	41	42	43	44	46
UK/US	14	14	15	15	16	16	17	17	18	-

Men's Underwear

Continental	5	6	7	8	9	10
UK	34	36	38	40	42	44
US	sm	med		lar	xl	

Note: sm = small, med = medium, lar = large, xl = extra large

Children's Clothes

Continental	92	104	116	128	140	152
UK	16/18	20/22	24/26	28/30	32/34	36/38
US	2	4	6	8	10	12

Children's Shoes

Continental	18	19	20	21	22	23	24	25	26	27	28	29	30	31	32
UK/US	2	3	4	4	5	6	7	7	8	9	10	11	11	12	13
Continental	33	34	35	36	37	38
UK/US	1	2	2	3	4	5

Shoes (Women's and Men's)

Continental	35	36	37	37	38	39	40	41	42	42	43	44
UK	2	3	3	4	4	5	6	7	7	8	9	9
US	4	5	5	6	6	7	8	9	9	10	10	11

Weight

Avoirdupois	Metric	Metric	Avoirdupois
1oz	28.35g	1g	0.035oz
1lb*	454g	100g	3.5oz
1cwt	50.8kg	250g	9oz
1 ton	1,016kg	500g	18oz
2,205lb	1 tonne	1kg	2.2lb

Length

British/US	Metric	Metric	British/US
1in	2.54cm	1cm	0.39in
1ft	30.48cm	1m	3ft 3.25in
1yd	91.44cm	1km	0.62mi
1mi	1.6km	8km	5mi

Capacity

Imperial	Metric	Metric	Imperial
1 UK pint	0.57 litre	1 litre	1.75 UK pints
1 US pint	0.47 litre	1 litre	2.13 US pints
1 UK gallon	4.54 litres	1 litre	0.22 UK gallon
1 US gallon	3.78 litres	1 litre	0.26 US gallon

Note: An American 'cup' = around 250ml or 0.25 litre.

Area

British/US	Metric	Metric	British/US
1 sq. in	0.45 sq. cm	1 sq. cm	0.15 sq. in
1 sq. ft	0.09 sq. m	1 sq. m	10.76 sq. ft
1 sq. yd	0.84 sq. m	1 sq. m	1.2 sq. yds
1 acre	0.4 hectares	1 hectare	2.47 acres
1 sq. mile	2.56 sq. km	1 sq. km	0.39 sq. mile

Temperature

°Celsius	°Fahrenheit	
0	32	(freezing point of water)
5	41	
10	50	
15	59	
20	68	
25	77	
30	86	
35	95	
40	104	
50	122	

Notes: The boiling point of water is 100°C / 212°F.

Normal body temperature (if you're alive and well) is 37°C / 98.6°F.

Temperature Conversion

Celsius to Fahrenheit: multiply by 9, divide by 5 and add 32. (For a quick and approximate conversion, double the Celsius temperature and add 30.)

Fahrenheit to Celsius: subtract 32, multiply by 5 and divide by 9. (For a quick and approximate conversion, subtract 30 from the Fahrenheit temperature and divide by 2.)

Oven Temperatures

Gas	Electric	
	°F	°C
-	225–250	110–120
1	275	140
2	300	150
3	325	160
4	350	180
5	375	190
6	400	200
7	425	220
8	450	230
9	475	240

Air Pressure

PSI	Bar
10	0.5
20	1.4
30	2
40	2.8

Power

Kilowatts	Horsepower	Horsepower	Kilowatts
1	1.34	1	0.75

APPENDIX E: MAPS

The maps on the following pages show the borough and postcode boundaries in outer and inner London and details of roads, congestion charge area, main railway lines and airports in and around Greater London. The 33 London boroughs are listed below; details can be found in Chapter 1.

Barking & Dagenham	Hounslow
Barnet	Islington
Bexley	Kensington & Chelsea
Brent	Kingston-Upon-Thames
Bromley	Lambeth
Camden	Lewisham
City Of London	Merton
Croydon	Newham
Ealing	Redbridge
Enfield	Richmond-Upon-Thames
Greenwich	Southwark
Hackney	Sutton
Hammersmith & Fulham	Tower Hamlets
Haringey	Waltham Forest
Harrow	Wandsworth
Havering	City Of Westminster
Hillingdon	

OUTER LONDON BOROUGHS & POSTCODES

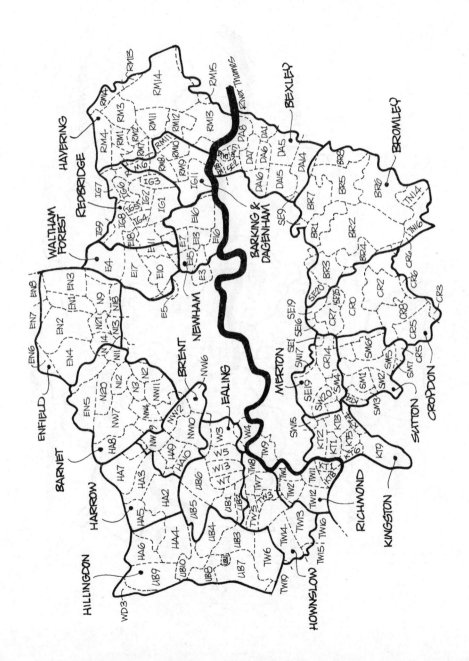

INNER LONDON BOROUGHS & POSTCODES

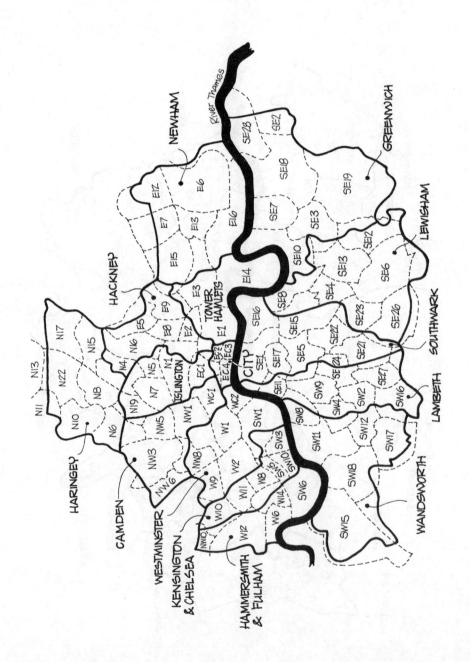

CONGESTION CHARGE ZONE

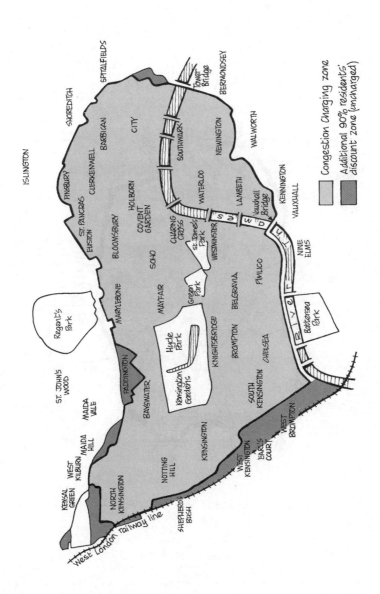

Congestion charging zone

Additional 90% residents'
discount zone (uncharged)

MAJOR ROADS & AIRPORTS

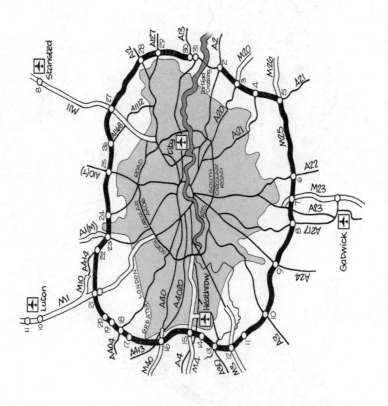

MAJOR RAILWAY LINES & STATIONS

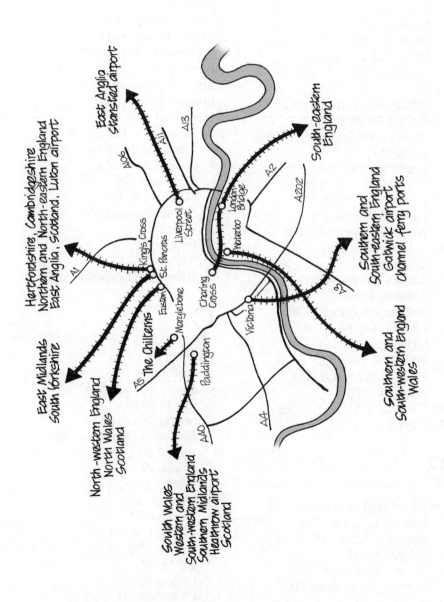

INDEX

A

Air Travel 106
  City 109
  Gatwick 107
  Heathrow 106
  Luton 108
  Stansted 108
Appendices 379
  Embassies & Consulates 380
  Further Reading 389
  Government Departments 386
  Maps 412
  Tourist Guides 389
  Tourist Information 387
  Transport & Travel 387
  Useful Websites 394
  Weights & Measures 408
Arrival & Settling in 87
  Checklists 99
  Council Tax Registration 97
  Customs 93
  Embassy Registration 98
  Finding Help 98
  Immigration 93
  Permits & Visas 89
  Police Registration 96
  Retirement 96
Art Galleries & Museums 278
Au Pairs 92

B

Banks & Building Societies 197
  Building Societies 198
  Business Hours 199
  Complaints 199
  Deposit Protection 199
  Opening An Account 200
Barking & Dagenham 23
Barnet 25
Bexley 27
Births & Deaths 273
Brent 29
British Homes 142
  Information 143
  Types Of Home 143
Bromley 31
Buildings Insurance 214
Bungee Jumping 307
Buses 121
  Green Line 122
  International Services 122
Buying Property 144
  Contracts 154
  Council Tax 151
  Estate Agents 152
  Flats 145
  Information 155
  Internet 153
  Relocation Consultants 151

C

Camden 33
Checklists 99
Chemists & Medicines 259
Childbirth 265
Choosing The Area 19
  Barking & Dagenham 23
  Barnet 25
  Bexley 27
  Brent 29
  Bromley 31
  Camden 33
  City Of London 35
  Croydon 36
  Ealing 38
  Enfield 40
  Greenwich 41

Hackney 44
Hammersmith & Fulham 45
Haringey 47
Harrow 49
Havering 51
Hillingdon 53
Hounslow 55
Islington 57
Kensington & Chelsea 58
Kingston-Upon-Thames 60
Lambeth 63
Lewisham 65
Merton 66
Newham 68
Redbridge 70
Richmond-Upon-Thames 72
Southwark 74
Sutton 76
Tower Hamlets 77
Waltham Forest 79
Wandsworth 81
Westminster 83
Cinemas & Theatres 282
City Airport 109
City Of London 35
Climate 346
Complementary Medicine 256
Congestion Charge 129
Cosmetic Surgery 265
Cost Of Living 208
Council Tax 210
Council Tax Registration 97
Cricket 307
Crime 347
Croydon 36
Customs 93
Cycling 133, 307

D

Dentists 266

NHS Treatment 267
Doctors 256
Driving in London 126
    Breakdown Assistance 129
    Car Hire 127
    Congestion Charge 129
    Parking 129

E

Ealing 38
Earning A Living 175
    Job Hunting 178
    Qualifications 177
    Regeneration 191
    Self-Employment &
        Doing Business 184
East London 338
Embassies & Consulates 380
Embassy Registration 98
Emergencies 248
Enfield 40
English-Language Schools 243
Eurostar 111
Eurotunnel 112
Evening Classes & Distance
        Learning 243

F

Family Planning Services 270
Football 308

G

Garages 164
Gatwick Airport 107
Getting An Education 221
    Courses 238

English-Language Schools 243
Evening Classes &
    Distance Learning 243
General Information 222
International & Foreign 234
Pre-School 223
Primary & Secondary
    Schools 224, 228
Private Schools 228
Religious Schools 231
Specialist Schools 232
State Schools 225
Universities & Colleges 236
Vocational Courses 242
Getting There & Getting About 103
Buses 121
Cycling 133
Driving in London 126
London River Transport
    Services 123
Rail 111
River Ferries 123
Sea 109
Taxis 125
Underground 118
Golf 310
Government 350
Greenwich 41
Greyhound Racing 311
Gymnasia & Health Clubs 311

H

Hackney 44
Hammersmith & Fulham 45
Haringey 47
Harrow 49
Havering 51
Heathrow Airport 106
Heating & Air-Conditioning 167

Hillingdon 53
Home Security 168
Horse Riding 313
Hospitals & Clinics 261
Hounslow 55
Houses 149
    New 149
    Old 150
Housing Market 139
    Housing Schemes 139
    Property Prices 140

I

Ice Skating 313
Immigration 93
Insurance 213
    Buildings Insurance 214
    Home Contents Insurance 216
    Private Health 254
International & Foreign
    Schools 234
Internet Shopping 341
Islington 57

J

Job Hunting 178
    Employment Agencies
        & Consultants 181
    European Employment
        Service 180
    Government Employment
        Service 179
    Newspapers & Magazines 182
    The Internet 182

K

Kensington & Chelsea 58
Kingston-Upon-Thames 60

L

Lambeth 63
Leisure Centres 314
Lewisham 65
London For Children 301
    Theme Parks 302
Luton 108

M

Magazines 393
Maps 412
Medicines 259
Merton 66
Metric System 410
Miscellaneous Sports 321
Monarchy 353
Money Matters & Insurance 195
    Banks & Building Societies 197
    Building Societies 198
    Cost Of Living 208
    Council Tax 210
    Mortgages 202
Mortgages 202
    Fees 207
    Foreign Currency
            Mortgages 207
    Income 203
    Interest Rates 206
    Size Of Mortgage 203
        Term 204
        Types 204
Motorsports 315
Moving House 170
Music 284
    Classical 284
    Jazz 287
    Pop 286

N

National Health Service 250
Newham 68
Newspapers & Magazines 182
Nightlife 287
North London 339
    Camden Town 339
    Hampstead 339
    Islington 340

O

Opticians 268
    Laser Surgery 269
    Sight Tests 269
Order Form 429

P

Parks 290
Permits & Visas 89
    Au Pairs 92
    Entry Clearance 90
    Permanent Residence 92
    Students 92
    The Self-Employed 91
    Training & Work Experience 91
    Visas & 'Visa Nationals' 89

Working Holidaymakers 91
Work Permits 90
Pets 354
    Animal Welfare 357
    Dogs 354
    Kennels & Catteries 357
    Pet Passport Scheme 356
    Quarantine 355
    Vets 357
Police 358
Police Registration 96
Postal Services 359
    Letter Post 360
Pre-School 223
Primary & Secondary Schools 224
Private Health Insurance 252
Private Health Treatment 254
    Drop-In Medicentres 255
Private Schools 228
Property Prices 140
Pubs & Bars 291

Q

Qualifications 177

R

Racket Sports 316
Radio 375
    BBC 376
    Commercial Radio 376
    Digital Radio 377
    Satellite Radio 377
Rail 111
    Channel Tunnel Rail Link 112
    Eurostar 111
    Eurotunnel 112
    The Rail Network 113

Redbridge 70
Regeneration 191
Religious Schools 231
Relocation Consultants 151
Rented Accommodation 155
    Bedsits 158
    Costs & Standards 159
    Rental Contracts 161
    Shared Accommodation 160
Restaurants & Cafés 293
Retirement 96
Richmond-Upon-Thames 72
River Ferries 123
River Trips & Excursions 297
Rugby 318

S

Sea Travel 109
    Belgium 110
    Denmark 110
    Fares 111
    Netherlands 110
Security 168
Self-Employment & Doing
            Business   184
Sexually Transmitted Diseases 271
Skiing 319
Somewhere To Live 137
    British Homes 142
    Buying Property 144
    Council Tax 151
    Flats 145
    Garages & Parking 164
    Heating & Air-Conditioning 167
    Home Security 168
    Houses 149
    Housing Market 139
    Moving House 170
    Property Prices 140

Rented Accommodation 155
Types Of Home 143
Utilities 165
South London 340
Southwark 74
Specialist Schools 232
Spend, Spend, Spend 325
East London 338
Internet Shopping 341
North London 339
South London 340
West End 328
West London 336
Sport & Fitness 305
Bungee Jumping 307
Cricket 307
Cycling 307
Football 308
Golf 310
Greyhound Racing 311
Gymnasia & Health Clubs 311
Horse Riding 313
Ice Skating 313
Leisure Centres 314
Miscellaneous Sports 321
Motorsports 315
Racket Sports 316
Rugby 318
Skiing 319
Swimming Pools 320
Watersports 321
Stansted Airport 108
State Schools 225
Staying Healthy 247
Births & Deaths 273
Chemists & Medicines 259
Childbirth 265
Complementary Medicine 256
Cosmetic Surgery 265
Dentists 266
Doctors 256
Emergencies 248

Family Planning Services 270
Hospitals & Clinics 261
Information & Help 272
Medic-Alert 250
National Health Service 250
Opticians 268
Private Health Insurance 252
Private Health Treatment 254
Private Hospitals & Clinics 262
Sexually Transmitted
Diseases 271
Sutton 76
Swimming Pools 320

T

Taxis 125
Black Cabs 125
Minicabs 126
Telephone 361
BT Bills 366
BT Call Charges 365
BT Chargecard 365
Companies 362
Installation & Registration 363
International Calls 367
Mobile Phones 370
Public Telephones 368
Using The Telephone 364
Television & Radio 371
Cable 374
Digital 373
Satellite 374
Standards 371
Stations 372
Television 371
TV Licence 373
Video & DVD 375
Time Difference 377
Time Off   277, 280

Art Galleries & Museums 278
Cinemas & Theatres 282
Excursions 299
Internet Cafés 297
London For Children 301
Music 284
Nightlife 287
Parks 290
Pubs & Bars 291
Restaurants & Cafés 293
River Trips & Excursions 297
Theatres 283
Tower Hamlets 77

U

Underground 118
East London Line Project 118
Information 121
Stations & Tickets 119
The Tube Network 118
Travelling By Tube 120
Universities & Colleges 236
Accommodation 240
Courses 238
Further Information 238
Living Expenses 239
Tuition Fees 239
Utilities 165
Electricity 165
Gas 166
Water 167

V

Vocational Courses 242
Childcare 242
Cookery 243

W

Waltham Forest 79
Wandsworth 81
Watersports 321
West End 328
Carnaby Street 330
Covent Garden 335
Old & New Bond Street 331
Oxford Street 328
Piccadilly 331
Regent Street 329
Soho 332
St James's 332
Tottenham Court Road 330
Trocadero 332
West London 336
Chelsea 337
Kensington 337
Knightsbridge 336
Westminster 83

BUYING A HOME SERIES

Our 'Buying a Home' books, including *Buying, Selling & Letting Property*, are essential reading for anyone planning to purchase property abroad. They're packed with vital information to guide you through the property jungle and help you **avoid the sort of disasters that can turn your dream home into a nightmare!** Topics covered include:

- **Avoiding problems**
- **Choosing the region**
- **Finding the right home and location**
- **Estate agents**
- **Finance, mortgages and taxes**
- **Utilities, heating and air-conditioning**
- **Renting and letting**
- **Permits and visas**
- **Travelling and communications**
- **Health and insurance**
- **Renting a car and driving**
- **Retirement and starting a business**
- **And much, much more!**

Our 'Buying a Home' books are the most comprehensive and up-to-date source of information available about buying property abroad. Whether you want a detached house, a townhouse or an apartment, a holiday or a permanent home, these books will help make your dreams come true.

They will also save you time, trouble and money!

Order your copies today by phone, fax, post or email from: Survival Books, PO Box 3780, YEOVIL, BA21 5WX, United Kingdom (☎ +44 (0)1935-700060, ✉ sales@survivalbooks.net, 💻 www.survivalbooks.net).

Living and Working Series

Our 'Living and Working' books are essential reading for anyone planning to spend time abroad, including holiday-home owners, retirees, long-term visitors, business people, transferees, students and even extra-terrestrials! They're packed with important and useful information designed to help you **avoid costly mistakes and save both time and money.** Topics covered include how to:

- **Find a job with a good salary & conditions**
- **Avoid and overcome problems**
- **Find your dream home**
- **Get the best education for your family**
- **Make the best use of public transport**
- **Endure local motoring habits**
- **Obtain the best health treatment**
- **Stretch your money further**
- **Make the most of your leisure time**
- **Enjoy the local sporting life**
- **Find the best shopping bargains**
- **Insure yourself against most eventualities**

Our 'Living and Working' books are the most comprehensive and up-to-date source of practical information available about everyday life abroad. They aren't, however, boring text books, but interesting and entertaining guides written in a highly readable style.

Discover what it's *really* like to live and work abroad!

Order your copies today by phone, fax, post or email from: Survival Books, PO Box 3780, YEOVIL, BA21 5WX, United Kingdom (☎ +44 (0)1935-700060, ✉ sales@survivalbooks.net, 🖥 www.survivalbooks.net).

OTHER SURVIVAL BOOKS

Alien's Guides: The Alien's Guides to Britain and France will help you to appreciate the peculiarities (in both senses) of the British and French.

The Best Places to Buy a Home in France/Spain: The most comprehensive and up-to-date guides to where to buy property in France and Spain, containing detailed regional profiles.

Buying, Selling and Letting Property: The most comprehensive and up-to-date source of information on buying, selling and letting property in the UK.

Earning Money From Your Home: Essential guides to earning income from property in France and Spain, including short- and long-term letting.

Foreigners in France/Spain: Triumphs & Disasters: Real-life experiences of people who have emigrated to France and Spain, recounted in their own words.

Lifeline Guides: Essential guides to life in specific regions of France and Spain. See order form for a list of current titles in the series.

Making a Living: Essential guides to self-employment and starting a business in France and Spain.

Renovating & Maintaining Your French Home: The ultimate guide to renovating and maintaining your dream home in France.

Retiring: Retiring in Spain and Retiring in France provide up-to-date information about the two most popular retirement destinations.

Rural Living in France: The most comprehensive source of practical information available about life in rural France.

Shooting Caterpillars in Spain: The hilarious but compelling story of two innocents abroad in the depths of Andalusia in the late '80s.

Surprised by France: Even after living there for ten years, Donald Carroll finds plenty of surprises in the Hexagon.

Order your copies today by phone, fax, post or email from: Survival Books, PO Box 3780, YEOVIL, BA21 5WX, United Kingdom (☎ +44 (0)1935-700060, ✉ sales@survivalbooks.net, 🖳 www.survivalbooks.net).

Qty	Title	Price (incl. p&p)			Total
		UK	Europe	World	
	The Alien's Guide to Britain	£7.45	£9.45	£12.95	
	The Alien's Guide to France	£7.45	£9.45	£12.95	
	The Best Places to Buy a Home in France	£14.45	£16.45	£19.95	
	The Best Places to Buy a Home in Spain	£14.45	£16.45	£19.95	
	Buying a Home in Australia & NZ	£14.45	£16.45	£19.95	
	Buying a Home in Bulgaria	£14.45	£16.45	£19.95	
	Buying a Home in Cyprus	£14.45	£16.45	£19.95	
	Buying a Home in Florida	£14.45	£16.45	£19.95	
	Buying a Home in France	£15.45	£17.45	£20.95	
	Buying a Home in Greece	£14.45	£16.45	£19.95	
	Buying a Home in Italy	£14.45	£16.45	£19.95	
	Buying a Home in Portugal	£14.45	£16.45	£19.95	
	Buying a Home in South Africa	£14.45	£16.45	£19.95	
	Buying a Home in Spain	£15.45	£17.45	£20.95	
	Buying, Selling & Letting Property	£12.45	£14.45	£17.95	
	Buying or Renting a Home in London	£14.45	£16.45	£19.95	
	Buying or Renting a Home in New York	£14.45	£16.45	£19.95	
	Earning Money From Your French Home	£14.45	£16.45	£19.95	
	Earning Money From Your Spanish Home	£14.45	£16.45	£19.95	
	Foreigners in France: Triumphs & Disasters	£12.45	£14.45	£17.95	
	Foreigners in Spain: Triumphs & Disasters	£12.45	£14.45	£17.95	
	Brittany Lifeline	£12.45	£14.45	£17.95	
	Costa Blanca Lifeline	£12.45	£14.45	£17.95	
	Costa del Sol Lifeline	£12.45	£14.45	£17.95	
	Dordogne/Lot Lifeline	£12.45	£14.45	£17.95	
	Normandy Lifeline	£12.45	£14.45	£17.95	
	Poitou-Charentes Lifeline	£12.45	£14.45	£17.95	
	Provence-Cote d'Azur Lifeline	£12.45	£14.45	£17.95	
	Living & Working in America	£17.45	£19.45	£22.95	
	Living & Working in Australia	£17.45	£19.45	£22.95	
	Living & Working in Britain	£17.45	£19.45	£22.95	
	Living & Working in Canada	£17.45	£19.45	£22.95	
	Living & Working in the EU	£17.45	£19.45	£22.95	
	Living & Working in the Far East	£17.45	£19.45	£22.95	
	Living & Working in France	£17.45	£19.45	£22.95	
	Living & Working in Germany	£17.45	£19.45	£22.95	
	Total Carried Forward (see over)				

ORDER FORM

Qty	Title	Price (incl. p&p)			Total
		UK	Europe	World	
	L&W in the Gulf States & Saudi Arabia	£17.45	£19.45	£22.95	
	Living & Working in Ireland	£17.45	£19.45	£22.95	
	Living & Working in Italy	£17.45	£19.45	£22.95	
	Living and Working in London	£14.45	£16.45	£19.95	
	Living & Working in New Zealand	£17.45	£19.45	£22.95	
	Living & Working in Spain	£17.45	£19.45	£22.95	
	Living & Working in Switzerland	£17.45	£19.45	£22.95	
	Making a Living in France	£14.45	£16.45	£19.95	
	Making a Living in Spain	£14.45	£16.45	£19.95	
	Renovating Your French Home	£17.45	£19.45	£22.95	
	Retiring in France	£14.45	£16.45	£19.95	
	Retiring in Spain	£14.45	£16.45	£19.95	
	Rural Living in France	£14.45	£16.45	£19.95	
	Shooting Caterpillars in Spain	£10.45	£12.45	£15.95	
	Surprised by France	£12.45	£14.45	£17.95	
	Wild Thyme in Ibiza	£10.45	£12.45	£15.95	
				Total	

Order your copies today by phone, fax, post or email from: Survival Books, PO Box 3780, YEOVIL, BA21 5WX, United Kingdom. (☎ +44 (0)1935-700060, ✉ sales@survivalbooks.net, ▭www.survivalbooks.net). If you aren't entirely satisfied, simply return them to us within 14 days for a full and unconditional refund.

I enclose a cheque in payment/Please charge my Amex/Delta/Maestro (Switch)/ MasterCard/Visa card as follows. (delete as applicable)

Card No. _ _ _ _   _ _ _ _   _ _ _ _ _ _ _ _   **Security Code*** _ _ _ _

Expiry date   ____/____ **Issue number(Maestro/Switch only)** _____

Signature _____   **Tel. No.** _____

NAME _____

ADDRESS _____

* The security code is the last three digits on the signature strip.

NOTES

NOTES